Routledge Revivals

The Origins of Early Christian Ireland

The cultural developments of Early Christian Ireland have long been recognised and described. There have, however, been few attempts to date to explain why the flowering of culture should happen at the time and in the way that it did.

First published in 1992, *The Origins of Early Christian Ireland* (now with a new preface by the author) explains changes in the period up to AD 800 in Ireland. External stimuli, most notably from Irish settlers in western Britain acted as catalysts which transformed a relatively moribund Iron Age culture into one of extraordinary vigour. All aspects of the culture changed radically, and changes in each had knock-on effects on others. Beliefs were revolutionised by Christianity; society was transformed by the church as an institution and the rise of the individual; agriculture was expanded by more advanced technology and the entrepreneurial flair of individual decision-making; craft production became more widespread and offered a vehicle for the display of personal wealth and status. Long-distance trade and ecclesiastical contacts integrated Ireland with the rest of Europe more effectively than ever before.

The book has two distinctive features, which means that it relates to two forms of academic market, each of which can be defined. Firstly, it deals with a particular culture-historical period, that of Early Christian Ireland, and presents an explanation of its origins and development to AD 800. This appeals to archaeologists and historians of Ireland, Britain and, indeed, Europe. Secondly, it takes a specific theoretical position and develops it using primarily archaeological but also extensive historical information. This is the most detailed application of processualist theory yet undertaken for a historic period in Europe. This appeals to archaeologists and anthropologists in Britain, and also North America where the processualist approach is the most popular theoretical position.

The Origins of Early Christian Ireland

Harold Mytum

Routledge
Taylor & Francis Group

First published in 1992
by Routledge

This edition first published in 2024 by Routledge
4 Park Square, Milton Park, Abingdon, Oxon, OX14 4RN

and by Routledge
605 Third Avenue, New York, NY 10017

Routledge is an imprint of the Taylor & Francis Group, an informa business

Publisher's Note
The publisher has gone to great lengths to ensure the quality of this reprint but points
out that some imperfections in the original copies may be apparent.

Disclaimer
The publisher has made every effort to trace copyright holders and welcomes
correspondence from those they have been unable to contact.

A Library of Congress record exists under LCCN: 91015727

ISBN: 978-1-032-87575-0 (hbk)
ISBN: 978-1-003-53337-5 (ebk)
ISBN: 978-1-032-87576-7 (pbk)

Book DOI 10.4324/9781003533375

The Origins of
Early Christian Ireland

HAROLD MYTUM

ROUTLEDGE

LONDON AND NEW YORK

First published 1992
by Routledge
11 New Fetter Lane, London EC4P 4EE

Simultaneously published in the USA and Canada
by Routledge
a division of Routledge, Chapman and Hall Inc.
29 West 35th Street, New York, NY 10001

Typeset in 10/12 pt Baskerville, Monophoto

Printed in Great Britain by Butler & Tanner Ltd
Frome and London

British Library Cataloguing in Publication Data
Mytum, H. C.
  The origins of early Christian Ireland.
  1. Ireland, history, 410–1086
  I. Title
  941.501

Library of Congress Cataloging in Publication Data
Mytum, H. C.
  The origins of early Christian Ireland/Harold Mytum.
        p.   cm.
  Includes bibliographical references and index.
  1. Ireland—Civilization—To 1172.   2. Ireland—Church history—To
1172.   I. Title.
DA932.M95   1991
941.501—dc20   91–15727

ISBN 0-415-03258-X

To my parents

New Preface

This book was written at a time when processualist archaeology was confronting the role of ideology in past societies, highlighted by the critique of its materialist, functional emphasis by the developing post-processualist approaches including contextualism (Hodder 1991). The concept of a cognitive form of processualism had not been elaborated in print (Renfrew 1993, Renfrew and Zubrow 1994) so this volume is a parallel exploration alongside those that subsequently appeared at about the same time. It takes an explicitly systemic approach.

The volume was one of two book-length explorations of Early medieval/Early Christian Ireland in the early 1990s, one a standard textbook (Edwards 1990), and this an explicitly theoretical exploration. No extensive archaeological synthesis for the period, despite its importance in Irish identity, had been produced previously, and indeed there still are no more recent single-author perspectives. Some edited volumes will be considered in a brief summary below to show how and in what respects the subject has developed since this book.

An innovative feature of *The Origins of Early Christian Ireland* was that it was the first developed argument in Irish archaeology of any period that applied explicit theory. Despite developments from the late 1960s in the application of theory within archaeology in Britain, North America, and parts of Europe, Ireland remained a bastion of empirical observation and classification. Following a Germanic tradition, describing and ordering data and making limited inductive interpretations was the norm. Irish archaeology gradually began to accept the relevance of theory, but this has been slow, limited, and draws on a wide range of theoretical positions as diversity of approaches widened in the post-processualist/post-modern intellectual environment. Book chapters reviewing theory in Irish archaeology produced three and six years after this book was published noted the antipathy to theory (Cooney 1995, Tierney 1998), and O'Keefe still commented on the limited shift to more explicit theory over two decades later (O'Keefe 2018). Most Irish archaeology still remains largely empirical, though with some implicit influences from a variety of theoretical positions; it is largely foreign archaeologists in Ireland who continue to more prominently indicate their theoretical positions (e.g. Crabtree 2004, Orser 2013); for the period covered by this book calls for greater use of theory are still being made by Gleeson (2022).

The theoretical position as set out in this volume is not one which I would follow unmodified today, though significant strands of the argument would remain. Despite my efforts to consider what would now be termed agency in the volume, this would be explored in a more sensitive and multiscalar way, considering the relationships between people and people (from individual interrelations to group relations), people and things (from particular artefacts to categories of objects and to landscapes), and things with things. Ideology is presented in *The Origins of Early Christian Ireland* as a system that affected personal belief and action. The original interpretation does emphasise individual decision-making would now be framed differently, and far more could be drawn out concerning multiple meanings and values. Further work on the anthropology of conversion (e.g. Hefner 1993, Hann 2007) would also be important to consider, and historians and archaeologists have taken greater interest in conversion to Christianity and its implications (Carver 2005, Flechner and Ní Mhaonaigh 2016).

The social structure relies on applications from the contemporary law tracts, which would be now much improved by use of some recent scholarship (e.g. Charles-Edwards 2000), but discussions regarding the best-known settlement form, the ring-fort, and the documented grades of society has continued to be of interest (Stout 1997, Kerr et al 2013). What is most notable, however, due to the results largely of developer-funded archaeology, is the greater diversity of settlement forms than realised in 1992. The most notable sponsor of archaeological work, often extensive, has been that of the Irish Roads Authority, and the investment in excavation and analysis of cultural and environmental evidence has greatly increased understanding of early medieval Ireland (Kerr et al 2013, O'Sullivan et al 2014a, 2014b). This diversity is not represented in the law tracts, and the binary division of enclosed settlements into ring-forts and large, presumably monastic, enclosures can now be seen as overly simplistic (Kinsella 2010). Open and palisaded settlements on lowland areas have also been located, expanding the range of landscape contexts for such settlements. Some larger enclosed settlements may have domestic structures but also zones for burial but are not necessarily thought of as linked to a monastery; indeed, some may have had fields or paddocks as well as craft areas, and more forms of lower status settlements have been revealed (Boyle 2004). Research on burials has moved apace, both on burial practice and skeletal analysis (Corlett and Potterton 2010), and the study of the churches has intensified (Ó Carragáin 2011). The environmental context for changes in the early medieval period has also received attention (McClung and Plunkett 2020).

The extensive use of radiocarbon dating has given greater clarity to the popularity of settlement forms, and most cover the period of this book. However, numbers of archaeologically dated settlements appear to decline towards the end of the period covered in *The Origins of Early Christian Ireland*. This may have been caused by socio-economic changes brought about by the introduction of a silver bullion economy, perhaps starting before the Viking settlement and the development of a Hiberno-Norse component to the settlement, socio-economic, and cultural landscape of Ireland.

Whilst *The Origins of Early Christian Ireland* is a book of its time, many aspects can still stimulate questions about early medieval Ireland and the ways in which a more theoretically informed and explicit investigation of a period and place can move beyond description. Irish archaeological interpretation is now more sophisticated but there are still many opportunities to exploit the early medieval archaeological record to ask more ambitious questions about this iconic period of Ireland's past.

Harold Mytum, August 2024

References:

Boyle, J.W., 2004. Lest the lowliest be forgotten: locating the impoverished in early medieval Ireland. *International Journal of Historical Archaeology* 8, 85-99.

Carver, M. ed., 2005. *The Cross goes North: processes of conversion in northern Europe, AD 300-1300*. Boydell Press.

Charles-Edwards, T. M. 2000. *Early Christian Ireland*. Cambridge University Press.

Cooney, G. 1995. *Theory and Practice in Irish Archaeology*. Routledge.

Corlett, C. and Potterton, M. (eds.) 2010. *Death and burial in early medieval Ireland in the light of recent archaeological excavations*. Wordwell.

Crabtree, P.J. 2004. Ritual feasting in the Irish Iron Age: Re-examining the fauna from Dún Ailinne in light of contemporary archaeological theory, in Jones O'Day, S., Ervynck, A. and Van Neer, W. (eds.) *Behaviour Behind Bones: The Zooarchaeology of Ritual, Religion, Status and Identity*, Oxbow Books, 62-65.

Edwards, N. 1990. *The Archaeology of Early Medieval Ireland*. Routledge.

Flechner, R. and Máire Ní Mhaonaigh, M. (eds.), 2016. *The Introduction of Christianity into the Early Medieval Insular World: Converting the Isles I*, Cultural Encounters in Late Antiquity and the Middle Ages 19. Brepols

Gleeson, P. 2022. Reframing the first millennium AD in Ireland: archaeology, history, landscape. *Proceedings of the Royal Irish Academy: Archaeology, Culture, History, Literature* 122.1, 87-122.

Hann, C., 2007. The Anthropology of Christianity per se. *European Journal of Sociology/Archives Européennes de Sociologie*, 48.3, 383-410.

Hefner, R.W. ed., 1993. *Conversion to Christianity: historical and anthropological perspectives on a great transformation*. University of California Press.

Hodder, Ian. 1991. *Reading the Past: current approaches to interpretation in archaeology*. Cambridge University Press.

Kerr, T., McCormick, F. and O'Sullivan, A., 2013. *The Economy of Early Medieval Ireland* (No. Early Medieval Archaeology Project (EMAP 2) Reconstructing the Early Medieval Irish Economy EMAP Report 7.1). Early Medieval Archaeology Project

(EMAP), UCD School of Archaeology, and School of Geography, Archaeology and Palaeoecology, Queens University Belfast.

Kinsella, J., 2010. A new Irish early medieval site type? Exploring the 'recent' archaeological evidence for non-circular enclosed settlement and burial sites. *Proceedings of the Royal Irish Academy: Archaeology, Culture, History, Literature* 110.1, 89-132.

McClung, L.C. and Plunkett, G. 2020. Cultural change and the climate record in final prehistoric and early medieval Ireland. *Proceedings of the Royal Irish Academy: Archaeology, Culture, History, Literature* 120.1,129-158.

Ó Carragáin, T. 2011. *Churches in Early Medieval Ireland: architecture, ritual and memory.* Paul Mellon Centre for Studies in British Art.

O'Keefe, T. 2018. Theory and medieval archaeology in Ireland and beyond: the narrative tradition and the archaeological imagination. *The Journal of Irish Archaeology*, 27, 99-116.

Orser Jr, C.E., 2013. *A Historical Archaeology of the Modern World.* Springer Science & Business Media.

O'Sullivan, A., McCormick, F., Kerr, T. and Harney, L. 2014a. *Early Medieval Ireland, AD 400–1100. The evidence from archaeological excavations.* Dublin: Royal Irish Academy.

O'Sullivan, A., McCormick, F., Kerr, T. R., Harney, L., and Kinsella, J. 2014b. *Early Medieval Dwellings and Settlements in Ireland, AD 400–1100.* British Archaeological Reports, International Series 2604. Archaeopress.

Renfrew, C. 1993. Cognitive archaeology: some thoughts on the archaeology of thought. *Cambridge Archaeological Journal* 3.1, 248-250.

Renfrew, C. and Zubrow, E.B.W. 1994. *The Ancient Mind. Elements of cognitive archaeology.* Cambridge University Press.

Stout, M. 1997. *The Irish Ringfort.* Four Courts Press.

Tierney, M. 1998. Theory and Politics in early medieval Irish archaeology, in Monk, M.A. and Sheehan, J. (eds.) *Early medieval Munster: archaeology, history, and society.* Cork University Press, 190-199.

Contents

Plates

Preface

To produce a synthesis and interpretation of the archaeological material recovered from Early Christian Ireland, and combine it where relevant with historical material, is an ambitious project. It is also one that is far greater than I had optimistically anticipated when the process of writing began. I am grateful to Barry Cunliffe for his invitation to write this book, to the publishers (particularly Andrew Wheatcroft) for forbearance in the delays and to my employers, the University of York, for sabbatical leave which has provided the essential blocks of time required for immersion in the theory and data, and the subsequent outpourings of text and illustration.

The results of my deliberations are produced here, and will be continued in a subsequent volume, *The Vikings and Early Christian Ireland, AD 800–1100*. In some respects a single volume for the whole period would have been preferable, but the quality and range of the data, and the recent developments in refining archaeological chronologies, have meant that some division was necessary to do justice to the important changes that can now be not only recognised but, it is claimed, interpreted.

The division between the two volumes has been on a chronological basis, and the date of AD 800 could be considered somewhat arbitrary. However, it does reflect a turning point in the development of Irish culture. By 800 the origins of the Early Christian period were well over, the church established and the indigenous Iron Age culture eclipsed by a new cultural phenomenon. Up to 800, political and social fragmentation was gradually reduced but still dominant. The subsistence economy and craft specialisation operated within a system of patronage and intimate social relations; long distance trade was relatively unimportant. After 800, different structures became significant: urbanism and long distance trade led to the growth of states, albeit unstable, and to the concentration of wealth and power at fewer monastic centres.

One is never satisfied with the results of research; there is always more that could be done, additional data incorporated, further aspects to be drawn in. This book has already been too long in its gestation, and needs to be delivered to the world in all its frailty. Some will be surprised or annoyed by the approach, and others by some of the interpretations. I hope that the book will cause reflection amongst those who work on Early Christian Ireland. It is time to move from description to interpretation, and if this book draws out further explanations, even if contradictory to those expressed here, then it will have served its purpose. Indeed it is to be hoped that a subsequent revision will be made desirable by the rapid progress that is now possible within this field of study.

It may seem to some that a chapter on theory and method is both distracting and self-indulgent in a book about a particular place at a particular time. But there are two distinct purposes of this book; one is to understand this particular place and time – Early Christian Ireland to AD 800 – but the other is to examine the use of a particular theoretical approach to the past. That approach is one termed processualism, and has not often been applied in a rich archaeological and historical context. Moreover, this theoretical approach has become more sophisticated since its early days when it could be seen as potentially mechanistic and overly functionalist in its applications. As other approaches have highlighted more aspects of the past, so processualism has evolved. The sophistication of the theory in modelling cultural change and explaining the interrelating factors causing this can be demonstrated through the study of Early Christian Ireland.

In conclusion, I would like to thank my wife for all her support during the book's production; and my parents, for their loving support and encouragement in so many ways. Their toleration for so many years of my archaeological obsessions can only in the smallest way be repaid by the dedication of this book.

Acknowledgements

I would like to thank the following for permission to reproduce photographs as follows: Plates XXXIII–XXXIX, The Board of Trinity College Dublin; Plates I–IX, Cambridge University Committee for Aerial Photography; Plates X–XIII and XVIII–XXXII, the National Museum of Ireland; Plates XIV–XVIII, the British Museum.

I am indebted to Julien Parsons who has produced to a uniformly high standard many of the illustrations used in this book, the original sources of which are acknowledged in the captions. He has been responsible for the following figures: 2:3, 2:4, 2:7, 2:8, 3:1–4, 3:7–9, 3:13–15, 3:18, 3:19, 3:21, 4:1–9, 4:13–15, 4:17, 4:24, 4:26–30, 4:34, 4:35, 5:2–6, 5:15, 6:7, 7:8, 7:11. The other figures were prepared by the author, with the exception of Figure 4:20 which is reproduced with permission of the Royal Irish Academy.

I would like to thank all those who have contributed to this book in various ways. The bulk of this book has been written during two sabbatical terms generously provided by the Department of Archaeology, University of York. Staff and students in the Department have helped refine my ideas both about theory and about the interpretation of material from Early Christian Ireland. Roberta Gilchrist, Chris Lynn and Mick Monk have kindly read parts or all of the work and made many useful comments. They do not agree by any means with all that I have said, and I have rashly not taken all their advice to heart. Nevertheless, they have all contributed significantly to what is worthwhile in this book. My father helped in the compilation of the index.

1
Theory and method

Introduction

One purpose of this book is to outline the major changes that led to the creation of Early Christian Ireland in about the fifth century, and then its subsequent development through to around the end of the eighth century. Another purpose, at least as important, is to explain these changes.

Some archaeologists and historians emphasise the continuity between the late Iron Age and the Early Christian period (Warner 1988, Jackson 1964). Whilst there are clearly important strands that carry on into the fifth century and beyond, there are in turn very many major elements of discontinuity. Settlement forms and patterns emerge clearly for the first time, the material culture is transformed; the language changes rapidly and becomes preserved in written form. A new religion becomes dominant and different patterns of external relationships emerge. Moreover, once these features can be recognised in the fifth and sixth centuries they do not remain static but continue to change over the centuries. These are not random, chance fluctuations but complex trends which require analysis.

To date, most publication for the Early Christian period has concentrated on the description of particular categories of data, whether classes of artefact, settlement form or material from a geographical area. Whilst this is a necessary part of archaeological research, at some time an overview is necessary to put these detailed researches into perspective. The only attempts in recent times have been by de Paor and de Paor (1958) and Laing (1975) who also covered western Britain. Both these concentrated on description, however, and the same can be said for the historical syntheses of Mac Niocaill (1972) and Ó Corráin (1972). Description alone, however, is unsatisfactory in the longer term and explanation is necessary for the development of the subject.

In order to explain changes through space and time effectively, it is necessary to have a defined analytical methodology and this will be briefly and simply outlined in this chapter. Archaeological theory can be written in the most obscure and jargon-ridden style. Whilst certain defined terms are useful, and are recognised as necessary in all disciplines, creation of jargon is in itself no progress unless it is related to the development of new concepts that cannot be

1

explained concisely using existing terminology. In the discussion set out below it is hoped that the minimum of jargon is used.

All works of synthesis are written within a theoretical framework, whether this is appreciated by the author and readers or not. No one can escape from having preconceived ideas about how the world works – and worked. Likewise, everyone has ideas about what constitutes sufficient evidence to support a certain view and what is a reasonable explanation of a phenomenon. The differences between mainstream archaeologists and parapsychologists in their explanations of stone circles indicate in dramatic form the differences in what may be considered reasonable hypotheses and relevant evidence to support them (Cole 1980). It is clear to all of us from our daily lives that for any problem there is no one simple and right answer to which everyone would agree; so much depends on viewpoint. And viewpoint is related to theoretical position, often itself dependent on sociopolitical factors. This has been recognised in studies of the history of archaeology (Daniel 1962, Trigger 1980), but is also true of the present (Leone 1978, Kristiansen 1981). This does not mean that there is no correct interpretation, and any one person's view is as good as another, which would be called a relativist position. Rather, progress can be made as new explanations are put forward that fit the data better than those that have been offered previously. Also, tests can be made of theories and explanations by collecting new data relevant to that particular problem. The relevance and significance of such results need to be assessed; measures of fit may be based on statistical comparison, visual inspection or intellectual evaluation. However, different attitudes and interests will highlight different aspects of the past. All we can hope for is an approximation to past reality, and the closer to this the better.

Inductive and deductive approaches

Many archaeologists and historians believe that by examining the evidence thoroughly, imbuing themselves in the data, the correct picture of the past will be obtained. This method of working from the data to the interpretation is called the inductive method, and is considered by many to be 'common sense'. The problem that faces those that espouse this inductive, empirical approach is one of seeing the relevant data from the great mass available; indeed, data can be considered infinite. Even one isolated object or archaeological site has very many immediately obvious characteristics or attributes, and vast numbers of others that could be discovered by, for example, physical scientific analyses. 'Common sense' cannot tell us which of these attributes are intrinsically the most important; their importance depends on their relevance to the questions being asked of the data. The Ardagh chalice, for example, is a complex artefact (Plate XXVII). Numerous measurements could be taken to analyse its overall size, shape and weight, but the same could also be done for each of its constituent parts such as the applied glass studs. There is also the way each part was manufactured and assembled, and the overall design of the decoration. Parallels could be found for the motifs, shapes and techniques but this could be just within Ireland, or western Europe, or the world; and perhaps a time period or stage of social or economic development should be set for relevant material. But all these decisions have to be made, in considerable detail, by an inductive researcher. Even in the case of a single artefact the data is not obvious, and can only be considered within the framework of relevant questions.

The deductive approach, by which the questions are phrased first and the data examined to answer them, is the opposite of the inductive method. Criticism of the deductive approach is that the enquirer is biased and will look only for evidence that supports his argument. This is not so; asking questions does not pre-suppose that one particular answer will be found. It is recognised that the deductive enquirer is biased, but no less so than the inductive one. It is just that he sets out his own position clearly at the outset. Inductive discussions are just as biased in data selection as deductive ones, but because of the unclarified approach to the data, this is not immediately obvious because of the claim to 'common sense'. There are many ways in which deductive analysis can take place, and it is not necessary to examine these closely here. In practice most research involves a combination of inductive and deductive work. Some idea of the data has to be obtained to appreciate the type of questions that can be asked. For example, knowing that there are detailed legal documents for Early Christian Ireland allows the formulation of more detailed questions about land use and ownership than would have been possible from just archaeological material; or knowing that several waterlogged sites have been excavated means that assessment of the use of wood and leather can be incorporated into an analysis of craft specialisation. The documents or wood on their own, however, do not convey any information; only by asking questions of them can progress be made.

Many archaeologists still feel that it is necessary to gather more data before any interpretation can be offered. For example, of the 60,000 or so ring-fort settlement sites known from Ireland only just over 100 have been excavated even in part. With only 0.17 per cent examined, many would argue that it is too early to make suggestions as to their status and function, and these should await further excavation. However, as has been explained, data collection can only be effectively carried out within a programme where clear questions have been formulated. Without problem-oriented research there is less chance of further excavations revealing relevant attributes of sites that would help to provide answers (expected or not) to our questions.

The survey of Co. Down carried out in the late 1950s and early 1960s was extremely effective because it was, at least in part, problem solving (Jope 1966). Besides collecting information on all sites known from the county, certain issues were intensively studied by survey and excavation. The one of greatest relevance to Early Christian Ireland involves a form of ring-fort known as the platform type which can be similar in surface appearance to a medieval castle motte. The question to be answered was were these native sites copies of the Anglo-Norman mottes or did they have an indigenous origin? As a result of an intensive campaign it has now been clearly established that platform ring-forts were not imitations of mottes but were first built centuries before, in the Early Christian period. This was achieved, however, only by careful selection of sites where evidence relevant to the question under examination was likely to be found. Undirected data collection would not have led to this advance in our knowledge.

Many questions posed about Early Christian Ireland are detailed ones, concerned with particular bodies of data. But there is one initial and fundamental question: why did the Early Christian period begin in Ireland at all? Because of the term Early Christian, the answer seems to have been given already in the name – Christianity arrived – but even at that simple level an explanation for its arrival is still required. In about the fifth century Ireland changed from a static, isolated culture to a vibrant, lively, expanding, developing and dynamic one. Explanation is required as to why this happened in Ireland at all, and why at that particular time. The effects were wide-ranging and led indirectly to many unforeseen repercussions in all aspects of the culture.

The multidisciplinary approach

This book is primarily based on archaeological and historical material. It is seen as a considerable advantage to analysis and interpretation that Early Christian Ireland is within the historic period; the archaeology can be text-aided; the synthesis can be multidisciplinary. With the academic trend towards specialisation it is not possible to be expert in all fields. Each scholar comes from a particular background, and this colours his approach to any subject. A grounding in theoretical archaeology at Cambridge, though initially not fully appreciated, has had its effect on the author's desire to produce a synthesis within a particular analytical framework. Having turned to Early Christian Ireland initially through archaeology, the interests and approaches of that particular discipline have coloured the way in which this book has been envisaged. In that sense, and through a closer and more intimate knowledge of the archaeological database with its potential and its problems, this book can be seen as primarily archaeological. The historical sources have been used to examine the problems seen as important to an archaeologist, though the types of evidence available are all treated as of equal value.

Multidisciplinary synthesis and interpretation come in formulating relevant models that can be tested against the data, and not assuming that the evidence from any one subject should be dominant. Unfortunately there has been a tendency in the past to consider that historical evidence is of greater value than the archaeological. At a time when archaeology was a very young discipline, with little grasp of the data available and with an undeveloped methodology, it was not surprising that mature historical studies should be used not only as the framework, but also as a guide to new directions and areas of interest. In recent years archaeology has matured as an independent discipline; much of the preliminary spade-work in data collection and ordering, and in methodological and theoretical approaches, has been done. Archaeology can now be considered alongside history.

The increasing self-confidence felt by prehistorians has not, however, been greatly in evidence in those studying historic western Britain and Ireland. The leading proponents of archaeology in these areas, notably Thomas (1981a) and Alcock (1971, 1981), have all tended to see the record of the past in terms of superior historical evidence and inferior archaeological data. Both scholars have been extremely active in both fieldwork and the synthesis of material from the early historic period in the Irish Sea province – the areas bordering the Irish Sea. They have excited interest in the subject, and created order in much of the scattered and fragmentary data. Their analytical methods, however, may now be considered critically, and may be found to need emendation in the light of the developments in archaeological theory and method already briefly discussed. Rather than appreciating the potential of text-aided archaeology, they have tended to consider (and Alcock more than Thomas) that archaeology should be text-dominated. Thomas believes in the deductive approach to archaeological research, though he considers that the higher levels of synthesis tend towards inductiveness, even though this is not necessarily desirable. Alcock, too, uses a deductive approach in his fieldwork. It is in the matter of combining history and archaeology that serious differences of approach between their work and this emerges.

Thomas considers historical sources to be primary, and has fortunately set out his reasoning at length (1981a, 19–24). He believes that the historian mainly depends on statements made in the past by human beings and which he can comprehend. Though some might be considered more objective, and others more subjective, all give evidence. This evidence is information processed by another mind in the past, but he admits that it has no direct correspondence to truth or past reality. archaeological material, on the other hand, is seen by thomas as fundamentally different from historical data. This is because he considers that archaeological material has not been previously processed by any human mind; the primary archaeological information is at a lower level than that of historical material, and only by inference can it be raised to the same level as the document. Therefore, whilst history deals with evidence, archaeology deals with inference.

Thomas has made an incorrect assumption about archaeological evidence, however. The material culture of a society has not been created by chance, but must have been processed by the human mind (Clarke 1968, Miller 1982). The design of a brooch or the building of a house involves human decision-making, and so has been processed by a human mind, as much as writing an entry in an Annal. Sometimes the decisions are related consciously to the carrying of meaning, such as the sculptured scenes on a high cross; indeed this active role of material culture in past and present societies is now much appreciated by archaeologists (Hodder 1982). At other times archaeological material reflects the organisation of society which may be acting only subconsciously within past individuals in, for example, the arrangement of buildings within a settlement (Fletcher 1977). Even the recognition of certain material as refuse and its subsequent pattern of disposal are the result of human mental processing and not a distortion that should be eradicated to get back to the pristine past.

There are post-depositional processes that affect the archaeological record, such as physical decay of objects and the disturbance of buried layers in the soil (Wood and Johnson 1978), but these are the equivalent to processes that affect historical sources. Physical decay affects documents themselves, and disturbance affects texts through transcribing, editing and altering (deliberately or not). The technical aspects of archaeological and historical research require these difficulties to be overcome before interpretation is possible. The diplomatic edition of a text can be compared with the archaeological excavation report or corpus of finds. Neither contains 'the truth', both contain all that the scholar thought was useful, in an appropriate (often traditionally established) format. Archaeologists are aware of the difficulties in selecting which data to publish, but the picture is not necessarily any clearer for historians with their texts, as a recent review indicates (Dumville 1985b).

This does not make archaeology more secure than history; rather both rely totally on inference. The problem, then, is how to infer effectively. Binford (1982, 160) stated about archaeological material:

> the past is gone, mute and only recognisable as such through inference. We cannot use a 'direct' strategy of describing the past ... the past cannot cry out and protest against our descriptions. Quite literally our descriptions of the past are constructions. The accuracy of such inventions can only be evaluated by evaluating our ... methods.

This applies equally to historical sources since, though they may speak initially in words rather than patterns, they too cannot cry out at our constructions made from those words. Progress can only be made by applying the correct methods. And these do not include ones which assume the primacy of the historical material.

Alcock was trained as an historian, and relies in his research strategies even more than Thomas on the primacy of documentary sources. Alcock's research design for locating high status sites in Scotland (Alcock *et al.* 1986) is a good example of this approach in operation. It appears an elegant deductive approach, with clear hypotheses derived from documentary sources set out and tested against the archaeological evidence recovered from carefully selected research excavations. There is, however, one major flaw in his method. Archaeology is only allowed to support the historically derived hypotheses, and cannot refute them. If the archaeological evidence should not support the historically derived hypothesis, the archaeology is considered erroneous or incomplete. The dominance of any one source of information in this way, whether historical or archaeological, cannot be logically supported and makes the supposedly deductive approach in fact inductive, since there can be no real testing.

In any one specific piece of research one source may be more fruitful and relevant to the question in hand than another, and in certain cases the two sources may appear contradictory. This can be caused by erroneous data (poor excavation or misread text) or processes not recognised by the scholar (residuality of artefacts or a document altered deliberately or otherwise during copying in the past). The most likely problem, however, is that the two sources are not compatible because of the circumstances under which they were created. They may, for example, relate to different periods, different areas or indeed different contemporary groups within the same society. A 'poor fit' between two different sources of information may not cloud the issue but allow it to be examined from a wider spectrum of perspectives.

Synthesising a variety of sources of evidence has always been recognised as difficult. It is frequently so within one discipline – different recensions of a text vary, or apparently similar settlement sites produce different artefact assemblages – and it is no wonder that greater difficulties emerge with the use of material from several disciplines. The information in this book is mainly drawn from archaeology, environmental studies and history in its various forms. All the disciplines provide evidence for Early Christian Ireland, and the book would be the poorer without any of them, but the questions of particular interest are those of an archaeologist, and as such the book is primarily archaeological.

Both Thomas (1971b) and Alcock (1971) have produced syntheses for the Irish Sea province as a whole, but the only archaeological work devoted solely to Ireland was the popular and now out of date book by de Paor and de Paor (1958). Indeed, most of the changes noted for Early Christian Ireland have indeed had little or no interpretation. As Kathleen Hughes wrote in 1972 (p. 17):

> Historians would often like archaeology to ... give definite answers to fundamental general questions about the material culture of a people. But this is what archaeology does least well, for such answers would imply a synthesis of a large body of material.... Not only is the archaeologist's interpretation of his material, just like the historian's, sometimes in dispute, but also his evidence is often scattered and scanty. He is therefore reluctant to offer a general analysis.

This may have been what many archaeologists did up to the early 1970s, and some continue to do, but it is not all that can be done. Hughes reflects the historian's view of archaeological potential, and one held by others, such as Ó Corráin (1972, 1981, 1983), who are also sympathetic to the use of archaeology but are not yet aware of its present potential, newly acquired through developments in theory and methodology. The historian's lack of expectation is really the result of the inductive culture-historical approach of most archaeologists who see their subject only as the 'handmaiden of history'.

Most culture-historians use archaeology either to augment historical sources, or to create pseudo-history. Many art-historical studies discuss motifs as if they were invading, migrating and mutating entities in their own right, and the relationship between these and society as a whole is not fully appreciated or considered in any detail. The recent recognition of the potential richness of meaning within art (Richardson 1984) may indicate a change for the better in this regard, though some are pessimistic (Ryan 1987). In the past, scholars who have taken a multidisciplinary approach have had a pessimistic view of what archaeology can contribute (even though they may have been primarily archaeologists themselves).

Reece, in a reaction to the approaches of Alcock and others, does not believe in the multidisciplinary approach to archaeology, and the creation of syntheses using archaeological and historical data (1984a). He considers that archaeologists should just work with material culture evidence and interpret it without the use of historical sources; these cannot be definitively related to archaeological material and the conflation of material from the two disciplines cannot be rigorously carried out. He considers this the creation of myths and historical fiction, yet in doing so severely restricts his ambitions, it might be argued to the point where the effort hardly seems worthwhile for limited increase in understanding of the past.

The testing of suitable hypotheses formulated from within one discipline against the data of the other would seem to be an opportunity within an historic period that prehistorians would envy. Both archaeological and historical sources can derive from the same past society; the skill comes in understanding to which parts of that complex past they relate.

Initial editing of texts or recording of excavations should be based on rigorous application of historical and archaeological methodology respectively. But beyond that, and indeed in the choice of texts to edit or sites to excavate (and how), multidisciplinary questions should have a role. The data should be presented without the synthesis, but then deserves the fullest possible assessment in the light of all potential information. It would seem inconceivable that a prehistorian would not consider using environmental evidence to deduce climatic and vegetational changes in a region, yet according to Reece this would be fanciful since only archaeological data should be used in an archaeologist's synthesis. Indeed, Reece's own numismatic work (1984b) would not have been possible if earlier scholars had not correlated the words on coins with historically documented individuals and places, and so dated and attributed them. Reece holds a position that is retrograde and by claiming that nothing can be gained by co-operation with other disciplines he threatens to render ineffective the recent methodological advances made in archaeology. It could be as divisive as the early sideswipes of some new archaeologists who claimed, totally wrongly, that history was mere descriptive narrative (Binford 1962). Now that archaeology has gained an equal footing with history, combination seems even more desirable than ever before.

The culture-historical approach

The culture-historical archaeologist or historian provides an explanation for events by their peculiar prior circumstances. The antecedents of an event are therefore seen as providing the cause, and events, though perhaps seen as part of more general trends, are seen as the vital elements needing explanation. Thus, many of the changes that took place in Early Christian Ireland have been explained in terms of the effects of plagues (Mac Niocaill 1972) or, at a later date, the violence of Viking raids (Hughes 1966, Henry 1967). Longer term processes are rarely considered, nor indeed are the mechanics of how a plague or raid would dislocate a society or economy. That such things happened can in itself be considered sufficient explanation for what followed after them; description is therefore often seen as explanation.

The traditional approach within a documented period often places exceptional importance on recorded people, places and events. Thus, Hencken used the references to the royal site of Lagore to provide the chronological framework for the stratigraphy, even though he was not completely happy with this on the basis of the artefactual evidence (Hencken 1950). Modern culture-historical archaeologists are more critical of the sources and the ways that they can be used (Warner 1986b), but there is still a desire to associate archaeological evidence with the particular historical reference, even if this is recognised as difficult. This is not an unreasonable aim, but should not be seen as an end in itself but rather as a way of linking otherwise disparate evidence in order to ask yet more sophisticated questions.

Another aspect of the culture-historical approach is that there is no desire for wider, cross-cultural comparison. The study is of interest in itself and for itself. It throws no light on any wider questions of human development, social changes or interactions with the environment. Linked to this is often a reluctance to recognise trends and similarities in data. For example, despite the fact that ring-forts have been excavated in considerable numbers and some clear patterns are now visible, explanation of features on any one site tends to be site-specific, rather than on a wider cross-site comparative basis.

In the case of processualist approaches, particular historical data is as important as particular archaeological information, but all can be used for generalisation and the formulation of hypotheses – models – concerning changes through time and space.

The processualist approach

The main thrust of the processualist paradigm is that large scale forces of change (and indeed stability) act within and between societies. These are larger than individuals, and provide a background against which individual action takes place. The actions of an individual, however brilliant, will not have any lasting effect until the time, the context, is right. Only when the larger processual changes are moving in a direction can an individual have the opportunity to act, and the results be taken on by others. Certainly in archaeological terms it is only the changes that are taken on by at least a segment of a society, and more than just briefly, that can be picked out from the background 'noise' of variability. For this reason the processualist approach fits well with many archaeological aims and the nature of the database available.

Processualists also believe in generalising about societies past and present. Comparison with other societies or cultures from different times or places is seen as valuable, indeed a vital part of the subject. Making generalisations about human behaviour (often group behaviour in the case of archaeological data) is seen as an important aim. This is in stark contrast to the culture-historical approach which sees each culture in isolation and as a unit of study which does not throw light beyond its immediate sphere.

In the processualist interpretation events are not denied; they are just seen within a wider process of changes. Events are symptoms of these larger scale factors, not their cause. Archaeological evidence by its nature is better suited to this broader canvas, though there is no reason why the historical sources, with their (fairly) precise dates, should not be used similarly. Many culture-historians do, of course, generalise but normally from the events or objects outwards. This is part of the inductive approach that is normally associated with culture-historical interpretation and which has already been criticised.

The extent of interpretation

We can never know everything about the past, but what aspects can be studied from material remains? During the 1950s, there was a pessimistic view of how far interpretation or inference based on the archaeological record could go. Even Childe, who wrote many syntheses of European prehistory, saw many problems in interpretation as insurmountable (Trigger 1980). The most dramatic negative statement was that of Smith (1955), but it was Hawkes (1954) who provided a detailed statement on the limitations of archaeological data, and elaborated a hierarchy of inference. He considered that the techniques used to produce past artefacts and structures could be inferred from archaeology, and it was relatively easy to interpret subsistence-economics. Social and political institutions were harder to infer, however, and religious institutions and spiritual life were most difficult of all.

The new archaeology on both sides of the Atlantic had a profound effect in changing attitudes to the past and, after all the initial rhetoric was over, led to the development of many useful (and contrasting) approaches to the study of material remains. The most important of these have been critically outlined by Hodder (1986). Central to the theoretical and methodological developments in new archaeology was the use of a processual approach, rather than a particularist culture-historical one. In other words, general processes were seen as more important and suitable for analysis than individual events in the past. Just as archaeology was better suited to study societies than individuals (Flannery 1967), it needed to work at a higher level of interpretation in explaining past change.

With the theoretical developments (Clarke 1973) came the realisation that the archaeological record was a far more complex and richer source than had previously been recognised and, through the use of analogy at different levels, it could be interpreted not merely in terms of technology and economy. Some have denied the need for analogy (Gould 1980, Wylie 1985) but all inference is, in the end, founded on analogy based on our shared (direct or indirect) experience. Out of this discussion comes an important issue of dispute: whether there are general laws of human behaviour that could, if recognised, help interpretation of the past. If it could be proven that people have always reacted in certain ways to certain circumstances, then this would greatly ease interpretation of fragmentary archaeological (and indeed historical) evidence since the missing parts of processes could be worked out using the general laws. The laws necessary for this to be applicable have to be at a high level of interpretation (Watson *et al.* 1971, Plog 1977), but the only ones that have been successfully promoted are so trivial that they have been described as 'Mickey Mouse laws' (Flannery 1973, 51). For this reason, the search for general laws of human behaviour has not continued as a major aim of new archaeology, at least in Europe.

After the initial period of unbounded optimism the practitioners of new archaeology have developed less ambitious but much more effective approaches by which generalisations are formulated about human behaviour in certain situations (Renfrew 1984, 18). This is the position followed here, and by many European processual archaeologists (for example, most authors in Renfrew and Shennan 1982, Renfrew and Cherry 1986).

Individual human behaviour

In the early years of new archaeology the individual had been seen as an insignificant part of a passive society upon which great forces acted and to which society could only react (Binford 1972, Wobst 1977). Some processualist archaeologists have recently, however, given greater emphasis to the role of the individual. The degree to which the individual is seen to have significance varies greatly from a relatively limited role (Binford 1982) to a wide ranging significance (Renfrew 1984) and even a version of the 'great man' mentality (Hodges 1982). In these studies, however, the processual approach has remained, and it is the combination of processual archaeology with a dynamic role for the individual that is the stance taken in this book.

An important assumption underlying many archaeological analyses, usually unstated but here briefly elaborated, is that of optimisation, often expressed in terms of group or systemic behaviour (Keene 1979, Hill 1977, 63). Humans do not behave in what modern western economists may consider an optimal way, and therefore social and ideological factors have to be taken into account in calculating optimisation (Jochim 1983), but there is some hope of carrying this out in a text-aided context. Individuals may still behave inefficiently within their own cultural desires as well as our own; however, the sum total of many individuals making decisions can be considered as more predictable and can be used as a vital contribution to wider, systemic change. Within the context of the present analysis it is the individual's desire to do as well as possible given certain circumstances that is considered a basic driving force behind change (Barth 1966, Paine 1974).

The way in which optimisation is perceived and enacted has been discussed by Kunkel (1970, 31). There are, however, many constraints on the individual. Optimising decisions also depends on the information available, how that information is interpreted and the ability to carry out the desired action (Moore 1983). For this reason perfect maximisation rarely occurs, and of course decisions could be completely wrong; there can be success and failure. An extremely important factor to consider also is that the benefits desired may be of many different kinds; material gain is only one alternative (Bee 1974). In the context of Early Christian Ireland documentary sources suggest that the main objectives were the acquisition of power or social status on the one hand, and salvation in the world hereafter on the other. These two forces acted at times against each other, at others in conjunction. In all societies what the individual considers most beneficial is culturally determined, based on the norms and values of the society at large, and the particular segment of the society in which the individual acts. For the same individual, norms would also vary through time and space.

Despite the ubiquitous applicability of the maximisation thesis, it is in the field of economics that this assumption can be seen most clearly, and economic models are now frequently used in archaeology. The dominant economic position espoused by archaeologists is that of the substantivists. This view holds that what was desired by past individuals, and the ways in which this could be achieved, was constrained by and enacted within the social system and accepted mores (Dalton 1961, 1971; Doherty 1980; Hodges 1982). In this respect, the economy could be said to be embedded in social relations. The advantage of this approach for archaeologists is that it allows greater appreciation of a past society through the remains of its economy. Formalist concepts, derived from the western capitalist system, can also be occasionally applied, for example where there is a recognition of supply and demand, and in the entrepreneurial role of individual activity in promoting change.

Although not always the case, maximisation is often only to be achieved at the expense of other individuals or groups. This provides the basis of competition, operating at a variety of levels and in many forms. There is considerable disagreement amongst anthropologists and archaeologists as to whether all simple hunter gatherer societies exhibit competitive tendencies, but certainly this seems to be the case with settled agriculturalists. Competition also provides the driving force in maintaining the status quo, or in initiating change, explained below in processualist terms. Intrinsic competition as a human trait provides the base line explanation for individual and (more frequently in archaeological analysis) group decision-making. Given that universal human behavioural traits can be defined, these can then be studied within particular geographical, temporal and cultural settings. Although competition may be universal, its particular manifestations are culturally related, and so explanations, whilst maintaining a generalising element, need to be more specific. It is in this light that Early Christian Ireland can be considered.

There is considerable evidence, particularly documentary, from Early Christian Ireland to support the view that individuals then were essentially competitive. Gerriets (1983) holds this view in her analysis of the clientship system used in Early Christian Ireland, and competition in many forms can be found throughout the secular literature. It is also an assumption which underlies recent historical syntheses of the period (Ó Corráin 1972, Mac Niocaill 1972). Archaeological evidence can also be adduced to support the identification of a competitive society, through ostentatious display in the form of personal adornment such as brooches, and in ecclesiastical art and architecture. In order to compete successfully, the individual works within the indigenous value systems and behavioural codes of the culture, but this does not negate the universal presence of competition, at least within all agricultural societies.

Symbols

Whilst processualist archaeology is the most appropriate approach by which to examine large scale changes through time and space, other approaches can also have value in examining other aspects of the past. For example, it is also important to study the way in which interrelationships at any one point in time were articulated. Structuralism has recently been applied to archaeological data. As Hodder points out (1986, 34), it can have many similarities with the systemic approach because of its emphasis on the relationships between different entities. In structuralism, the detection of rules of behaviour can, through formal analysis, lead to the recognition of organisational rules or grammars. These may be in art (Washburn 1983), buildings or settlement planning (Glassie 1975, Fletcher 1977) or a wider range of material culture (Deetz 1977). The grammars so identified may be recognised by the actors, or may be subconscious. The problem with any grammar is that the meanings that lay behind it are largely if not completely irrecoverable because there is no set relationship between symbol and meaning. However, in an historic period the documentary evidence can provide indications about meanings of material culture symbols. Many of the texts available – law tracts, Saints' Lives, secular tales – are highly structured and loaded with levels of meaning. A structuralist, or semiotic, approach has been used in literary studies of the Early Christian period (see Merdrignac 1987 for a study of a Continental text). The structure in artefacts of Early Christian Ireland, and the symbolic meanings attached, has only just been recognised (Richardson 1984), but the use of symbols can be seen as particularly important in the ideological and social systems (see Chapters 3 and 4). Grammars can change through time, and Deetz (1977) has associated this with major changes in world view, a process of possible relevance in the transformation from Iron Age to Early Christian Ireland.

Systems approach

A number of archaeologists have considered that a systemic approach to past societies can help elucidate the main processes operating in maintaining a stable society, or in promoting change. Some of the basic concepts and terminology of systems analysis in archaeology have come from general systems theory (von Bertalanffy 1962, Ashby 1965, Buckley 1967). However, only a few archaeologists (Watson *et al.* 1971) believe general systems theory and its tenet that basic systemic relationships exist in many phenomena, including human societies. Most archaeologists who use systemic analysis do not consider, however, that there is a body of theory associated with the approach; rather they see it as a method or technique by which complex inter-relationships can be defined, elaborated and explained (Renfrew 1972). Some scholars have considered that this weakens the explanatory value of systems analysis (Salmon 1978) but supporters of the approach argue that it is a technique to be applied within one of a range of theoretical positions (Lowe and Barth 1980).

The real world is extremely complex, and systems analysis allows simplification of this real world. The simplification is done, however, to allow examination and explanation of a particular part of the complex whole, and has no independent existence (Munton 1973, 686). A system chosen for study is 'a set of elements so interrelated that changes in any one require changes of some sort in others ... [and] the whole [system] is greater than the sum of its parts' (Saxe 1977, 108). Any subsystem could be likewise chosen for analysis alone, and considered a system in itself, made up of an interrelated set of elements. What is considered a system and what are its subsystems are decided by the particular problem in hand. A common level of analysis in archaeology, however, has been to see a culture or specific geographic region as the system.

Clarke was one of the great early proponents of systems analysis (1968). He saw that sociocultural systems (societies) were integral whole units, with economy or religion being subsystems. These intercommunicate with each other, forming a system. A change in one subsystem could have effects on other subsystems. Other sociocultural systems and the environment were external, but had an influence on and were influenced by the sociocultural system under analysis. An example of such a system is illustrated in Figure 1:1. Most systems can be affected from outside and are so called open systems.

Early Christian Ireland can be thus defined for this book as a sociocultural system comprising a series of subsystems (ideology, society, subsistence economy, craft production and trade). Each of these subsystems is examined separately (Chapters 3–7), and further subdivisions and internal interrelationships analysed. The subsystems are also considered interacting with each other to inhibit or increase change. Changes in Early Christian Ireland can be explained through the links between subsystems, and how one can promote or inhibit changes in others. The whole essence of systems analysis is that simple one-to-one cause and effect explanations do not reflect the sophisticated nature of real life. The complex interrelationships of variables can be more suitably investigated through systemic analysis. Whilst some argue that the explanations thus produced are merely complex descriptions of past processes (Hodder 1986) and so not explanations, they incorporate complex cause and effect relationships and so must constitute a relatively high level of explanation.

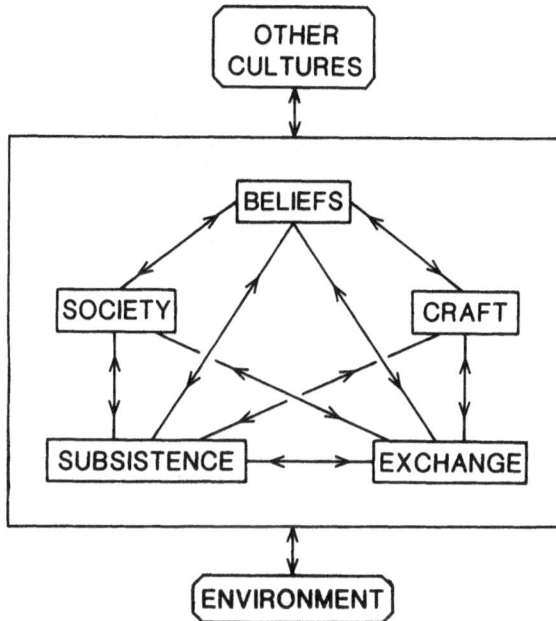

Figure 1:1   A model indicating the systems operating within Early Christian Ireland, and the relationship with the environment and other human groups.

The use of systems analysis is inappropriate in much culture-historical archaeology. If individual events, such as invasions, are considered as sufficient explanations for changes, then systems analysis has no place. Processual archaeology does not deny that invasions could and did take place, but would see them as part of wider trends, processes, of which the migration was just one element. Invasion does not explain change, since the invasion itself needs explanation, and the process of absorption of any foreign traits that are then incorporated into the indigenous culture also needs analysis. The explanatory inadequacy of the simple invasion hypothesis was recognised in British prehistory by Clark (1966) and the applicability of the criticisms to Ireland has been emphasised by Waddell (1978). As yet, there has been little attempt to widen discussion to the historic period in Ireland, though there are now moves to re-examine Anglo-Saxon archaeology from different perspectives (Hodges 1982, Arnold 1988). Though there are well documented movements of peoples in post-Roman Britain, in themselves these do not explain the main sociocultural changes that took place.

One of the most important concepts in systems analysis is that of feedback. A change in one subsystem can have an effect on another, but that effect often in turn has implications (directly or indirectly) for the first subsystem. This is termed feedback, which comes in two forms. Negative feedback has the effect of reducing any tendency for change in the subsystem, whilst conversely, positive feedback increases the propensity for change. Systemic analysis has an underlying assumption that systems tend towards stability. This goal-seeking may be conscious in that individuals or groups seek to maintain the status quo. It is often unconscious, however, and works at a level much higher than that conceptualised by those involved. Thus, individuals may all be attempting to better their social or economic position, but the overall structure of these social and economic subsystems will tend to remain stable since a certain level of competition can be accommodated, and indeed may even be required.

Systems are maintained by the operation of regulators. These consist of elements in a subsystem that mediate between other subsystems or between one system and another. They remove or muffle the variability and so reduce stress elsewhere in the system. A good example in the first few centuries of Early Christian Ireland was within the social system where the complex succession rules prevented secure unilineal dynastic domination over many generations, and so the concomitant accumulation of power that this might have allowed (Chapter 4). Only in the Viking Age was the regulator made less effective through economic changes which allowed the large scale purchase and manipulation of political support (Mytum forthcoming).

It is important to recognise that not only can the elements within a system change, but the relationships between them (indicated diagrammatically by arrows) can also change. For example, a king may have a client who owes him a set of obligations in return for a loan of land. If these obligations are doubled from one cow each year to two, the relationship remains the same but the flow along that link varies. Increased flow round a system may not affect its structure, but often it can lead to changes. For example, a rise in agricultural production could lead to major adjustment in the level of support for craft production, and so allow specialisation (which would not be just an increase in the scale of the existing elements of the system but the creation of new ones). Intensified agricultural production and the effects of this in Early Christian Ireland are one of the central themes of this book.

When the system alters its form, then this is termed structural change. Thus, changes in the amounts of flow (e.g. number of cows paid as obligation) do not constitute structural change; nor does an increase in an element (e.g. the number of clients held by a king). If, however, the number of elements in the system alters (e.g. the king becomes a client of an over-king) then this is structural change, as is a change in the direction of flow or the addition of new flows (e.g. obligations paid not only to the king but also directly to the over-king by the former's clients). Structural change does not always involve increasing complexity in a system; it can in some cases involve reductions (e.g. abandonment of direct payments to an over-king from a king's clients).

The apparently contradictory forces of stability and change provide a tension which exists within every system. Given the natural tendency of systems to be stable, however, how can any one model incorporate both stability and change? Perlman (1977) considers that these should not be necessarily viewed as opposites, but as extremes on a continuum. In a stable system there will be some movement, and in a changing one some of the old order will be preserved. However, in the former negative feedback will be dominant, and in the latter, positive feedback. Given that a system is constantly adjusting to maintain or return to equilibrium, how can these systemic changes take place? Perlman (1977, 332) expresses this in terms of corrective action (negative feedback) that may, whilst attempting to maintain equilibrium, be too great or too little, thus overshooting or undershooting the mark and causing continued instability in a subsystem (thus being positive feedback). Initially, this will only take place in one subsystem, but this maladjustment may have effects elsewhere. Unless other subsystems can adjust inputs and outputs to regulate this maladjustment they, too, will be affected and the full effects of positive feedback will be felt and will lead to structural change.

The relationship between stability and change has also been discussed by Renfrew (1984, 273). He explains the dichotomy through the multiplier effect. This is the tendency by which change in one subsystem tends to promote modification in another and, as this works through into other parts of the whole system, further promotes change in the first subsystem. He considers that this is how innovation is often produced, in that the acceptance of new ideas in one aspect of life often allows acceptance of others in other domains. This can be seen most clearly in Ireland with the introduction of Christianity into the ideological system and the parallel adoption of new ideas in the social and economic systems. For Renfrew, the multiplier effect can only operate if sustained change, positive feedback, can be maintained in at least two subsystems. If there is only change in one, then there is no structural change, no transformation of the system. The regulators are preventing effects being transferred beyond that one subsystem, and negative feedback is dominant in the system as a whole.

It is clear that Perlman and Renfrew are both indicating similar processes. Perlman provides the initial cause of change, in that apparently negative feedback can in fact be positive. Renfrew emphasises the necessity of cumulative effects being geared by reactions in at least two subsystems.

External and internal causes of change

There are two major schools of thought concerning the cause of change in systems analysis. In one school, most closely linked with general systems theory, it is claimed that change can only come from outside the system. The leading exponent of this external trigger for change is Hill (1977). Left alone, a system would maintain itself indefinitely, so it can only be upset by some external input. For example, in relation to the system shown in Figure 1:1 there may be an environmental change, or a change in relations with another sociocultural group. Any changes of input to the system will if possible be absorbed by internal adjustment, but if the external inputs alter too much, a chain reaction could lead to positive feedback and structural change. Popular choices of external forces that are often evoked by archaeologists to explain changes in a system are: the environment, an invasion, or culture contact (often with a more advanced society). This is termed exogenous systemic change, and an example from historic archaeology would be that of Randsborg in his analyses of Viking Age Denmark (1980, 1982).

The other school of thought believes that, though change can be instituted from outside the system, it also can and does develop from within. Here, the stable system operates with constant slight adjustments up and down, thus maintaining equilibrium. If at some point the reaction of one subsystem to the input of another is inappropriate, then the positive feedback can begin with the scenario envisaged by Perlman, and be sustained by the multiplier effect described by Renfrew. Internal change is often, though not always, involved with growth in some form (Wright 1977, Johnson 1982). This relates back to the discussion of the amounts of flow around a system leading to structural change. Renfrew (1972) is the leading proponent of this position, which can be termed endogenous systemic change.

It is recognised here that systemic change is often internal – endogenous – and most of the changes within Early Christian Ireland were generated internally (see Chapters 3–6). But there can be no doubt that the very origins of Early Christian Ireland itself were external. The significant forces (such as the adoption of Christianity) acting on the Iron Age sociocultural system in the fourth and fifth centuries were from parts of the Romanised world, and led to major irreversible structural changes to the system (see Chapter 2).

Environment and population

Two major forces often invoked to explain past cultural adaptation are environmental change and population pressure. Both causes have been invoked as prime movers in initiating change, and have been popular with processualist archaeologists and others. However, such explanations need to be treated with care since changes in the record may be effects of other changes not the original triggers for wider change. Causes and effects can be very difficult to disentangle using archaeological and historical sources since sequences and chronologies are often not fine enough to be certain of priorities. Moreover, hidden, further factors may have been even more significant in promoting change and it always needs to be remembered that two changes may not be related, but caused by a third process.

Environmental change is thought to play a minor role in the changes described and explained in this volume, though it was not absent during the period as both pollen analyses (Mitchell 1965, Lynch 1981) and soil studies (Culleton and Mitchell 1976, Dillon 1983) show. The climate by the eighth century seems to have been colder than the present day, and there may have been a gradual decline in the weather pattern from the Iron Age, something recognisable in Britain as a whole where there was a withdrawal from upland exploitation and settlement in the post-Roman period, followed by later colonisation once more (Mytum 1986a). In Ireland, however, this gradual deterioration can be set against major developments in agricultural technology and investment in land management (fencing, drainage, manuring) which progressed at a pace greater than the opposing factors of any climatic decline, and so the impact of the climate was small. The other environmental changes such as alteration of the vegetative cover, soil erosion and degradation were effects of man's more intensive exploitation, not the cause. These various factors are discussed in Chapter 5. Whilst climatic change can be seen to be an external factor in systemic change, most other environmental changes can be the result of human action rather than its cause. These aspects of the environment then form elements within the complex system rather than being an external force for change.

Estimating past populations is a difficult business, even within recent documented periods (Hollingsworth 1969, MacFarlane *et al.* 1977). In archaeological studies the methods are even more difficult, but attempts have been carried out using settlement sizes and densities, and cemetery studies (Hassan 1981). The problems of chronology, relative survival and representativeness of the record all present enormous problems (Boddington 1987). Nevertheless, there has been progress in recognising trends in population growth and decline, whatever the actual numbers may have been. What is more difficult, however, is to establish that an increase in population was the primary cause of cultural change.

Historical demographers, anthropologists and archaeologists fall into two camps: one sees population growth as a cause of change, the other as an effect. Boserup (1965) has proposed that population increase is an autonomous force which leads to cultural change; it is the greater number of mouths to feed that forces adaptation, but greater labour intensification and specialisation are also possible. This is a view with which many archaeologists have concurred (examples include Renfrew 1972, Cunliffe 1978b, Johnson 1982).

Population growth and so pressure cannot, however, be treated as an external autonomous variable. Hassan (1981) has emphasised that population levels are not externally regulated, although plague and famine could in the short term have dramatic effects. Rather, population size and structure are dictated by a complex interplay of social and physical factors. All societies operate internal controls on population including contraception and marriage rules. In Early

Christian Ireland other important controls were celibacy within the church and endemic warfare. Population increase cannot be seen as appearing externally; it must be internally created.

At any level of technology, labour input and manipulation of the landscape, a certain output is possible. The level of population this output will support can be called the carrying capacity. This concept can be further refined. The theoretical maximum carrying capacity achievable is in fact never reached because of short-term fluctuations in resources, so a lower level, the critical carrying capacity, reflects a level which can be relied upon. In fact, societies tend to operate below even this level, at the optimum carrying capacity (Hassan 1978). Moreover, in complex societies such as Early Christian Ireland, only part of the product will be used for basic subsistence needs. Various social and economic strategies such as craft specialisation, exchange and conspicuous consumption absorb much of the produce. Changes in any of these strategies can lead to pressures on production without an increase of population.

Whilst widespread environmental, subsistence and social factors affect demography, much of the decision-making associated with population levels takes place at the family level. Investment in more children is only one choice open to a family in the allocation of its finite resources; it should not be assumed that an increase in population is a major driving force; rather the social and economic advancement of the family is often paramount. In Early Christian Ireland, for example, social status was a major concern, and the desire would be to maintain or if possible improve the family's social standing over time. With the practice of partible inheritance too many male children would dissipate wealth unreasonably, but too few could lead to loss of succession through chance deaths and would limit social manipulation through fosterage and marriage.

Transfer of ideas

One of the most important issues to consider when discussing and analysing change through time is that of the mechanics of change, in particular how a new attribute (whether an abstract idea or practical technique) was integrated into society. This spread, diffusion, may be from a source external to the society – such as from Britain in the case of Early Christian Ireland – or internal – from one craftsman in a monastic community to another. The way in which innovations take hold and spread is an important component of processualist analysis, and several approaches are used here.

Acculturation

The arrival of Christianity and many of the aspects of its material culture was from areas within the Roman empire. The processes involved in the transfer of ideas and objects from a complex society, as in the empire, to a simpler one, as in Iron Age Ireland, can be analysed using the principles of acculturation. This is an approach much favoured by some anthropologists (SSRC 1954, Ervin 1980) and more recently by archaeologists (de Laet 1976, Brandt and Slofstra 1983).

Acculturation is seen to take place between discrete, independent cultures, and there can be little doubt that Ireland was, in the fourth century, functioning in a quite different way to Romanised Britain. It is doubtful whether all of Roman Britain perceived itself as a single entity, and Ireland certainly did not, but in cultural terms they can be so considered. Each can be viewed as a separate system, separated not only physically by the Irish Sea but ideologically, socially and economically by different recent histories. The contact situation was one of a relatively populous western Britain, with a developed form of agriculture, wide range of material culture, spreading Christian ideology and acceptance of change. Ireland maintained a conservative hierarchical social structure and with it an underdeveloped economic base. The pagan belief system reinforced the beliefs in an unchanging world. However, the physical environment and resource base in both Ireland and western Britain were similar. The transfer and subsequent practical implementation of ideas were easy. Once the situations whereby acculturation could take place had been established then transformation was rapid.

The transfer of cultural traits is seen to take place at the personal, individual level, though the overall effect is discerned on a societal scale. These conjunctive relations can be seen as structural (SSRC 1954, 980), and are discussed in Chapter 2 under the headings of military, kinship and religious links. Exactly what is communicated can be difficult to evaluate, even in ethnographic situations. Individual contacts only are exposed to a limited part of the other culture. Moreover, these aspects of the other culture are then perceived and evaluated within the world view of the recipient, leading to distortion. Some of what is then perceived may be adopted, and from thence integrated into the donor culture. In some societies the introduction of new ideas has led to complete cultural disintegration and collapse. This has been most frequent where the differences in complexity between the two societies have been too great for the recipient to adapt whilst maintaining its own identity. The differences between Ireland and Britain at this period were not sufficient, however, to lead to such difficulties. A policy of selective acceptance of new ideas used to protect other, original aspects of the culture (transculturation) can lead to the appearance of superficially acculturated societies, whilst in reality they retain old values and systems (Ervin 1980). This may have been the case in Early Christian Ireland, for example with groups apparently becoming Christian but in reality maintaining a pagan world view.

The ideology of those exposed to influences is an important element; cultures have boundary-maintaining mechanisms in the form of institutionalised control of contact with outsiders and rules, generally covert, governing acceptance of new ideas. Therefore it may only be the social 'entrepreneur' who will, in advantageous contexts, begin to break down conventions. Therefore, the nature and frequency of contacts affect the degree, nature and speed of acculturation. That individuals are in close contact does not necessarily lead to adoption of new traits; some forms of contact are intrinsically far more potent factors in cultural change than others.

In historical and archaeological studies it is possible to ascertain what has been transferred by examining the cultural change over time in order to see, for example, artefact types and loan-words enter the recipient culture from the donor. By examining which artefact types and loan-words entered Ireland, and when, it is possible to test the hypotheses concerning contact situations.

Early studies of acculturation saw societies as uniform, but it is now widely appreciated that every society is a complex weave of sub-groups who had varying degrees of opportunity and desire for external contact. Some anthropologists have emphasised the role of certain individuals as initiators of acculturative change, acting as 'cultural brokers' (Wolf 1965). It is here that individual decision-making with regard to the appropriation of new cultural traits acquired from more complex societies is related to the idea of maximisation already discussed.

Once traits are accepted into the donor culture, integration can take several forms (Spicer 1961). Replacement is where a new trait is substituted for an old one; this can involve very little stress to the system, though if there is a large amount of replacement many of the inter-relationships between the parts of the system will not function in the same way, and this can lead to stress. Incorporation involves a new trait being added to the existing culture package. The system is not structurally altered but is made more complex by the addition. Again, if there is a large amount of addition, the system would need to adjust, as with the expansion of agricultural practices. In fusion or syncretism, the two traits are mixed, something seen in religious practice and art styles.

It is relevant here to emphasise the varying roles of, say, similar artefacts within and between cultures, and the processes in the integration of symbols and ideas (van der Leeuw 1983). In analysing the origins of the Early Christian period, therefore, it is essential to examine the context of these various stages in detail. It is also important to realise that changes can also be derived from other processes apart from acculturation, and that during the fifth century Ireland was not necessarily obtaining the momentum for change only from the areas once in the Roman empire; it appears, however, that it was thence that most stimuli emanated. Acculturation is an approach by which a systemic analysis of externally derived change can be formulated.

Peer polity interaction

Renfrew has recently developed the concept of peer polity interaction to explain internal change (Renfrew 1986). A group of independent, roughly equal political units (peer polities) within a region often have social and economic contacts. These involve competition which may be manifested in a range of forms. Renfrew lists those which he considers most important: warfare, competitive emulation, transmission of innovation including symbolic entrainment (the use of a common system of symbols), and exchange of goods. If these processes are cumulative they can lead to structural change within the political units. Renfrew considers that peer polity interaction lies between exogenous and endogenous change, and so is a third and intermediate form of change. However, it is really endogenous since the largest unit of analysis – the system within which subsystems operate – is the region containing a number of political entities. Within this regional system the peer polities each act as a subsystem, with links that include the various processes that are listed above. It is merely that analysis is of a regional inter-societal system rather than a smaller scale one. It does not constitute a new explanatory framework, but is a useful tool in examining regional change. As such, it is valuable in the analysis of Early Christian Ireland which throughout the period contained many political units.

Peer polity interaction is a useful concept by which to explain the surprising uniformity of culture throughout Early Christian Ireland, and the spread of many ideas and techniques through the country. Cherry (Renfrew and Cherry 1986, 150) recognised that with historical sources, the mechanics of peer polity interaction can be studied in much greater detail than in the case of prehistoric examples. There are, however, still problems in understanding the operation of the processes recorded archaeologically and historically, and particularly in recognising those which were of greatest importance.

One of the greatest problems in systems analysis is in measuring the levels of flow of, say, information or materials between the various elements or entities within the system, and in what way and to what extent these change through time. The evidence for this is often not amenable to numerical presentation or statistical testing, but this problem of assessing the degree of change is not confined solely to systems analysis. Wherever possible, the scale of changes discussed in this book is stated, and some quantitative evidence presented, but this is not easy, especially where there is both archaeological and historical evidence relevant to the problem.

Many processualist archaeologists are now confident that real progress can be made in analysing past social and ideological systems through material culture. Not all would necessarily accept the attitudes expressed above with regard to the individual, ranking and the relationships between the economy and society, but all would believe that past systems are reflected in the material culture record and can, using suitable methodology, be understood. It is a major aim of this book to show the relevance and explanatory value of processual archaeology in the case of Early Christian Ireland.

2
The beginnings of the Early Christian period in Ireland

The transformation from the early Iron Age to the Early Christian period is, to students of the past, one of the most exciting periods of Ireland's development. Some have considered that the name Early Christian has been too loaded, and have preferred the terms later Iron Age (Warner 1983), early historic (Ó Corráin 1983) or early medieval (Doherty 1980). The first of these emphasises the continuity with the previous period. Whilst there definitely are elements of continuity, these seem insufficient to warrant the use of the phrase Iron Age in the light of the major structural change which is so profound in the fifth century. Therefore a different term is preferred. 'Early historic' and 'early medieval' are perfectly acceptable, but the traditional terminology of Early Christian is preferred here because it seems that the ideological change to Christianity underpinned so many of the other changes. Also, the proliferation of terms for a widely accepted and defined body of material seems unnecessary. What caused Ireland after AD 500 to become so different from before was the new religion and with it the institution of the church. Even though many were not initially converted, the whole nature of society was transformed; the change was far more than just one of religion. Indeed, archaeologically most of the change appears to be related to settlement, subsistence agriculture and technology. The old order was completely revolutionised in all aspects of life.

The change between the Iron Age and Early Christian period is dramatic, and it is important to set out the differences very clearly so that the scale of the change can be appreciated. This will be explored largely within an archaeological framework, since historical sources only exist from the later period, and therefore direct comparison can be made satisfactorily only on the basis of material culture. There was also change within the Iron Age and Early Christian periods, but the major structural transformation took place as Ireland moved from the Iron Age to the Early Christian period. This was of a totally different order to any of the earlier or later changes within the two periods. Transformation occurred in all the major subsystems: ideology, society, subsistence economy, technology and trade. The systemic framework of Iron Age Ireland was so radically altered within about a century that return to the earlier system was impossible; a new trajectory of change had been initiated. A new order can be recognised by the beginning of the sixth century, an order that lasted through all Ireland for 600 years, and in parts for over a millennium.

The fundamental change between the Iron Age and the Early Christian periods cries out for explanation, but as yet no developed exposition has been given. The common view (de Paor and de Paor 1958) is that the early church was responsible for bringing more advanced agriculture and a range of artefact forms to Ireland. This explanation, however, is not in itself rigorous or exhaustive. A much fuller and more detailed explanation is necessary, and a processual one using a systemic approach allows the complexity of such major changes to be analysed. Laing (1985) provides a long check-list of similarities in artefact types between Early Christian Ireland and Roman Britain but offers little in the way of the explanation of 'Romanisation'.

Despite considerable effort on the part of several scholars in recent times, notably Bateson (1973), Caulfield (1977, 1981), J. Raftery (1951, 1972), B. Raftery (1976, 1984) and Warner (1976, 1983), the amount of evidence available for the Irish Iron Age is slight. Large ceremonial sites which had functioned in the later Bronze Age continued in use (Raftery 1976), and some network of communications can be inferred from the timber trackways laid across boggy ground (Raftery 1987). External contacts, whilst not negligible, produced little impetus for change. What evidence there is suggests a relatively static society and an undeveloped economy. This is in stark contrast to all parts of Britain where evidence of various kinds for the Iron Age is plentiful (Cunliffe 1978a).

The archaeological record for the Early Christian period, however, is totally different. There are numerous settlements which can be placed into a social and economic hierarchy, and some evidence of field systems. The artefactual record is also much richer, with not only numerous small personal objects found on excavations, but also many casual finds which can therefore be more directly compared with the known Iron Age artefactual assemblage. All this archaeological material will be used to support the discussion of how and why a structural systemic transformation occurred in Ireland in the middle of the first millennium AD, and how this was manifested within and between the subsystems. It is first necessary, however, to examine the processes that initiated this transformation.

In order to understand causes, it is essential to construct some sort of chronology. From such a sequence of events it may be possible to test hypotheses concerning cause and effect. In carrying this out, however, it is essential to realise that correlation does not prove association. Just because two changes took place at the same time, it does not necessarily mean that they were causally interrelated. However, the use of the systemic approach allows relationships to be established and examined even between apparently unrelated subsystems. It is in this context that the difficulty in understanding the internal dynamics of the Irish Iron Age means that external factors in the origins of Early Christian Ireland are emphasised. It may be that if the previous period could be better understood then part of the florescence seen from perhaps the fifth but certainly the sixth century can be seen to originate from internal changes begun earlier. Much, however, can be linked to external stimuli and influences, and these are the ones invoked in the following discussion.

Most interrelationships were not recognised by those participating in the system. Nor were the effects of change in one part of a subsystem necessarily designed to have any effect on that subsystem as a whole and thereby perhaps other subsystems, though this in fact could and did happen. Indeed, many of the trends analysed here were initiated by the structural transformation which had taken place in the fifth century, but how these trends would develop would not have been known to those at the beginning of the period, nor could they since the trajectory taken over the next half millennium was one dictated by actions and reactions throughout that time.

The systems approach does not assume any inevitable trajectory, nor is this necessarily one of 'progress' towards greater complexity, though both the structural transformation at the beginning of the period and the processes that encouraged change throughout tended towards increased complexity, though at a slow rate of development.

Systemic change can be seen as occurring internally, or as a result of external change. Whilst internal stimuli led to most of the changes within the Early Christian period, the evidence overwhelmingly indicates that the prime mover for change in Ireland came from outside. Christianity could not, by definition, be independently developed; moreover, numerous craft and agricultural activities were inspired by Romanised prototypes.

Some of the problems associated with the explanation of culture change have been outlined in Chapter 1, where the importance of ideology was emphasised in allowing for the acceptance of new ideas, whether imported or internally generated. Individuals and groups can be resistant to innovation and in such circumstances change can be minimal. Indeed, the Iron Age in Ireland was such a period of relative stability, even stagnation. When change does come, the directions it takes are not inevitable; there is no one 'obvious' reaction to stimuli and not all reactions are effective.

Acculturation between Britain and Ireland

There is little doubt that many of the changes that occurred in Ireland in the fifth and sixth centuries which produced a rich material culture where there had not been such before were caused by external contact, and mainly from Britain. What is important for a processual interpretation is the understanding of the context and nature of the contacts and how and why these led to change. Acculturation – the acceptance by one society of features from another which is technologically, economically or socially more complex – happens when two are in stable contact. There is a significant difference between the transfer of objects and the transfer of ideas, and whilst the former may have happened in Iron Age Ireland, it is the latter (along with artefacts) that occurred from the beginning of the Early Christian period.

Thomas (1987) has recently set out a preliminary model for the transmission of ideas to Early Christian Ireland. The contact may be with Britain or the Continent, most likely the former. For the purposes of discussion here, this will be assumed. Thomas sees three main ways by which these are transmitted to Ireland (Figure 2:1). Anything can be transferred but in the first instance (and in most of Thomas's discussion) artefacts and designs are used to illustrate the process.

In case 1 a Roman Briton, B, producer of artefact Y migrates to Ireland and in association with an Irishman, A, produces X. This would be a reproduction of Y or a modification of it and having the same function. In case 2 the Irishman comes to Britain, meets the Roman Briton and sees artefact Y. On return to Ireland he produces X. He may do this from an example of Y that he has brought back, from a drawing or just from memory. In case 3 neither A nor B travels (though someone has to) and artefact Y reaches A from B by trade. X may be a copy of Y but may not necessarily have the same function.

This simple model highlights some of the stages of the transmission of material, but needs much further elaboration. The first essential matter to differentiate is between object and meaning. Artefacts can be transferred and used, as in case 3, but their function or social, ideological or even economic meaning can be lost. Thus, a Roman coin in Britain had a function and many potential meanings. Its function was as a unit of currency and so could be exchanged

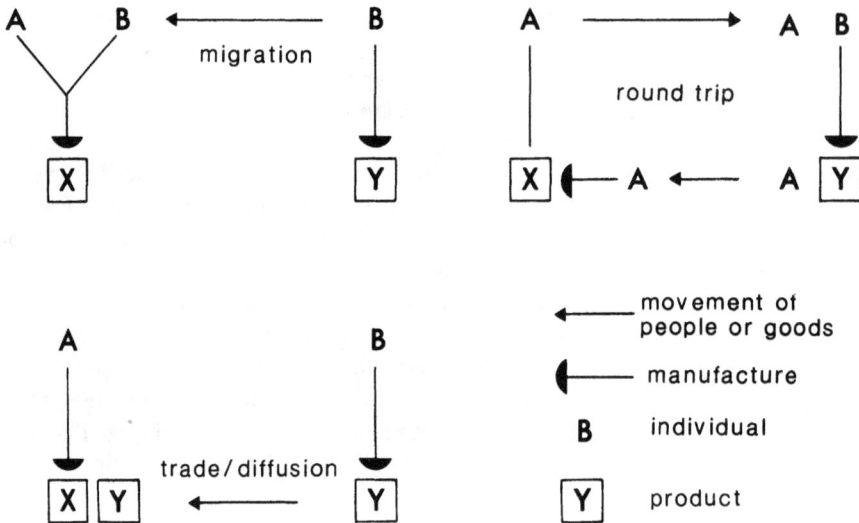

Figure 2:1   Preliminary model for the transmission of ideas, set out by Thomas (1987).

for goods or services. It carried a social meaning (the head of the emperor and his titles affirmed the hierarchy), an ideological meaning (the use of certain deities) and an additional economic meaning in that the user was participating in a market economy. Moreover, within Roman Britain the coin would have had different meanings in different contexts. To a rich urban dweller a silver coin had a different significance than one owned by a poor farmer; the same coin, as it moved through society, changed its significance. It meant one thing whilst used in the market, another when being given as part of a dowry, another when deposited at a temple. In Ireland it was just a decorated metal disc from afar, having possible social prestige and even religious significance, but now perceived from a perspective within the indigenous Irish system and values.

Thus, there is a large difference between Thomas's cases 1 and 2 as to whether content or just form is transferred. Irishman A's understanding the social contexts of use and meanings of artefact X in Britain (from B or other people), and then emulating this in Ireland when producing Y, is quite different from straight copying or borrowing. Indeed, it is because of the importance of context and meaning that some forms of trade and exchange were such poor translators of culture. During the Iron Age there was contact with Roman Britain but not in a way that led to assimilation of ideas, only the acquisition of a few artefacts.

A more complex processual model therefore needs to be set up to explain how ideas, techniques, artefacts and motifs were introduced into Ireland. That meanings were transferred is apparent from the coherence of the new Early Christian culture. It is not just a selection of borrowings adapted to the indigenous social, economic and ideological subsystems but is a transformation of these into a different, independent, vibrant, growing, adapting system. This would not have happened with just transfer of techniques and motifs. The ideas that made them coherent, the rationales that allowed adaptation and change, must also have been transferred. The context within which such full acculturation could have taken place must be seen as the

Irish settlements in Britain. The evidence for these comes from ogham inscriptions and placenames (Figure 2:4) as well as historical sources. Here, the Irish were absorbed within the indigenous native Romano–British culture, itself not highly Romanised. This is itself interesting since acculturation is most effective when the differences between the more and less advanced cultures are not too great. If there are major differences, the lesser culture often collapses under the pressures of too much change.

In a more refined model, related to four processes outlined below, the roles of form and meaning can be brought together. This allows assessment of the varying quantity and quality of possible association between individuals, and so the potential acculturation, under various contact situations (Figure 2:2). There are many dimensions to the appreciation of an alien culture and its multi-faceted nature. To obtain even a passing understanding it has to be viewed through time, space and varying context. Where any of these are constrained, the communication must be limited. Some of the contacts between Britain and Ireland in the fifth century were little different to those limited ones of the Iron Age, but others were completely new. What is important is that the various processes acting together (thus increasing the range of temporal, spatial and contextual situations) meant that not only was contact established but structural change within Ireland was initiated. Previously, the conservative forces within the country had prevented any significant change from taking place. The combination of a number of processes together made assimilation of new ideas and techniques possible, with considerable unforeseen knock-on effects that led to internally generated changes over the following centuries.

Military links

During the fourth century the Roman empire was undergoing stress of various forms, of which infiltration (both violent and peaceful) by migrating groups was but one. The Continental mainland was suffering particularly badly whilst parts of Britain, such as the south-west, were in contrast flourishing. Nevertheless, even here social instability was increasing. How far this was due to external forces, and how much to internal stress, is unclear, but the documentary references to invasions and raiding may throw undue emphasis on the former. Indeed, events such as the Barbarian Conspiracy of 369 are now doubted. The building of town defences, the decline of villas in some areas and the erection of coastal defences along the Saxon Shore and in Wales all point to threats from both within and without.

The contribution of the Irish to the raiding problem is uncertain. The few late Roman finds from Ireland do not seem to represent booty, and silver hoards of hack silver may represent mercenary service (Mytum 1981). Raiding may have been for less visible items such as slaves; certainly this was the fate of Patrick who was seized on such a raid and taken back to Ireland into captivity (Hanson 1983). Raiding, however, does not seem to have contributed in itself to any change in the Iron Age society or economy. It was almost certainly a traditional activity, both within Ireland and on occasion beyond. The insecurity in parts of the Roman province might have encouraged slightly more raiding there, but this is not recognisable archaeologically. Any burning of villas (Branigan 1977) could have had a variety of causes, none of which necessarily involved Irish raiding.

No matter what the scale of raiding by the Irish, this was not an activity conducive to the absorption of new ideas. Material goods appear to have been ignored, or if taken were re-worked into native products. Slaves were taken for menial duties, and the Irish were unlikely to absorb new ideas from such low status individuals. Dumville (1984) has suggested that Latin

Roman design rules not
understood or needed

Roman design rules
understood and needed

1st generation copy

2nd generation copy

Rapid disintegration of
Roman design, using
indigenous elements
(acquiring new meanings,
losing old ones)

Slow disintegration of
design (maintaining old
meanings or slowly losing
them)

Stable design: no innovation
(meanings may not change)

Development of design
within Roman rules of style
(maintaining old meanings
or developing new ones)

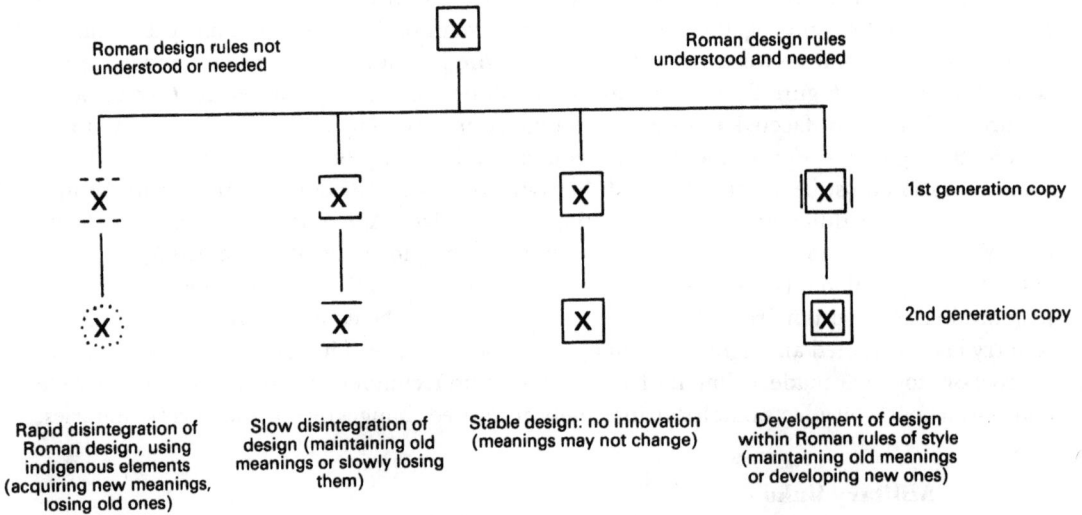

	MERCENARIES	KIN	TRADERS	MISSIONARIES	PRODUCERS
COVERT	small	large	very small	large	limited (meanings)
OVERT	small	large	limited	large	large (technology)

Figure 2:2 Refined model for the transmission of goods and ideas.

loan-words and the British pronunciation of Latin were introduced by slaves but this seems inherently unlikely compared with the other contexts of association described below. Raiding activity, whilst causing some artefacts and individuals to move from one society to another, is not a context that is likely to lead to systemic change through the influence of the captured. This must have been particularly so when those enslaved were given no opportunity to use the skills developed in their homeland, but were used as free labour on low status activities. Therefore, in the search for causes of major change in Ireland, raiding can be dismissed as insignificant.

The movement to Ireland of refugees from Britain with the fifth century collapse of the political, social and economic systems in the province was highly unlikely. Some groups in north Britain still had important kinship links with those in north-east Ireland, but there could have been little across the water to encourage migration. Those who had become Romanised would have seen little attraction in Irish Iron Age society. The few who had never more than tolerated Roman rule were now freed from it, and migration would have seemed unnecessary. Whilst an influx of refugees from the initial Roman conquest of Britain might have been a factor in the presence of a group of southern British type burials at Lambay Island, Co. Dublin, the effect of four centuries of Roman influence was sufficient to limit the desirability of flight across the Irish Sea at the end of Roman rule. If any refugees had then arrived in Ireland and conquered some territory, they would have been in an extremely weak position to survive as an independent unit, and without any established social relations with neighbouring groups which were essential to maintain stability, they were bound to fail. The only hope for survival would have been rapid acceptance of the indigenous Irish Iron Age ways. In such circumstances, the chances of initiating cultural change would seem at best remote.

The adoption of some Roman ideas may have occurred through those Irish who had spent time in Britain. There is now convincing evidence that some Irish served as mercenaries in Roman Britain, and were paid at least in part in scrap silver. It has been suggested that the hoards at Balline, Co. Limerick and Ballinrees, Co. Derry represent the results of raiding, but both contain ingots which were made as pay for soldiers (Painter 1965), which suggests otherwise. Young men anxious to make a name for themselves could have done so by acting as mercenaries in Britain for a few years, then returning with their pay in kind, possibly leaving votive offerings such as the gold coins and items of jewellery found deposited at Newgrange in thanks for a safe return. The presence of some Irish who were taking on continuing Romano–British traits even after the removal of the Roman army is attested by the funerary inscription CUNORIX MACUS MAQUI COLINE of about 460–75 at Wroxeter (Thomas 1987, 9). The work of Barker (1979) has indicated that large timber buildings were in use in the centre of the town, and some form of Romanised life was still being propagated at Wroxeter during the fifth century.

How far any ideas acquired in Britain could be applied in Iron Age Ireland by the returning mercenaries is unclear. Parallels from more recent times suggest that the military only acquire a limited concept of the society in which they are employed. They tend to spend most time with their own cultural group, and have limited contacts with the indigenous population, especially when language is an important barrier to communication and appreciation of ideas.

The Irish would have been exposed at a distance to possibly a wide range of situations in Roman Britain. They would have worked at villas or towns as military personnel, mixed with native militia and spent time and money in local markets. But there would have been limited opportunity to appreciate the meaning and role of material culture in these circumstances, and even less to discover a coherent view of Romano–British ideology. For many mercenaries with only the most rudimentary knowledge of the British or Latin language the understanding of motives, aspirations and ideology must have been beyond their grasp even if not their interest. There would only have been two sorts of exception to this. One was the employer of the mercenary, who may have explained his aims and priorities to his employees and thus given some overt indication of his values. The other, more potent, context would have been if any mercenary were converted to Christianity. In such cases there would have been substantial explanation of the religion, and this would have provided a conceptual framework within which the mercenary could order the evidence from the alien culture. Even then, though, there may have been difficulties in conveying the real ethos of the message because of the Romano–British Christians' poor understanding of the Irish culture and values from which the mercenary came.

In general, a considerable covert amount of information observed in a variety of contexts within Roman Britain would have been understood (but from an Irish perspective) by mercenaries. Thus, any one artefact could be observed as utilised by a variety of individuals in a variety of contexts. But perhaps only from the employer (with whom contact was sufficiently long) could there come much understanding of the artefact's varying symbolic role. A large repertoire of Romano–British activities and material culture would have been experienced by a mercenary, but there would have been only limited contextual understanding of this. In such situations, the mercenary is unlikely on his return to Ireland to have initiated development along lines parallel to those in Britain, though he may have been ready to absorb such traits once they were introduced by others who did understand them. He may have been prepared, in other words, for acculturation, but was not a major initiator.

Kinship links – migration

Another cause of the contacts across the Irish Sea was sustained kinship links, often associated with migration. This is extremely relevant in the understanding of social change, particularly the beginnings of Early Christian Ireland, because the greatest and most important context within which observation and understanding of alien culture could be combined was within the kin group. Visits to Irish kin living within Britain may have been common and included, perhaps, fosterage when young members of the family would have been particularly responsive to new stimuli. The potential of acculturation via the Irish in Britain was therefore enormous, simply because the behavioural, social and ideological contexts could be understood. The covert use of artefacts in different ways in different contexts could be recognised, and the variations in the social system between kin in Ireland and Britain could be seen and appreciated. The Romano–British system, operating as normal, could be observed and absorbed as a whole, yet because of the kin-based relationship the environment would not have been felt totally alien by an Irish observer. Some at least of the context would have been familiar; the rest could be slotted around this. The Irish mind could adjust, reorder, explain and thus incorporate.

Many cultural differences, moreover, would have been overtly recognised and could be defined and explained. The advantages of the Romano–British methods of, say, land organisation or craft production could be discussed. This, of course, was not the Romano–British villa owners' organisation but a less sophisticated western British version, a more traditional meld of Iron Age and Roman. Moreover, all explanations could be given in the Irish tongue, though of course with the use (and vernacular definition) of British Latin loan-words for new techniques, ideas, artefacts. As many of the British Irish became Christian, this would have led to further communication and acculturation, but this is discussed further below under Christianity. Those who travelled back to Ireland after visiting British kin, or British kin visiting Ireland, could easily and comfortably transfer values as well as artefacts across the Irish Sea. Indeed, Thomas (1987) suggests that some of the features which make the British Irish recognisable may be examples of traits and ideas moving in an easterly direction. The movement of ideas was not all one way, but as the British culture was in many aspects more complex, the more important flow in the fourth and fifth centuries was westwards.

Acculturation is inter-personal, and its nature and extent depend on the relationship of the people involved and the context of the meeting. A kin-based relationship and a domestic setting provided the ideal constituents for acculturation, and at a depth rarely available in other contexts. A full range of social relations would have been present within dimensions of time, space and situation. Much would have been covert, but within a partly recognisable framework, other parts would have been overt.

North Britain

Recent reassessment of the artefactual material from northern Ireland, southern Scotland and northern England suggests that contacts between these areas were maintained throughout the Romano–British period (Warner 1983, 1987). Earlier contacts are visible through the metalwork (Jope 1955) but a continuity of contact can also be demonstrated through to the period of interest here. The traits that show links are the combination of the returned bird head motif from Ireland with the penannular brooch from Britain, and the development of the hand-pin (Figures 4:19, 4:21; Plate XVI) and perhaps the 'latchet' dress fastener (Plates XIV, XV). There is also a small amount of settlement evidence of contact, such as the vitrified fort at Banagher Glebe, Co. Derry which could belong to this period and suggests a link to the Scottish vitrified forts. Warner (1987) also suggests parallels between some stone-walled forts with intramural passages in the north of Ireland but these probably have closer links with later indigenous Irish souterrain developments. Indeed the Scottish forts with intramural features are more likely to have been influenced by the Irish structures. Problems over the dating of these sites makes further discussion futile at present.

Warner (1983, 183) suggests that there was a migration into lowland Scotland in the first two centuries AD after which the artistic developments (seen in the metalwork) took place. At a later date there was a reflux movement and the descendants of the Irish settlers moved back to northern Ireland. There seems to be no need to postulate actual migrations of people but rather continuing kinship links between the aristocracy either side of the northern part of the Irish Sea during the first half of the first millennium AD. In this environment craft specialists would have travelled, absorbed new ideas and created styles dependent on both traditions.

Raiding, warfare, small scale movements and disruption probably occurred intermittently between those either side of the Irish Sea, but probably no more so than within Ireland or Britain beyond the Roman military frontier. The movement of artefacts may have been through trade or raiding, but the most significant context was probably social relations between elite families. The north British–north Irish link was clearly of some importance in cultural transfer, but as there was little social and economic development on the British side there was no opportunity for acculturation to take place.

South of Hadrian's Wall the native population became heavily Romanised, but appear to have maintained only limited contacts with those to the north. The Wall had divided the region, and whilst it is likely that some contact continued, only limited amounts of Roman material penetrate beyond the Wall after the second century AD, perhaps as the population to the south become more integrated into the Roman economic system. The extent of this integration can be well gauged by the extensive settlement and field systems identified in the north-west (Higham and Jones 1985). However, at the end of the military occupation in the early fifth century contacts appear to have increased, probably indicating a resurgence of the old tribal identities. The more complex, Romanised culture was now effective in leading to structural transformation, containing within it additional stimuli, most notably Christianity. Thomas (1981a) has elegantly outlined a most convincing case for Patrick coming from this Romanised, Christian mural zone. But whilst Patrick provides a documented model for links between Britain and Ireland, this is not one based on kinship links.

Wales

Contact between Wales and Ireland can be identified both archaeologically and documentarily. The problems come, however, in defining the chronology of such interaction. Whilst this certainly persisted through the sixth and seventh centuries and beyond, the crucial question concerning the origins of Early Christian Ireland needs to be addressed during the fourth and fifth centuries. It is difficult to isolate such early activity, but there is some evidence to indicate the important part played by Wales in the process of culture change. Most notable in this regard were the initial movements of Irish to settle in parts of Wales, and so come into contact with Romanised populations.

There may have been some movements of population to north Wales, particularly Anglesey (Coplestone-Crow 1982), but these were probably on a relatively small scale. The immigrants – whatever their status – would have come across a society which, at least in the case of the elite, was considerably Romanised; there was also the presence of the army at centres such as Caer Gybi on Anglesey and Segontium. It is difficult, however, to assess the significance of the Irish in north Wales simply because their role, and so their context within the existing society, cannot as yet be defined. Dillon (1977) suggests that the placename evidence indicates considerable settlement with, for example, the Llyn peninsula derived from the Latin; a small number of inscriptions bearing Irish names come from that area. The migrations to south-west Wales seem to have been more substantial, however, or at least had a more lasting and recognisable effect, and so can be discussed at greater length.

The area of Britain which provides the most relevant context for large scale Irish acculturation of Romano–British ways is that of south-west Wales. The traditional historical view is that there was an initial movement to Dyfed from southern Ireland by the Déisi in the late fourth and early fifth centuries, followed by contact with Ireland for several centuries (Richards 1960, Dillon 1977). But Coplestone-Crow (1982) considers that, whilst there was an initial invasion at the early date, there was a second migration in the late fifth and early sixth centuries, and it is with this that the archaeological material, such as the inscribed stones, and much of the placename evidence belong. The division into two separate waves of movement may more accurately be perceived within the traditional framework of continued contact across the Irish Sea, of which two phases may have been given particular documentary emphasis. There is growing support, moreover, that some of the archaeological evidence in the form of inscribed stones relates to the early part of the period, namely the late fourth and fifth centuries, and not merely later settlement.

Inscribed stones with ogham have been found mainly in Dyfed but also elsewhere in Wales and south-west England. Whether one follows the theory that it was a late fourth century Irish response to the grammar of Donatus or considers it to be an earlier Celtic development (Carney 1975), there is no doubt that the script was derived from the Latin, but designed for use on surfaces where only simple incised lines could be easily cut (Figure 2:3). Inscriptions were written vertically, up the edge of a stone. Irish presence can be indicated by the presence of Irish names, Irish written in ogham, Irish written in Latin script, or by writing Latin vertically in a way which imitates ogham. All these forms of inscription indicate strong Irish influence if not presence and, whilst some are clearly sixth century in date, others are probably earlier.

Some of the earliest inscriptions in Latin alone may belong to the late fourth or early fifth centuries. This early date is probably applicable where the inscriptions are in horizontal lines of well cut letters. In this case the archaeological evidence begins at the crucial period of interest, and can be seen to involve the Irish settlers at an early stage. Thomas (1987) has suggested that the first use of ogham on memorials was in Ireland, though the idea of an inscribed memorial had been taken originally by the Irish from the Roman world. He further suggests that the earliest Latin memorials in western Britain were copies of these Irish prototypes but transmuted back into the classical language and milieu. Whilst this may be possible, and the flux and reflux of ideas and motifs across the Irish Sea makes locating the origins of ideas difficult, it is likely that in such circumstances the Latin inscriptions, copying the ogham, would have been written vertically. But as these monuments have good, horizontal lines and in some cases well shaped letters the derivation seems to have been directly from Romano–British inscriptions.

Another category of evidence to indicate Irish settlement is that of placenames (Richards 1960). Whilst these provide very impressive distributions which correlate well with the inscribed stones (Figure 2:4), they are not amenable to close dating. The same applies to the use of saints' names though it is highly likely that they reflect significantly later links between Ireland, Wales and south-west England.

The reasons for the movement of the people later called the Déisi are unclear; they were presumably an unsuccessful group ousted from territory near to Waterford. There is no information about their number; it was most probably a fairly small group of opportunistic aristocracy with their supporters rather than a large scale folk movement, but perhaps when their settlements are located the position will become clearer. As there was no Roman military opposition to this settlement in Dyfed, Alcock (1971, 123–4) has suggested that the movement took place whilst Wales was short of troops when Magnus Maximus was making his bid for emperor. However, it is not clear exactly when the movement took place, and the reliance on one such historical event would be unwise without other strong support. Indeed, the lack of later Roman action might be taken as evidence that the settlement was deliberate government policy.

There can be little doubt that the western coast of Britain was under threat of attack in the fourth century. This is suggested by the forts at both Cardiff and Caer Gybi on Anglesey which were smaller versions of the Saxon Shore forts on the south and east coasts of England. The south-west of Wales was traditionally left alone by the Roman army apart from the gold mining at Dolaucothi. It may have been that as no roads or local supply system existed west of Carmarthen, the settling of a foreign population seemed an easier response to raiding there, whilst in the north and south-east of Wales an infra-structure was well developed and direct military protection could be organised.

It might be argued that the migration of the Déisi was just the type of incursion that the forts to the north and south-east were designed to prevent, and that in the militarily unoccupied

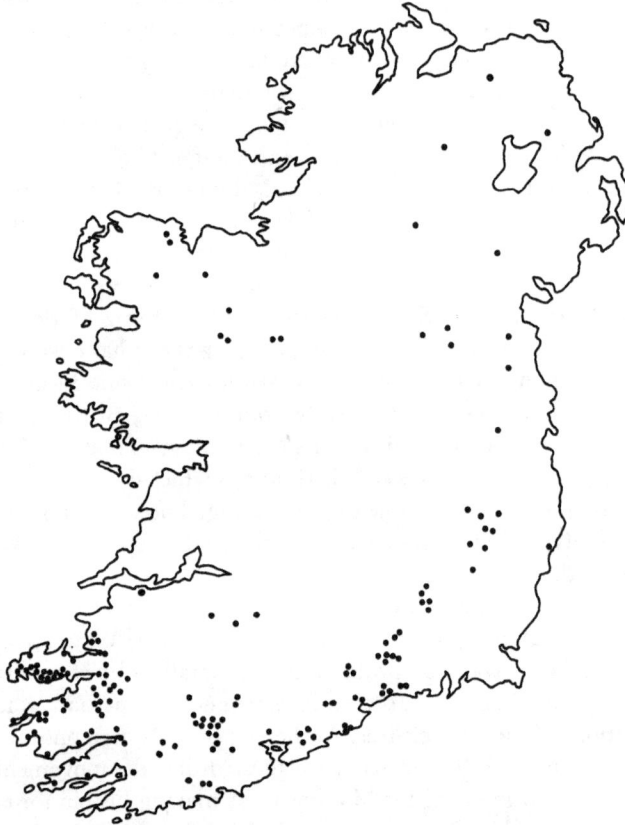

Figure 2:3 The ogham alphabet and the distribution of ogham inscriptions in Ireland (Thomas 1971a, Mac White 1961).

south-west no response to the invasion was possible or considered worthwhile. Haverfield (1923) suggested that they might have settled there because it was thinly populated and undefended, and without the Romans' consent. But modern archaeological survey and excavation in the region have shown a great density of native settlement at this time (Mytum 1988, Williams 1988). Likewise, the claim of Dillon (1977, 11) that 'the mass of British people must have feared and hated the Romans who had robbed them of liberty and self-esteem' has little support from archaeology in any part of the province after the initial period of conquest; indeed much of the indigenous social structure was used by the Romans to ensure rapid and effective Romanisation;

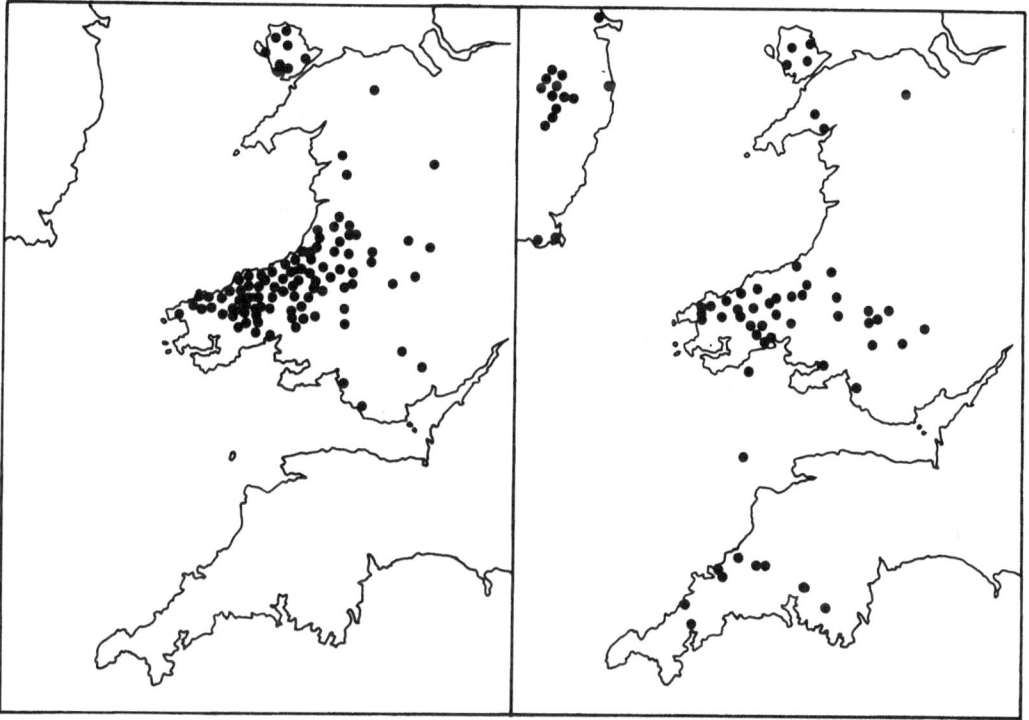

Figure 2:4 Distributions of indicators of Irish settlement in south-west Wales. *Left:* name-forms *cnwc*, *cnwch*. *Right:* ogham stones and Latin inscriptions containing Irish names (name-forms, Richards 1960; inscriptions, Nash-Williams 1950 with additions).

the elite was encouraged to Romanise to maintain and even strengthen its position. In south-west Wales, moreover, there was no reason for such a feeling since there never had been any dominant military presence there. All the archaeological evidence points to a continuing trend of expansion in south-west Wales that had begun in the first or second century BC and lasted till the sixth or even the seventh century AD. In Pembrokeshire where recent excavations have been concentrated the abandonment of defences around, and gateways into, settlements during the Roman period suggests calm and security.

There are other indications that south-west Wales was not as isolated during the Roman period as might once have been thought. The west coast was an important supply route to the Roman army in the north, and Carlisle was the major entrepôt for the garrisons on the western half of Hadrian's Wall. This trade can be most easily traced by pottery, notably the Black Burnished 1 ware produced around Poole in Dorset. The Irish, if unwelcome, would have disrupted trade along the coast of north Pembrokeshire and Cardiganshire, and would have caused Roman imports to the excavated site at Castell Henllys to cease (Davies 1984). In addition, the Llawhaden sites of central Pembrokeshire show no disruption during this period (Williams 1988). The evidence therefore supports either an invitation to the Déisi to settle, perhaps to protect this important western trade route, or a small scale elite intrusion taking over the existing social and political systems.

That the Déisi chose to migrate across the Irish Sea suggests that the prospects were better in Dyfed than in southern Ireland. How many came is totally unknown. Certainly an elite was able to establish itself within a century or so, and retained a certain degree of Irish identity since many of the fifth or sixth century inscriptions show the use of Irish names; the presence of the ogham script also indicates such a continuity. There is also evidence from the genealogies which confirms an Irish origin for some of the rulers of Dyfed from the fifth century (Miller 1978).

Once in south-west Wales, the Irish appear to have been absorbed within the indigenous social and economic systems. There are no typically Irish finds, though the Déisi came from an area with a tradition of impoverished material culture, and the absence of diagnostic artefacts may not be conclusive. However, the mixture of British and Irish names and the use of British Latin on inscriptions indicate that there must have been admixture with the local population. Therefore, although the Déisi established a ruling elite in Dyfed, they quickly became enmeshed in the indigenous culture of south-west Wales.

Although the Irish settlers were culturally absorbed into the late Roman fabric of Wales, they nevertheless maintained contacts with kin and political allies in Ireland, and therefore were able to transfer ideas and techniques across the Irish Sea. Although Dyfed was not heavily Romanised, a wide range of provincial artefacts was in use. Moreover, agricultural and craft activities had been absorbed from groups to the east by processes that had begun before the Roman conquest of Britain and continued during the occupation. Acculturation was little enhanced by the Roman town at Carmarthen and probably of more importance was contact with more Romanised areas such as south-west England and south-east Wales via traders along the coast.

The social and economic structure of south-west Wales in the first half of the first millennium AD was in many regards similar to that of Ireland in the second half of the millennium. Small, single family unit farmsteads were built on the agriculturally desirable brown earth soils, each defined by a bank and ditch with limited defensive significance (Figure 2:5), and similar in form to the ring-forts of Early Christian Ireland. A strategy of mixed farming was adopted, but with probably greater emphasis on arable than had previously been the case (Mytum 1988). Surviving material culture on many sites was poor, but rotary querns, hones, spindle whorls, perforated stones and glass beads have been found. Apart from imported Roman pottery, the settlements were practically aceramic. Timber roundhouses were the normal dwellings. The material culture assemblage of Romano–British south-west Wales was therefore similar to, though not identical with, that of Early Christian Ireland. It is not the similarity of particular artefact or settlement types that is of greatest importance, however. What is of relevance is the similarity in systemic structure between these two areas, particularly with regard to economy and social organisation. Contact only leads to acculturation and change when the relations between the two societies are such that the more sophisticated donor can impart some of its attributes in a context which enables these to be integrated within the existing recipient culture. This was not the case with the raiding activities, but it was possible within a situation of flux and reflux – migration and continued social and economic contact – across the Irish Sea.

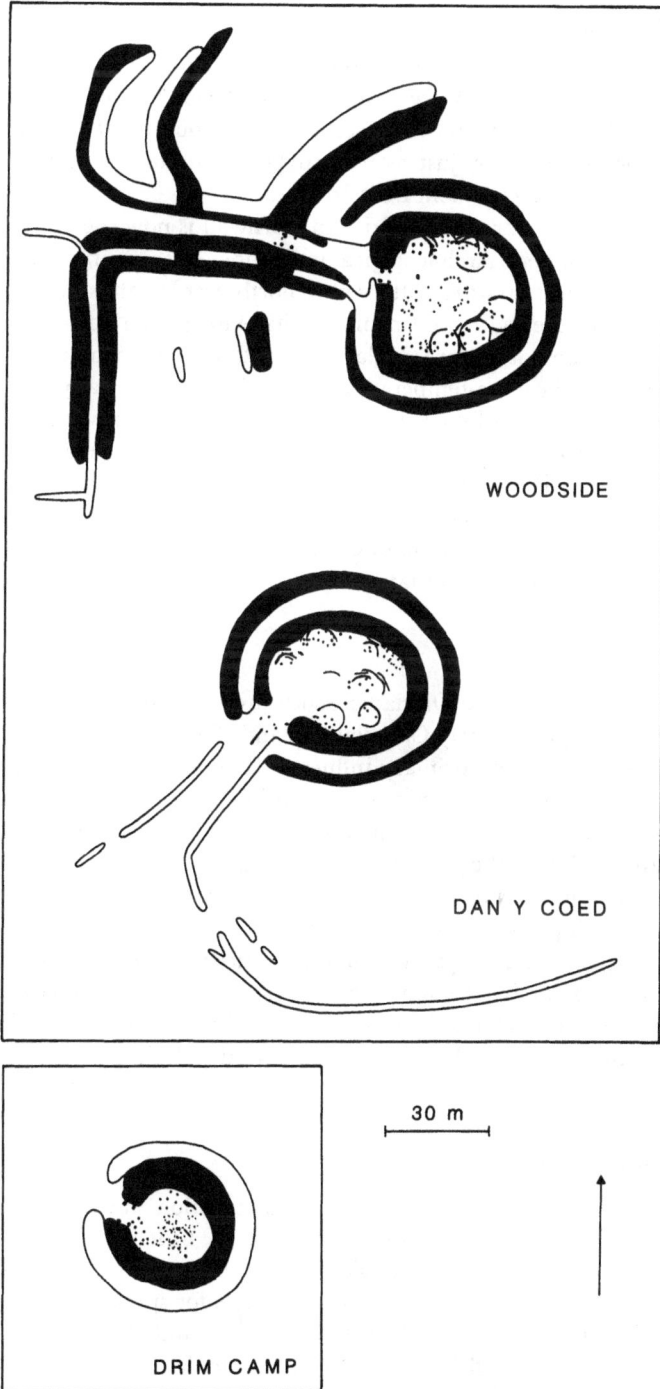

Figure 2:5 Enclosed settlements from south-west Wales (Williams 1988).

South-west England

Evidence for Irish links with south-west England is strong (Thomas 1972, 1973), but only a few examples relate to this early phase. A few Irish may have been present in Cornwall by the sixth century, as indicated by the bilingual inscribed stone of around 500 at Lewannick (Thomas 1981a, 298). This could, however, just as well suggest secondary movement from the Irish settlements in Wales as direct settlement from Ireland.

The other evidence put forward for the Irish in Cornwall is now shown to be later than the period under consideration here. Archaeological indications of population movements based on the similarity between souterrain ware pottery from north-east Ireland and grass-marked vessels from post-Roman sites in the south-west peninsula have long been postulated (Thomas 1986, 76). Whilst the forms of the pottery are similar (Figure 2:6), the technology is different in that whilst souterrain ware can be grass-tempered, grass-marked pottery was just stood on vegetable matter before firing. Moreover, of particular concern here is the growing evidence to suggest that souterrain ware in Ireland does not appear until perhaps the seventh or eighth century (Lynn 1982, Baillie 1986). If any substantial population movements occurred at all, which is doubtful, they were in the seventh century or later. The widespread contacts around the Irish Sea area recognisable by the distribution of early saints' names (Bowen 1969, 1972) can now be mostly dated to the tenth century or later.

Scotland

The migrations to Scotland by the Dálriadic Scotti are of little relevance in a discussion on acculturation and the origins of Early Christian Ireland, since they happened too late – in the early sixth century – to have any primary influence (Bannerman 1974). The continuance of Dálriada in both Ireland and Scotland provided an important context for cultural exchange from that time onwards, and the establishment of Iona ensured an ecclesiastical link as well as the secular one. As in Dyfed, the Irish settlers were politically successful, and indeed their descendants gradually gained control over most of Scotland. The area of primary settlement may be indicated by Irish placenames (Nicholaisen 1965); only two memorial stones in ogham come from the area (Jackson 1965) and their very paucity in this region would suggest that they were no longer popular by the sixth century. Some other archaeological finds, such as those from the royal centre of Dunadd, show very close Irish affinities, but these again do not relate to the very beginnings of the Early Christian period in Ireland.

Religious links – Christianity

Christian conversion was an important medium of acculturation, and occurred both within and beyond kinship links. Conversions within kinship bonds are little recorded in the documentary sources but, given the nature of much conversion in the western provinces of the Roman empire, it is likely that the kinship pattern was a powerful vehicle for spreading the word. Within the family context Christian ideology could be easily explained and although it is clear that in the early centuries of Christianity in Britain and Ireland many families contained both Christians and pagans, the dominant trend was towards the new religion. The social ties of the extended family gave opportunities for contact in established ways, without threat, and discussion could be in the language and at the level normal in that group. Moreover it could be intermittent;

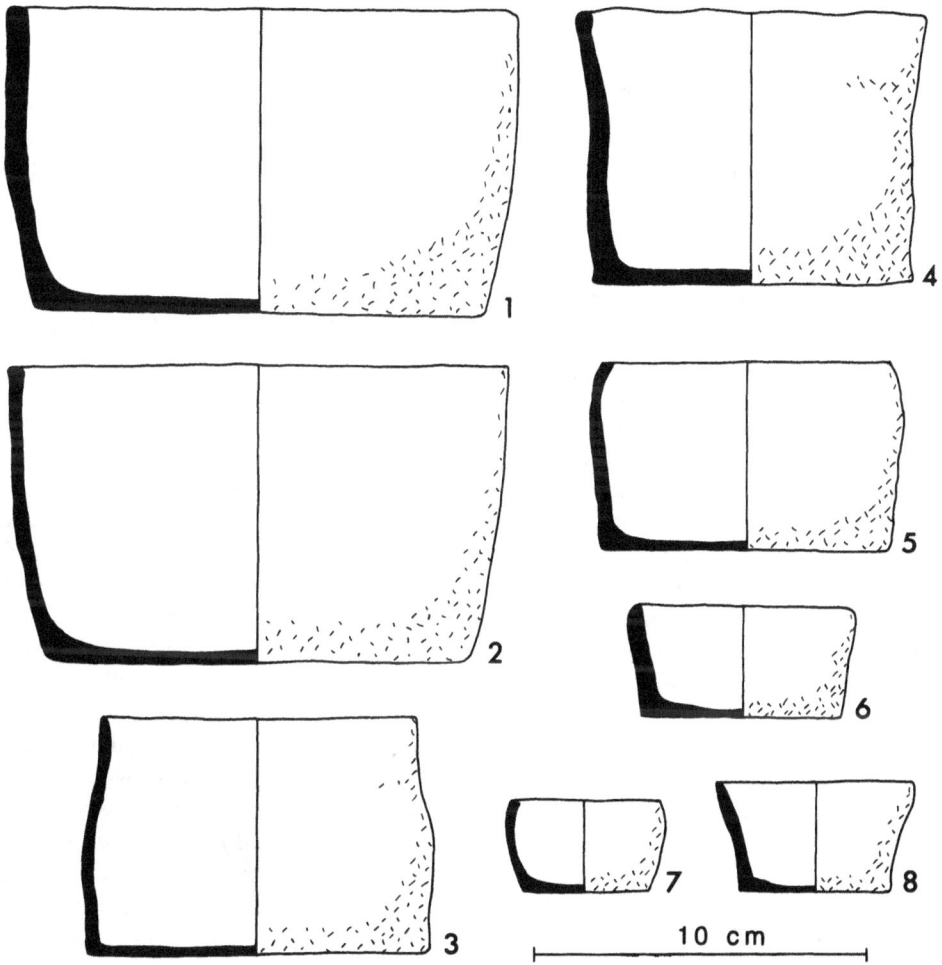

Figure 2:6   **1–3** Grass-marked pottery from Cornwall; **4–8** souterrain ware from the north of Ireland (**1–3** Thomas 1968, **4** Ivens 1987, **5–8** Ryan 1973).

there were always other opportunities to return to the issue, which was not the case with the few peripatetic missionaries. There was also the possibility of converting by example; the lives of Irish Christians were in some respects very different to pagans. Mutual support must have been a great comfort, and the family structure would have helped kin remain Christians and not return to pagan ways.

Within the family there was also the opportunity to introduce far more than Christian teaching. Acculturation would also have included many other aspects of Romano–British life which had come as part of the cultural baggage. The gospel teaching justified the status quo in Britain, and though it was also used to justify it in Ireland, aspects of the more complex social and economic subsystems could be easily incorporated as this adjustment of world view took place. Christianity would have been a particularly effective vehicle for wider acculturation because the communication would have been largely overt, openly discussed, explained, argued, understood. Thus, it would have been incorporated into the Irish culture and have augmented and altered it. Also, once the mind was opened by conversion to a new faith, it was open to other more worldly traits from a similar source.

Within the unstable political and social environment of the western provinces during the fourth century the church was a growing force and, despite military and political disintegration, appears to have survived in some form in both Gaul and Britain. Whilst the migration peoples were pagan, the Christian population was not specifically persecuted, and there was no halt to Christian activity. For many anxious to assume or retain a degree of *Romanitas*, Christianity might have indeed seemed almost a requirement in the circumstances. It was through the church that Latin was perpetuated, and thereby writing and learning.

Christianity acted as a force for change, but largely within the existing social and economic framework. Therefore, it was the mercenaries, migrations and kinship ties that provided the context and opportunity for much of the conversion. Patrick's story of capture, enslavement, escape and final return to Ireland to proselytise has tended to dominate the nature of missionary activity in Ireland to the exclusion of other, less dramatic but probably more common processes. Much conversion from paganism to Christianity probably took place on a familial, kin-based level, permeating through society at any level. The limited distribution of churches traditionally associated with some of the earliest missionaries can be taken to support this small-scale conversion (Figure 2:9). The migrations meant that a large number of Irish were exposed to British Christianity, and if converted, could have easily transferred their faith to relatives still in Ireland. From thence the spread within Ireland could have gained pace, perhaps spurred on and at times directed with more vigour by the early Christians whose names survive in church dedications but about most of whom nothing reliable is known. These early saints may have been Britons, Irish from Britain or native Irish. Flanagan (1984) has suggested that the distribution of the placename *domnach*, Anglicised later as Donagh-, may be a reliable indicator of an early phase of church foundations (Figure 2:7). The Latin word *dominicum*, in its meaning of church building, ends in the fifth century.

The Irish in Wales were converted to Christianity and were using Latin at least alongside ogham in the fifth century. This indicates indigenous Christian communities already in southwest Wales at the end of the Roman period, and this was almost certainly through contacts coming from lowland Britain where Christianity was already well established. In north Wales, Boon (1960) considered that the destruction of the Mithraeum at Segontium was the work of Christians, although alternative causes are equally likely. Later inscribed stones could imply continuity, however, from a late Roman Christian community in the area.

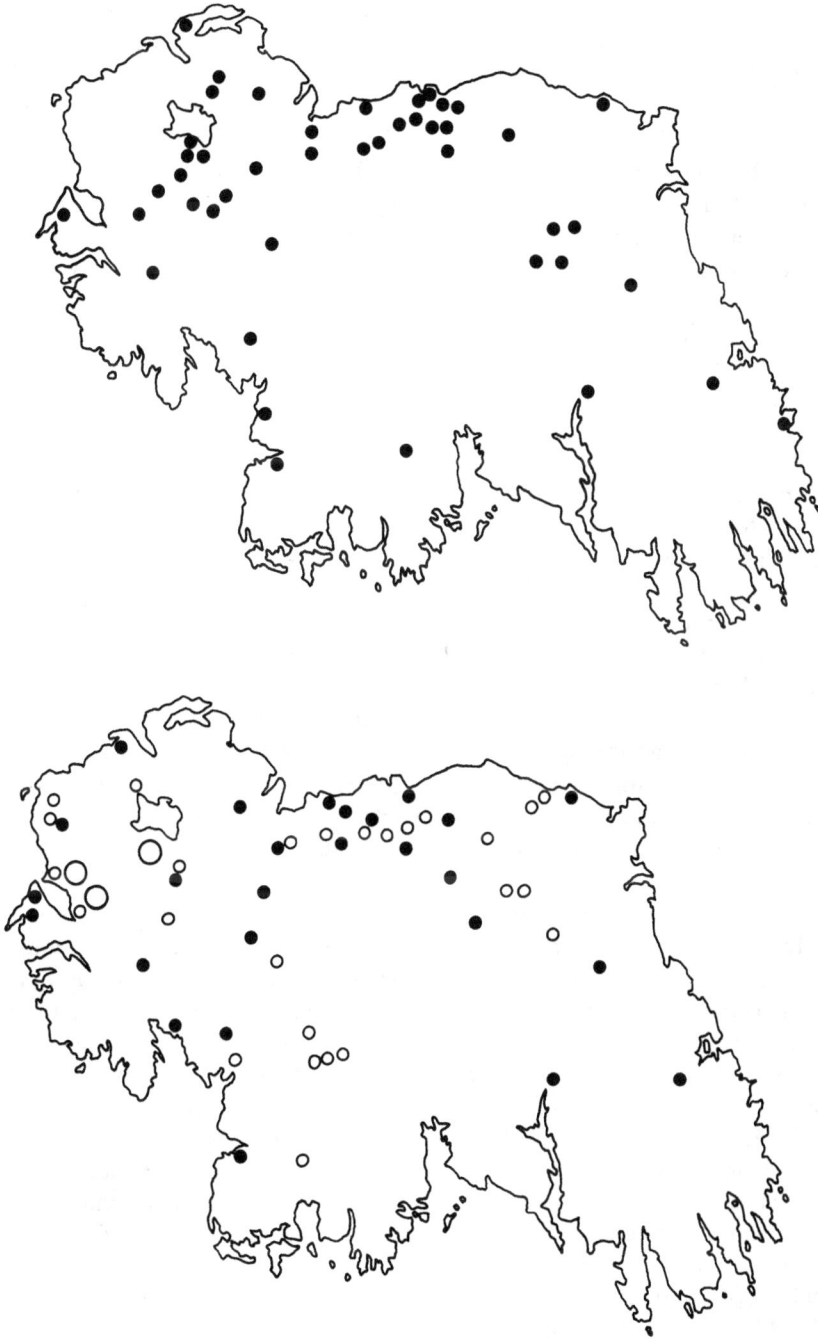

Figure 2:7 Map indicating early placenames. *Left: domnach* names from documentary sources. Solid circles – established; open circles – possible; large open circles – units of 7. *Right: donagh* and variants from Ordnance Survey maps (Flanagan 1984).

There is linguistic evidence to suggest that much of the earliest proselytism in Ireland was from Britain. The Christian terminology used in Ireland was borrowed from British, or from Latin pronounced in a characteristically British way (Jackson 1953), and many such words were brought into Ireland in the fifth century before the linguistic evolution of archaic Old Irish (Greene 1968) though, once started, the process of borrowing continued for some time (McManus 1983). The multilingual Irish in Britain seem a more likely vehicle for this transfer, however, than the British slaves in Ireland proposed by Dumville (1984). But it is also possible that Christianity could have been introduced into Ireland in a small way by returning mercenaries who had been converted whilst in Britain. There is certainly considerable evidence to suggest that some Christians were wealthy villa owners (Thomas 1981a), and they could well have employed mercenaries to protect their estates.

Although British Christianity continued to gain strength throughout this period, it was not an isolated church and had links abroad. Documentary sources provide evidence for continuing contact between Gaul and Britain in the crucial period of the fourth and early fifth centuries. The bishops from British cities who attended the Council of Arles in 314, Sardica in 347 and Rimini in 359 (Hughes 1966, 21) attest to a continuing link between Britain and the Continent through the fourth century. That this carried on into the fifth is made clear through the Pelagian heresy. Though called an Irishman by Jerome, Pelagius was probably a British cleric, who claimed that man had a powerful will independent of God's grace (Grosjean 1957). By 418 this view was condemned, but had by then many supporters in Britain. Such was the strength of support for his ideas in the island that the bishops Germanus of Auxerre and Lupus of Troyes were sent in 429 with a mission to Britain to eradicate the heresy. These efforts were clearly not successful since another mission came from Gaul in the 430s, and even then full removal was not achieved, since Pelagius was still quoted centuries later in Ireland (Hughes 1966, 21). More details of the controversy, and the light it sheds on the theology and thereby ideology of the fourth and fifth centuries, are discussed later. For the present it is sufficient to note that, through the church, contact was maintained between western Britain and the Continent during the last decades of the Roman empire and continued beyond its fall.

That Ireland had Christian communities from the early fifth century is undoubtedly indicated by the dispatch by Pope Celestine of Palladius as the first bishop to 'the Irish believing in Christ' in 431. These Irish Christians probably inhabited the parts of southern Ireland from which those who had migrated to Britain had originated (Hughes 1966, 31), and so may have been converted through contacts with Britain. The Christians in Ireland, through their close contacts with Britain, may have been implicated in the Pelagian heresy, and that was the reason for sending Palladius; an alternative explanation may be that the community was becoming so large that a bishop was required. It is interesting, however, that it was not a Briton that was sent. Doherty (1984a) has suggested that there may have been some limited Gaulish activity in the north of both Leinster and Connaught, but even if this was so it was a minor contribution compared with that coming from Britain. However, it may have been these communities that sent for a bishop who was from Gaul (Thomas 1981a, 302 suggests Auxerre). Certainly there is plentiful evidence for later contact between Ireland and Gaul.

One artefact has been found in Ireland that might have been associated with early Christians. Raftery (1984, 242) has drawn attention to a jet spoon which has close parallels with late Roman loop-handled silver spoons some of which have been found with Christian inscriptions and in association with other Christian material (Figure 2:8). It was found in a tumulus at Carberry Hill, Co. Kildare containing inhumations with grave goods, but did not come from

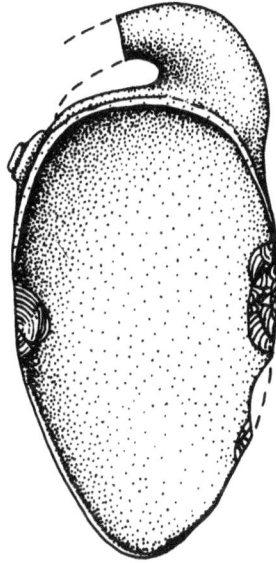

Figure 2:8 Jet spoon from Carberry Hill, Co. Kildare, with possible Christian associations (Raftery 1984).

a burial itself. This is the part of Ireland most likely to have been exposed to early Christian influences, but the spoon may have had a purely secular function.

The only documented early missionary activity belongs to the later fifth century, and is that of Patrick. Whatever his exact dates, Patrick was active in the last third of the fifth century in the north-east. Other early Christians are known to have been active at much the same time down the eastern and central parts of Ireland (Figure 2:9) but their actual role is unknown. Whence they came is unclear. Thomas (1979, 1981a) has shown that there was a flourishing centre of Christianity in northern Britain around Carlisle in the late Roman period, and the archaeological evidence suggests a region as far west as Galloway and as far north as the Forth–Clyde line was at least partly Christian by the later fifth century. It may be from the Carlisle region that Patrick was taken at this time (Thomas 1981a, 310–14).

In Wales, there is early evidence of Christianity in the south-east; Aaron and Julius may have been martyrs at Caerleon (Thomas 1981a, 133; Stephens 1985), and though the postulated church there has been discredited, other evidence from the town has been put forward to suggest a Christian presence (Boon 1976). West Wales was probably rather later in conversion, but this may well have been happening in the late fourth century; inscriptions with good lettering in horizontal lines may be of late fourth or early fifth century date. Ceramic evidence suggests contacts with the Severn estuary area in the fourth century, and Preceli slate was sent to south-east Wales for roofing. There was thus at least a trading context within which conversion could take place, but as yet there is no archaeological evidence to suggest when this happened. Wilson (1966) outlines historical evidence which supports the idea of Christian continuity within south and west Wales, and the vitality of the church in those regions from the fifth century onwards. This was a time of rapid and extensive Christian activity in western Britain and from thence to Ireland. Though indirectly and intermittently supported from Gaul, the main stimulus was directly across the Irish Sea, and was deeply integrated with social relations based on kinship ties. Thompson (1985) has emphasised how unusual – and possibly unique – Patrick was in his attempts to convert the barbarian population; in the fifth century clerics were expected only to

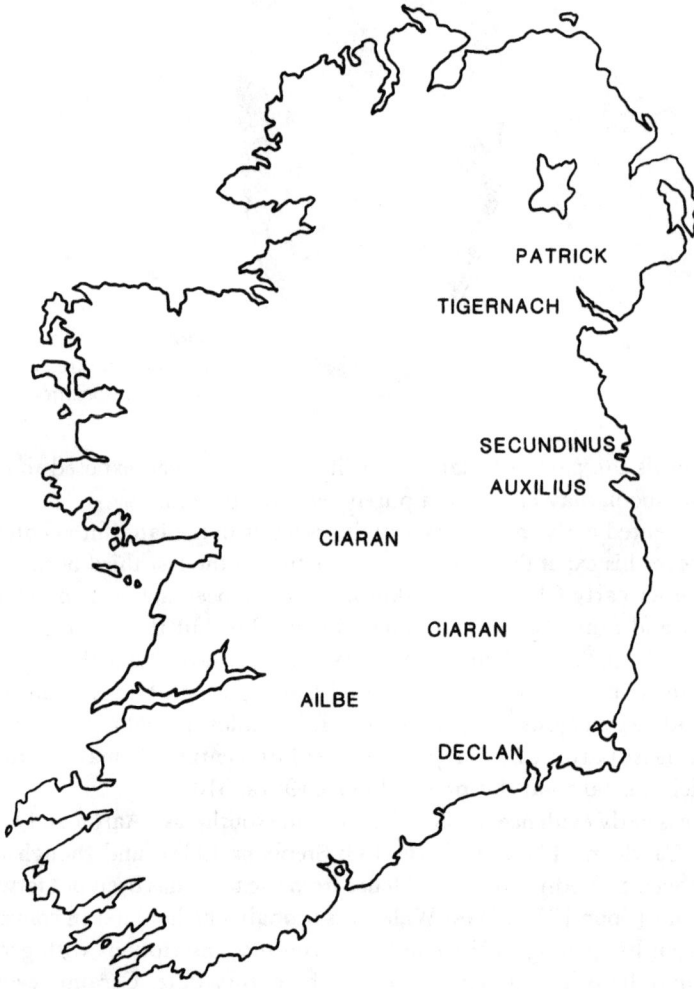

Figure 2:9   Map showing areas associated with early saints which may indicate early Christian activity in Ireland (Mac Niocaill 1972).

support existing Christians rather than, as later, invest time and effort in the dangerous activity of conversion.

Summary of the processes that led to change

The evidence from archaeology and history suggests that contact between Ireland and Britain came in many forms during the crucial fourth and fifth centuries. Actual trade was slight and raiding, however great, could not provide a suitable context for cultural assimilation. Mercenary service in Britain may have led to some transfer of ideas, perhaps even Christianity, and though the mercenaries do not appear to have been very numerous, they may have been powerful enough to create an impact. Of greater importance were the Irish migrations possibly into Cornwall, certainly into north Wales and, largest of all, south-west Wales. The links between these groups and their homelands provided a vehicle along which ideas could travel. That links were maintained can be archaeologically recognised by the spread (in whatever direction) by ogham inscriptions, and is also historically attested. The most important of these ideas, and probably the earliest, that was transferred to Ireland was Christianity. It is also likely that a few missionaries made their own way to Ireland from the main centres of Romano-British Christianity independent of the Irish settlements; this, at least, is the story given by Patrick. He had, albeit by force, been taken there and saw the potential for conversion. The role of missionaries may have been much less than some historians have assumed, however, and Patrick may not have been typical. For most of those living in western Britain exposure to Ireland must have been through social and kinship links.

Thus, the two main forces for external change, which ran in parallel and were largely interwoven, were contacts between Irish groups each side of the Irish Sea, and Christian missionaries, either British or Irish in origin. Both these forces led to change in all the subsystems – ideology, society, subsistence, technology and exchange. The rest of this chapter examines each of these as a discrete system, but emphasising the links between them and how all the changes were part of a complete transformation of the Iron Age structure, thus creating Early Christian Ireland.

Structural change from the Iron Age to the Early Christian period

Having examined the nature of the conjunctional relations – the various links – that provided the context for change, the effects of these on the Iron Age system can be examined. As part of the systemic approach, these can be considered under broad headings, each corresponding to one of the major systems operating in Ireland.

Beliefs

The first and most vital issue to examine must be the reasons for a change in attitude in Ireland that allowed the absorption of many new ideas over a very short period of time, ideas that revolutionised the whole culture.

The advent of Christianity can be suggested as the most important single catalyst for change, since it changed attitudes which allowed other forces, some already present to some degree, to become effective in promoting change. The pagan religion espoused by the Irish was similar to that found throughout western Europe, with an emphasis on water cults, sacred groves and the cult of the severed head (Ross 1967). There was a panoply of greater deities associated with fertility and power, and lesser ones associated with more specific activities and localities. Of particular relevance here, however, is the innately passive nature of pagan religion, unlike Christianity which had a strong missionary drive. This drive was successful because it was supported by a dramatic emotional power, particularly the promise of eternal salvation, something lacking in pagan beliefs where the afterlife, if it existed at all, was vague and uncertain. In addition, Christianity was supported by intellectual arguments which could be passed on and studied through the written word. Although there was a pagan tradition, and a body of oral knowledge, this was controlled, hidden and emotionally rather than intellectually constructed.

Whatever one's personal belief in the working of miracles by the early saints (and most evidence for these is late and recognised as accretion once Christianity was well established) the early missionaries must have had great personal presence. Their faith and vision were such that they would have arrested the attention of many whose pagan religion provided little emotional comfort. The promise of eternal salvation from men such as Patrick must have been attractive.

Anthropological studies of Christian conversion suggest that women and younger people are more likely to accept Christianity than older men. The Anang Ibibio are a West African society where this process has been analysed (Messenger 1959). The elders refused to accept Christianity at all, though in many other societies in the region their equivalents were able to accept Christian beliefs and rituals within their own existing understanding of the world. Those who were young men when the missionaries arrived became nominal Christians but maintained many aspects of their pagan faith. Those brought up in Christian education were true converts, though traditional beliefs still continued concerning malevolent forces.

The writings of Patrick (Bieler 1953) indicate that he had success in converting two elements that were unsuccessful in the indigenous system: women and the unfree. Those with little stake in the existing system were more likely to be prepared to listen to an alternative. Dumville (1984) considers that many of the slaves were Britons and perhaps some were already converted. Patrick worked in the north where raiding across the Irish Sea may have been more prevalent. Elsewhere it is not easy to see what elements in society were being converted, but there is no evidence that it was primarily the elite.

The processes recognised in Africa equate well with what is known for Britain and Ireland. At first either most people refused to be involved, especially those who were older or had authority and so vested interests in the status quo; or if there was any acceptance it was frequently merely a syncretism of pagan and Christian beliefs; a duality of belief must have been even the norm in the first phases of Christian expansion. That certain mystical beliefs continued can be seen in the slightly later rules or canons which mention that magic should not be practised. The Saints' Lives, though written much later than the period of concern here, indicate a continuity of magic associated with Christianity which must have been a relic of pagan beliefs; indeed some continue right up to the present and continue to be recorded by folklorists.

Whilst a ground-swell of conversion 'from the bottom up' appears to have been one strategy in Ireland, it was also necessary to obtain at least the acquiescence of the elite in order that missionary activity could take place. In this regard it is worth remembering that the church in the later Roman empire was frequently dominated by the aristocracy; Patrick came from a family of some standing (Thomas 1981a, 307). Therefore it may have been no great challenge for the early leaders of the church in Ireland to negotiate with local chieftains. Moreover, in areas where the Irish settled it is likely that, given their secular political success, they would also have filled some of the highest religious posts, and so those leading expeditions back to Ireland would have been of recognised status within the indigenous native social system.

For those working in southern and eastern Ireland kinship ties are likely to have been vital in establishing acceptance with the aristocracy. Whether working closely within kin-groups or travelling more widely, Christians would at least have been able to fit into the native social structure if they had some recognised position to which they were entitled by blood.

The elite may have been more interested in Christianity for some of the material benefits that could be associated with it. Missionaries coming from Britain would bring with them portable objects of interest and could tell tales of the more complex world from which they came. Some groups in southern Africa supposedly were converted specifically to obtain access to westernised goods and an education which would allow social and economic advancement (Pauw 1965, 251). This could undoubtedly have been a factor in the success of religious conversion in Ireland. If Christianity were just part of a total package which included more sophisticated agricultural and craft techniques and new material culture goods, it might have been at least superficially recognised in order to guarantee the material gains. Thus the elite may have been converted in order to obtain ideological support for their position from a new religion which was already gaining ground amongst the less privileged, and to obtain exotic resources which would also maintain their rank. Christianity from the earliest times supported the social and political status quo, and so in that respect was no threat to the elite (de Ste Croix 1975); conversion could, however, cause or at least be associated with social change (Chadwick 1985).

Association between absorption of Christianity and other aspects of foreign culture has been widely noted, though best documented in areas of recent conversion. The Mfengo of southern Africa are an example of a society with many converts and a positive attitude to education, the introduction of new agricultural methods and various other betterment schemes (Pauw 1965, 247). In Ireland, after centuries of stagnation, the prospect of new potential may have been attractive, especially with the ideological support of Christianity and with the conviction clearly shown by those, perhaps related, who had already been converted in Britain. Here, perhaps the ideological aspects can be seen to have priority; it was the absorption of Christianity which was considered desirable, incidentally (or perhaps as a God-given right) bringing with it material changes. Hanson (1968, 114) has suggested that Patrick may have intimately associated Christianity with the Roman empire; this might well include, therefore, taking on all the artefactual types listed by Laing (1985).

The Christianity to which some Irish were being converted in the fifth century emphasised a number of theological points. It is necessary to examine the main tenets of the early faith in Britain to see how these affected the wider, world view. Many of the changes in world view probably affected not only those converted to Christianity but others as well. Therefore it is particularly important to examine this aspect since it would have had a wide significance in the development of cultural change.

The immediate popular image of early Christianity in the west is one of monasticism, but this did not begin to appear in western Europe until the late fifth or even the early sixth century (Thomas 1981a, 348). The early church in Britain was derived from the church active in the Roman empire (Chadwick 1967), with a little appropriate adaptation to indigenous cultural systems.

Pagan religion had been submissive, fearful, emphasising placation of the gods (Ross 1967).

It also placed great stress on communal responsibilities. Christianity offered hope, but that hope was generally individual. In some circumstances there was wider responsibility; kings, through their actions, affected their territory and their subjects (Byrne 1973). But this was taken on as part of the absorption of native beliefs, and necessary to reinforce the special position of the elite. Generally, the message was one of individual responsibility. This New Testament emphasis, contrasting with the group responsibilities of the Old Testament, gave the individual a special place in the new ideology.

The theology of early Christianity was based firmly on the idea of Christ as God, but also as man; his body was the church. An intimate relationship with Christ and God is conveyed in the slightly later Irish poems, helped by the fact that within the Irish social system the king was a familiar figure since the political units were so small. Though distant, perhaps, socially, the secular king was physically close. To the Irish, Christ, too, was near (Ó Laoghaire 1984). An aspect of Irish theology relevant to much of the later discussion is the emphasis on the individual in prayer and salvation. Godell (1963, quoted by Ó Laoghaire 1984) makes clear the stress placed on 'I' rather than 'we' in the documented prayers. The individual was also expected to carry out penances for his own sins. Pilgrimages were journeys of personal exploration, both topographically and also, more importantly, spiritually. It was the individual, not the group, that was saved or damned. On the basis of individual faith and action was the final judgement to be made. This emphasis was particularly relevant to the debate concerning the Pelagian heresy of the early fifth century.

It is possible that Pelagianism affected the early church in Ireland as it did in Britain (Dumville 1985a), though the extent of the belief is unclear. This heresy stated that man possessed free will, could dictate his own destiny and did not rely on divine grace. This was in direct opposition to the views of St Augustine of Hippo who saw man as helpless and dependent on God's will. In Roman Britain Pelagianism may have had a short-lived success, but it was Augustine's supporters who triumphed. Nevertheless, Pelagianism highlights an important issue which runs through Christianity: the role of the individual in life and salvation.

It is worth remembering that ideological change did not have to come about only through Christian missionaries. Some of the Irish settled in Britain may not have been converted, but would still have acculturated other aspects of Romano–British culture. They could have spread many of the same ideas that Christians would have transferred. They were all involved in a developed social system with defined ideas about land ownership. Whilst individual ownership of portable objects was no doubt recognised throughout the Iron Age in Britain and the early Iron Age of Ireland, the position was rather different for land. In Britain individual ownership of land seems to have begun to be recognised in the immediate pre-Roman Iron Age, and the concept became widely applied in the Romano–British period (Hingley 1989). By the time the Irish reached Britain, therefore, land there was owned by individuals, which gave them a sense of place and commitment to their property that was different to that which had been held under communal ownership. Moreover, other aspects of Roman law emphasised the individual's responsibilities and obligations.

The freeing of the individual from ideological constraints emphasising group obligations was largely through Christianity, but was also inherent in some pagan Roman beliefs too. This meant that optimising strategies could be perceived and carried out on radically different lines. The 'entrepreneur' could experiment, less encumbered with the conservatism inherent in wider group responsibilities, able to succeed or fail in new ventures. Innovation was open to those who wished to try it; change was ideologically acceptable.

Society

The change away from an emphasis on tribal or kin-group ownership of land took place in western Britain near the end of the first millennium BC and profoundly affected social structure. With the division of the communal land into smaller units under the ownership of families, settlement could become dispersed, each being smaller and accommodating individual family units. Large settlements such as hillforts and promontory forts stopped being constructed in naturally defensive locations augmented by substantial banks and ditches. Instead, smaller settlements were built in open terrain and surrounded by lesser earthworks. Where the old settlements continued in use or were re-occupied, it was by family groups and the defences were not refurbished. This change from larger defended sites to smaller enclosed ones has been well documented in many areas such as south-west Wales (Mytum 1988) and Cornwall (Johnson and Rose 1982).

At the same time as the recognition of individual land ownership, tribal organisation at a higher level must have become more structured. There was sufficient authority to negate the need for stringent levels of defence, whilst a greater flexibility for individual actions was introduced by the dispersed settlement pattern. There was a move from small, independent social and political units organised on a kin-group basis, in conflict with each other and living in highly defended sites, to larger and more stable units controlling a dispersed settlement pattern, within which each small group farmed its own land.

The Irish settlers were quickly absorbed into the British social and economic system, and must have recognised its effectiveness. This may then have been transferred back to Ireland through continued contact based on kin-group ties, providing a purely secular context by which changes were transferred to the Irish scene. There, dispersed settlement already seems to have been the norm, though communal defended forts were also necessary. What was new, however, was the change in tenurial pattern away from sharing among a large kin-group to individual claims. The later documentary sources suggest a continual weakening of the communal control over land. The idea of individual landholding came from Britain, possibly through the Irish settlements, and was reinforced by the ethos of the individual, already discussed at length.

Whilst the attitudes of personal ownership originated long before the adoption of Christianity in Britain, they could be easily associated in the Irish context with the new faith's ideology. The social, economic and tenurial systems of parts of western Britain could have been transferred to Ireland simply through kinship links, but it is likely that such ideas came along with Christianity. Together they would have formed a package of superior religious, technological and economic ideas.

Christianity itself affected social structure in several ways. Whilst there was already a hierarchical social structure in the Irish Iron Age, and individual power and prestige were recognised, the pagan rituals associated with kingship emphasised communal responsibilities. By the time documented accounts of inauguration are recorded some changes may have been encouraged by the church, but there were still heavy pagan overtones (Byrne 1973). These included royal responsibility for the wealth, health and security of the kingdom through the king's actions; he was seen as representing his territory, and the whole suffered for any of his faults. Christianity did not undermine secular authority, and indeed supported the elite as having God-given rights to rule, but the emphasis on the individual allowed personal ambition to become an ideologically acceptable quality. As shall be seen in Chapter 4, the social system developed in such a way that certain successful dynasties gained power over wide areas. These dynasties were successful in a competitive environment based on individual power play where kinship was used as only one element in the struggle for supremacy.

Increasing egocentrism led in part to the demise of the wider kin-group throughout society. The *derbfine*, membership of which was based on the sharing of a common great-grandfather, was replaced during the Early Christian period by the more limited *gelfine* to which those with a common grandfather belonged. The social system was becoming less based on blood relationships and inherited position, but more on personal relations and property ownership. By the time that the law tracts were written down in the early eighth century they still contained elements of communal, kin-based rules but the grading of society was basically by property and private patronage.

The emphasis on personal choice led to the development of patronage through clientship. Social relations were instituted and maintained between two individuals, the lord and the client. In theory at least, both sides were free to choose their partners and could end the relationship by payment of dues, the amount depending on circumstances. This form of social relations could only have developed once a sense of the individual outside and even above the kin-group had been awakened. It is possible that some form of clientage as documented in Ireland may have already existed in western Britain.

Subsistence

Only a little is known of the subsistence practices of the early Iron Age, but the palaeobotanical evidence is consistent in showing a relatively empty, under-exploited landscape (Mitchell 1976). Though recent evidence of timber trackways across bogs indicates a complex pattern of communications (Raftery 1987), very few settlements are known. Field systems are completely absent, but the large numbers of beehive querns suggest some arable cultivation (Caulfield 1977). It is likely that the economy was predominantly pastoral. Subsistence strategies were extensive and low in labour input, rather than intensive and supporting a dense population.

In contrast to the Iron Age there is ample evidence for agricultural intensity in Ireland from perhaps the fifth and certainly from the sixth century onwards. This expansion of agricultural production was linked with a growth in population, but this growth was not the cause of the changes to more intensive farming, but the result. Social factors rather than population pressure started this trend towards intensive agriculture which was one of the fundamental characteristics of Early Christian Ireland, though once the upward spiral of agricultural production and population had begun, this was a dynamic for continued development.

One effect of the ideological change to greater individualism was the social acceptance of individual 'entrepreneurial flair', even at the expense of kin-based obligations. This liberated the more dynamic from a stifling framework of joint tenure and agricultural practice and allowed innovation. Even whilst most land remained under the control of the kin-group (and as described in Chapter 4, it was only in the eighth century that private ownership was finally dominant) the recognition of individual flexibility of practice would have allowed some development.

The contacts maintained by migrants between Britain and Ireland exposed those in the latter to various developments in subsistence technology. However, the structure of communal agriculture would have tended to inhibit the incorporation of new techniques, and there may have been resistance to invest in more advanced capital equipment. As more decision-making was done by individuals, then the more innovative members of society could try out new ideas.

It is often the young who are most prepared to accept new ideas of all sorts in traditional societies, and this was the case in Ireland, too, in Patrick's experience (Thompson 1985, 91). The kin-group structure, with most power resting with the elder members, would have been resistant to change in subsistence patterns.

The subsistence system operating in western Britain would have offered several innovations for the Irish. Some developments spread through Britain in the third to first centuries BC (Jones 1981) at a time when land ownership became dominant. Since the tenurial changes had not reached Ireland in the early Iron Age it is likely that these had not reached there either. Further advances took place in the third century, and it is highly unlikely that any of these had percolated across the Irish Sea before the period under discussion here.

The social structure based on clientage that developed out of the increased emphasis on personal relations also had an important benefit for subsistence agriculture. Clientship allowed those lords with a surplus – often of cattle – to loan this out to clients, thus increasing the lords' status within the elite. Each lord had greater control over individuals through clientship than he could have had through kinship relations. His power base was also flexible and could be expanded by loans to further clients. Furthermore it had the effect of increasing subsistence production; the freemen to whom the loans were made needed sufficient returns to pay for them. It also allowed clients to expand since they were provided with the necessary capital to make a surplus using innovative methods and so reinforce their social and economic position. Whilst loans were normally of cattle, they could be of seedcorn, equipment or even land. Clientship may have been an Irish adaptation of a British method of capital loan, designed by the elite to maintain and expand their power within the changing social and economic system.

The nobility were constrained by social convention from too close an interest in agricultural production, but by loaning their surplus out to the freemen grades who could use it as efficiently as their technology allowed, subsistence production could be considerably enhanced. Through the process of clientage, subsistence innovations to which the elite were exposed, but could not personally use, could be passed on to their clients. This social control of innovation allowed the elite to continue their domination but did not prevent the development of new techniques.

Technology

The level of technological development in Iron Age Ireland was high, but there is little evidence that the skills were used for the production of a wide range of goods. Whilst the manufacture of personal ornaments and ritual-associated artefacts for the elite was common, particularly in the north, a wider range of artefacts apart from querns has not been recognised. The potential for craft production was not realised in the Iron Age, probably because of elite control over both the materials and craftsmen. By limiting production, output was demonstrably valuable and reinforced the existing hierarchical social order through display of prestigious material culture.

Whilst the social order was not fundamentally disturbed with the coming of Christianity, and the hierarchical structure continued, a new attitude to material goods became prevalent. As has been seen in other systems, the individual became more flexible. This may have affected craftsmen directly, but also created additional demands for products from others who could break free from the earlier constraints. Craft production turned away from limited, individual works to mass produced goods. Pins, ringed pins and penannular brooches were made in large numbers, and whilst some may have been made in the Iron Age (dating is extremely difficult for the earliest forms), most were clearly produced in the Early Christian period.

The change in perhaps the fifth and certainly the sixth century to larger scale production of less ornate artefacts suggests that controls on craftsmen were broken down. Demand may have been stimulated by contact through the migrated Irish who would have been exposed to the mass produced Roman trinkets such as bronze brooches, glass beads and armlets. In Ireland, however, the artefacts produced show the local desires since craftsmen did not slavishly copy late Romano–British forms. For example, the hand-pins were developed from the British type, and the ringed pin is predominantly an Irish development; forms may be related to traditional costume.

Later, the patronage of an organised institution, the church, affected craft production greatly (see Chapter 6), but at the beginning of the period this was not so. Anyone from Britain would only have had an effect on craft production through the giving of artefacts from their homeland in gift exchange which could then be emulated. Far greater importance should be attached to the spread of the idea of Romano–British specialist production. This is unlikely to have come directly through missionary activity and must represent contact through the migrated Irish and movements of British encouraged by such migrants. Excavations suggest a small amount of craft activity at certain south Welsh sites but there is more impressive evidence from both Cornwall and north Wales. In Cornwall tin was of particular importance, whilst in north Wales the varied rich mineral deposits of Snowdonia were exploited by native craftsmen (Kelly 1980). It is likely that these extractive methods may have been transferred back to areas such as the Wicklow Mountains, and from thence elsewhere. The practice of large scale production of finished goods could have been similarly transferred across the Irish Sea.

Therefore, it can be seen that the Irish migration and continued contact with the homeland could have provided the manner by which Romano–British craft techniques and organisation could have reached Ireland. There had been earlier links but these had not led to technological change because the social control over production made innovation unwelcome. However, as this social system changed under the growth of individual choice, the demand for personal adornment by craft products could be satisfied. Social conditions allowed the demand to be expressed; the indigenous technological skills were augmented by some from western Britain along with the methods of larger scale production, thus allowing this demand to be satisfied.

Exchange

Gift exchange within Iron Age Ireland must have been an important process by which goods were transferred within the elite. The earliest Christians certainly used gift exchange to create suitable social relations so that their missionary activities could take place. Patrick gave presents to kings and supported their sons who came with him, and also, interestingly, appears to have paid the brehon class also, despite their pagan associations (Hanson 1983, 118). He would, from his period of captivity in Ireland, have learnt the correct responses to encourage good social relations among the elite, and at this early stage of missionary activity would have had to work at times with a pagan elite in order to carry out his proselytising work. In contrast he refused jewellery given to him by female converts, to their annoyance (Hanson 1983, 16), but perhaps considered that amongst those within the church such gifts were unnecessary, or was concerned that he did not appear to charge any fee for conversion. Other missionaries presumably managed because the manner of gift exchange was already appreciated by them, or rapidly learnt from either those already converted in Ireland or the pagan Irish to whom they wished to direct their attention.

The great impact of Christianity on trade and exchange in Ireland, however, was the opening up of the country to new trade routes. This has commonly been recognised, particularly with reference to the wine trade necessary for the mass (Thomas 1959). Whilst Iron Age Ireland could continue to survive although basically isolated, Early Christian Ireland had to have an international dimension. The need for wine and oil by the church provided a constant, steady and significant demand that promoted trade which could then include other items. By associating the elite with this trade through gift exchange, the early Christians also allowed them access to rare goods. As these then reinforced the position of the elite, it did not offer any opposition to the trade. Wine could reach Ireland since it was already acquired by Christians in south-west Britain, and presumably south-west Wales. The later inscribed stones show a Gaulish connection, and that particular link may have been facilitated by the wine trade. That such inscriptions do not occur in Ireland might be taken to suggest transhipment in Britain, and most foreign contact with Ireland during the earlier part of the period came through British merchants or even through social relations as gift exchange across the Irish Sea.

The earliest trade recognisable in the imported ceramics, that of Mediterranean A and B wares, falls just beyond the period of concern here (see Chapter 7). The lack of earlier imported vessels may suggest that a well organised trade did not get under way until the late fifth or early sixth century, but more likely it indicates that Gaulish wine in wooden containers was all that reached Britain and Ireland in the earliest decades of the Early Christian period. It does, however, make archaeological detection of earlier trade of this kind impossible at present.

The links between the Irish abroad and those at home would no doubt have led to some trade between these areas, since there was some variation in the range of goods available on each side of the Irish Sea. It is unlikely, however, that trade would ever have become a major element in the economy, and long distance trade in particular was unlikely. All the evidence points to traders coming to western Britain from the south and east during the Roman period, rather than the local population sailing off to ports in lowland Britain and Gaul. With the collapse of the Roman economy this trade would have ceased, and western Britain would have become more economically isolated. Since it had not been heavily dependent on a complex economic network of relations, this had limited effects in western Britain and settlement evidence suggests no major changes till the sixth or seventh century. However, contact with areas beyond western Britain was maintained in a limited way partly through the medium of missionary activity, education of clerics and a limited wine trade. It was this link that was the vital factor in initiating long distance trade with Ireland. Although the secular authorities quickly became involved with the trade, as seen by the large quantities of A ware at Garranes, the initial spur came through the spread of Christianity.

Internal trade and exchange can be recognised in Iron Age Ireland only through the distribution of particular artefacts such as the Navan type brooches, and the more general spread of La Tène material beyond the main areas of its use. However, this exchange activity must have been limited by the stagnant nature of the wider economy, and the socially limited markets that were available. With the move to greater individual choice, technological developments were possible and craft production expanded. This of necessity must have led to a far more dynamic exchange network; not only were the finished goods distributed to clients, but larger amounts of raw materials were required. As agricultural activity intensified, the surplus could be absorbed by the specialist craftsmen, and even agricultural produce was exchanged.

Furthermore, a pattern of clientage – a network of social obligations between the elite and the rest of the population – allowed for the local movement and redistribution of goods.

In the early stages of the Early Christian period, it seems that the development of complex local exchange networks and long distance trade links was the result of changes in the ideological and social systems outlined above. Only later in the period did these economic patterns themselves have an effect on other systems. Initially, developments in the exchange subsystem were caused by changes – positive feedback – from elsewhere in the economic system and particularly by stimuli from outside it, in beliefs and social structure.

Plate I Cahercommaun, Co. Clare. A stone-built ring-fort with outer enclosure.

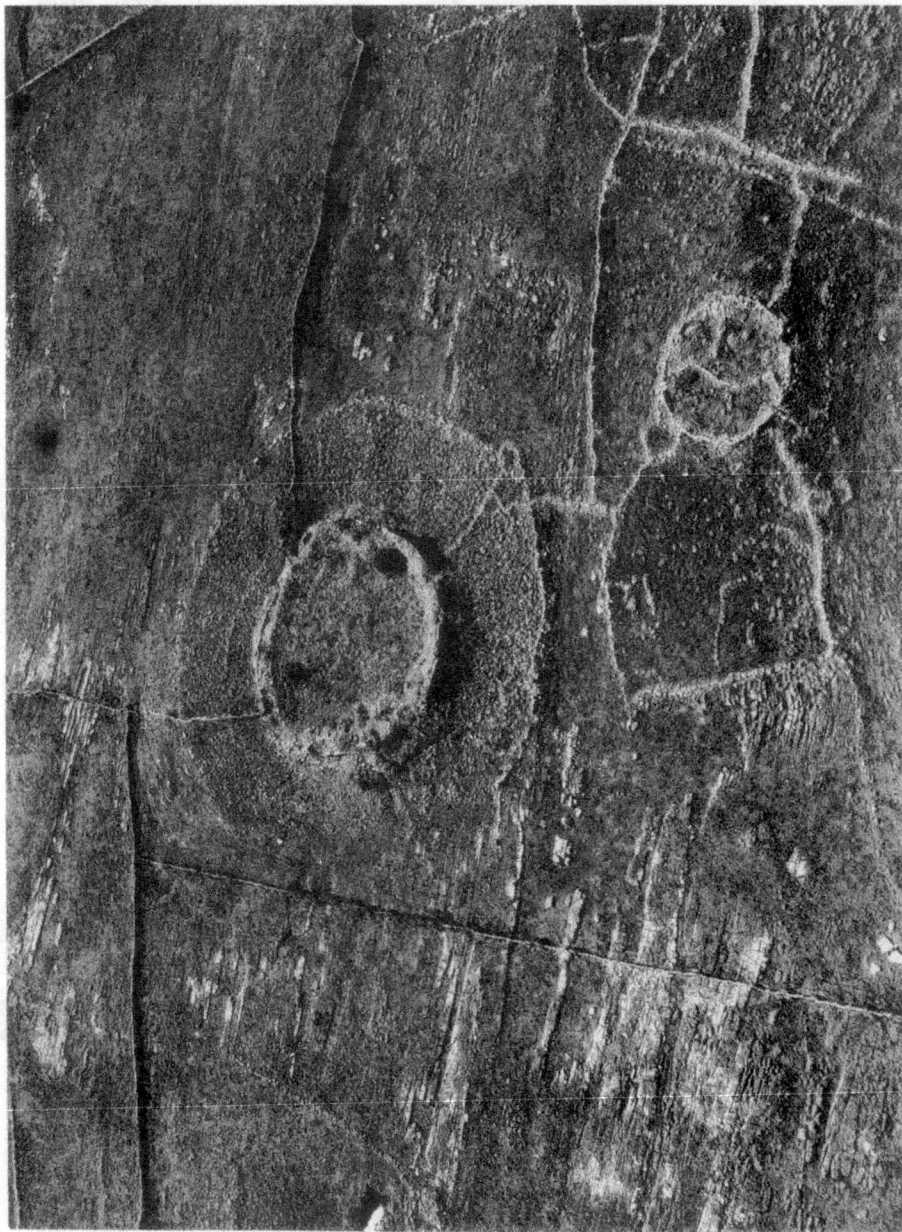

Plate II Stone fort of Ballykinvarga, Co. Clare, with its *chevaux-de-frise*. Note also a less substantial ring-fort with abutting fields.

Plate III A large multivallate ring-fort and nearby two smaller univallate ring-forts in a lowland landscape.

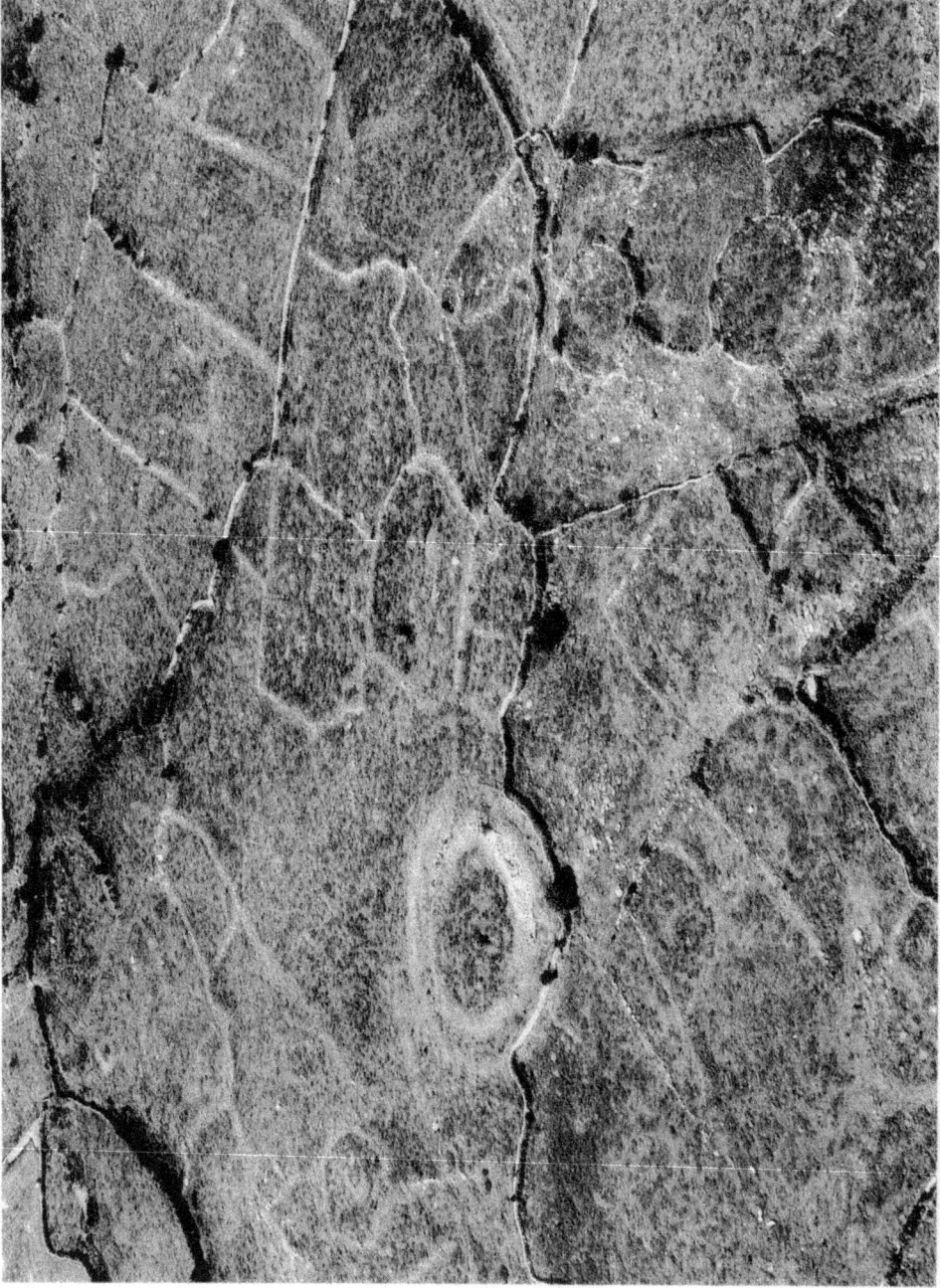

Plate IV Stone-built ring-fort and less substantial curvilinear enclosures within a complex of fields.

Plate V Cashel, Co. Tipperary. A royal and religious centre which has continued to be used to the present day.

Plate VI Tara, Co. Meath. A political centre which has visible monuments dating from the neolithic onwards.

Plate VII Nendrum, Co. Down. A monastic complex consisting of concentric enclosures, near the shore of Carlingford Lough.

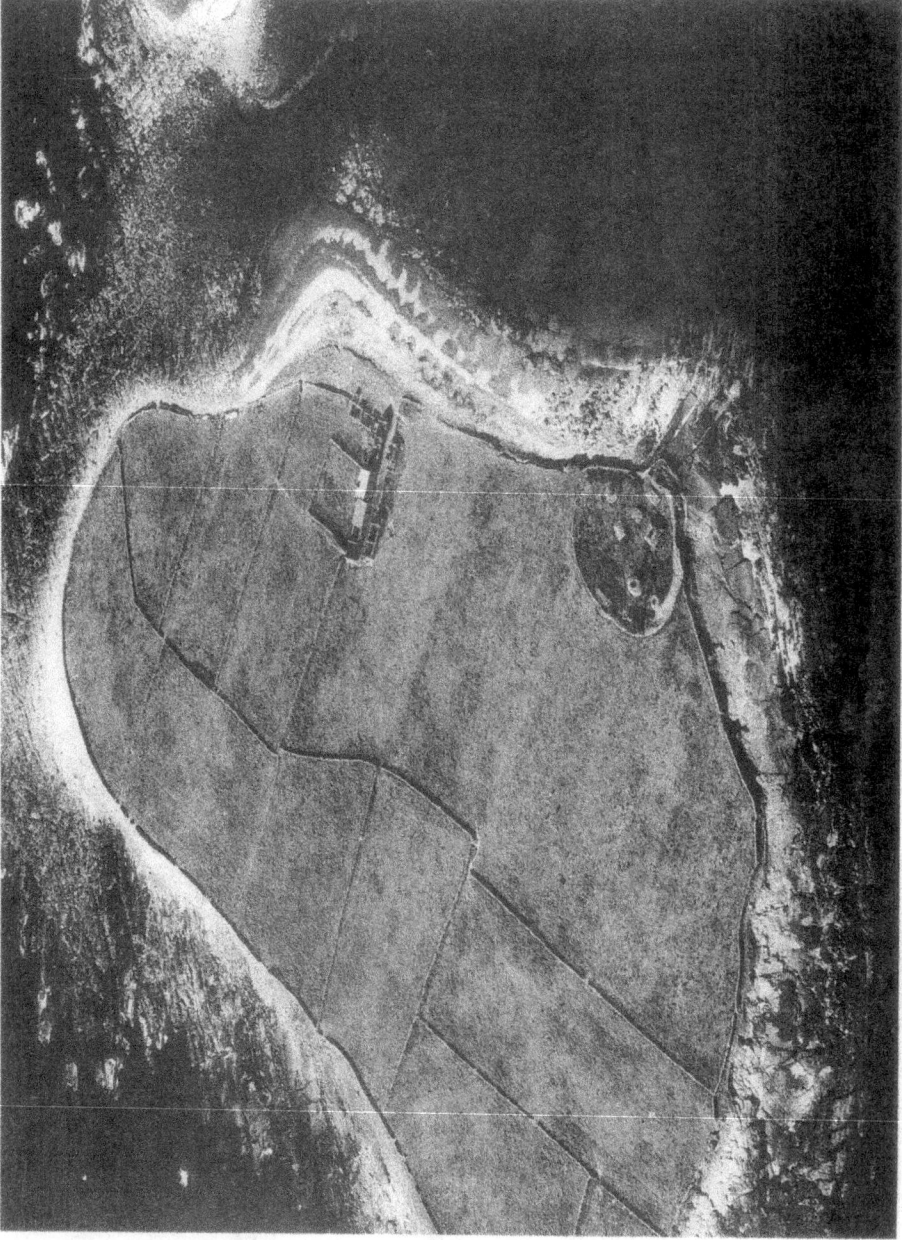

Plate VIII Illauntanig, Co. Kerry. A religious settlement consisting of a stone-built enclosure containing roundhouses and an oratory on a small island.

Plate IX The centre of Armagh. The boundaries of the ecclesiastical enclosures have been preserved in the street plan.

Plate X Stone pillar, Aglish, Co. Kerry, with an ogham inscription. At a later date the stone was inverted, and had a Maltese cross, swasticas and a spear or arrow added.

Plate XI Decorated stone belonging to the beginning of the Early Christian period from Mullaghmast, Co. Kildare. Reminiscent of Iron Age standing stones, the decoration can be paralleled with metalwork of the fifth and sixth centuries AD.

Plate XII Motif-piece of antler, from the earliest phase at Dooey, Co. Donegal. The spirals, marigold and multiple lozenge designs suggest that it may be fifth or sixth century in date.

Plate XIII Motif-piece on a cattle bone, from Lagore, Co. Meath. The designs are incised or chip-carved, the latter being comparatively rare. Parallels for the geometric designs are known; the date of this motif-piece may be eighth or early ninth century.

Plate XIV Copper-alloy latchet dress fastener of the sixth century from near Newry, Co. Down. One of four found together but varying slightly in design and originally decorated with enamel.

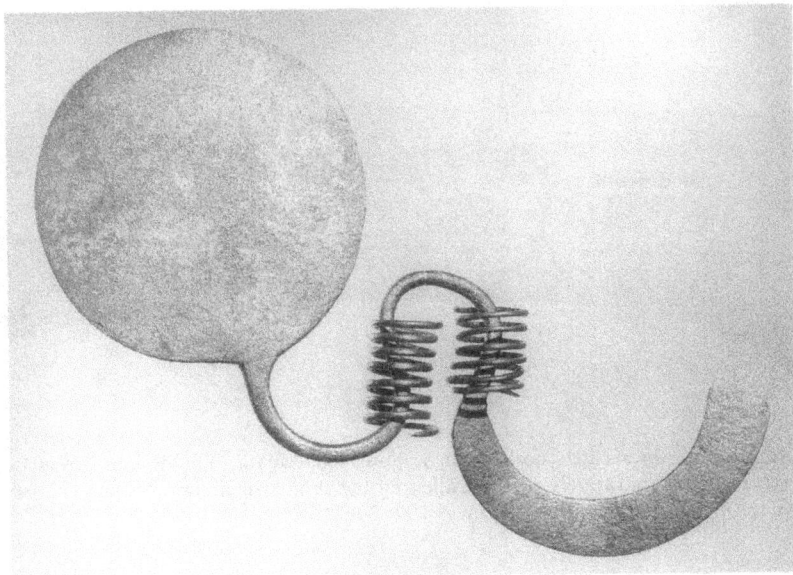

Plate XV Copper-alloy undecorated latchet dress fastener with attachment coil, from the Shannon at Athlone, Co. Westmeath.

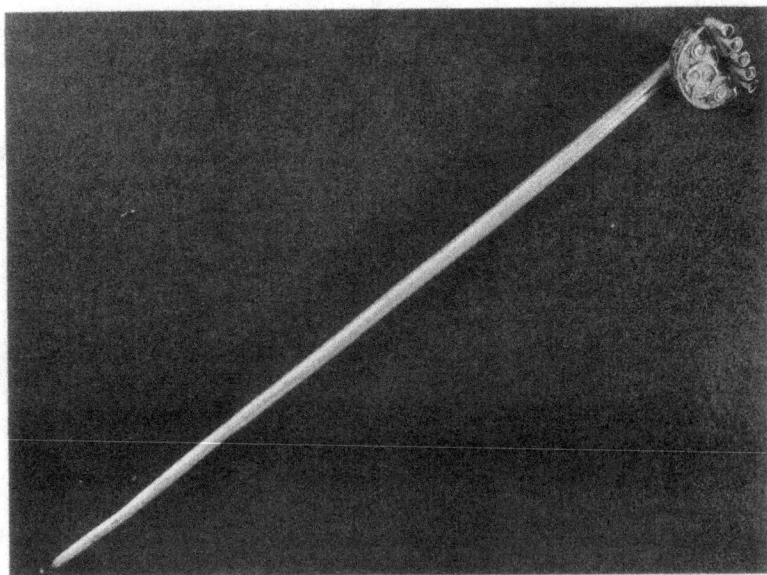

Plate XVI Copper-alloy handpin of the seventh century from Craigywarren Bog, Co. Antrim. Both the five projecting 'fingers' and the semi-circular decorated plate are inlaid with red enamel.

Plate XVII Copper-alloy drinking horn terminal from Lismore, Co. Waterford. Derived from earlier Anglo-Saxon designs, it is eighth century in date.

Plate XVIII Copper-alloy belt-buckle from Lough Gara, Co. Sligo, decorated with red, green and yellow enamel together with one blue and white and two brown glass studs. The buckle form and the angular settings for the enamel are derived from Germanic jewellery. The object is seventh or eighth century in date.

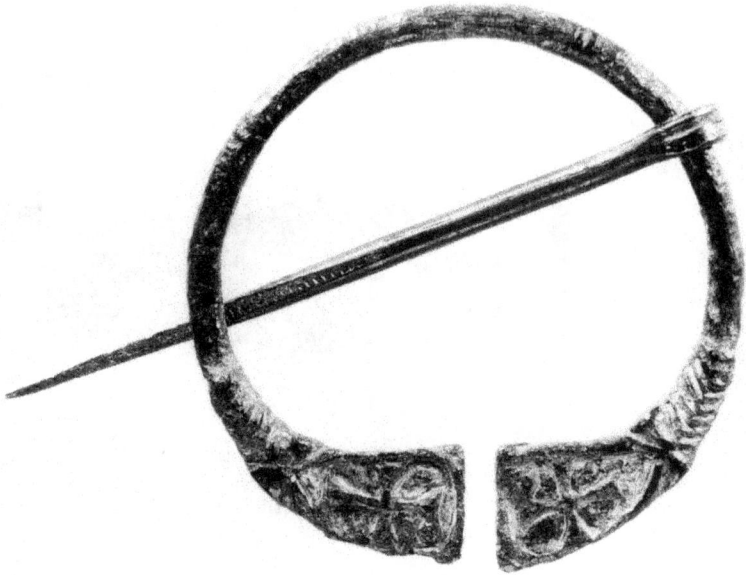

Plate XIX Copper-alloy penannular brooch with a Maltese cross on each terminal.

Plate XX Copper-alloy penannular brooch from near Castedermot, Co. Kildare. Originally decorated with enamel and millefiori studs, of which two in blue and white survive. This brooch is similar to that found at Ballinderry 2, Co. Offaly (see Figure 4:20) and is late sixth or early seventh century in date.

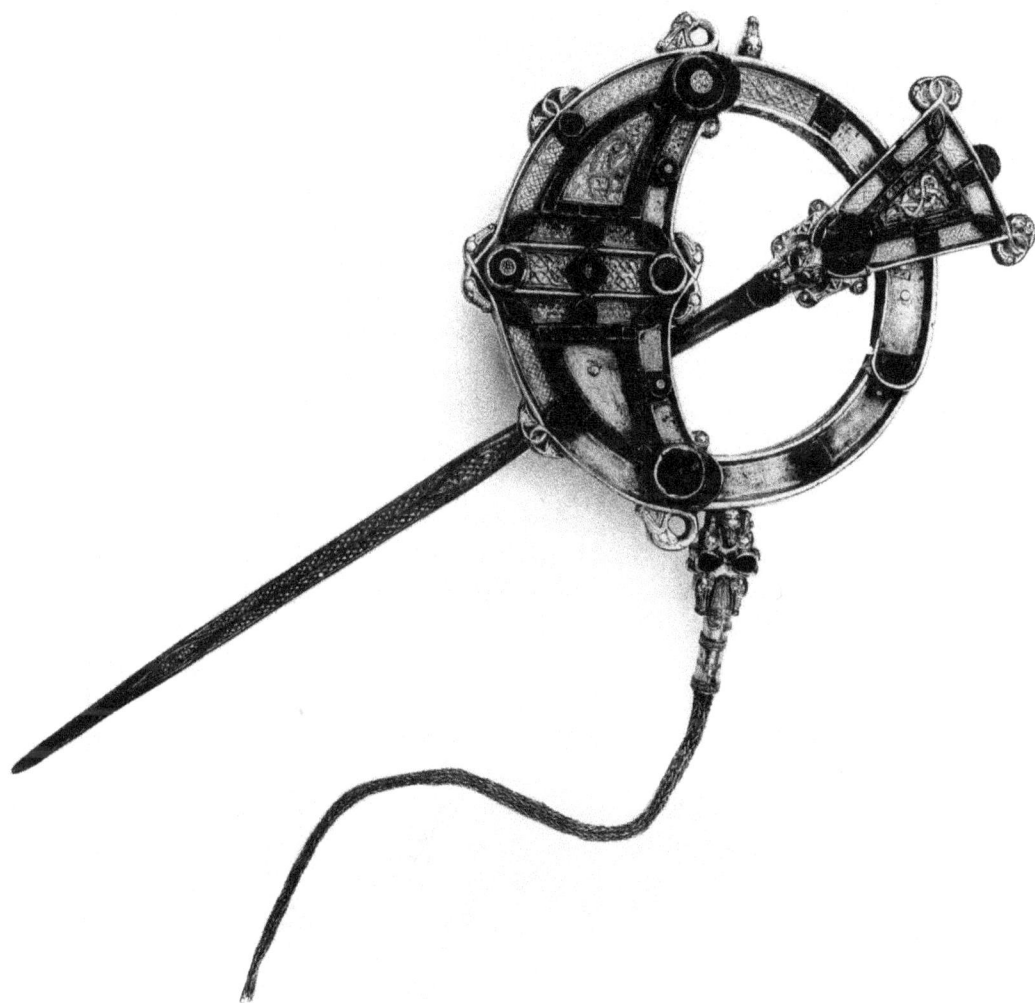

Plate XXI Tara brooch from Bettystown, Co. Meath; front view with gold filigree panels and extensive use of amber studs. This eighth-century silver-gilt pseudo-penannular brooch is the most complex and intricate example of personal jewellery to survive from the period.

Plate XXII Tara brooch from Bettystown, Co. Meath; back view with decoration including cast imitation chip-carving, inlaid red and blue studs and panels decorated by selectively polishing away a surface coating.

Plate XXIII Copper-alloy house-shaped shrine from Lower Lough Erne, Co. Fermanagh, found inside Plate XXIV. The only decoration may have been on the now lost ridge-pole.

Plate XXIV Yew wood house-shaped shrine from Lower Lough Erne, Co. Fermanagh, containing Plate XXIII. It was covered with tinned copper-alloy sheets and decorated with cast imitation chip-carved medallions and ridge-pole. The reliquary is late eighth or early ninth century in date, although the binding strip with angular interlace was a tenth-century addition to the front of the shrine.

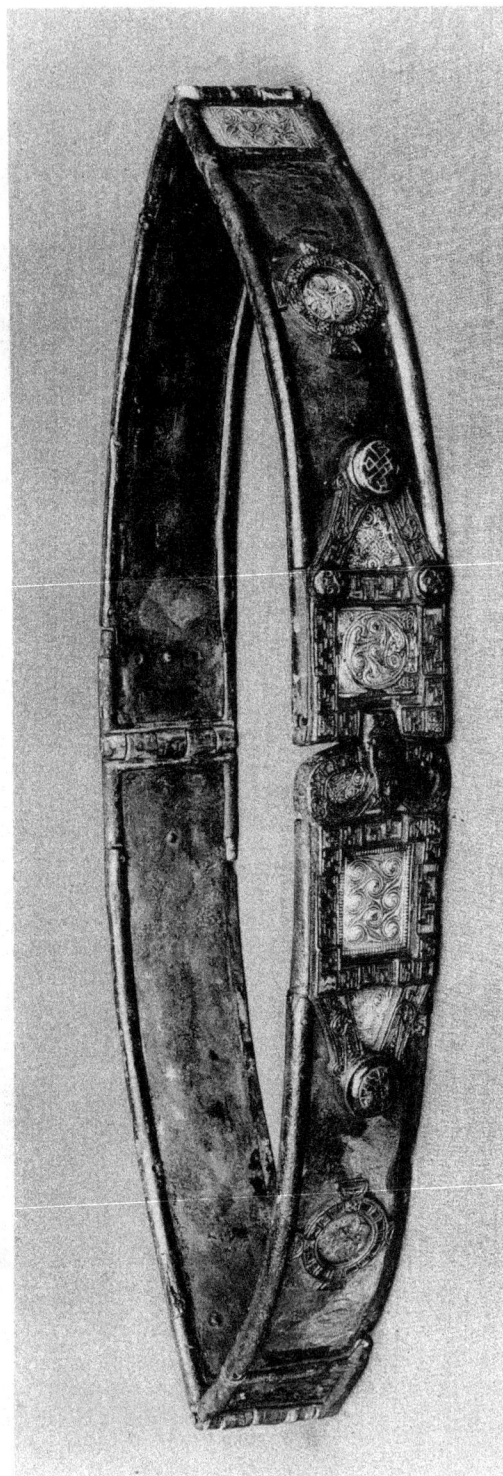

Plate XXV Tinned copper-alloy belt-shrine from Moylough, Co. Sligo, containing leather strips. This eighth-century shrine is decorated with cast medallions and a false buckle and counterplate infilled with silver panels, millefiori and enamel.

Plate XXVI Copper-alloy crucifixion plaque from St John's church site, Rinnagan, near Athlone, Co. Westmeath. Of eighth century date, this is an early Crucifixion scene that may have been part of a book cover or on an item of church furniture.

Plate XXVII Silver chalice from Ardagh, Co. Limerick, dated to the eighth century. Gold filigree, gilded bronze, crystal and glass studs are utilised in the complex decorative scheme. The names of the eleven original Apostles and St Paul stand out against a stippled band around the body of the vessel.

Plate XXVIII Copper-alloy chalice from Ardagh, Co. Limerick.

Plate XXIX Detail of the rim of the paten from Derrynaflan, Co. Tipperary. The paten is made of silver, with knitted silver and copper wire mouldings between which are gold filigree panels set in gilt copper-alloy imitation chip-carved frames, and elaborate glass studs. The edge of the paten is also highly decorated, with gilt copper-alloy settings for enamels and gold foil panels.

Plate XXX Iron bell from Armagh, made from two sheets riveted together and then coated with copper-alloy. Attributed to St Patrick, and documented from an early date in the Annals as a relic.

Plate XXXI Tinned copper-alloy animal-head handle from Donore, Co. Meath. This would have been attached to a door of a church or shrine, and was found with a disc and circular frame into which it would have fitted. The assembly is of early eighth century date.

Plate XXXII Wax tablets from Springmount Bog, Co. Antrim.

Plate XXXIII Book of Durrow, fol. 3v. Carpet page with elaborate La Tène spirals. Mid-seventh century.

Plate XXXIV Book of Durrow, fol. 21v. Man, symbol of Matthew; a stiff, geometric representation compared with later manuscript illustrations (see Plates XXXV, XXXVII). Mid-seventh century.

Plate XXXV Book of Dimma, fol. 30v. Portrait of St Mark. Mid-eighth century.

Plate XXXVI Book of Dimma, fol. 104v. The Eagle, symbol of St John. Mid-eighth century.

Plate XXXVII Book of Kells, fol. 7v. The Virgin and Child with angels holding *flabella*; a complex figurative scene. Mid-eighth century.

Plate XXXVIII Book of Kells, fol. 33a. This carpet page illustrates the complex cross forms that could be used. The communion scene to the right of the foot of the main cross can be seen in more detail in Figure 3:19. Mid-eighth century.

Plate XXXIX Book of Kells, fol. 188a. Opening page of St Luke's Gospel. Designs such as the lozenge had symbolic meaning. Mid-eighth century.

3
The belief system

The way in which individuals perceive the world around them, and their place in it, is dictated by their beliefs. In prehistoric contexts, these can be reached indirectly and at present can only be perceived in a generalised form. In historic periods it may be possible to have a more detailed understanding since many documentary sources indicate beliefs explicitly, and others contain implicit statements. In the case of Early Christian Ireland there are many sources, both religious and secular, which can be used to construct systems of beliefs. Most are concerned with the elite, and whilst there may have been other systems amongst other groups these cannot be so easily appreciated. In addition, the society had both pagan and Christian elements which meant that there was no single, coherent set of beliefs even within the elite. During the period, however, the Christian viewpoint became dominant and, whilst its fundamental message did not change, its interpretation and manifestation altered because of influences from the indigenous pagan belief systems and wider changes that took place in Christendom.

Pagan beliefs

The pagan religious framework is not well documented, and some of the most detailed sources were written by Christian clerics who would not have wished to present a balanced picture even if they fully understood the ritual that they were describing. Much is hidden in mythological tales that later had entertainment value but which had originally been an active support for the pagan belief system. As the meanings were removed and obscured by changes to the stories, much coherence was lost. Nevertheless, there are several clear strands that can be identified.

Dumezil (1968) has interpreted Irish mythology by relating it to a wider Indo-European background, including Gaul at the time of Caesar. He recognises three functions of the deities: administration of the universe (in magico-religious and rational or juridical spheres); exercise of physical force; fertility and prosperity. The tripartite division can in some respects be paralleled in the social structure, and relates to the primary activities of the major social groups. Mac Cana (1970, 61) suggests that later adaptation of the mythological cycle may have obscured many relationships. It certainly seems that the pagan religious framework was confused and even contradictory by the time that Christianity appeared. Nevertheless, there was a basic tripartite division of society, and each section had ideological support for its position, role and actions. It is worth examining the ideology associated with each of these.

Religious elite – the filid

The religious life of the pagan Irish was organised by the druids, *druid*, and seers, *filid*. Originally, they may have all been aspects of the same person, and Mac Airt (1958) suggests that specialisation may have occurred as learning was disrupted and increased in the Early Christian period. The *filid* were poets but also uttered prophecies (Byrne 1973, 13). They were graded according to ability, and came from literary schools where the repertoire and technique of oration were learnt. The seer could, however, be critical and use satire to ridicule authority. The *filid* wielded such control because, according to Byrne (1973, 15), there was a widespread recognition of the power of the word. Anyone satirised, whatever their rank, lost their position in society and could become ill or even die. In the Life of St Berach, Diarmait was a head poet and chief master of druidism to the King Áedh. The latter was afraid that, if satirised by the druid, blisters would appear on his face (Plummer 1923a, 33).

This ability to control aristocratic behavioural norms meant that the *filid* were extremely powerful. They also maintained the belief system though this had to be modified when Christianity became dominant. The ideals and values of the elite were disseminated and reinforced through literature. Not only pure mythological but also heroic tales and poems emphasised the power of spirits, demonstrated the special position of the elite, and the inevitable subservience of the freemen grades. It also supported the structure and power of the *filid*; they could predict and even control divine intervention, and prophesy the future. Though feared by the rest of society they were also respected and obeyed. Control of unknown forces ensured that their position was unchallenged until the appearance of Christianity. Even after the arrival of this rival belief system and the successful conversion of many to its monotheistic faith, many aspects of the knowledge held by the *filid* were still required.

The *filid* adapted to the changing times, though not without a struggle, and maintained their power by adjusting their role. They eventually became converted to Christianity, but were often amongst the most resistant to the new faith. The ritual aspects were then relegated whilst the literary, historical and legal responsibilities were accentuated. It was the control of these duties that continued to give the *filid* their dominant role, even within a Christian world. By allowing these elements to continue the Christian church could become absorbed within the system with the minimum of social disruption and turn what were originally opponents into supporters of the religion, the religion which could in other aspects give support to the values which the *filid* held so dear.

The oral transmission of knowledge was normal, and the best *filid* could recite very large numbers of items. The *ollamh* according to one source could recount 250 principal stories, *prim-scela*, and a further 100 anecdotes, *fo-scela*, though this may have been some exaggeration (Mac Airt 1958). There was no developed system of pagan writing, though Binchy (1961) and more recently Carney (1975) have suggested that the ogham script was in use for several centuries before the coming of Christianity, perhaps from as early as the first century BC. Ogham had been dated to the fourth century AD because it was structured on the four-fold organisation of the Latin alphabet which was believed to have been first set out by late Roman grammarians such as Donatus (Jackson 1953, 151). It is now clear, however, that a system for dividing the

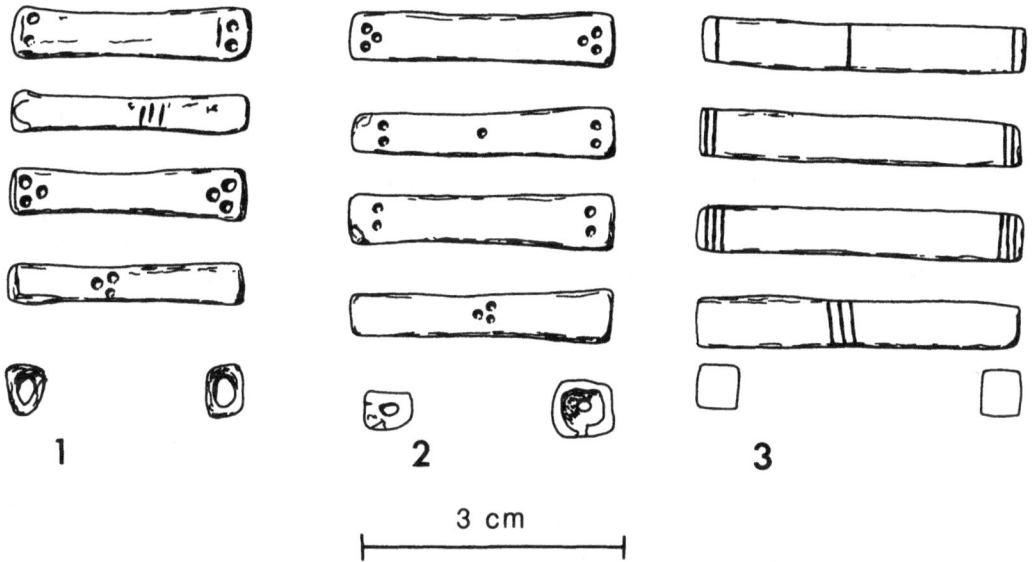

Figure 3:1 Dice from Ballinderry 2, Co. Offaly. **1** Bone, with the number 5 in ogham script; **2** bone; **3** wood (Hencken 1942).

alphabet similar to that used for ogham was current in the Roman world from the first century BC (Figure 2:3).

There are no early ogham inscriptions except on the memorial stones, and it is on this archaeological material that further assessment of date relies, though even here most discussion is linguistic. The problem is that most stones have no secure or chronologically meaningful context or associations. Mac Neill (1931) thought that no stone was earlier than the middle of the fifth century. More recent work on the Welsh stones has dated the earliest there to that period, but Mac White (1961) considers that as the earliest Welsh oghams are later in form than the earliest in Ireland, the dating can be pushed back. The problem, however, is how far. The only evidence cited by Mac White comes from a bone die from the crannog Ballinderry 2, Co. Offaly which has the number 5 in ogham (Figure 3:1). In a re-dating of the site, J. Raftery had claimed this as second century AD. The evidence from the crannog, however, indicates nothing that need be earlier than the Early Christian period, though there was a much earlier Bronze Age site beneath this (Lynn 1983a). Therefore, secure dating for the beginning of ogham is still unavailable.

Carney calls ogham a cipher, and suggests that it may have been developed in an area where it could not be read by those who knew the Roman alphabet. In other words, it was a code which could not be read if intercepted (Carney 1975, 63). This might link it with anti-Roman factions, including the druids, and thus it may have acquired a religious significance. Certainly in the secular tales the script was a potent magical force, and was used to write spells. The abandonment of ogham on a large scale (its use and meaning were, however, never completely forgotten) may have been because of Christian disapproval of the script rather than its mere replacement by writing with the Latin alphabet. The use of ogham on memorials seems to have given them special power. Some mention deities as tribal ancestors such as Dovinia of the Corcu

Duibne. It seems that ogham stones were important markers indicating property ownership (Mac Airt 1958), and perhaps these rights were all the stronger through their statement in a magical script.

The importance of the rights of ownership and place was further emphasised by 'history', *senchas*, the aristocratic genealogies which were memorised and recited alongside the more literary works. As the tasks of the *filid* became divided, a separate class of *seanchai* performed this task. They were able to move about the country relating tales and histories to different kings, and were given special protection in the laws. Their very mobility gave them an important role in spreading concepts throughout Ireland and they were an important force in the creation of a uniform ideology.

The laws also provided a continuing force in supporting the current ideology. They were, like the literature, learnt by heart by special officials. Originally, they may have been in verse to aid memory, or in the form of maxims or instructions (Charles-Edwards and Kelly 1983, 24). The latter part of the *Bretha Déin Chécht*, written in verse, has been identified by Binchy (1966b, 3–4) as pre-Christian because of the lack of loan-words that came into the Irish language from Latin and British dialects with the new faith, and various other linguistic pointers. This is a clear example of an early form surviving into the written tract.

The role of legal expert was later devolved onto the brehons, *brithemain*, who were part of the *filid* and held a special place in Irish society and were ranked according to skill. They had not only to know the laws but to be able to interpret them in the light of custom and within the ideology which they supported. Whilst written law tracts may have aided the brehon, as the Early Christian period went on society became more complex, and this resulted in an ever-growing legislation. This is clear from the eighth-century tracts that survive, which show numerous subsequent additions. Other evidence comes from new laws written on subjects that had previously not had any particular legislation, such as the mid-seventh century *Bechbretha* covering bees (Charles-Edwards and Kelly 1983).

A brehon was constantly in the king's court and travelled with him. By having legal advice constantly available the king was both controlled in what he could do and controlling what others could do. Whilst this political power was obvious, the ideological support given to the king by his association with the law was considerable, and the ethos provided by these tracts further reinforced the social hierarchy and the structure of the economy.

The secular elite

The aristocratic elite from which the kings were drawn were supported in their social position by an heroic tradition of which the most famous tale was the Tain, the Cattle Raid of Cooley (O'Rahilly 1967). The stories were concerned with the lives, and deaths, of a warrior aristocracy who fought each other over points of honour and worked within a fierce and harsh ethical code. Slaughter of lesser people took place on a grand scale and destruction of property during such escapades was deemed acceptable. Despite the clear exaggeration associated with story telling, these tales had a definite message. The elite were expected to fight to win, or die in the attempt, and only they and their code were of value. The gods supported those that followed the code; those that did not, or were of low status, suffered. This attitude, repeated time and again in the heroic literature, must have influenced the views of the aristocracy, and given them the confidence to rule. It would also have provided justification both to them and to those of lesser status who would also have heard the stories. The heroic literature can be seen to fit into Dumezil's scheme associating the elite with physical force.

Origin myths also provided ideological support for the social order. Ancestors, including some who figured in the heroic literature, carved out territories and subjugated lesser peoples who now formed the lower strata of society. Genealogies then provided the link between the remote past and the present.

The king in particular, however, had responsibilities to a wider audience, representing in person the kingdom, *túath*. This included links with the deities, and so with the interests of the *filid*, and also with the land and productivity, and so with the *féni*.

The role of fertility underlies the rituals associated with the inauguration of kings. These pagan aspects can be identified even where later Christian influence has amended the ceremonies. The details of most early inauguration rituals are now unclear, but often seem to have included standing on a stone slab, *lecc*. At Tara there were two such stones which had to part to allow the chariot with the king through if he were to take the throne (Byrne 1973, 63). A sacred tree, *bile*, or grove stood at the inauguration site which was usually a mound (Byrne 1973, 27). In some territories, the king took a bath in a large container of stew. Giraldus Cambrensis, writing in the twelfth century, described an account of an inauguration where the king had intercourse with a mare which was then killed and put in a stew in which the king bathed and from which all present imbibed. Though a late and second-hand description, there may be some element of pagan ritual at the heart of the story (Byrne 1973, 17–18).

It is clear that the union of king and country was central to inauguration; the king was wedded to his country (Carney 1955, 334). The standing stone Lia Fail at Tara, originally on the Mound of the Hostages, was a phallic symbol. In the well documented examples of Tara and Connacht the king underwent a symbolic mating, *feis*, *banfeis*, with the local earth-goddess (O'Rahilly 1946). This was to ensure that there should be prosperity throughout his reign; the king himself was quasi-divine, and this affected his actions whilst king. The Feast of Tara has been shown by Binchy (1958) to have been a fertility rite which deified the king. So potent was this that it was suppressed by the increasingly powerful church in the later sixth century. It seems that similar feasts also occurred at Navan in Ulster and Cruachain in Connacht.

The freemen – the féni

The freemen grades, the *féni*, also had a literature of their own, but being of lower status it was not considered of interest and so not written down until comparatively late. The tales associated with the *féni* were first transcribed in the twelfth century, but apparently reflect a long tradition with pagan origins (Mac Cana 1970). In these stories it is not fighting that is emphasised but nature and man's place in it. This is expressed most frequently in terms of hunting, which provided the excitement and action, but within a milieu concerned with the natural world and fertility. The overall ambience emphasises a lowly position for man, above the animals, but intimately associated with the earth. This would have both interested the socially inferior, and reinforced their views of their position. They were unable to relate to heroic tales, but could do so with these stories. The attitudes to the use of the landscape and resources reflects a life involved with producing a surplus from the land. This was the obligation of the *féni*, and part of this surplus was taken by the elite. These tales take the social order as it was and confirm it as a static and correct way of organising the world. The lower orders of society recognised and accepted their lot, and did so at least in part through the ideological legitimation of their position. Whilst the warrior aristocracy could physically crush any minor disturbance, they relied on the *féni* for the surplus. An ideology to support the hierarchical structure of society was essential to maintain the system. The *féni* relied on the elite to provide some form of protection against rival political groups, though this may not have been totally reliable. It was only by the ideology, however, that they recognised that they themselves could not become the elite, nor that a more egalitarian system was possible.

The origin myths of the elite gave further support to the lowly position of the *féni*, since they were descended from inferior stock that had been defeated in the distant past and relegated from political power to become primary producers. The concept of inherited inferiority must have been a powerful force in the acceptance of the status quo. The laws, much amended through the Early Christian period before being written down around the eighth century, also emphasise the agricultural responsibilities of the lower free grades, in contrast to the ambitions, activities and responsibilities of the elite. This is further discussed later in the context of Christianity.

Pagan thought seems to have recognised Ireland as a discrete entity, and saw it divided into five 'fifths'. Uisneach, the umbilical centre of Ireland where the five fifths joined, was the site of a druidic fire ceremony at Beltaine (Byrne 1973, 64). It and Tara were later likened to the two kidneys of an animal (Byrne 1973, 58). The division into fifths was seen by Rees and Rees (1961) as cosmological and represented the grades in society, like the castes recognised more widely in Indo-European tradition (Figure 3:2). This association of tribes with occupations lasted beyond the period of dominant paganism, as can be seen from the obligations of the various tribes to the king of Munster listed in the *Frithfholaid* texts (Byrne 1973).

The role of magic and superstition

Magical beliefs were attached to many actions. One of the most important was that of fasting against a king (Binchy 1973a). This technique allowed a subject to shame a king into changing his decision on some legal matter over which there was disagreement. It was later taken up by saints, and merged with the ascetic traditions of fasting, but has a clear pagan origin, and probably was practised by the druids themselves. This and other measures gave the religious grades important control over the secular authorities. It could also be carried out by any claimant against one of higher grade, and thus provided a mechanism by which domination by the elite against the rule of established law could be somewhat reduced. The accused could settle the claim, or undertake a fast himself, thus negating the magical effect of the suitor's action. Whilst this was originally a continual fast, it later was reduced to a period from dusk to dawn each night outside the house of the offender, who had to similarly starve, until settlement was reached. This method was the one employed according to various versions of the Life of Ruadan, founder and first abbot of Lorrha, Co. Tipperary, and by many other saints.

The pagan ideology was one based on the common threads of Indo-European polytheism. Fertility, the earth, sun, fire and water were all important. Sacred groves were important foci for ritual, though they are difficult to detect archaeologically. Use of water can in some cases be easier; ritual deposits such as the Lough-na-shade musical instruments in the bog or lake at the foot of the hill on which Navan stood is an example; many of the other La Tène artefacts recovered from Ireland may have similarly been deposited in lakes or rivers, including the finds from Lisnacrogher and Toome.

The cult of the severed head, predominant in so much of the Celtic world, is also well

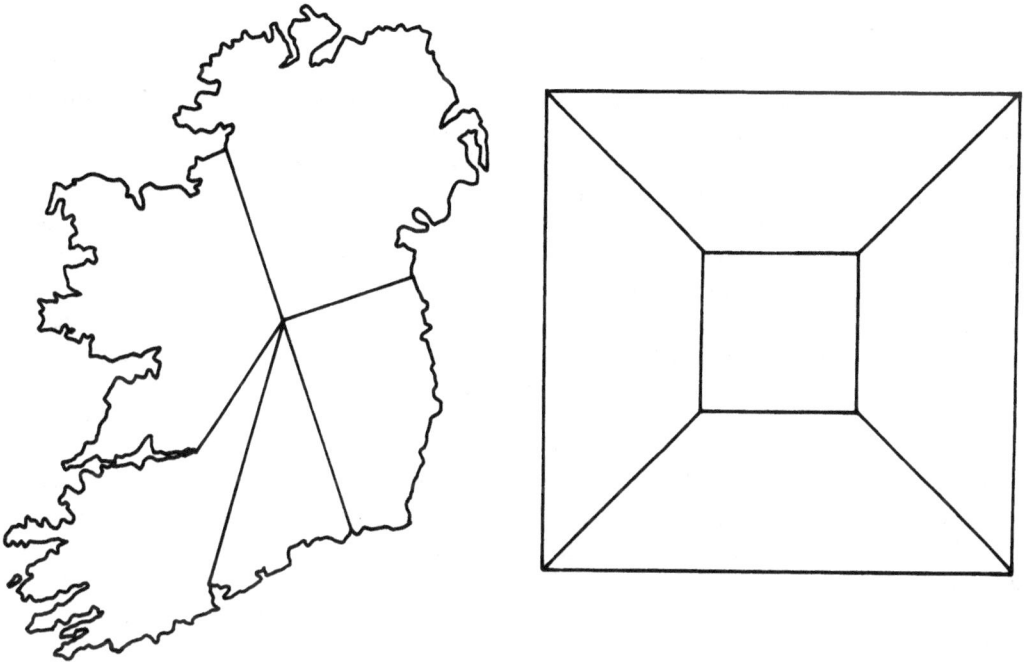

Figure 3:2   The division of Ireland into fifths (Rees and Rees 1961).

represented in Ireland, though many of the carved examples are at present very difficult to date. They occur widely throughout the country, and are often crudely produced. Most stones have single faces, but a few have two or even three (Rynne 1972). Documentary evidence gives further information about the cult of the head. The brain was particularly revered, those of slaughtered warriors being preserved and used as visual props in the boasting and tale-telling associated with elite feasting.

The king was a vital figure in maintaining the moral and physical health of the country. The use of ritual actions was widespread, and the royal taboos (Dillon 1951) were just the most powerful. The role of man was to attempt to avoid encounters with the numerous evil forces. Though the deities could be beneficial on occasion, the world was fundamentally antagonistic; all men could summon up evil spirits to do harm and the druids could be deadly. And death held no great promise either. The prospect of the everlasting feast was not of great comfort, supervised as it was by the devious god of the Otherworld.

The pagan belief system was not based in any intellectual framework, and worked on the basis of fear. It is perhaps not so difficult, therefore, to understand how Christianity could have had relatively rapid success in some areas. By the seventh century Christianity had gained a dominant position, but by then it had been in some respects influenced by pagan custom.

Christian ideology

Christianity came into Ireland in the later fourth and fifth centuries and was in part the cause of changes in the social and economic systems. Without the new religion, the traditional framework of society could have stifled any innovation. It is therefore extremely important to examine the role of Christianity in the ideology of Early Christian Ireland. At first it was a minority religion, having to work within a pagan environment. As conversion became more prevalent, and as Christianity became the dominant belief system, it began to take a more central role in society and the economy. Christianity as it first arrived in Ireland was an exotic religion. During two centuries it adjusted to the existing cultural milieu, and in the process incorporated earlier indigenous elements into its organisation. The vital Christian message was not affected, but the way in which it was communicated and interpreted was modified. This Celtic adaptation of Christianity may well have already begun in areas such as south-west Wales from whence it had come, since these were only partially Romanised regions, but the major changes came in Ireland itself (Bethel 1981).

It is useful to examine the role of Christian ideology in two sections: one covering the period of expansion when Christianity was still largely a minority faith not integrated into Irish society, the other the period of consolidation when Christianity was the dominant (but not exclusive) belief system and social integration was under way. The ideological position of Christianity, in terms of relevance to the other social and economic systems, was quite distinct in these two periods.

The period of expansion

The earliest Christian beliefs have already been outlined in Chapter 2. Whilst the Bible and early Christian teaching do discuss group responsibilities, particularly based on the Old Testament, this was not the main thrust. It was individual sin and repentence that were central, as were the idea of God's forgiveness and therefore the hope of salvation. These ideas were developed further in the penitentials, texts which set out the penances required to obtain forgiveness for particular sins. These documents form one of the most important sources for Christian priorities in beliefs during this period. In the very earliest phases of Christianity in Ireland, those of the new faith must have felt isolated in a pagan world. This feeling continued during the sixth and even into the seventh century, and it is clear from the sources discussed below that as far as possible Christians cut themselves off from contact with pagans. Spread of the faith continued by the conversion of kings, and thus whole kingdoms, but the more usual and effective spread was through family conversion with a much deeper understanding of the new religion.

We are here concerned with the ideology of conversion to Christianity and the development within the faith itself. There were social and economic aspects to this that are discussed elsewhere, and it must be remembered that ideology should not be considered in a vacuum. Although there were no doubt very many conversions brought about by deep religious experience, others were more pragmatic. Conversion would not have automatically brought about a real abandonment of the old ideology. This is clear in the penitentials where the practice of magic by Christians was seen as a problem throughout the sixth century (Bieler 1963, 57). Nevertheless, the inexorable spread of Christianity gradually relegated pagan practices and beliefs to the fringes, where they linger still today.

The dating of some of the significant documentary sources for the sixth century is contentious. The document called the 'First Synod of Patrick' consists of canons supposedly drawn up by Patrick, Auxilius and Iserninus. It has been considered fifth century by many scholars (Bury 1905, Bieler 1963, Cornish 1971, Doherty 1984a). Cogent reasons for a date in the mid-sixth century have been set out by Binchy (1968) and Hughes (1972). Whatever its date, however, it can be taken to represent the first phase of an established but minority church.

In the early sixth century, the church was organised on a similar basis to that in Britain, with bishops each controlling a *paruchia* (Hughes 1966, 44). The secular legal system was viewed as pagan and to be avoided (Bieler 1963, 57). This may have been in part because the *filid* class who administered the law also included the druids and pagan ethical codes must have been strong. There may also have been risks in associating with pagans who might not honour their obligations and, by defaulting, hold Christians accountable for payment. The general impression is one of the church apart from society rather than incorporated within it. Hughes (1966, 47) points out that clerics could range in social status from slaves to nobles, but the church had not adjusted its organisation and legislation to account for the indigenous social structure. This can be clearly seen in the penalties for wrongdoing, which within the Christian judgement were penance and excommunication (Hughes 1966, 45). The complex of payments to the aggrieved party which was the basis of secular law did not figure at all in this early church legislation. The church was determined to prevent dilution of the faith, and serious offenders were excommunicated, and were not to be contacted by any of the faithful. If penance was accepted, offenders could be re-admitted and new converts were also accepted, though a 40 day fast was first required to prove their faith.

The early bishops were independent of each other, there was no organised hierarchy, and the church was therefore extremely fragmented (Sharpe 1984). Within their territories bishops were particularly concerned to prevent secular influence. Any individual who obtained permission for actions from a secular authority rather than the bishop was excluded from the church. Patronage by the aristocracy must have been desirable in order to obtain land and resources for churches, but priests could not build churches without permission. The bishop was required to consecrate each new foundation (Bieler 1963, 59). In this way, unsuitable associations could be minimised.

The church wished to expand, but not at the cost of diluting the Christian message and commitment. Alms were not to be received from pagans, and there was no way that non-Christians were to obtain any perceived or actual benefit by being associated with the church. Just as Christianity legitimised the power of an elite that was converted, so it undermined the power of pagans by deliberately having a strong policy of non-association.

It would appear that the monastic ideal became relevant in Ireland from the sixth century onwards, within this early phase and as part of the strategy of withdrawal from the pagan world. It is in this light that it is easier to explain why so many Irish monks were only laymen; they had taken to a strict Christian life, perhaps even as whole families, but had no direct role in the wider community. Sites that can certainly be considered to be within an eremitic tradition are those in isolated and physically undesirable areas such as Skellig Michael (Figure 3:3) and Illauntanig (Plate VIII), though the standing remains on such sites may be late within the Early Christian period. Most monastic sites, however, are in areas containing large numbers of secular settlements such as ring-forts. In such cases it was presumably not such an isolated style of monasticism that was intended.

Many early foundations seem to have been family churches, and this probably mirrored one

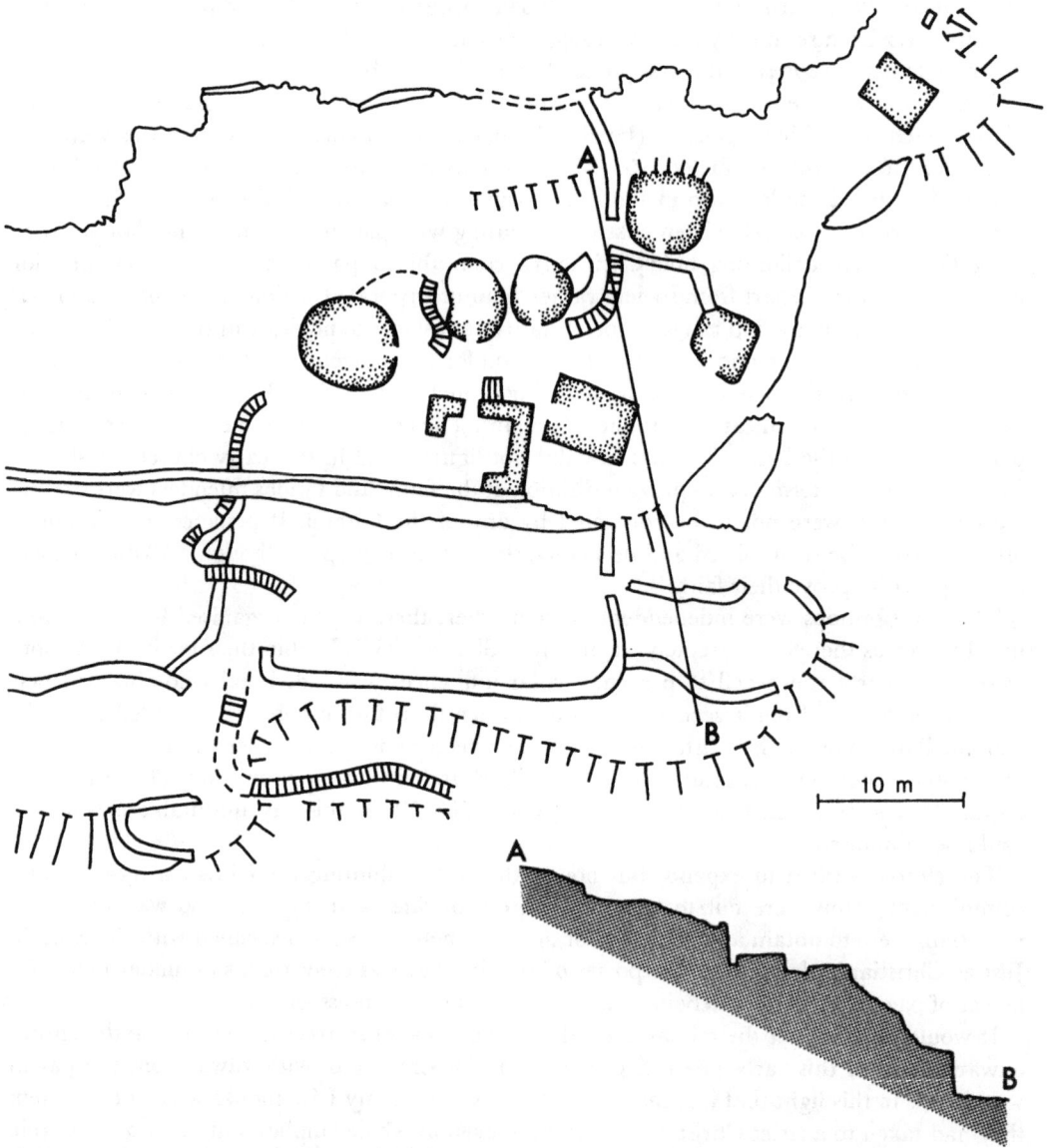

Figure 3:3   Eremitic monastery of Skellig Michael, Co. Kerry (de Paor 1955).

important pattern of conversion. A family would all become Christian, would require a church and perhaps give some or all of their land for a small monastery to be set up. They would not, however, then lose all interest in it, and probably had one of their own kin as abbot. Indeed, there would have been considerable economic benefits in setting up a monastery. An association would remain for decades and descendants of the donors often held offices generations later. This family pattern of conversion seems similar to that in both the Romano–British church, with the private churches in villas (Thomas 1981a, Morris 1989), and the church as it spread through Wales. The Life of St Samson indicates this family church structure in western Britain (Hughes 1966, 76–7).

In its early phases (fifth to seventh centuries) Reask, Co. Kerry may represent the family secular monasticism of Ireland (Figure 3:4). Fanning (1981) discusses the difficulty in recognising a monastery in archaeological terms. He suggests that cross-slabs and burials might be found on a secular Christian settlement; two of the earliest lintel-graves might, from their size, have contained children but unfortunately no skeletal evidence survived at the site because of the acid soils. The sequence of changes at Reask is not perfectly clear because of the paucity of stratification linking the various structures, but a tentative reconstruction can be put forward based in the comments of the excavator, and using comparative data where possible from other similar but unexcavated sites (Mytum forthcoming). The first phases of occupation at Reask can be taken as representative of one strategy chosen by Christians during the period of expansion. The initial timber roundhouse was perhaps unenclosed, though a wooden fence may have lain beneath the later stone enclosure wall. To the east of the first house was a small burial ground, its northern end at least marked by a standing stone (Figure 3:5). There may have been a small timber church at this time, but only two post holes survived and they could have been for another type of structure or even wooden crosses. In the next phase the stone enclosure wall was built, two small stone roundhouses replaced the single dwelling, and the stone oratory was erected. The cemetery increased in size slightly but, as in all phases, suggests no more than a family using the site. The later phases at the site indicate a formal division of space into sacred and profane, and can be seen to relate to developments belonging to the phase of consolidation (see below).

The other major pattern of conversion was when the king was converted, leading to the nominal conversion of the whole of his territory. Whilst this was an effective way of linking the church with the elite, and thus gaining political and probably economic security, it did not necessarily lead to a great change in ideology. In these circumstances the churches were probably still considered marginal, or liminal. This attitude of ambivalence can perhaps also be recognised in the location and treatment of the early church.

Many of the early church sites known today are in isolated and marginal areas. Whilst this may be partly a factor of survival, the evidence is sufficiently strong to suggest that past patterning is represented archaeologically. In the Burren, churches are found mainly along the edge of the territory of the Corco Mruad (Figure 3:6), possibly to act as boundary markers which could give sacred support to the political position, possibly merely to keep the church at a distance and on land which was no great loss for the kin-group (Mytum 1982). In the more fertile areas of Cork and Kerry, many sites are on marginal land. These include those incorporating the *dísert* placename element which are in damp, riverside locations, whilst others with the element *cluain* suggest foundations within forest clearings (Hurley 1982, 307–10). In the early days of expansion, the church may have preferred marginal locations in order to distance itself from the overwhelmingly pagan secular world; as it gradually

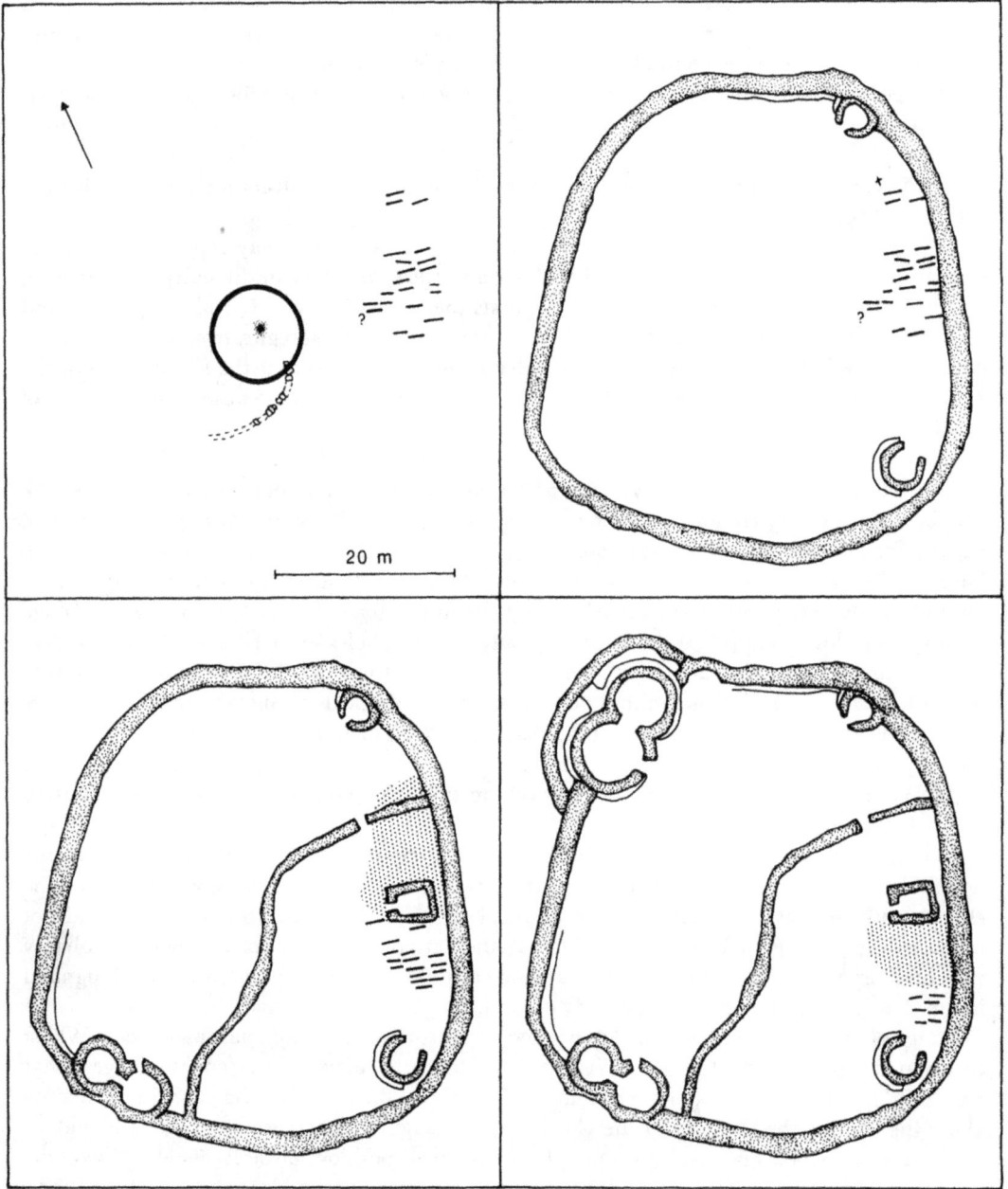

Figure 3:4   The various phases of Reask, Co. Kerry (interpreted from Fanning 1981).

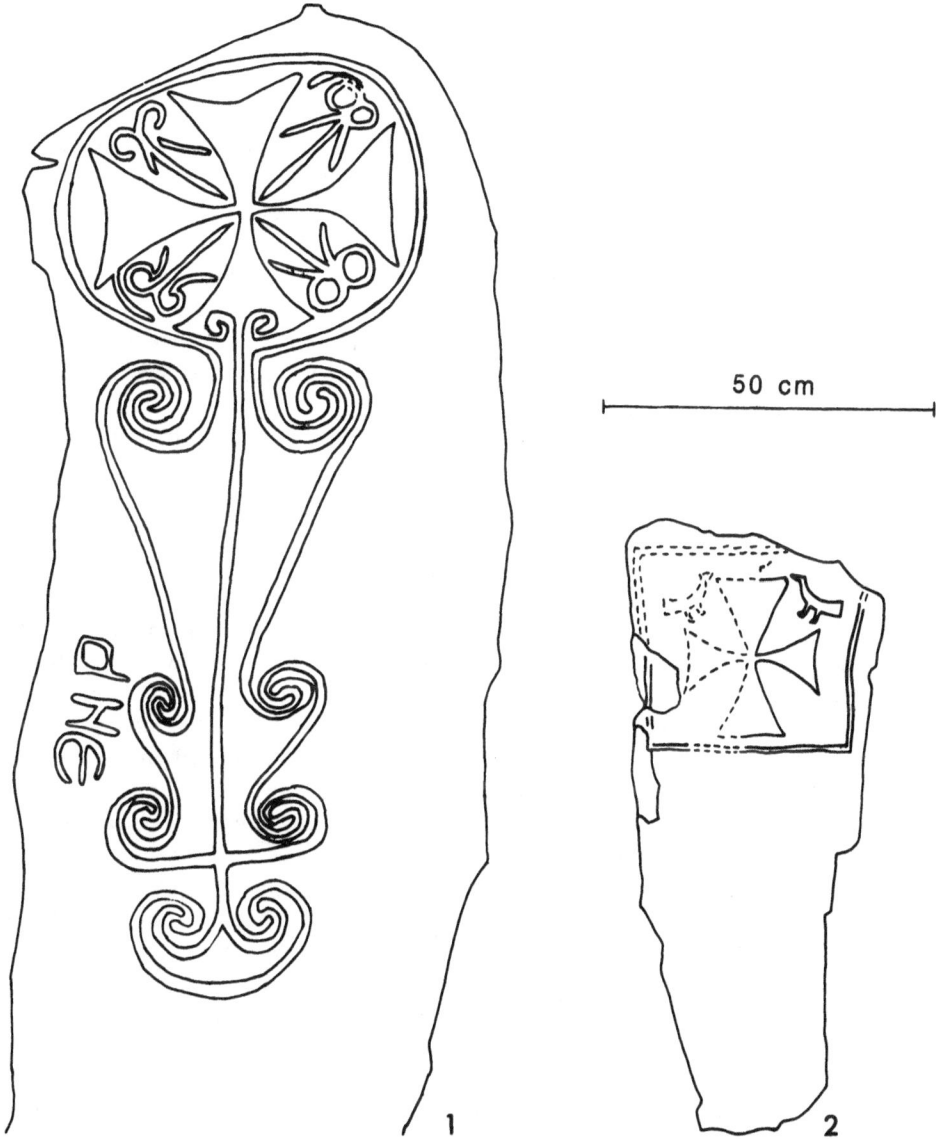

Figure 3:5   Carved stones from Reask, Co. Kerry. **1** Stone A; **2** Stone H (Fanning 1981).

became more dominant so it acquired physically more central locations within the settlement pattern.

In some cases, religious sites grew up on existing settlements. This can be demonstrated at Millockstown where, despite limited excavations in difficult circumstances, it was possible to establish a sequence of enclosures, a cemetery and a souterrain (Figure 3:7). Unfortunately no other structures were located, so it is unclear whether there was a church or domestic buildings for any of the phases. However, the site probably represents a typical secular settlement belonging to the earliest part of the Early Christian period which there was then changed to the typical ring-fort. Around this time the occupants may have been converted to Christianity. A family burial ground was then started in the settlement, which may possibly have become monastic in some form at this stage; it was probably of such a status by the third phase.

Any association with pagan practices was firmly condemned in the early canons. Belief in witches was not allowed, and a year's penance was demanded for swearing before a druid. As far as possible the church was to stay separate from pagan society. Alms were not to be received from pagans, and many customs acceptable within pagan society, such as having second wives, were forbidden (Bieler 1963, 57). Clerics, however, were not required to be celibate, merely monogamous. Christians were in some senses living apart and had a different set of values affecting behaviour, but it was impossible to avoid all contact with the remainder of society. The reality of interdependence and interaction was recognised in the canons, and arrangements were made for the payment for hostages. Pagans were in daily social and economic contact with Christians, and change was bound to come to both.

In the later sixth century a set of canons was written by Vinnian (Bieler 1963). They show a more mature church and one becoming attuned to society. Far more people had by this time become Christian, and this ideology was beginning to become dominant. As the secular population became Christian, so the demands on the clergy were increased. There was now a requirement that priests should leave their wives and become celibate; the monastic movement was beginning to grow. This can be seen as a natural development. Christianity was tightening the moral code in the fifth and early sixth centuries by allowing only monogamy; this was a dramatic enough change, and celibacy would have been unacceptable. Once the Christian ideology was becoming dominant, the logical consequence was to move towards a celibate clergy.

Vinnian was concerned that priests should be celibate, but they still appear to have lived with their families (Bieler 1963, 83); enforcement must have been difficult. Magic was seen as an evil practised by women and even by priests. Lay Christians also now had stricter regulations on behaviour (Bieler 1963, 87–93). It was explicitly stated that a wife could not be divorced because she was barren, and if one spouse left, the other could not be remarried. If a female slave should prove a temptation to adultery, then she should be sold unless pregnant in which case she should be freed. In addition a series of proscriptions were imposed on sexual behaviour between married couples.

During the sixth century, Christians were increasing in numbers but were still a minority, at least in many areas. Christians may have felt threatened by the still powerful pagans, yet the pagan establishment may have likewise felt under stress since their constituency was dwindling away. In these circumstances, the use of symbols as a visible statement of ideological position may have become important. Christians at first seem to have only used plain ogham stones for memorials but soon they were including symbols in the designs. Thomas (1987) considers that

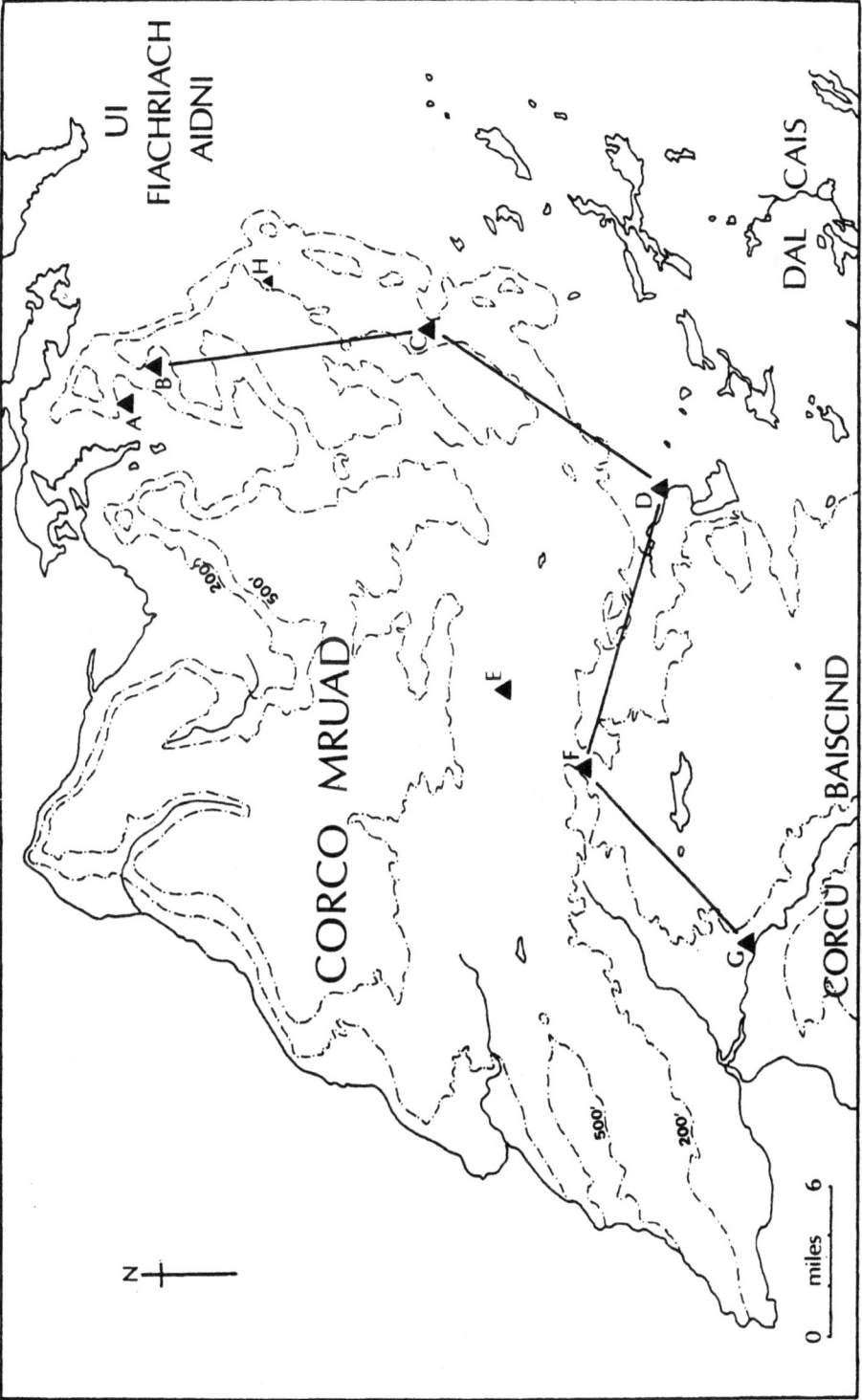

Figure 3:6 The peripheral location of early church sites in relation to the territory of the Corco Mruad, Co. Clare (Mytum 1982).

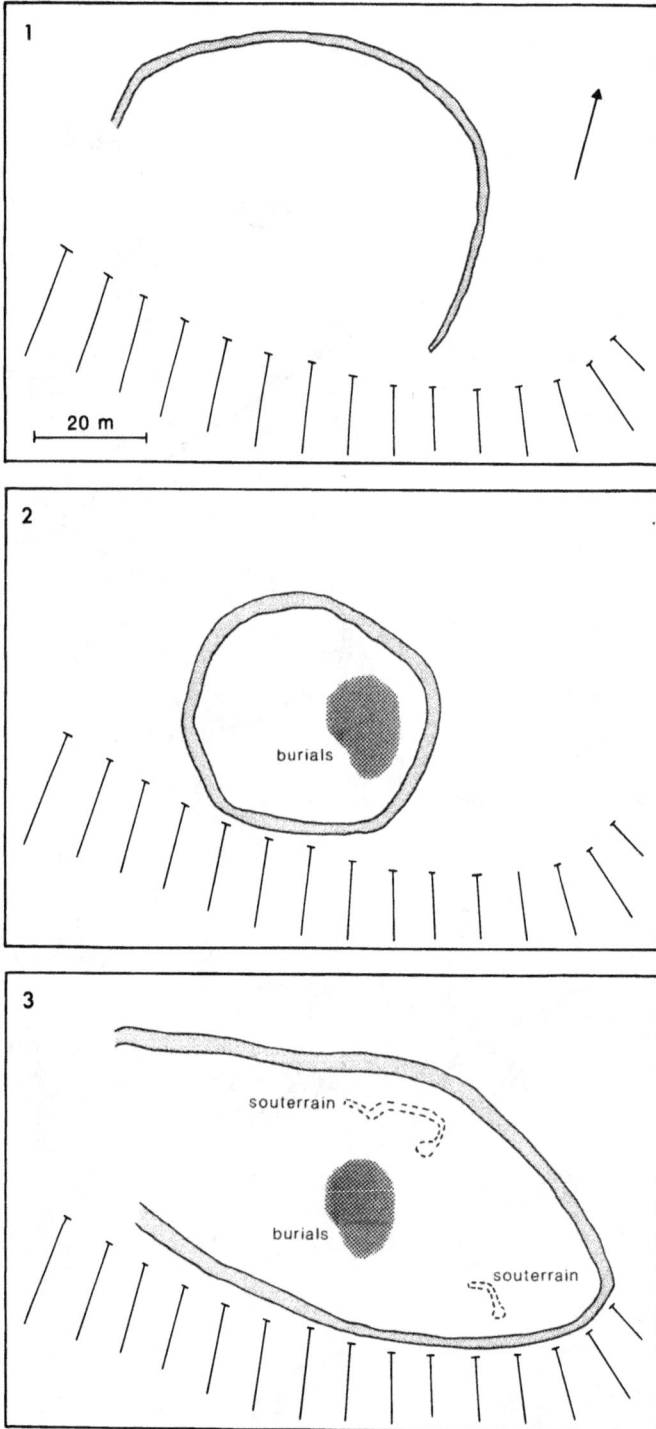

Figure 3:7 Phase plans of enclosed site at Millockstown, Co. Louth (Manning 1986).

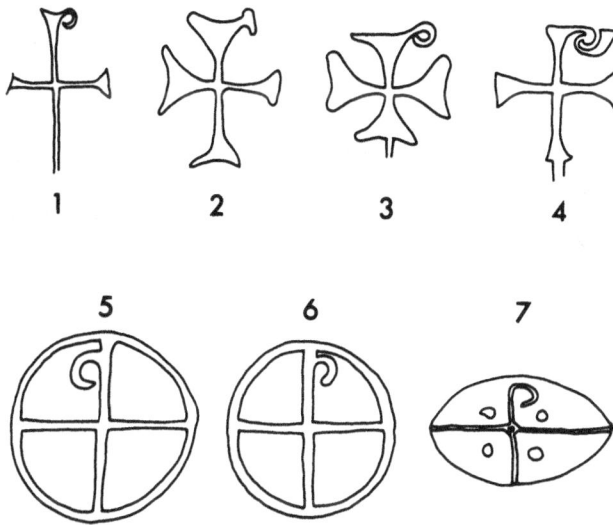

Figure 3:8 Examples of the chi-rho motif from Early Christian Ireland. **1** Kilshannig, Co. Kerry; **2** Arraglen, Co. Kerry; **3** Knockane, Co. Kerry; **4** Iniscealtra, Co. Clare; **5, 6** Drumaqueran, Co. Antrim (east and west faces of stone); **7** Kilcorban, Co. Galway (**1–3** Cuppage 1986, **4–6** Hamlin 1972, **7** Higgins 1987).

designs with a clear Romano–British pedigree are early, and Higgins (1987, 161) suggests that a 'package' of motifs may have come into Ireland in the fifth century.

The chi-rho (Figure 3:8) appears to have been used in western Britain and Ireland from the late fifth century, and continued directly out of a Romano–British tradition (Thomas 1981a). The form used was the 'monogram' style, sometimes set in a circle which may have been the inspiration for the simple ringed cross (Thomas 1971a, 114). The chi-rho was a distinctive Christian symbol but never very popular, probably because its original function as the first two letters in the Greek for Christ had been lost. It was sometimes carved back to front, having been copied perhaps off a signet ring or engraved glass; only seven certain examples are known from stone sculpture (Hamlin 1972, 1982). The alpha and omega are also occasionally found (Figure 3:9). The carved example at Loher, Co. Kerry was perhaps copied from a manuscript design such as that on the *Codex Usserianus*. Sometimes, however, the form and perhaps the detailed symbolic meaning were confused if not lost when the letters were positioned reversed, as at Cloonlaur, Co. Mayo (Henry 1947).

Simple crosses also appear early in the sequence but, as with so many motifs, continue to be produced for a long period of time. The examples considered earliest by Henry (1967) and Thomas (1971a, 1987) are plain incised designs. Stones carved with simple crosses without any inscription were erected from at least the sixth century. They were placed within Christian settlements, on boundaries or along routes. Some isolated standing stones such as that at Ballintermon, Co. Kerry may have been converted into Christian use by the addition of an inscribed cross (Cuppage 1986, 77), but such re-use or Christianisation was rare and generally new ones were set up (Hamlin 1982). Another early cross type is that with an anchor motif

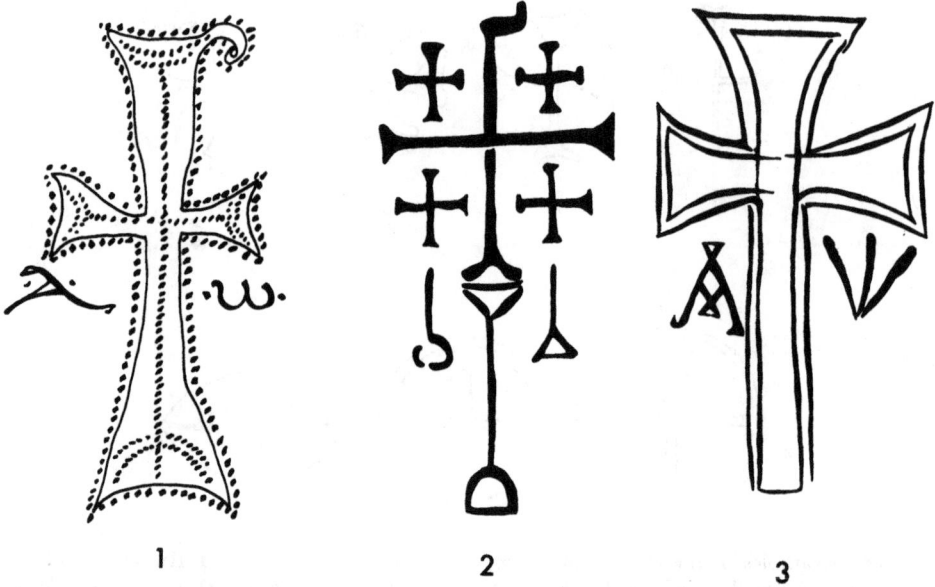

Figure 3:9   Alpha and omega on sculpture and in manuscript art. **1** *Codex Usserianus Primus*; **2** Cloonlaur; **3** Loher (**1, 3** Henry 1965, **2** Henry 1947).

added at the base, though this is rare in Ireland. Much more frequent was depiction of the *flabellum*, a liturgical fan (Figure 3:10). This was a symbol of vigilance and appears early in designs. It was readily combined with the cross motif to make an encircled cross on a stem or shaft. In the later stages, Higgins (1987, 113) suggests that the original meaning may have become lost.

Face crosses have at their top a face instead of a simple cross arm, presumably representing Christ (Figure 3:11). They may be inspired by sixth-century Coptic or Syro-Palestinian designs, but could be independently developed (Roe 1960; Thomas 1971a, 129–31). These are unusual within Irish art of this period in that they include figural depiction, but this is a trend which becomes increasingly important as Christianity becomes fully established. Other probable early representational designs are birds (Figure 3:5) and fish, though these are also rare.

The Christian art at this period shows very little evidence of any indigenous La Tène influence, and this cannot be mere accident. There is some curvilinear ornament present on a few relatively early stones, such as stone A at Reask (Figure 3:5), and on a range of stones with the Mediterranean *flabellum* motif decorated with spirals, but this is generally in a symmetrical layout and not comparable with earlier Irish La Tène art. There is no evidence in any of the sculpture belonging to the period of expansion for any admixture of pagan mythology and Christian scripture in the ways so well documented in northern England (Bailey 1980). At a later date curvilinear art in the manuscript tradition became acceptable (Plate XXXIII), but this was no doubt only after the pagan meanings associated with La Tène ornament had been lost, and also under the influence of Christian Anglo-Saxon art styles where such interlace was found acceptable.

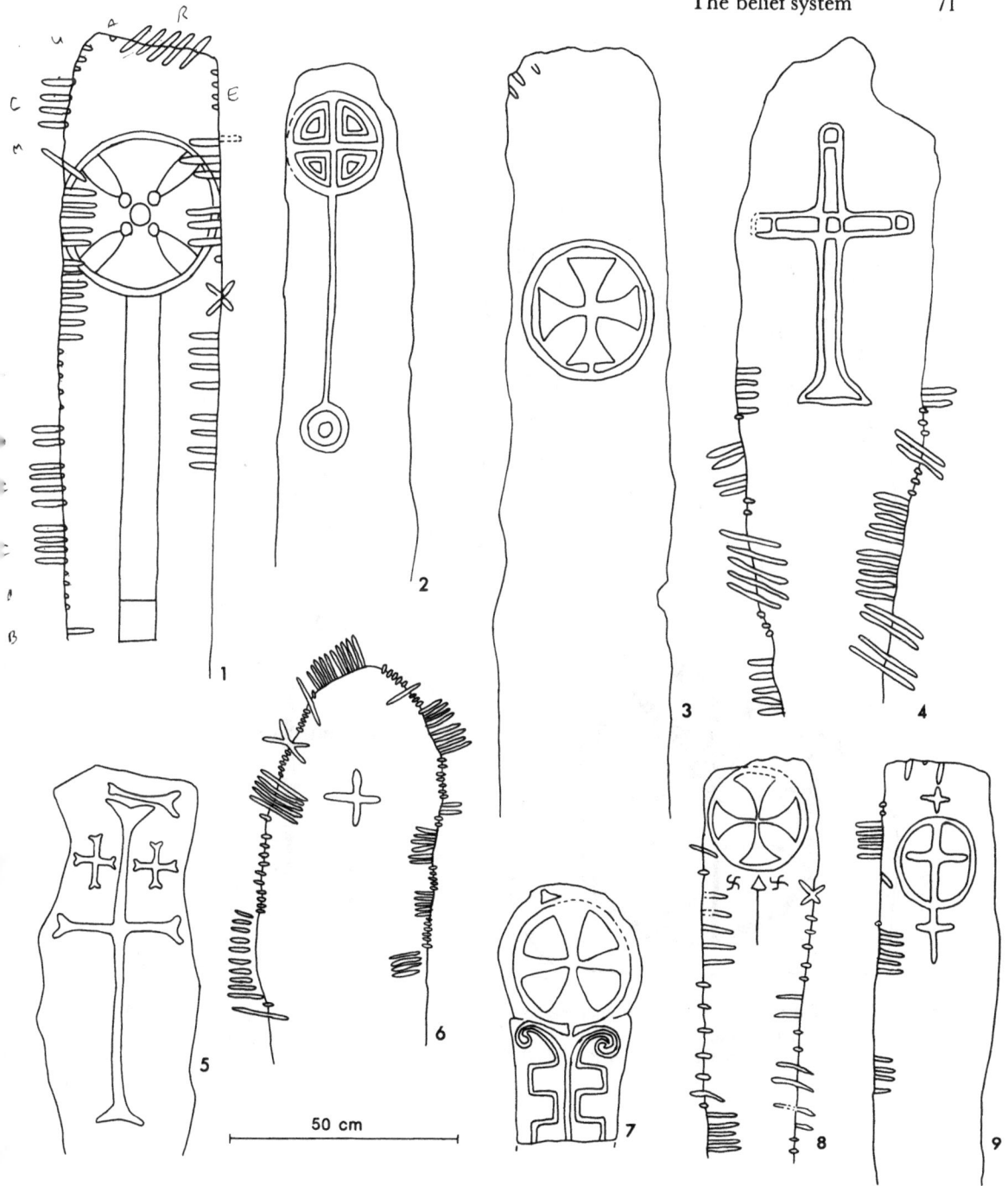

Figure 3:10 Motifs on early inscribed stones. **1** Church Island, Co. Kerry; **2** Cashel, Co. Donegal; **3** Arraglen, Co. Kerry; **4** Ballynahunt, Co. Kerry; **5, 7** Reask, Co. Kerry; **6** Ballintaggart, Co. Kerry; **8** Aglish, Co. Kerry; **9** Rathduff, Co. Kerry; **1** and **2** are motifs derived from the *flabellum* (**1** O'Kelly 1958, **2** Lacy 1983, **3, 4, 6, 8, 9** Cuppage 1986, **5, 7** Fanning 1981).

Figure 3:11 Face crosses and slabs, some possibly altar fronts. **1** Kilbroney, Co. Down; **2** Skellig Michael, Co. Kerry; **3** Caher Island, Co. Mayo; **4** Knappaghmanagh, Co. Mayo; **5** Mason Island, Co. Galway; **6** Tobernacroisseneve, Co. Galway (**1–4** Roe 1960, **5, 6** Higgins 1987).

It seems likely that there was an avoidance of as much indigenous art as possible on the earliest Christian monuments, since it would have had pagan associations. Craft activities were related to those of the *filid*, and most if not all La Tène art probably had symbolic meaning within it. In this period of expansion, not only were new motifs such as the cross, titulus, birds, chi-rho and alpha and omega introduced to the repertoire, but motifs popular in pagan society were deliberately excluded. It would be quite wrong merely to claim that it was lack of expertise that limited the sophistication of the early designs; they carry a clear and simple message and ably contained all that was desired. The impression given in the canons of, at first, separation from the rest of society and, later, only gradual absorption can also be seen to be reinforced through the art. The material culture here acted as a deliberate representation of ideological belief and division within society. Thus, the standing stone from Mullaghmast, Co. Kildare (Plate XI) continues the pagan Iron Age tradition of decorated stones, and can be considered a survivor of pagan sculpture contemporary with the Christian ones. It uses the traditional repertoire of motifs and symbolic associations for their traditional, pagan purposes. The Christian sculpture incorporates new motifs and styles to indicate new beliefs and symbolic associations. Fusion of style can only come with either fusion of beliefs (partial conversion) or, more likely in most cases, the abandonment of the pagan symbolic associations with the indigenous artistic repertoire, thus making it suitable for Christians' use.

The period of consolidation

Reaction to internal influences

From the start, Christianity was prepared to give ideological support to the existing elite, as it had done elsewhere in its spread. There was no conscious policy of changing social or political organisation, though changes inevitably followed from the adoption of the new faith. Whilst pagan beliefs were not to be given any credence, Christian beliefs could overlie native ones and subsume some of their superficial characteristics. This included the choice of days previously used for pagan rituals being associated with Christian festivals. Plummer (1910) saw this as a major theme in the Saints' Lives, and whilst this may have been exaggerated, it did still on occasion take place.

The Irish church, despite its efforts to stay apart from the rest of society, could not fail to be influenced by the wider culture. Relatively few foreign clerics came to Ireland; the overwhelming majority of the Christians were born and bred there. The early church organisation, based on bishops controlling *paruchia*, came from Britain but adapted well to the Irish small scale political structure. Although it is not certain, it is likely that each *paruchia* was coterminous with the basic political unit, the *túath* ruled by a king. In this way, the bishop could be seen to provide ideological support for the king and his territory.

As time went on, the monastic organisation also became widespread. The kinship system was reflected in this structure, and the abbot was seen as head of the monastic family. The wider monastic federations were, in contrast, based on a different Irish system, that of clientship. Major monasteries had subservient, dependent houses elsewhere. They were in the same relationship to the mother house as clients were to their lord. As the political importance of the individual *túath* lessened with the increased concentration of power in over-kings and provincial kings, so this was mirrored and legitimised by the monasteries following along the same route. The type of arguments put forward by the larger monasteries such as Clonmacnois or Armagh to justify their position were also applied by the more powerful kings.

The form of early Irish monasteries is not well known, but when they can be identified, some at least are not dissimilar to the secular ring-fort of the higher levels of society. At Reask, in phase 2 the site becomes enclosed by a stone wall similar to the numerous cashels in the area (Figure 3:4). Kathleen Hughes (1966, 148) pointed out that the church was able to use the secular law of precinct to protect an area containing church and cells within an enclosure. In the seventh century when Christianity was becoming widespread, such an area, *termon*, was to be consecrated by not only the bishop, but also the king and his people, thus ensuring widespread recognition of the sanctity of the site. This shows an acceptance of direct contact and co-operation with secular authority not visible a century or so earlier.

In the seventh and eighth centuries, important changes are visible in the secular laws. These can be seen to reflect changes directly caused by the growth of Christianity, and the need to recognise it. There is also a clear acceptance by the church that secular law was something that Christians should obey and with which they should be involved. This is a contrast from the earlier phase when it was viewed as alien and dangerous, and isolation was preferred. Now, integration is obvious.

The integration of the church into secular law was to the benefit of the church because not only did it firmly establish the social ranking of the clergy but it also gave secular legal support for the defence of the church and its property and dues. These can be stated outright, such as in the seventh century *Bechbretha*, dealing with bees. Here, in an early example of a prose text with no Christian loan-words (Charles-Edwards and Kelly 1983, 26), the church is just becoming involved. Along with the head of a kin-group, the church had rights over a portion of a stray swarm found by a man in unclaimed land (Charles-Edwards and Kelly 1983, 85). The church was integrated into the secular legal framework by being treated as a new kin-group; it was not granted any special position (Melia 1982). It is likely that the legal position of churches varied within Ireland as arrangements were made with each secular authority.

In some cases, secular laws referred to religious ones and stated that they must be obeyed; for example, the early eighth century *Críth Gablach* included the *recht Adamnain* (Mac Neill 1923, 303). There is some doubt over the original coverage of this legislation, but it was probably to prevent damage to church property and personnel, including clients, during secular conflict. The *Cáin Adamnain* is an eighth century document that outlines the provisions of the *recht*, and a narrative describing its apparent origin. This includes the saint fasting against God, something which Melia (1982) sees as being derived from secular, pagan law and suggests continuity of world view. This is an example of the ideological compromise which the church accepted.

The *Críth Gablach* itself is a good example of the combination of the secular and the ecclesiastical. Though a secular legal text, it was written down in a form heavily influenced by the Latin grammarians. The categorisation of society into seven rather than the older three grade system was inspired by the seven grades of cleric (Binchy 1941).

Hughes (1966, 152) considers that the ecclesiastical story telling was a potent force in changing attitudes to violence. The Saints' Lives, often composed in the form in which we now find them in the seventh and eighth centuries, appear to show early missionaries with fiery tempers and unpleasant characters. They are, however, mild and forgiving when placed beside the heroes in the secular heroic literature. This form of entertainment, combined with the legal backing, may have reduced wanton violence during the seventh and eighth centuries by creating a more peaceful ideology. Fighting still took place within the politically active elite, but perhaps with less damage to the rest of society. This may have also been desired by the whole of society since there was little benefit in obtaining political and thereby economic domination of an area if by so doing its wealth was destroyed. The very presence of more material wealth spread over a wider social spectrum may have made legislation that controlled wanton destruction desirable. Whatever the reasons, the church could through legislation and religious stories provide ideological support for the desired actions within society. These rules were broken not infrequently, but at least it was recognised that they were being broken and that punishment should be severe, even if enforcement was not necessarily politically feasible.

The Irish church was able to spread its ideology through education, which it gave to boys placed in fosterage. The use of the secular tradition of fosterage from perhaps the seventh century allowed the church to become enmeshed in a wide series of social links, with inevitable political benefits. However, the spread of its own learning, and the certain conversion and faith of the younger generations of nobility, must have been the most powerful long term benefit. Not only religious tracts were studied, but also secular law and heroic tales. However, set within a religious framework the dominant message was that of the church ideology. Indeed, by including the secular sources, and at times modifying them, there was no alternative educated tradition to which the elite could turn. By incorporating the material of the *filid* and brehons, and 'capturing' it by writing it down, the church was able to become dominant. The storage of accumulated knowledge through the written word was undoubtedly one of the most important factors in the gradual dominance of the church in society.

By the eighth century, the Irish church was fully integrated with secular society. It was recognised in law, and its officials were respected members of the community. Such was the integration, however, that there seems to have been some shift away from the high ideals of the earlier ecclesiastical leaders. Despite a widely recognised requirement that clergy should be celibate, it is clear that this was not always so.

Abbots from the later seventh century onwards were not always clergy (Hughes 1966, 159–60). Whilst earlier abbatial succession had often been on a kinship basis, this did not mean that celibacy was not followed since more distant relatives could succeed. By the eighth century the laws recognised celibate bishops and priests, and also those with a wife. Hughes (1966) illustrates a single family controlling Lusk, Co. Dublin at the end of the eighth century; at Slane, Co. Meath, two families kept control, a pattern reminiscent of the alternating possession of secular kingship in some areas (Figure 3:12). Though in many respects religious life may not have been less rigorous there are indications of a slackening of the ascetic spirit in many monasteries. Their success in acquiring lands and wealth led to an increasing involvement with wider political issues. This particularly affected those in the highest positions, and in some establishments these must have been much more comparable with the now Christian secular leaders than had been the case two centuries earlier.

The monasteries by the eighth century were concerned to obtain funds from many sources, besides their own lands (Hughes 1962). The saints' laws were sources of income through the fines that were imposed on those who violated them. Doherty (1984b, 97) points out that the term *cáin*, with its secular meaning of not only law but also rent and tribute, appears from the late eighth century as the replacement for the Latin term *lex*. As time passed, the income aspect seems to have increased in importance. Often associated with the promulgation of such a law was a circuit of relics. This was an increasingly recognised form of taxation by which each district visited was required to make payment to the monastery from which the relics had come

SLANE
(entries from *AU*)

Colmán of the Britons,
ab. Slane, +751

Cormac of Slane

Máenach, ab. Slane
and Cell-Foibrich, +773

Muiredach,
ab. Louth
+758

Fedach
ab. Slane,
Louth and
Duleek
+ 789

Ailill
ab. Slane
+802

Robartach,
econ. Slane and
ab. Cell-Foibrich
+787

Congal,
ab. Slane
+806

Colmán, ab. Slane
+839

Colmán,
ab. of Slane and
other churches in
France and
Ireland +825

Labraid
ab. Slane
+845

LUSK
Crundmáel ab. Lusk, +736

Óengus,
ab. Duleek
+783

Conall,
ab. Lusk
+779
(*AFM*)

Colga,
ab. Lusk
+787

Muiredach
ab. Lusk
+791

Máenach
secnap Lusk
+796

Cormac,
economus
Lusk
+804

Máenach, ab. Lusk
+805
(infeliciter)

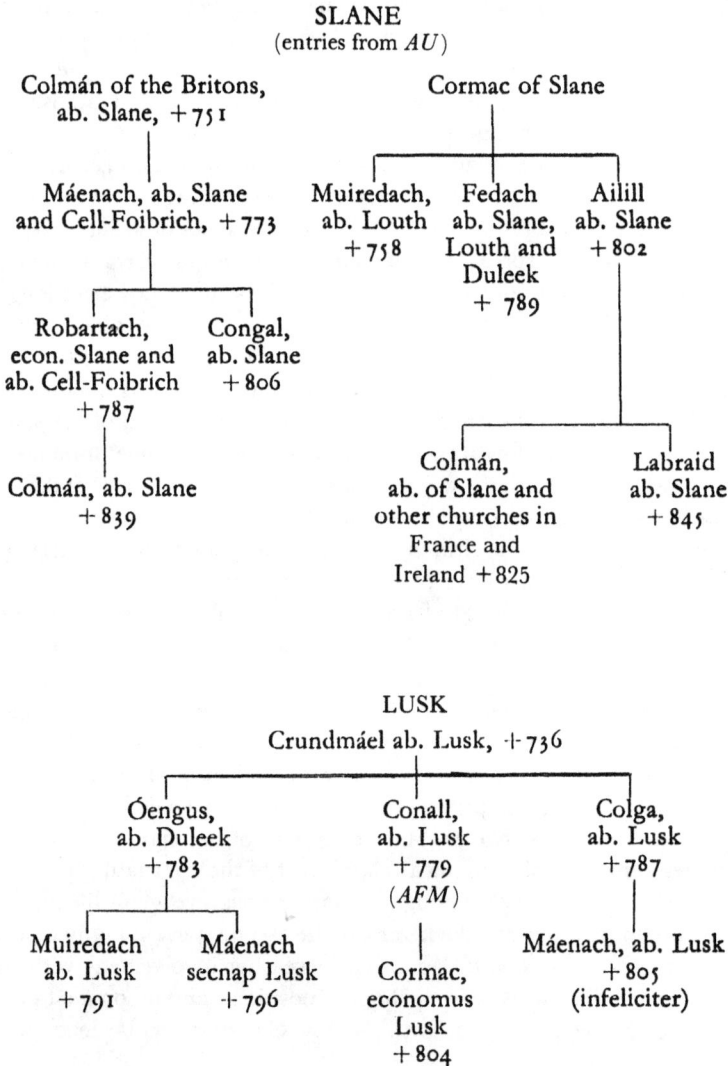

Figure 3:12 Control of the monastery of Lusk, Co. Dublin, by a single family in the eighth century, and an alternating control between two families of Slane, Co. Meath (Hughes 1966).

(O'Briain 1940). Those monasteries with important relics could clearly benefit in direct financial terms as well as through the spiritual benefits that such items were supposed to bring.

The final way in which the church was seen to become incorporated within the wider Irish culture was that certain abbots were prepared to resort to violence. Whereas earlier legislation and writings were against violence, in the later eighth century Armagh and Durrow were involved in incidents. Secular affairs were sometimes the cause, other times it was the rivalry between internal factions. The church was less of a unity at this time; synods where all the church leaders met were held regularly in the sixth and seventh centuries, but by the eighth century they were no longer relevant. Hughes (1966, 171) considers that by this time the abbots often saw kings rather than other abbots as allies. The power of the church was now fragmented in the same way that the secular power was, and the leaders of a monastic community or secular dynasty wished to use similar means to reach similar ends. Whilst there were still many within monasteries who were fervent Christians living out a life of service to God, the leaders of the major houses were more distant than ever in their attitudes and ambitions from the founders of those very establishments.

A widening world view

Christianity had from the start widened the world view of the indigenous population by the incorporation of the Roman, Mediterranean world within their experience, albeit indirectly through much of the established teaching and the Bible itself. But as the church became established within Ireland, it was able to develop its wider contacts even more. Columbanus founded monastic houses on the Continent, at Annegray, Luxeuil and even Bobbio in northern Italy. His code was extremely harsh, and Hughes (1963, 59) has pointed out how it may not be very representative of insular Irish practice. What may have been more important ideologically, however, was the expansion of the world view. Columbanus with his extensive travels through Europe was the most impressive clerical traveller. By the later sixth century, Ireland was not merely a passive recipient of ideas from Britain and Gaul. The Irish church was active within a wider European tradition and as such in contact with ideas from many areas, although as James (1982) points out this Irish influence was later exaggerated on the Continent. Nevertheless, the Irish who went abroad, such as Fursey who founded a house in East Anglia and later moved on to north-east Gaul, and those who evangelised in Bavaria, continued to have contact with their homeland (Hughes 1966, 92) whilst acquiring ideas from the regions in which they lived. Irish clerics went to Rome, and even further afield.

The thirst for knowledge was apparent in the work of Adamnan at the end of the century (Meehan 1958). Though he apparently did not travel to the Continent himself, scraps of information came from far-flung parts and were incorporated into his writings. This desire for new facts and ideas was widespread within Ireland by this time and can be seen clearly in the material culture.

Manuscripts were taken to the Continent, and others brought back to Ireland. Indeed, the links created at this time were maintained for generations, and even by the seventh century a complex web of relations was established that went even further than the Continental Irish houses. The links between the scriptoria in Ireland, Northumbria and the Continent such as Bobbio are numerous, and have led to debate, at times violent, on the place of production of many individual manuscripts (Henry 1965, Alexander 1978). The very fact that such debate continues suggests close interaction, and it is not relevant here to examine the detailed arguments for any particular case. Moreover, differential preservation further confuses discussion of origins and the relative importance of scriptoria; Continental Irish monasteries now contain the greatest number of documents, but this clearly cannot have been the case in the past.

Contacts with Spain are suggested by the speed with which the writings of Isidore of Seville were quoted in Ireland (Hillgarth 1961, 1962; Herren 1980). Isidore was concerned with the Hebrew, Greek and Latin languages, and these became major areas of interest to Irish monks. How far this learning was widely established in Ireland, however, is far from clear. The Fahan slab has an inscription in Greek uncials (Macalister 1948, 118). It is a Greek version of the *Gloria Patri*, in which honour is mentioned; this form occurs in the mid-seventh-century Antiphonary of Bangor, and the Fahan inscription was perhaps copied off a page of a Greek manuscript (Henry 1965, 127). Stevenson (1985), however, considers the stone later than the period of concern here. This does not necessarily indicate a source in Spain as suggested by Hillgarth, however. Other Continental links were also possible vehicles for transmission of such texts.

Merovingian links are attested through documentary references and parallels in motifs frequently cited by art historians (Henry 1965). The use of the marigold design, produced using a compass, is frequently found on early crosses. Another sculptural example includes the multiple cross decoration from Inismurray, Co. Sligo which can be closely paralleled on sarcophagi from the area of Nevers (James 1982, 384). It is also possible that the dotted background of the inscription on the Ardagh chalice owes something to the similarly finished but slightly earlier belt buckles from Aquitaine (James 1982, 385).

There is considerable evidence to suggest that motifs and techniques were not coming into Ireland alone, but were inextricably associated with ideas. In the case of manuscripts the ideas were actually conveyed in part through the writing, though the designs intimately associated with the texts could magnify or augment the power of the word. But art forms on other media would also have been transferred with any symbolic significance that lay behind them. Indeed, the two were probably seen by the Irish at the time as inextricably interrelated; therefore the presence of external motifs might indicate the presence of new ideas.

Whilst copying and re-copying might have only involved the transfer of material designs and not the ideas that had originally come with them, it is unlikely that the two could have been so easily separated. Art was not seen as mere decoration, but was viewed as a language, and so motif and idea were likely to have been linked. In a culture where most of the populace were illiterate, the use of symbols was well established and even expected. The difficulty comes in deciding how much of an idea may be passed on through generations of copying, or even whether new meanings might become associated with a particular motif. An incorrect chi-rho or alpha and omega could indicate 'down the line' transfer of ideas which might, in the process, have become somewhat transformed from the original. Nevertheless, it does suggest some transfer which, within the Christian tradition, can be expected to have retained much of the core meaning of the original.

One extremely important development in art styles was the introduction of the human form into the repertoire. This probably came from the Gospel books where at the beginning of each Gospel a picture of the saint was given, as in the Book of Dimma (Plate XXXV). The routes by which motifs reached Ireland could be tortuous; Henry (1965, 186) points out that the way in which St Luke holds a cross in one hand and flowering staff in the other in the Echternach Gospel is that of the Egyptian Osiris-judge. The attitude appears in Ireland with Christ in judgement in the Book of Kells and later sculptured crosses. The route may have been complicated, but the theme of judgement remained associated with the attitude of the figure. Motif and meaning remained integrated.

Thomas (1971a, 128) highlights a group of cross-slabs which have faces on them, and may be related to similar grave slabs from Egypt. Such a link may seem distant, but it is probable that decorated Coptic textiles were in Ireland by the seventh century, and it may have been through these that such a design was transferred. Icons have also been suggested as inspiration for designs. Henry (1965, 122) suggests that the Killen Cormac pillar with its engraving of a bust with a cross is derived from such a source. She also considers that two Crucifixion scenes from Inishkea North and Duvillaun, both in Co. Mayo, were derived from icons. Textiles and icons may have come along the Mediterranean and along the western seaboard or through Merovingian Gaul. Whilst the A and B ware pottery from the Mediterranean is the only certain, archaeologically detectable, residue of long distance contacts (see Chapter 7), it is likely that the art-historical evidence outlined above gives a correct picture, albeit a fuzzy one, of the complex web of contacts which Ireland maintained directly and indirectly with many parts of the Christian world.

During the seventh century two major controversies arose in the church. The first and most important was over the computation of the date of Easter, and the second was the use of the Celtic form of tonsure for priests. The latter dispute lasted longer than the one concerning Easter but was never so vehement. The Easter question was the most serious dispute. The Irish, along with those in Wales and other parts of western Britain, worked on a different system of calculating Easter from those elsewhere. Hughes (1966, chapter 10) emphasises that there had long been debate about this, and that many rival methods were used throughout Christendom. The matter came to a head partly through the expansion of the Irish church to the Continent and Britain, and in more obvious direct disagreement with other traditions. It also became an issue as the whole church matured and wished for a more standardised practice. This further emphasises the way in which Ireland was now part of a wider world, and long gone was the introverted and stagnant society of Iron Age Ireland. Though the dispute lasted decades, Ireland eventually conformed to the Roman method of calculation. Cummian was a leading figure in this change, and the southern part of the country, perhaps most in contact with the Continent, abandoned the Celtic Easter in the 630s, but it was only at the end of the seventh century that the north conformed to the Roman calendar. The debate over Easter lasted so long in Ireland because of the toleration there of diversity of practice. Numerous monasteries were not under the control of higher authorities and were used to their own ways; even Columbanus had been prepared to accept divergent practices (Hughes 1966, 108). The dispute was not the cause of major stress within the Irish church, though feelings at times ran high.

It has been suggested that the unity with Rome can be recognised archaeologically. An inscription on a cross-slab at Kilnasaggart, Co. Armagh states: 'this place has been given by Ternoc, son of Ciaran-the-Little, under the protection of Peter the Apostle'. The back of the stone has 11 crosses on it representing all the apostles apart from St Peter who is probably indicated by the large and ornamented cross under the inscription. Henry (1965, 119–20) suggests that this may have been an affirmation of loyalty to Rome. The Ternoc mentioned may be the one in the Annals who died in the second decade of the eighth century; the cross would be earlier than this, and so would have been set up soon after the final agreement on the Roman calculation of Easter.

Access to salvation – the church at work

The church held a central role in an Ireland converted to Christianity. There were no thoughts of schism, and so the power of the church was complete. It alone mediated between the secular individual and God, and it alone could facilitate salvation through baptism, communion and appropriate burial. The canons emphasised the attempted control of the lives of not only the clerics but also the secular congregations. How far this was achieved cannot be ascertained, but it was clearly the desire. Control of the route to salvation legitimised the church's authority on earth, and this was emphasised through the creation of suitable settings for religious services – the churches and monasteries – and suitable equipment for the sacraments. The material culture acted within the liturgical framework but also in itself created part of the message, being full of meaning in simile and metaphor. Whilst the earliest church in Ireland did not have elaborate equipment, this was considered essential within the mature, developed and established church from the end of the sixth century.

The physical setting

The setting for religious services was important. It was clearly easier for the celebrants to be spiritually prepared if they entered a suitable environment for worship. In the earliest phases of Christianity, services must have taken place in the open air at no particular sacred location or in the homes of believers, and this can perhaps be seen at the first phase of Reask with the simple round dwelling house and associated small, probably family, burial ground.

As the church became established, however, so too did its foci for religious activity. The sites were enclosed by a bank and ditch or wall and varied greatly in area. In the case of monastic sites, the *vallum* enclosed much more than areas related to strictly liturgical functions, and so such sites tend to be the largest. Indeed, most work has been done on the monastic sites or possible family churches, and relatively little is known about the communal churches that must have been so common.

Some monastic boundaries were defined by topography. In some cases part of an island or promontory (coastal or in a river bend) resulted in the construction of only a short length of boundary. Small islands were used as eremitic sites such as Skellig Michael and Illauntanig, Co. Kerry (Plate VIII). But even here, though, a boundary wall was still sometimes built. Church Island the stone enclosure wall was constructed in a late phase and is probably beyond the period of interest here. In the early phases of the site the shore line of the island itself was considered sufficient (Figure 3:15).

Within recent years many large enclosures have been found by aerial photography and field survey, particularly in the midlands and south-west (Norman and St Joseph 1969; Hurley 1982; Swan 1983). They form a distinct settlement type (Figure 3:13), often larger than the contemporary secular ring-fort sites. Their diameters range from 30 m to 400 m with the vast majority between 90 m and 120 m and, though Swan (1983) considers that they may be villages, the more general opinion is that they are monastic.

There are also a few sites with rectangular plans (Figure 3:14). Some of these have been known for some time, and were important sites such as Clonmacnois (Thomas 1971a, 29) and Iona (RCAHMS 1982, 36–9). In other cases, such as at Inch, Co. Down they were less important (Hamlin 1977, 1984).

At monastic sites, not only domestic activities but also agricultural and craft work was carried

BAWNATEMPLE

TEMPLEBRYAN

KILMACOO

FANLOBBUS

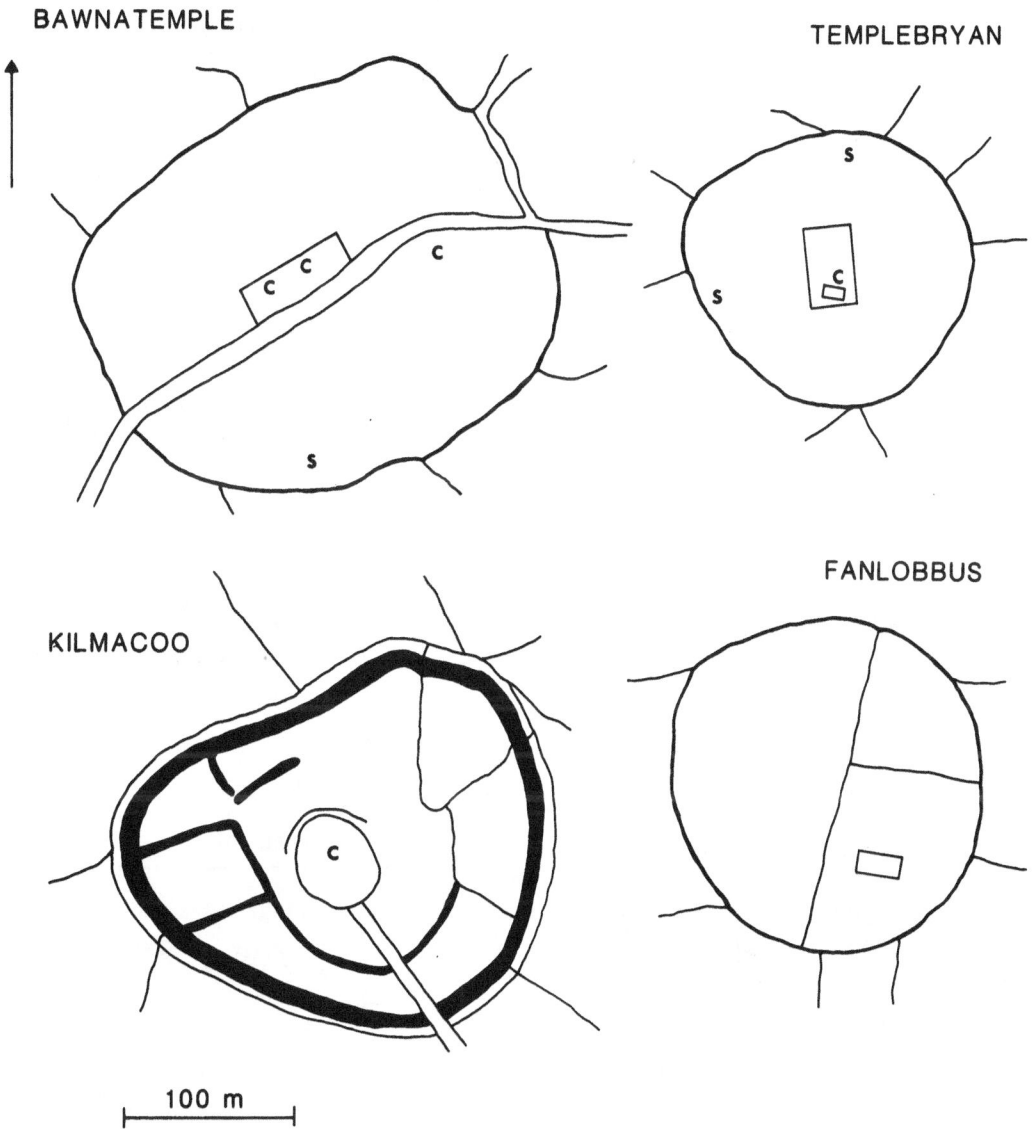

Figure 3:13   Large enclosures from Co. Cork. *Key*: **c** church; **s** souterrain (Hurley 1982).

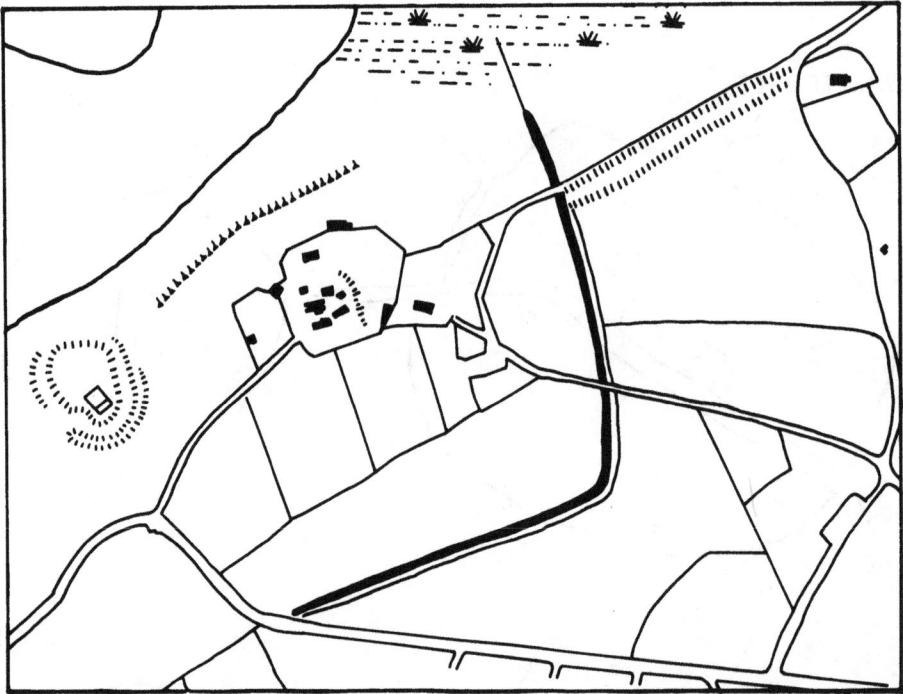

CLONMACNOIS

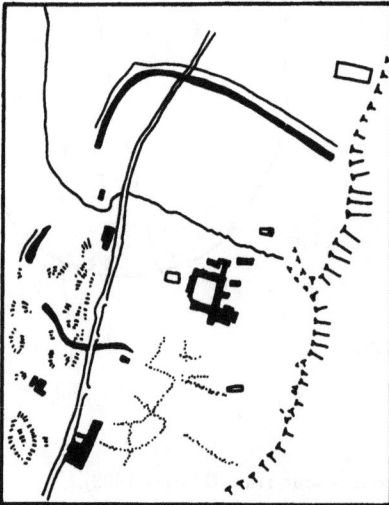

400 m

IONA

Figure 3:14   Monasteries in rectangular enclosures (Clonmacnois, Thomas 1971a; Iona, RCAHMS 1982).

out by members of the community within the large enclosure. In these cases there were clear spatial delineations between areas set aside for different activities. Although all the work of monasteries could be seen as related to the service of God on earth, and therefore allowed within the enclosure, the liturgical activities were of greater sanctity and required further separation within the enclosure (Doherty 1980).

The large enclosures have not yet been subjected to much excavation, with the exception of Nendrum, Co. Down (Plate VII) where the quality of excavation and recording was not very high. Aerial photography suggests that the interiors were often subdivided by banks, sometimes, as at Armagh, even where urban development has covered the area (Plate IX). At rural sites, more details are immediately visible; at Kilmacoo, Co. Cork there was a concentric arrangement with a central area containing the church and burials, an annular area around this and then an outer zone divided up by radial cross-banks (Figure 3:13). Care has to be taken with survey evidence, however, because at Moyne, Co. Mayo excavation has shown the internal subdivisions of a large oval monastic enclosure to be later, post-abandonment additions (Manning 1987). The church in the centre and more secular activities near the periphery do seem to have been the norm, however. At sites with no subdivisions surviving it is sometimes still possible to see intrasite patterning. At Templebryan and Bawnatemple, Co. Cork souterrains are found near the edges of the sites and the churches are at the centre. In some other cases it seems that the most sacred area can be to one side, as at Fanlobbus, Co. Cork (Figure 3:13). Excavations at 'Dunmisk Fort', now identified as a monastic enclosure, suggest that there were craft areas within the settlement. Heavy metalwork took place in the south-west, and elaborate work including bronze and glass in the north-east. The domestic area was in the north-west and the religious centre zone lay to the south-east (Ivens 1985, 1986).

A much better picture of the physical layout of religious enclosures comes from the smaller sites, mainly preserved in the west. The arrangements found in these may not be directly applicable to the larger, more complex sites, but even here spatial differentiation was often established from the beginning, later becoming more formalised. In many cases the surviving buildings may be late in the sequence and have been built after the eighth century, but in nearly all cases where excavations have taken place earlier, wooden remains beneath the stone structures suggest continuity of plan.

At Reask, excavations have shown the developments from a small Christian settlement without specialised buildings and only limited spatial differentiation within the enclosure to more complex arrangements (Figure 3:4). In the first phase a central timber building was constructed in the enclosure, and presumably was domestic. A slab-shrine and a small cemetery lay to the east, possibly with a small timber oratory but only two post holes survived the later disturbance. At the southern end of the cemetery was a small circular stone building which may belong to late in this phase. In the later phase, the eastern area was separated off by a stone wall, though this did not enclose all the burials and excluded stone A. Within the walled-off area burial continued and a developed cemetery was formed when the stone oratory was constructed. The rectangular building to the south may be much later, and should be disregarded from spatial analysis. In the larger domestic section to the west the dwellings (now all of stone but still circular in plan) moved to the periphery, leaving a large open area in the centre. It has been suggested that the open area west of the oratory and in the centre of the site represents the *plateola* where monks could walk (Herity 1984). In the west, where preservation of at least stone phases is relatively good, many other small enclosed monastic settlements have been located which have this division clearly marked without need for excavation.

At some of the smaller and more isolated sites the division into more and less sacred areas was not carried out. At the excavated site of Church Island the circular house 1 was inside the enclosure, along with the oratory (O'Kelly 1958). Both were originally in timber of which fragmentary evidence survived (Figure 3:15). Both buildings were then replaced in stone and it is possible to see a more detailed picture of the plan. The house and oratory were orientated facing away from each other, a situation emphasised by the distribution of refuse from the door of the house. The later, rectangular, house 2 was built outside the boundary wall and this may represent a greater differentiation between liturgical and domestic space.

At Skellig Michael (Figure 3:3) a row of six stone dwellings face down onto a small oratory with its cemetery, and though another oratory lies along the cliff edge to the north, there is no real separation (de Paor 1955).

It may well be that where the division between domestic and liturgical areas was not made then the site was a truly ascetic community fully devoted to contemplation and prayer. When there was a clear subdivision of the settlement then other, worldly activities were also carried out at the site. This may therefore be an archaeological method of differentiating hermitages and fully ascetic communities from small familial secular monasteries.

The church building

Information on church buildings comes from archaeology and descriptions in literary sources. Rectangular wooden churches seem to have been extremely common, though there was considerable variation in the materials used, depending on what resources were available locally. Oak timbers are implied in the term *dairthech* which means oak-house but was used for wooden churches; there are also references to wattled churches, and occasionally even to structures of turf or earth (Hamlin 1984, 118). Wooden shingles or rush thatch were probably the normal roofing materials. There are a few references in the Annals to stone churches but at only the most important monastic centres and not until the late eighth century (Harbison 1982). Hamlin (1984) considers that they were not common until the eleventh and twelfth centuries, though one at Duleek may unusually have been built in the sixth century.

The provision of rectangular buildings in a culture exclusively used to circular structures meant that the church itself would have been instantly recognisable, however small it may have been. Thomas (1981a) has suggested that the use of the rectangle was related to the number four, and so to the arms of the cross. If this were so, the central message of Christianity could be conveyed in the very structure itself. The churches were orientated approximately east–west, but the exact angle seems to have been dictated by topography.

Oratories were small, and if the congregation was of any size it would have had to stand outside such buildings, a situation common till the eleventh century (O'Kelly 1975, 21). In these cases, a temporary altar may have been set up outside, and a standing cross-inscribed stone may have acted as a focus; this may have been the case at the early phase of Reask, Co. Kerry. The oratory was then really just a repository for the altar and any liturgical equipment when not in use, or available for private prayer.

Many of the small chapels may, however, have only needed to serve small groups, a monastic family or scattered Christians from the locality. For example, the Reask type oratories may have been family chapels, in which case they would have been large enough for everyone to stand inside (Figures 3:4, 3:15). Though the stone oratories may in many cases be later than the ninth century, they do at least form a large enough group to be susceptible to analysis and

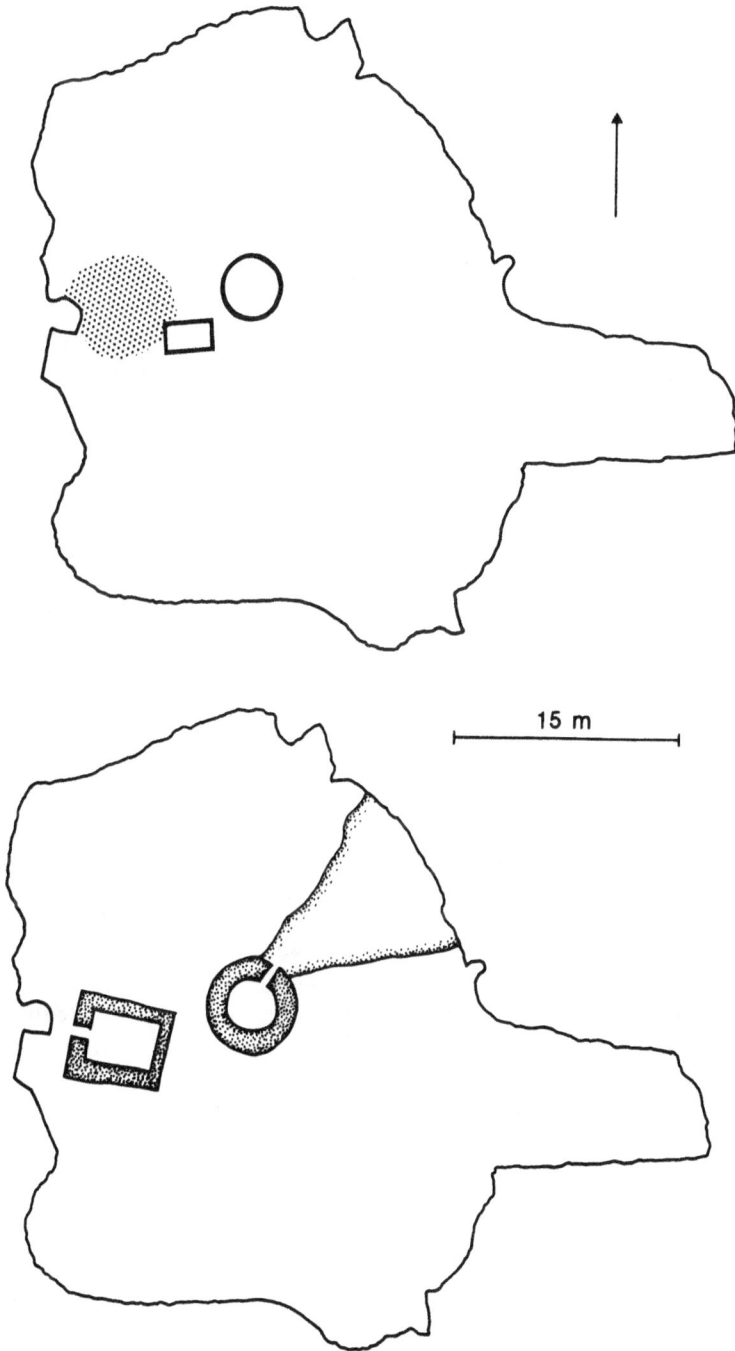

15 m

Figure 3:15   The early phases at Church Island, Co. Kerry (adapted from O'Kelly 1958).

show that they could accommodate a family that might live in the roundhouses found at Reask or other similar sites.

Most of the timber churches that have been excavated were found beneath later stone examples, with the result that they are rarely well preserved (Figure 3:16). At Church Island, Co. Kerry rock-cut post holes indicated a building roughly 2 m by 3 m though the east end had been destroyed (O'Kelly 1958). At Carnsore, Co. Wexford a complete rectangular plan of a wooden structure was recovered beneath a medieval stone church within a large oval enclosure (O'Kelly 1975). The post holes delineated an area measuring 2.25 m by 1.5 m and a radiocarbon date of AD 660 ± 80 (Har-1340) came from one of the post holes. Harbison (1982, 628) considers that this is too small to have been a church but may have been a shrine. Harbison also postulates an alternative plan using other post holes from the excavation to produce a building 6.25 m by 4.25 m but this is on a north-west by south-west alignment and looks less convincing though it is more reasonable in size as a church. A further example for which a plan could be reconstructed came from Ardwall Isle, Kirkcudbrightshire, Scotland (Thomas 1966). Wallace (1982) has suggested that the internal area of the churches might have been greater than that suggested hitherto if the post holes that have been recognised do not mark the wall lines but are the roof supports of hipped roofs. If this were so, the internal areas would be more similar to those of the stone phases, which seem to be slightly larger, but at Church Island at least, the timber phase roundhouse would be very close to, if not actually overlapping, a larger timber oratory.

The only timber church found on a site not disturbed by later activity is that excavated by de Paor at Inishcaltra (Harbison 1982, 628). The building, of two phases, was about 8 m by 5 m and aligned east–west. The wall was made of earth faced on both sides and supported in the centre by lines of wattling. It was thought by the excavator to be early in the sequence on the site, but detailed dating evidence has not yet been presented.

There is a growing number of instances of excavation producing fragmentary traces of timber churches. The stone church on White Island, Co. Fermanagh was built on the site of two successive timber churches (Lowry-Corry et al. 1959). At Derry, Co. Down a timber-framed building with stone footings was uncovered that may have been ecclesiastical (Waterman 1967). Whilst it is not closely positioned east–west, several of the early burials are aligned with it, and some would have been within the structure. Thomas (1971a, 74) mentions traces of a timber structure beneath a small stone chapel at Ardagh, Co. Longford excavated again by de Paor but not yet published.

The *Hisperica Famina* (Herren 1974) contains a long passage describing a chapel which, in the light of the archaeological evidence, is most illuminating. The building is rectangular with a single western door, and with a central altar. This differs from the evidence from the stone examples where altars survive, and also Inishcaltra where the altar seems to have been against the eastern wall.

A detailed description of the church dedicated to St Brigit at Kildare and newly constructed in the second quarter of the seventh century is given by Cogitosus (Kenney 1929, 356–60). This has been used by Radford (1977) to produce a tentative reconstruction, though there are alternatives (Thomas 1971a, 145). In particular, these concern whether it was the nave or the choir which was divided north–south, and therefore whether the altar and the shrines of St Brigit and Conláed either side of it were in the choir or nave (Figure 3:17). In the case of Radford's interpretation the congregation at large could see the altar and shrines, but not in the case of the second interpretation, when all they could see was the dividing wall highly

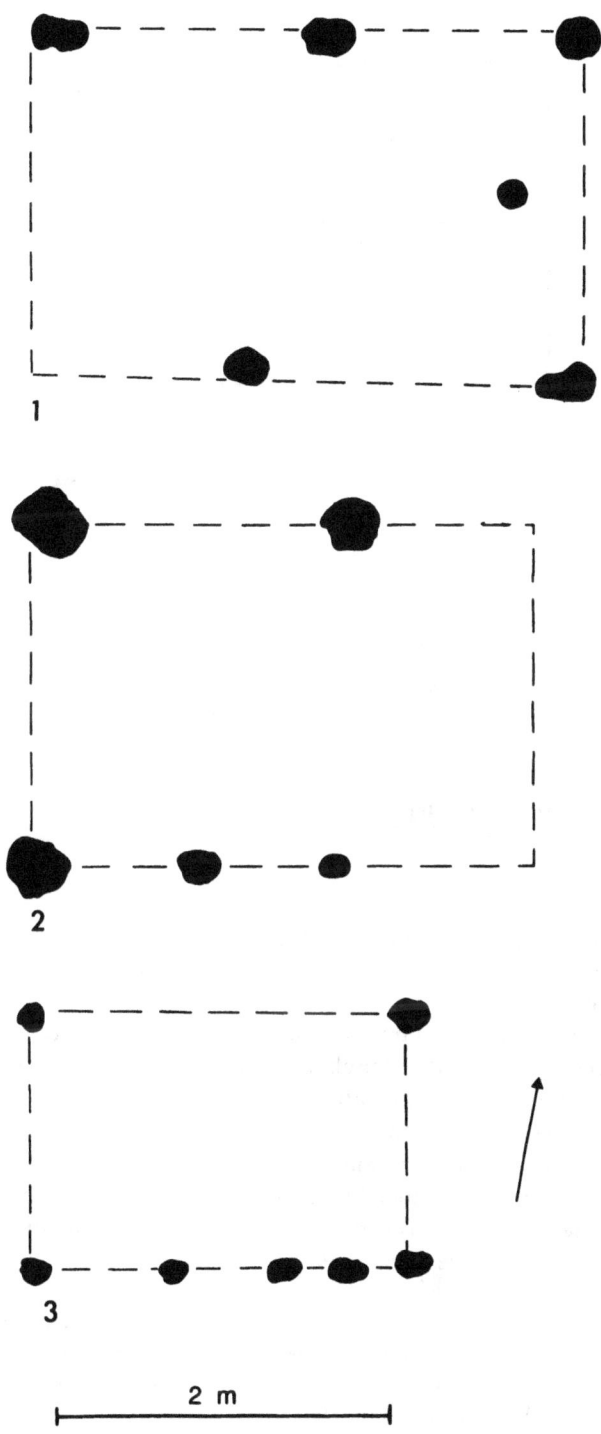

Figure 3:16 Plans of Celtic timber churches in Britain and Ireland. **1** Carnsore, Co. Wexford; **2** Church Island, Co. Kerry; **3** Ardwall Isle, Kirkcudbrightshire, Scotland (**1** O'Kelly 1975; **2** O'Kelly 1958; **3** Thomas 1966).

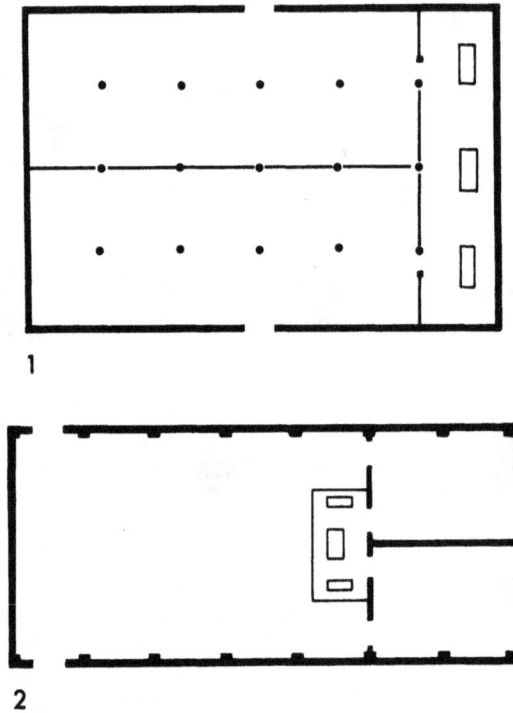

Figure 3:17 Alternative reconstruction plans of the wooden church of St Brigit at Kildare, based on the description of Cogitosus (**1** Radford 1977, **2** Thomas 1971a).

decorated with painted images and hangings. Whatever the details of the plan, there was a very substantial church at Kildare, and it may have been one of the largest ecclesiastical structures in Early Christian Ireland.

The internal arrangements at Kildare are of particular note in relation to ideology because of the conscious use of space within the church. Different areas were set aside according to status for the various constituents of the congregation. There is clear evidence of the northern half of the church being reserved for the women, and the south for the men. All women entered through a north door into the nave, whilst men came through a south door. The abbess with her nuns subsequently could pass through a door in the northern end of a transverse wall within the church to receive the sacraments. This female–north, male–south opposition was also followed with regard to the position of the shrines containing the bodies of Bishop Conláed and St Brigit.

The position of women on the north side of the Kildare church might be considered a subsidiary location, and it was proposed on the basis of documentary evidence that female religious were given lower status and gradually excluded from any significant religious role during the eighth and ninth centuries (Bitel 1984).

Most services for the secular population would have been held in communal churches rather than at monasteries or private chapels. Very little is known of these, and presumably many lie beneath the Romanesque churches, often now in ruins, scattered widely throughout the countryside. Thomas (1981a) suggests that many of the communal churches would have been large. However, the separation of the congregation from the altar which might be implied at Kildare may have been quite widespread and could account for the small size of the archaeologically attested oratories, used only by clerics whilst the congregation remained outside.

Relics

The cult of relics began very early in the development of Christianity, and was associated with tombs of early martyrs. From the earliest period, they seem to have formed an important part in the reinforcement of authority within the church as well as aids in prayer. In Ireland relics are known from the fifth century onwards but their major importance did not come until after 800. Nevertheless, there is archaeological and documentary evidence for relics and shrines earlier than this (Thomas 1971a; Doherty 1984a, 1984b; Lucas 1986).

Relics of St Peter and St Paul were probably brought to Ireland by Palladius in the fifth century to enhance his authority (Sheehy 1961); these and his own books and writing board were kept in Cell Fine, a small church in Leinster (Doherty 1984b, 91). It is possible that the few early church sites with the name *basilica* contained relics in the fifth century (Doherty 1984a). Those at Baslick, Co. Roscommon were later acquired by Armagh, which also probably obtained others directly from Rome through an embassy which returned from there in 632. These were then used to bolster Armagh's claims to supremacy within Ireland, the ideological support for these claims coming from the sanctity and power of the relics. By the seventh century relics could be derived from early Irish saints, and did not have to be imports; indeed the process of translation of remains may have begun at this time (Doherty 1984b, 94). On the one hand there were the major, national and international figures whose relics had widespread power, and on the other there were intensely local saints whose sanctity and power were restricted. An example of a relic associated with a major figure is St Patrick's bell (Plate XXX).

In south-west Ireland a group of slab-shrines have been identified which Thomas (1971a, 141–4) considers perhaps seventh century, but which may at least in some cases be as late as the twelfth (Hamlin 1985, 295). These are probably to be associated with locally important relics (Figure 3:18). At Killabuonia a cross-inscribed end slab was pierced with a hole, allowing the bones to be touched, but not all examples had such a hole. A slab-shrine at Reask has been excavated; the interior was paved and the phosphate level in the soil above the paved floor indicated the presence of bone, presumably that of a re-interred human body. This shrine was invisible on the surface, and many other sites may therefore have had such shrines. The only other excavated possible example also had a paved area. This was at Ardwall Isle, in Scotland, the only example known outside Ireland. In both the Ardwall and Reask examples the ridge of the shrine may have run north–south, rather than east–west as with other examples. Slab-shrines were probably widespread in Ireland, and examples are known from Donaghpatrick and Slane, Co. Meath (Westropp 1901, 418). Thomas identified rectilinear grave enclosures in association with the early slab-shrines, but the excavations at Reask indicated that, at that site at least, the enclosures were of much later date.

Excavations at Church Island revealed an external tomb that may have been a shrine. Though partly set below ground, it rose some distance above the surrounding level. It was not tent-shaped but would have had a flat top slab or slabs. It had been extended in the post-Norman period, but originally would have been of similar dimensions to the slab-shrines, and may have had a similar function. It is uncertain to which phase of the site the tomb belongs,

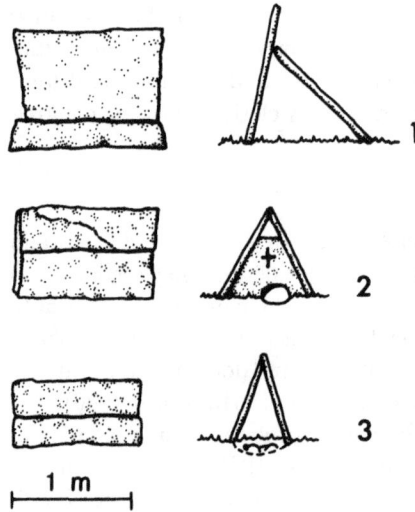

Figure 3:18   Slab-shrines from Co. Kerry. **1** Illaunloghan; **2** Killabuonia; **3** Killoluaig (Henry 1957).

but it did not act as a focus for burial, unlike the other excavated examples of Reask and Ardwall. The small oratory at Ardoilean may have had a shrine tomb on the external east wall and could have been a focus for pilgrimage from the eighth century (Herity 1987), but lack of excavation means that distribution of burials in the area is unknown.

By the seventh century, shrines were being placed within churches. At Kildare, St Brigit and Bishop Conláed were positioned on either side of the altar in shrines richly decorated in gold and silver and set with precious stones. These were not just local figures, but known throughout all Ireland. The contrast with the slab-shrines is only too apparent. Unfortunately no large internal shrines are known archaeologically, although some fittings that may have been attached to such structures or other ecclesiastical furniture have survived (Plates XXVI, XXXI).

Small reliquaries were made in a number of shapes, and are part of a wider tradition current in Britain and on the Continent. They seem to appear in the eighth century; Henry (1965, 99) notes that there are eight mentions of shrines being made in the eighth century, the earliest being in 743. Though there were important developments during the eighth century, the real flowering of reliquaries, and the most important period of their use in rituals, was to come later. Perhaps the most common shrines were the church-shaped ones like that from Lough Erne, Co. Fermanagh (Plates XXIII, XXIV). The late eighth-century Emly shrine is made from yew wood, inlaid in silver in step patterns which create cross-like patterns over much of the surface. Circular mounts and the ridge pole of the shrine, to which originally was attached the carrying strap, are bronze decorated with cloisonné enamels in green and yellow (Swarzenski 1954).

Not all reliquaries contained fragments of human body; many contained the belongings of a noted saint. Thus, the Moylough belt-shrine (Plate XXV) was an elaborate housing for a leather belt (O'Kelly 1965). It is dated to around AD 700 and displays more complex decorative ambitions than the earlier items. Some croziers made of bronze tubes encased wooden staffs that had belonged to saints, but these are difficult to distinguish from others which had used a new piece of wood to provide a solid core to the object (Ryan 1983, 45).

Entry into the church — baptism

Baptism is one of the most significant events in the life of a Christian, and there is both documentary and archaeological evidence for this in Early Christian Ireland. Four types have been defined by Davies (1962, 23–5): submersion, immersion (of the head), affusion (poured over the head) and aspersion (sprinkled on the head). The only form of baptism recorded is that of affusion, the form most used in Roman Britain (Thomas 1981a). No baptisteries are known from Early Christian Ireland.

No early fonts survive, although it is possible that some of the bullaun stones found at many monastic sites may have had such a function. Baptism was completed by anointing the convert with the chrism, holy oil. Some of the imported pottery often claimed as evidence for a wine trade may well have held the oil necessary for this part of the church service. Small buckets of wood, bound with decorated bronze bands, have been recovered as stray finds and from settlement sites. They date to the eighth or early ninth century, and some may have been used for liturgical purposes, in either baptism or the mass.

Communion

The regular attendance at church services, particularly mass, was the central part of the Christian worship. A recent survey of liturgy in Early Christian Ireland suggests that two types of service, the Gallican and Roman, may have been used in Ireland (Ní Chatháin 1980). The Gallican mass was the form that had been practised in Roman Britain, and was probably common in much of Ireland. The contact with Rome through Palladius in 431 could have meant that the Roman mass was also used in some areas. The general latitude of practice within the Irish church may well have applied even to the mass. Both services consisted of two elements, a fore-mass with readings, songs and prayer, followed by the sacrifice-mass including communion.

Evidence for readings and prayer comes mainly in the form of surviving manuscripts. From the earliest period there must have been Gospels, psalters and commentaries. The earliest surviving is that of the later sixth-century *Cathach* of St Columba, a translation of the Gallican psalter of St Jerome. The *Codex Usserianus Primus* is a pre-hieronymian text with the Gospels in the order Matthew, John, Luke, Mark; it is early seventh century in date (Lowe 1935). The early manuscripts were not heavily decorated, and were often small; the *Cathach* measures only about 6 inches by 9 inches. Later, larger Gospel books were produced to be used mainly on the altar. Examples include the Saint-Gall manuscript which Henry (1965, 196) considers was made in Ireland in the mid-eighth century and taken to the Continent in the ninth, and a group made in Irish monasteries on the Continent, including the Echternach, Trier and Maihingen Gospels. From Ireland itself comes the Book of Durrow which, though made of small pages, falls into this tradition because of the amount of ornamentation (Plates XXXIII, XXXIV) and the use of the majuscule script which limited the amount that could be written on each page. This manuscript again emphasises some of the archaic features of Irish Christian liturgy and tradition. Though the text is Vulgate the symbols of the Evangelists are depicted in the Old Latin order of Matthew, John, Mark, Luke (Lowe 1935).

Pocket-books were also produced that could be carried around to be read or used by priests attending scattered churches. The Books of Mulling and Dimma (Plates XXXV, XXXVI) were Gospels of this type, written in a minuscule script with numerous abbreviations to save space (Henry 1965, 199). Also of this portable type was the Stowe Missal, produced at the end of the eighth century, containing part of the Gospel of St John as well as the Missal, which includes a commemoration of St Mael Ruain of Tallaght, Co. Dublin. The text is mainly but not exclusively in Latin and there is only a limited amount of decoration (Mitchell 1977, 139). The Antiphonary of Bangor is an example of a mid-seventh century hymn book, again with very little illumination.

The mass had a range of other items besides books that were necessary for the full ritual, and a few of these have survived; others have been illustrated in manuscripts and carving or described in texts.

The most impressive item used in the mass was the chalice. Whilst early in the church any material could be used for this vessel, later only fine materials were acceptable. In Ireland, glass, bronze and silver were used. Richardson (1980) notes that there were two forms of chalice, both derived from the classical world: the first was the two-handled cup originated from the cantharus, whilst the second was set on a conical foot without handles. Two very fine examples of the handled chalice have been found in Ireland. The most famous is that of the Ardagh chalice (Plate XXVII), made of silver, whilst a recent discovery was another example in the Derrynaflan hoard. Both were decorated with goldwork and glass studs which conveyed symbolic messages. The presence of the handles and the size of the vessels (23 cm and 21 cm diameter respectively) indicate that they were probably ministerial chalices used for the communion of the congregation. They may also possibly have been used in the consecration of offerings at the mass (Ní Chatháin 1980).

Only one example of the smaller type of chalice without handles has been found (Plate XXVIII). It was smaller, under 14 cm in diameter, and made of copper-alloy. It was discovered with the larger Ardagh chalice. This type may originally have been common, and is frequently depicted on manuscripts (Figure 3:19); Richardson (1980) considers that, because of the colours used, such as blue, they were made of glass. Small chalices were probably used in private services which must have been common if the incidence of small oratories is any guide (Godel 1979, 65). Mass could have taken place daily in monasteries, and whenever a priest was present in private chapels.

The wine was poured into the chalice through a strainer, and one of these formed part of the Derrynavlan hoard. It acted as both a ladle and strainer, since the wine was strained by passing through a perforated central divider in the bowl; it must have been used in the manner depicted in the Book of Kells (Figure 3:19). As grapes could not ripen in Ireland, all wine had to be imported. Whilst most of it probably arrived in wooden casks, some seems to have been brought to Ireland in large ceramic amphorae (Figure 7:3). Though they derive from the eastern Mediterranean, they may have been re-used and the wine, if that was what they contained, could have come from closer areas such as Gaul.

Flabella were fans used to keep flies from falling in the chalice. Originating in the eastern Mediterranean, they were still used by Irish clerics. The *flabellum* became a symbol of Christian fidelity and is depicted on incised slabs (Figure 3:10), grave-slabs (Lionard 1961, 137) and in manuscripts such as the Book of Kells (Plate XXXVII).

Whilst the wine had to be imported, the bread for the mass could be made locally. It is possible that in Ireland, as elsewhere, the preparation of altar bread became a special activity separate from other baking. Only when extensive excavations have been carried out in monasteries and around early churches may it become clear whether this was the case, but Power (1939) suggested that querns decorated with crosses may have been used for this purpose (Figure 5:14). Illustrations in the Book of Kells give some indication of the loaves, and Henry (1974,

Figure 3:19   Representation of a chalice in the Book of Kells (Richardson 1980).

199) considers that one type was cross-inscribed. There is dispute as to whether the bread used in the mass was levened or unlevened (Ryan 1962, Crehan 1976), and it may have been the case that both were used. The Derrynaflan paten was certainly large enough to be used with levened bread. It has a raised rim which, whilst carrying elaborate decoration (Plate XXIX), also served to prevent crumbs falling to the ground. During the service there was also what appears to have been a stand used, perhaps, to again prevent spillage of any bread. The host was not necessarily passed to the communicant by hand. A spoon and a pronged object in the St Ninian's Isle hoard of around AD 800 may, for example, have been used to distribute the host (McRoberts 1965).

Moral control and penitence

Mention has already been made of the penitentials formulated by such church leaders as Vinnian. The church could control behaviour by having its own rules and regulations and, as was clear from the canons of Patrick, these were not related to secular law at an early date. Later, the two legal traditions became intertwined as the church became more directly involved with the secular powers and as they in turn were converted. However, the church retained moral control and could excommunicate miscreants or at least prevent them from attending services. For those who sincerely believed in the teachings of the church, this must have been a very real threat. Whilst many may have held a rather equivocal faith and were not greatly concerned with judgement in the hereafter, there was still social pressure to conform at least outwardly.

Secular authorities may have had, through the maintenance of order, control over life and death. But the church had a far more powerful weapon for the faithful through the administration of the sacraments, and thereby access to individual salvation and everlasting life. This great responsibility brought with it a power that ensured a dominant role for the church in Early Christian Ireland. As it acted within the existing social and economic sytems, maintaining and influencing them, the views of the church were vital in the ideological justification and support for all other systems. This power came in the last resort, however, from its control over the sacraments.

Burial

It was essential for Christians at this period to be buried in a suitable manner with the attendant services. Archaeological excavation and survey have provided much information about the form of burial and commemoration, but relatively little is known about the accompanying rituals.

Graves

Graves were constructed in a number of ways. They were normally dug with parallel sides and rounded ends, but some tapered towards the foot and a few had sharper corners and straight ends. Simple earth dug graves were commonly used, with no lining. Usually no trace has been found of coffins, indicated by either staining or nails; however, at *Ma Ferte* in Armagh oak log coffins have been discovered (Lynn pers. comm.). Presumably most bodies were buried wrapped only in a shroud. A small fragment of woollen cloth, possibly the hem of such a shroud, was found in an early grave at Church Island, Co. Kerry (O'Kelly 1958). Derry, Co. Down had one pit which may well have been a grave that was dug and, after a period of natural silting, was partially backfilled (Waterman 1967).

Some bodies at Knockea (O'Kelly 1967) were protected around the head by a few stones, but this was not common elsewhere. At many sites stone lined cists were used, and generally consisted of thin flags or slabs set on end, with several side stones placed end to end along the length of the grave, and one placed at each end. If further slabs were laid on top of these, thus sealing the body, these have been termed lintel graves (Thomas 1971a, 49). In a few cases where recumbent memorial slabs have been found in situ, as at Glendalough, Co. Wicklow, they were used as lintel stones covering graves. In many cases a full set of vertical slabs was not provided, and the lintels collapsed at a later date onto the skeleton. At Millockstown, Co. Louth (Manning 1986) and Boolies Little, Co. Meath (Sweetman 1983) the lintel slabs were sometimes so narrow that they could never have rested on the vertical slabs and must have been supported by the body. It was rare for the bottom of the grave pit to be paved, and Derry yielded only one such example (Waterman 1967). There is little evidence for a chronological sequence of grave types though at Derry the cist graves seemed to have been earlier than the simple rock-cut examples. Reask had both dug and lintel graves, but here there seemed to be no chronological order (Fanning 1981).

The body was normally laid supine, fully extended east–west. In most cases the head was to the west, though in a few cases it was to the east. It was medieval practice to bury priests with their heads to the east, so that at the resurrection they faced their flocks, and it is perhaps significant that the one example of this arrangement at Knockea was a male burial. The exact orientation of the graves varied considerably, and three, all children, at Knockea and a few adults at Church Island were placed north–south (Figure 3:20). Unfortunately, the reports do not state the stratigraphic sequence of the burials. The rock into which the Derry graves were cut partly influenced their alignment, but the excavator did not consider that this was the only factor. At Reask, orientation varied between 4 and 24 degrees south of east, and one small group of later burials contained those closest to east. It is possible that orientation at this site was approximately related to chronology. Often orientation was influenced by the alignment of nearby buildings such as an oratory. This was the case at Church Island according to O'Kelly (1958) where, of the burials near the oratories, all the earliest burials were parallel with the longer axis of the wooden building, and the later ones were aligned with the stone one.

Arms were normally laid at the side of the body. In a minority of cases the arms were crossed over the pelvis, though at Church Island this was the only position used. Crouched burials were rare; at Knockea one was found lying on its back with arms across the chest and knees pulled right up over them. In some of the burials at Booleys Little, the cist graves seem to have been made a little too small, and the bodies were pushed in with little ceremony. Many of the burials at this site had their arms folded across their chests.

It was normal for only one to be placed in each grave. There are, however, quite a number of exceptions. A woman was buried at Knockea with a very young baby lying on her chest, its head near the presumed mother's chin. At Derry two adjacent graves, 19 and 23, were found where part of a second skull was laid behind the head of the complete burial, and covered with a stone; in the case of grave 4 a complete skull was placed at the feet of a burial which was only partially excavated. A double burial also occurred at this cemetery, where in grave 31 one male was laid out in the typical position but north of him in the grave was stacked the skeleton, including the skull, of another male. Two graves at Reask may have been constructed together,

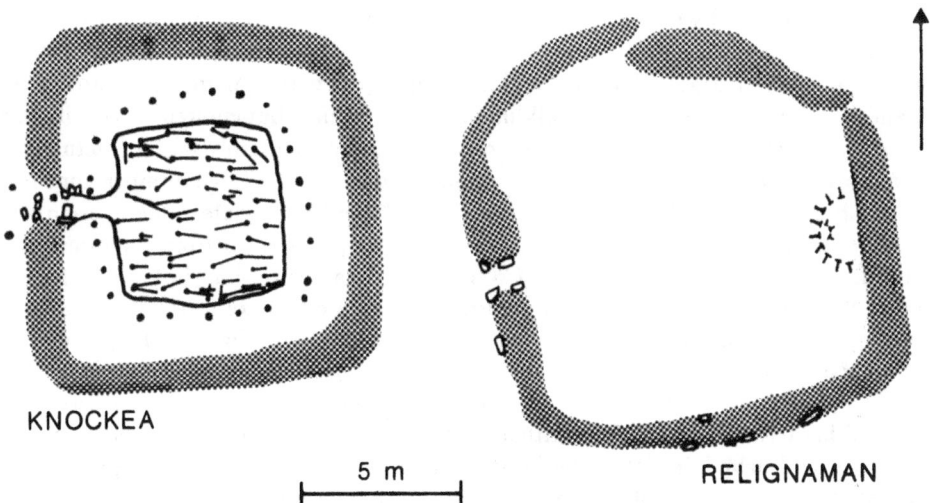

Figure 3:20 Rectangular undeveloped cemeteries (Relignaman, Hamlin and Foley 1983; Knockea, O'Kelly 1967).

since both graves 7 and 8 had a shared set of sidestones on which the lintels were placed. When disturbance of an earlier grave took place at Boolies Little, bones including the head were sometimes placed at the foot of the new interment.

Graves were generally backfilled with the earth that had been taken out. At Derry, some of the graves to the north of the cemetery contained considerable quantities of occupation material. One child burial at Knockea had small boulders round two sides whilst the lower grave fill contained 111 water-rolled pebbles. Grave goods were rare. The strike-a-light found near the Knockea child burial with the pebbles may have been deliberately placed near its left hand, but might have been included merely as one of the small rounded stones. A small bead of green glass came from Reask burial 23, but was not necessarily a deliberate deposit; the same can be said for the bronze strip and link from graves at Boolies Little.

Grave markers

A small number of graves, belonging to particularly revered individuals, were made into shrines, and some remains of saints were also translated to specially built shrines or fragments were enshrined in portable reliquaries. These have already been discussed so the great mass of ordinary grave markers known from archaeological sources are discussed here.

Graves were marked on the surface in many cases, though rarely does such evidence survive in situ. Sometimes the marking can be inferred, as with the early burials at Church Island where the graves are all neatly arranged and do not cut each other. The same must have been the case for most burials at Knockea where, considering the relatively small space available for inhumations, there were few intercutting graves; however, the excavator found fragments of other individuals in the topsoil suggesting that some had been disturbed. Whilst a few graves at Reask intersected slightly, no bodies were disturbed and the overall arrangement was in rows. Rows can be seen at both Millockstown and Boolies Little, but there was some intercutting of graves at these sites. Graves were often dug in line with an older interment, but cut through either the upper or lower portion. There must have been some form of marking for the alignments to have been maintained within this cemetery, though not sufficient to prevent disturbance of earlier remains.

The earliest burial markers that can be dated were those with ogham. Many are no longer in situ and have been re-used in later buildings and souterrains, but enough survive in place to show that, whilst some may have been only memorials others certainly marked actual graves. Some oghams may have been pre- or at least non-Christian, but a large number appear to be related to Christian usage. Whilst most are fifth or sixth century in date, oghams seem to have continued to be inscribed even later than this, after scripts derived from manuscripts were introduced. A stone from Church Island, Co. Kerry has an ogham inscription which overlays an incised cross of later seventh or early eighth century date (Figure 3:10). In most cases the relationship between oghams and inscribed crosses is uncertain (Figure 3:10), although the reverse sequence is known in the case of an ogham from Aglish, Co. Kerry (Plate X).

Ogham stones stood upright, and so did many but not all other early grave markers. Thomas (1971a, 112) has termed upright slabs with a simple cross primary cross-slabs, whilst recumbent slabs which would have lain flat at the head of the grave are termed primary grave markers. It seems that upright cross-slabs were the norm until the seventh century, after which the recumbent slabs became common. The cross-slabs that were still carved became larger and developed into the free-standing crosses. There was a period when both types were used in conjunction, and a tomb called Leaba Phadraig on Caher Island, Co. Mayo has a recumbent slab and an upright cross-slab marking it (Henry 1947). At Glendalough, Co. Wicklow a small cross was used at the head and also at the foot of some recumbent slabs. Some cross-slabs were set in a specially made socket stone; at Inishcaltra two such socket stones were cross-inscribed and so were in essence also small recumbent slabs. One of the earliest dated examples of a recumbent slab is a re-used millstone from Clonmacnois (Figure 3:21) and this may originally have held an upright of wood or stone. Indeed, the recumbent slab may have developed from the decorated socket stone for the cross-slab.

A few manuscripts survive from the sixth century onwards and so can be used to provide decorative and calligraphic parallels for the burial markers. The only Irish example at this early date is the *Cathach* of St Columba and this contains slight decoration on the large capitals; it may date from the time of the saint after which it is named (Lawlor 1916, Lowe 1935). Epigraphic evidence also comes from wax tablets set in wood, found near Springmount Bog, Co. Antrim (Armstrong and Macalister 1920; Plate XXXII). From these and later texts it is possible to construct an epigraphic typology which can help in the dating of inscribed burial markers. For example, the alphabet stone at Kilmalkedar has been dated on epigraphic grounds to the sixth century.

Stone A at Reask is thought to be a cross-slab of the late sixth or early seventh century, and has possible omegas between the arms of the incised cross (Figure 3:5). An inscription *dne* standing for *domine* in an early form of Irish script is found on the stone; a few other cross-slabs are known with this formula in a number of different contractions. The Reask stone also has decorative features that can be considered early. The Maltese equal-armed cross has peltas and spirals beneath, and can be compared with those in the late sixth-century *Cathach* manuscript (Henry 1965).

Dating of most early burial markers can only be done on typological grounds, since most have no inscription. Numerous pillars in western Ireland may well belong to this early phase, with simple crosses inscribed on an unworked or roughly hewn surface. More closely dated examples show that such designs began at an early date, but evidence from the recumbent slabs shows that simple designs continued throughout the Early Christian period, so caution has to be employed. However, the recumbent slab became popular from the seventh century onwards and it is likely that many of the standing cross-slabs are early.

There may have been many wooden markers that do not survive. Thomas (1971a, 92) considers that these, especially small crosses, would have been common. It is possible that the post holes in the Reask cemetery and over the early Carnsore burial held such crosses, or perhaps were supports for some wooden structure, possibly like the shrines discussed above.

The grave markers or recumbent slabs have been studied by Lionard (1961). The recurrent design is that of the cross, sometimes with subsidiary crosses. The recumbent slab became popular in the seventh century, but lasted through to the twelfth century; only the earlier examples are discussed here. Recumbent slabs were not generally shaped, even when elaborate designs were carved on them, and their size varies greatly. A few are the length of a body but most are much smaller. The smaller ones tend to be earlier, and some have a size, proportion and design very similar to contemporary manuscripts.

Many recumbent slabs are inscribed, though only one, from Clonmacnois, was in ogham; Latin is also rare. The early slabs have inscriptions with a formula like that on the ogham inscriptions *lec* followed by a personal name in the genitive (i.e. 'slab of X'). In some cases, *lec* is left off. There are also names in the nominative, and these can have a second word indicating

Figure 3:21 Recumbent slabs, datable by the identification of the commemorated deceased in the Annals; all from Clonmacnois, Co. Offaly, except **3** from Inishcaltra, Co. Clare. **1** Tetg ..., 709; **2** Chuindless, 720–4; **3** Diarmait macc Delbaid, 762; **4** Rectinia, 781–4; **5** Soirberge, 787–91; **6** Sechnasach, 709–12; **7** Ailgal, 751–5 or 760–4; **8** Snedreagol, 783–6; **9** Muirgalae, 789 (Lionard 1961).

ancestry or occupation. Later recumbent slabs have a request for blessing, *bendacht ar, bennacht ar* or *for anmain*, followed by the name of the deceased. A few of the names found on the slabs can be identified with individuals mentioned in the Annals. The dating by this method, at best tentative especially in the early period, suggests that some of the plain linear, outline and ringed crosses occur early in the sequence and belong to the seventh and eighth centuries (Figure 3:21).

Cemeteries

Thomas has differentiated between undeveloped and developed cemeteries (Thomas 1971, 50–1). The former consisted of burial grounds that had no associated structures and at most a few commemorative crosses. In contrast, developed cemeteries contain associated structures. In Ireland cemeteries of both types are generally enclosed and, whilst a circular or elliptical shape was normal, this was not always the case. The evidence from Ireland does not support a sequence of undeveloped to developed, but rather both forms running in parallel, the latter probably far more frequent but they may merely appear so because they are easier to locate.

Undeveloped cemeteries (Figure 3:20)

Undeveloped cemeteries were common in Ireland, and many have survived as infant burial grounds, *cillin*, in use until recent times. An almost certain early burial is the now destroyed example marked by an ogham stone within a circular stone setting described by Thomas (1971a, 63). It may be that originally many of the burials commemorated by ogham inscriptions were more elaborate than just the inscribed standing stone. Some graveyards were used for special groups, such as unbaptised infants, in the Early Christian period. Relignaman near Carrickmore, Co. Tyrone is a sub-rectangular enclosure which appears to have been reserved for women, though when this practice began is unknown (Hamlin and Foley 1983). Near Relignaman the Children's cemetery, Relig-na-paisde, and the Cemetery of the slain, Relig-na-firgunta, have been noted, though their origins are also uncertain. More commonly, undeveloped cemeteries contained the full range of local population. Site I at Knockea, Co. Limerick consisted of a rectangular ditched enclosure with an internal bank topped by posts, revetted internally and with an entrance to the west (O'Kelly 1967). It contained a minimum of 66 people, most of whom were aligned east–west with their heads to the west; they were probably Christian.

The early phase at the excavated site of Reask may have been an undeveloped cemetery, though two post holes may indicate that a small timber chapel was present from the beginning. The area used for burial seems to have been demarcated by standing cross-inscribed stones of which one, stone A, remained in situ. At Kilnasaggart, Co. Armagh dug and lintelled graves were clustered around the cross-inscribed pillar stone (Hamlin 1985).

Numerous stone lined graves have been found accidentally during earthmoving activities, but these have often been ascribed to the Iron Age (Raftery 1941). Whilst some do seem to be of this date (Raftery 1981), many of the others are probably later. Some, indeed, may be pagan cemeteries contemporary with Christian ones, but others could equally well be Christian themselves.

Developed cemeteries

Developed cemeteries are the most common forms now known for Early Christian Ireland. Several have been fully excavated, and at other monastic sites the location of cemeteries and their relationship to other structures can be recognised by surface features.

Church Island was a developed cemetery from its inception. It was very well organised, lying to the west of the early timber oratory. The graves and oratory were orientated 5 degrees north of east. A single circular timber building lay to the east, near the centre of the small island. At some point, it is not clear when, the oratory was replaced in stone imported from the mainland. It partially overlay the old chapel and a number of the early burials, and was on a different orientation – 5 degrees south of east – and subsequent burials were generally interred on this alignment.

The later phase at Reask was certainly that of a developed cemetery. A stone oratory was constructed, as at Church Island, over existing interments. Indeed, the excavator suggests that it was located where it was specifically because it was over earlier burials. When the oratory was constructed, a dividing wall was made, marking off the sacred area within the enclosure.

The cemetery at Derry, Co. Down was only partially excavated, and the overall arrangement of the cemetery is difficult to recognise (Waterman 1967). It appears that an early timber-framed structure was the first focus for burial, and this was later replaced by the south church in stone. The limited excavations at Boolies Little and Millockstown did not produce any evidence for a church, but both had souterrains and it is likely that more extensive excavation would have revealed other structures such as oratories. At 'Dunmisk Fort', Co. Tyrone a densely packed cemetery was excavated within a hilltop enclosure which also included a church (Ivens 1986).

Populations served by cemeteries

Of the cemeteries that have been extensively excavated, most are quite small. Reask had only 42 burials, including some children on the basis of cist size, and would seem to be a family burial ground for those living on the site. At those sites where aging and sexing of the bones have been carried out, a pattern of both sexes and all ages being buried is the norm. Infant burials seem to be much under-represented, and absent at some sites. This may in part be due to preservation factors, but it is also possible that young children were not buried in these cemeteries. It is possible that the St John's Point cemetery was originally male (though the sample is small), and later became a mixed cemetery.

Hamlin and Foley (1983) note that those who had been murdered or died in battle and so had not received the last rites might be buried on the north side of a church. This separation is perhaps more certainly indicated by the Church of the wounded (or slain) men, Teampull-na-Bhfear-ngonta, which was part of the monastic complex on Inishcaltra in Lough Derg, Co. Clare. Whilst some cemeteries may have had a special function such as this, most were mixed, and not very large or even long-lived. By taking the age structure from the identifiable remains at Millockstown and applying this to the estimated population of the whole site, it would seem that the site was used by only the equivalent of two extended families over a couple of centuries (or one family over four); the complete cemetery of Knockea (which was not analysed in detail) can be taken to represent just a single such extended family over two hundred years.

The major monastic sites must have had much larger cemeteries than those so far excavated; well over 400 grave slabs are known from Clonmacnois alone, and presumably far from all interments there were marked in such elaborate fashion. Many smaller cemeteries, however, were scattered over the landscape to serve the secular population, though some such as Reask and Millockstown may well have been used by small family monasteries.

4
The social system

Introduction

In recent years archaeologists have become less pessimistic about the recognition of past social systems through the study of material culture. Much of the effort in relating material culture to society has so far been directed to prehistoric contexts (Renfrew 1984, Bradley 1984) or, through ethnoarchaeology, to the present (Hodder 1982). Ironically, however, it is historically documented periods that provide the opportunities for fastest development. A few scholars have examined documented societies, both in the Near East (Adams 1966) and in western Europe (Hodges 1982, Randsborg 1980). But Ireland, despite having the richest contemporary documentation of any region of temperate Europe till the high Middle Ages, has been ignored. Hodges (1982, 193), in quoting Byrne (1973, 7) dismisses it as a 'failed civilisation'. This may or may not be true, depending on one's definitions, but it does not remove Early Christian Ireland's great potential for studying the role of material culture within a changing society.

With the recognition of the archaeological contribution to the study of past societies has come an increased awareness of the active role of material culture in society. Whilst some of the proponents of this approach are against processualist methods (Hodder 1986), the two are not necessarily opposed since the ways in which material culture acts can be seen in processualist terms. Material culture should not be viewed merely as a passive residue of past societies, but was active and important at the time. In this chapter, the role of personal adornment is emphasised, as is sculpture, a tradition that becomes most developed in Ireland during the ninth and tenth centuries. The enclosed nature of the ring-fort as a symbolic statement in a colonising environment has already been emphasised; further aspects of ring-forts, and indeed other settlement types, may also be interpreted as carrying social messages.

Social organisation at all levels seems to have been remarkably similar over the whole of Ireland during the Early Christian period. The law tracts have some regional variations (Binchy 1941) but these are relatively minor and merely emphasise the essential unity of the whole; the same impression is given by the genealogies, and the Annals which, though recording local events more thoroughly, record the same type of material in a similar format. Ireland is also remarkably homogeneous in its archaeology and again the few regional peculiarities such as souterrain ware pottery in the north-east only highlight the widespread uniformity in the range of material culture. It is therefore possible to generalise about Early Christian Ireland as a whole, using data from all parts of the island. How this uniformity was maintained, in contrast to the Iron Age diversity, is of particular interest and will be examined using the concept of peer polity interaction (Renfrew 1986).

Whereas there was a uniformity through space, it is clear that there were considerable changes in the social system through time. These changes, however, are not easy to recognise or date closely because the relevant documents and archaeological remains present difficulties which obscure the dynamic nature of Early Christian Ireland. Most of the earliest written sources belong to the 'classical' period of the seventh and particularly the eighth centuries (Mac Niocaill 1972). There were some earlier texts, but these are often extremely fragmentary and incorporated into later works where their original significance is now obscure. The period of compilation of ancient texts can often be calculated even though they only survive in the form of much later copies. The language and internal characteristics of a text can be dated, often to within half a century and sometimes even less.

That so many documents were written down in the seventh and eighth centuries is in itself an interesting phenomenon. The basic laws were then fossilised and did not recognise later changes, making them difficult to identify except from the later glosses and inferences from other sources. Their very static nature suggests that the law tracts themselves had ceased to be a major controlling force by the end of the eighth century and their writing down may have been either a last attempt to enforce the legal system that they embodied, or due to the well documented Irish monastic fascination with antiquarianism. Whatever the causes, the result is that social changes after the eighth century, even major ones, often have to be inferred rather than dramatically demonstrated through these documentary sources.

Changes have to be recognised, but they also need to be interpreted. As yet, few detailed explanations have been made concerning the development of the social system. Ó Corráin (1980, 155) has stated in a review of Byrne (1973), 'many of the major changes – decline of the *túath*, simplification of the *fine*, fossilisation of jurist-made law etc. – came about as a result of major social upheavals, plagues and famines of the late seventh and early eighth centuries – when as Byrne shows, many of the major dynasties appeared'. This catalogue approach does not explain change. It merely raises further questions about the cause of the social upheavals, if not also the plagues and famines. By using a systemic approach and combining historical and archaeological material, longer term processes can be seen to lie behind the individual events so frequently recorded in the written sources, and the particular sites and finds recovered by the archaeologist.

The material culture record for Early Christian Ireland is rich and varied, but has been notoriously difficult to date. Most settlement sites produce a limited repertoire of finds, and many of these are simple and may well have had a long period of manufacture and use. Nearly all the objects that can be considered high quality sophisticated works are casual finds, often recorded in the last century and with resultant vague or non-existent provenances. Stylistic dating has very few cross-checks to independently and firmly date items. The firmest evidence comes from illuminated manuscripts which can be dated by their contents and by the script used, but for the first part of the Early Christian period these do not exist. Even some of the most intensively studied classes of artefact, the stone high crosses, have recently been reassessed and most of the previously accepted criteria for their dating have been questioned (Harbison 1979), though traditional chronologies seem to have withstood this discriminating examination

(Henry 1980). For most other categories of artefact relative sequences have been attempted, but it is not easy to calibrate these typological schemes with any chronological precision.

The same site types remain in use all through the Early Christian period, and as a result it is possible only to assign many on surface evidence to the period as a whole. Changes within settlements are occasionally possible to identify, and can be of great value in recognising social changes. One example of this is the trend from round to rectangular buildings (Lynn 1978). It may also now be possible to date the introduction of souterrains and mills to the seventh century, though they only became common in the ninth.

In recent years there has been an increased use of scientific dating, particularly Carbon 14 dating and dendrochronology, to provide vital absolute dating to set beside the limited arte-factual evidence from settlement sites. Problems of calibration, inclusion of heart wood and errors associated with routine Carbon 14 analysis have, however, reduced the value of Carbon 14 dates within the Early Christian period. Whilst they can be useful in demonstrating that sites belong to the period, they are of very limited accuracy in assigning samples to worthwhile segments of time within the period. In the definition of rapid change in an historic period Carbon 14 has a very limited role, unlike that of dendrochronology which can routinely now date sites to the decade and in ideal circumstances date to a year (Baillie 1985, Scott *et al.* 1983). The various developments now recognisable archaeologically are crucial for the discussions in this chapter, yet many have only been identified during the last decade. It is hoped that further changes will be identified as excavation and analysis continue.

More difficult to study is the development of settlement patterns through time. The dating of individual excavated sites is difficult enough, and from field evidence no dating within the period is possible. Nevertheless, preliminary deductions, based on site distributions, have been made by a few archaeologists. Some studies were dominated by the distribution of settlement in relation to routeways, and explanation was based on the invasion hypothesis (Fahy 1969). Others (Proudfoot 1961) have emphasised correlations with soil types, and used interpretations based on agricultural colonisation of marginal lands which are discussed more fully in Chapter 5. At present, however, the archaeological evidence for settlement at a regional level is basically atemporal within the Early Christian period. This does not prevent all social analysis but it considerably impedes it. Only in a region where there has been extensive excavation providing secure dating will any firm conclusions be possible, and as yet no region has received this. It may, however, be possible within a decade to examine parts of north-east Ireland with more confidence; then some of the interpretations set out below may be tested. Sou-terrain ware may indicate a later phase of activity in the Early Christian period, and the aceramic and early undecorated pottery phases in the north-east may broadly belong to the period up to AD 800. Such a temporal division is not so easily established elsewhere, however.

This chapter considers both archaeological and historical evidence for social structure. The two types of evidence cannot be directly integrated; the search within the archaeological record for either textually documented individuals or exact, legal categories of individuals is almost always bound to end in unprovable assertions. However, it is possible to structure the material culture remains in a hierarchy of levels. General social groups can thus be archaeolog-ically recognised and set beside the grade system fully defined in documentary sources though these may in any case have been overly-divisive in their classification of society (Binchy 1943).

Social relations

Two sets of social relations bound Early Christian Irish society together: kinship and clientage. Before the social hierarchy can be examined in detail it is necessary to analyse these two subsystems and any archaeological correlates that can be identified for them. The twin sets of interrelationships provided the complex web which supported the structure of this fiercely hierarchical society. Once these have been examined, analysis can work through a number of levels, starting with the individual and working up to that of the regional and national framework. This order has been deliberately chosen because of the belief that the basic driving force for social change was the individual acting within society. Individuals, both named and as examples of people in particular grades, are identifiable historically, and a hierarchy of levels can be archaeologically defined. Although there is a careful attempt to mesh the archaeological and historical material, it will be no surprise to discover that for some aspects of social organisation one dominates at the expense of the other. This in itself may hint at where further research could be usefully directed. Nevertheless, at all stages the multidisciplinary approach is emphasised.

The effects of Christianity and the church in the development of the social system are discussed in the final part of the chapter. The church at first played a peripheral role in society, and there was a policy for Christians to have as little association as possible with secular authorities. This isolation was gradually broken down, however, and by the seventh century the church began to play a significant role. In the eighth century, the assimilation of Christianity into secular society was widespread, even if there were still many who were pagan. Moreover, the church had absorbed by this time a great deal of indigenous Irish cultural values and patterns of organisation. Whilst the ideology of Christianity was a vital component in beginning the Early Christian period in Ireland, it was only from the seventh century that the church as an institution began to hold a significant place in the social order. By the eighth century, the church was a dominant force.

The kin-group

The important social unit was the kin-group, the *fine*, to which loyalty was owed (Mac Niocaill 1972). The *fine* was responsible for overdue payments by any of its members, including those resulting from legal action or clientship obligations. As these were particularly heavy for free clientage, no member could enter into an agreement until permission had been given by the *fine*. The overall effect of these limitations was to inhibit social and economic activity beyond the kin-group. Wherever possible, transactions were between kin who were considered more trustworthy and certainly more easily dealt with if this confidence was misplaced. Indeed, the primacy of kin-based relations is emphasised in the regulations dealing with the ending of base clientship: much lower penalties were imposed when a client changed allegiance to a lord who had a closer kinship tie (Gerriets 1983).

Land was considered to be in some sense the property of the *fine*. It belonged to individuals within the *fine*, who had inherited it from their fathers. All sons were equally entitled to a share of their father's property, with the result that fragmentation could quickly take place. A childless man could not leave his land to anyone, but instead it was portioned out within the kin-group based on proximity of relationship. The selling of inherited land was not allowed without permission of the *fine*; only land acquired through purchase or, presumably, pioneering clearance could be bought or sold. Even this was counted as land of the *fine* after being passed on one generation, and so was not easily sold. It must have also caused great stress within the *fine* in many cases where land was given to the church; for example, the kin had to give permission for women to leave land to a church (Bitel 1984).

Early in the period, almost all land was owned communally. Common land was an important property of the *fine*. It was used for grazing, and probably some of the managed woodland was also held in common. As the population rose, each individual's share of common land was reduced and this led to considerable stress. The population increase was probably greatest during the sixth and seventh centuries, leading to an increased desire for private land since the communal share was dwindling for each individual. Related to communal land ownership were shared agricultural activities. These are discussed in Chapter 5, but the joint ploughing and herding among kin emphasise not only social but physical proximity. It may be possible to recognise archaeologically groups that worked in common; ring-forts and open settlements scattered within field systems may represent part of a *fine* intimately associated in landscape as well as economic and social terms (Figure 4:1). This can be no more than speculation, but the documentary sources suggest that the physical pattern of the social landscape must have been something like this.

The degree of kinship that was socially significant changed during the Early Christian period. The *fine* means any kin-group, but was usually more closely defined so that the extent of particular rights and obligations could be recognised. Relationships back as far as six generations could be significant, but only in exceptional circumstances. All those with a common great-grandfather belonged to the *derbfine*, and during the early part of the period this was the dominant social unit. By the eighth century, however, the more restricted kin-group related to a common grandfather, the *gelfine*, was increasing in importance (Mac Niocaill 1972, 49–50). These kin-groups are illustrated in Figure 4:2.

The limiting of responsibilities and rights by restricting the kin-group may have been caused by a combination of processes. The ideological changes brought about by Christianity discussed in Chapter 3 emphasised the individual. As a result, only the more immediate kin were considered relevant, and probably had a direct practical role in the operation of shared agricultural assets such as ploughs and mills. Related to the increased importance of the individual was the growth of clientship relations, personal agreements which were potentially more flexible and powerful than the inherited kinship links. There are hints of antagonism between the two systems, such as the control by the *fine* of free clientship obligations, and the parallel representatives for *fine* and lord at legal disputes. The elite may have been an influence in the reduction in size of the generally recognised kin-group since an increased dependence on clientship gave more control to the nobility.

Another important factor in the reduction of the kin-group may well have been the difficulties of decision-making at the level of the *derbfine*. With population increase the arrangements necessary for the meeting of the kin-group would have grown more complex, and communication between dispersed elements would have been slow. Control over transactions outside the *derbfine* would have been difficult and the head of the kin-group could have been overwhelmed with matters requiring decisions. Moreover, there was probably a rise in litigation and disputes as the population of the kin-group grew and as there was increased stress and competition for resources both within and beyond the *fine*. Distant kin would find obligations in such cases an unwelcome burden, especially as penalties were being increased for transgressions. The system of kinship obligations can be seen to become overstrained just through growth, with a resultant

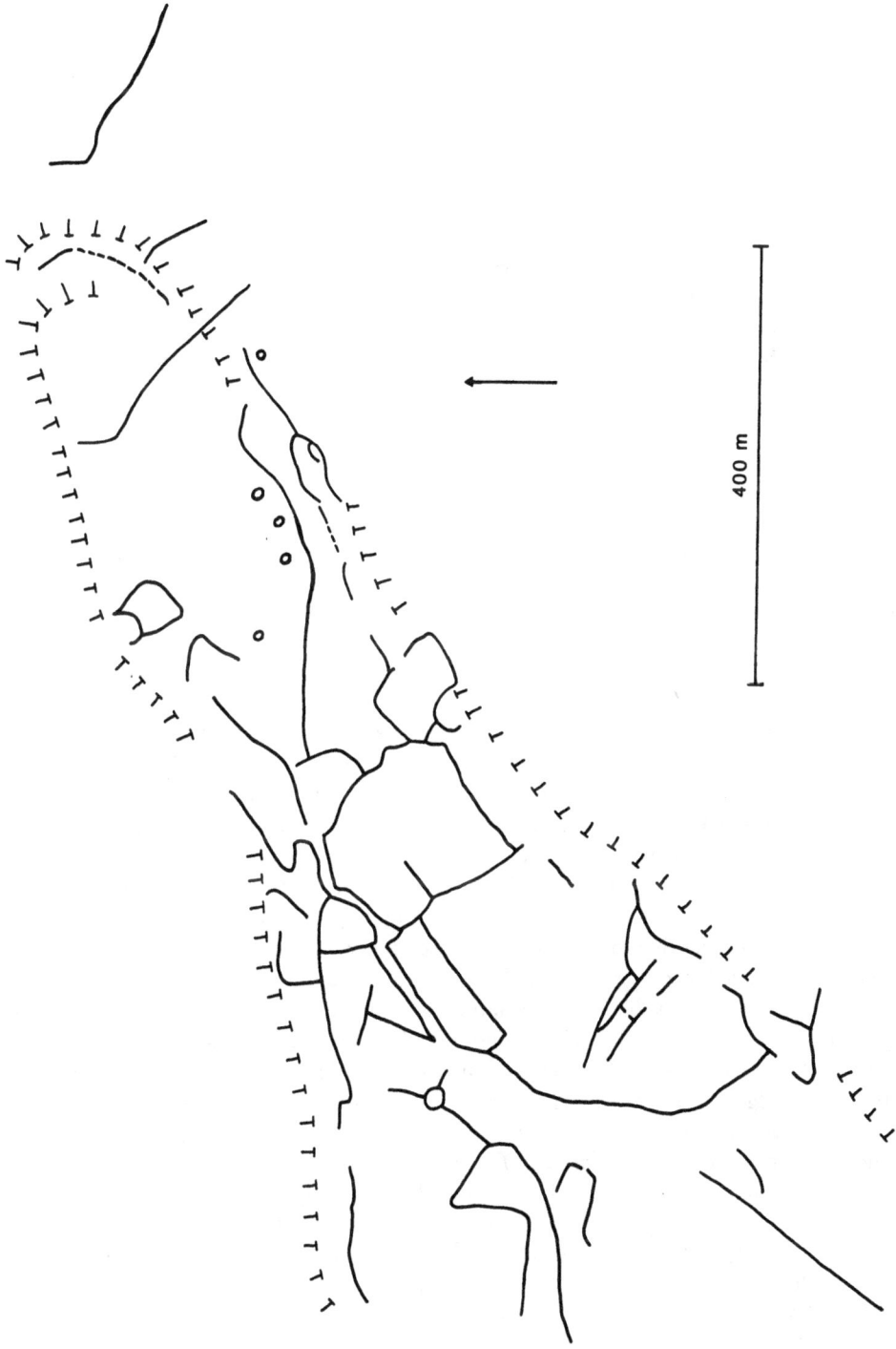

Figure 4:1 Settlement system at Twomile Stone, Co. Donegal (Davies 1942).

400 m

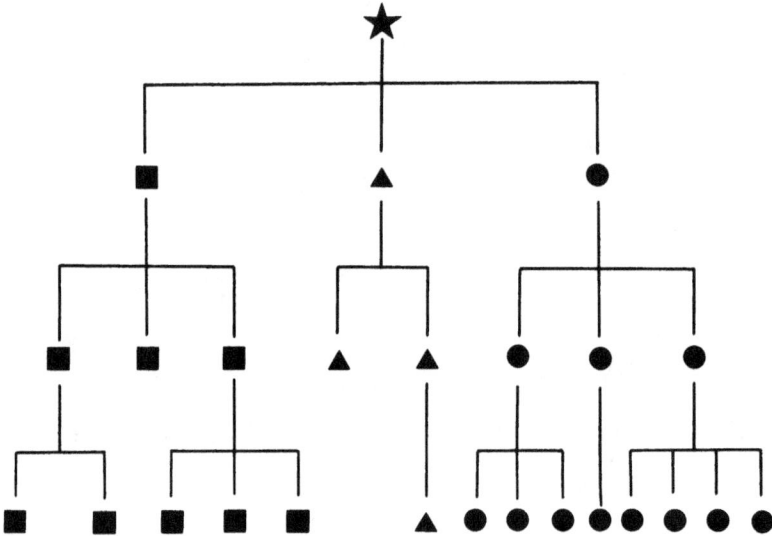

Figure 4:2   Diagram showing membership of the *derbfine*, descendants from a common great-grandfather (star). Each *gelfine*, descendants from a common grandfather within the *derbfine*, is shown by a different symbol.

crisis in information flow through the system (Figure 4:3). The problems of information processing within an expanding population have been discussed by Johnson (1982), but unlike the examples quoted by him, a solution was not found by increasing the complexity of the system by creating a bureaucracy. Instead, the stress was removed by implementing a policy of fragmentation, splitting down to the *gelfine*.

The choice of reaction to the stress within the *derbfine* suggests that there was a rising sense of individuality, as opposed to community. Rather than strengthen the existing kinship group by providing it with an executive to carry out its increasingly onerous functions as it grew in size, these functions were reduced by narrowing kinship ties considered relevant. An individual could readily appreciate the links between his father and uncles (with their links to a common grandfather); they were probably all in close physical association due to the laws of equal inheritance. But the links a further generation back were less concrete and far more diffuse. Although knowledge of descent was vital, and the genealogies show how the demonstration of pedigree was preserved (or when expedient, created) it was primarily seen to be for the benefit of the heir. The change from *derbfine* to *gelfine* constricted responsibility very considerably and cut down those whom any individual was obliged to help (Figure 4:2). It also reduced the numbers who could give help in return, and suggests a society moving towards the rights and privileges of an individual based on direct inheritance and clientship, and away from the wider kin-group with its powers of control and mutual support.

There are few archaeological sites that suggest concentrated secular populations that could represent a kin-group, but a class of large, oval enclosures containing numerous dwellings has now been recognised in Ireland. At Ballyutoag, Co. Antrim, a main oval enclosure had roundhouses positioned behind the bank, mainly opposite the entrance (Figure 4:4). A second

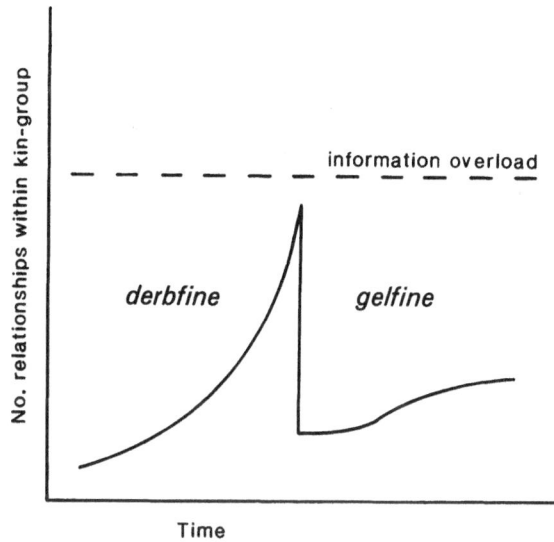

Figure 4:3   Effects of population increase on information flow leading to the rise in importance of the *gelfine* over the *derbfine*.

enclosure to the north-east contained a more scattered collection of about the same number of buildings. Excavations in the primary enclosure fully investigated building A. It had four constructional phases, followed by squatting occupation. Only in the final phase could the internal diameter of 4 m be securely established, but it must have been similar for all phases (Williams 1984). This could have only housed a nuclear family, and the other structures in the enclosure are all similar in size to that of building A. One trench through a second building, B, located further occupation material though, perhaps significantly, a similar trench through building C in the secondary enclosure contained no pottery. The Carbon 14 dates suggest an occupation in the eighth century.

Ballyutoag may be seen as the communal settlement of a kin-group, either a *derbfine* or a *gelfine*. It may have been related to the utilisation of upland communal grazing, though there could have been some arable also (see Chapter 5). Large lowland oval enclosures are thought by Swan (1983) to be secular enclosed village settlements, though many do appear to be associated with church sites. Excavation and detailed survey have as yet been extremely limited, but it may be that this category of settlement was a common one, indicating the presence on some scale of larger kin-group settlements. They may even have been some form of family monastic centres on a scale larger than the nuclear family.

The concentration of ring-forts at Cush, Co. Limerick may represent continued occupation of the site by a small kin-group. From the various stratigraphic relationships between the ring-forts a sequence of construction can be elucidated (Figure 4:5); it is not known, however, how long any site was occupied once constructed, or whether any were re-occupied during the use of the site. Nevertheless, there can be seen to be a gradual expansion from perhaps a single ring-fort to a conjoined complex, followed by a further group to the north. The range of finds suggests

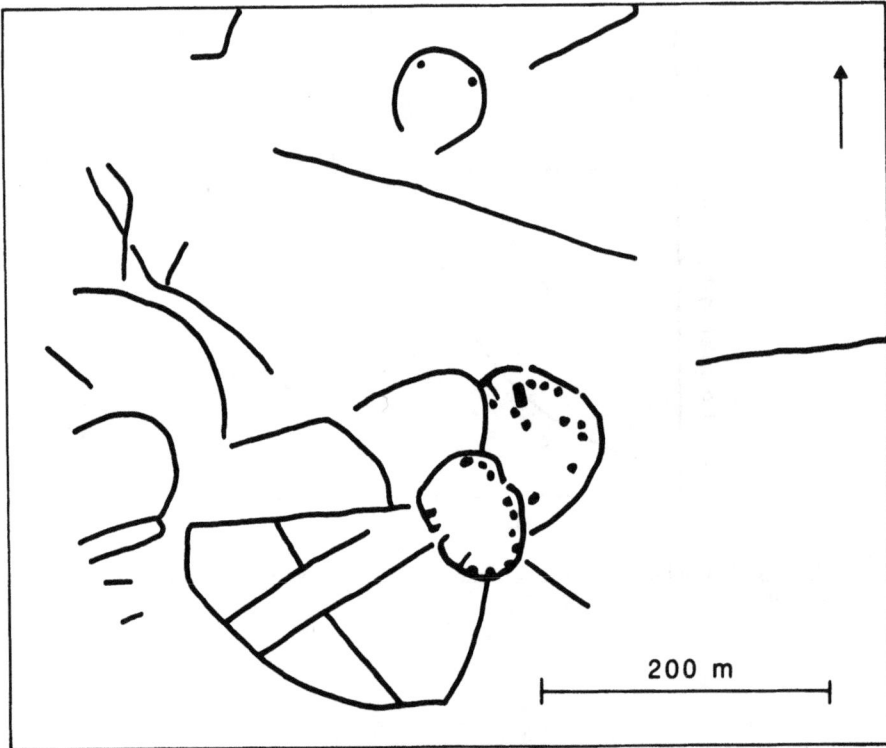

Figure 4:4   Upland enclosed communal settlement at Ballyutuag, Co. Antrim (Williams 1984).

that the settlement was only equal to the majority of ring-forts, and the arrangement here of so many individual enclosed settlements cannot be easily explained.

Pairs or clusters of ring-forts are often noted during survey (Plate III), but even where excavation has taken place it is often very difficult to demonstrate contemporaneity. At Garry-duff, one ring-fort was heavily used but the other had no evidence of human occupation and may have been a cattle pound (O'Kelly 1962). This may also have been the case at Ballypalady, Co. Antrim where three sites are in close proximity (Waterman 1972). Here, the unexcavated ring-fort 1 was earlier than ring-fort 2 which contained a roundhouse and possible byre. In contrast a limited range of evidence came from ring-fort 3; but it may well have been in use at the same time as ring-fort 2, since both contained undecorated souterrain ware (Figure 4:6).

The pairing of small late Iron Age, Romano–British and post-Roman farmsteads in south-west Wales has been attributed to an early version of the Welsh system of partible inheritance (Williams 1985; 1988, 43). This may also have been the case for some of the pairs in Ireland but as yet the evidence is far from conclusive. In some Welsh cases, one of a pair of enclosures was given over to the church and provided a ready-made circular graveyard enclosure (James forthcoming); some of these may have been either family donations of settlement and associated lands, or even the establishment of a family church or monastery on the old settlement site.

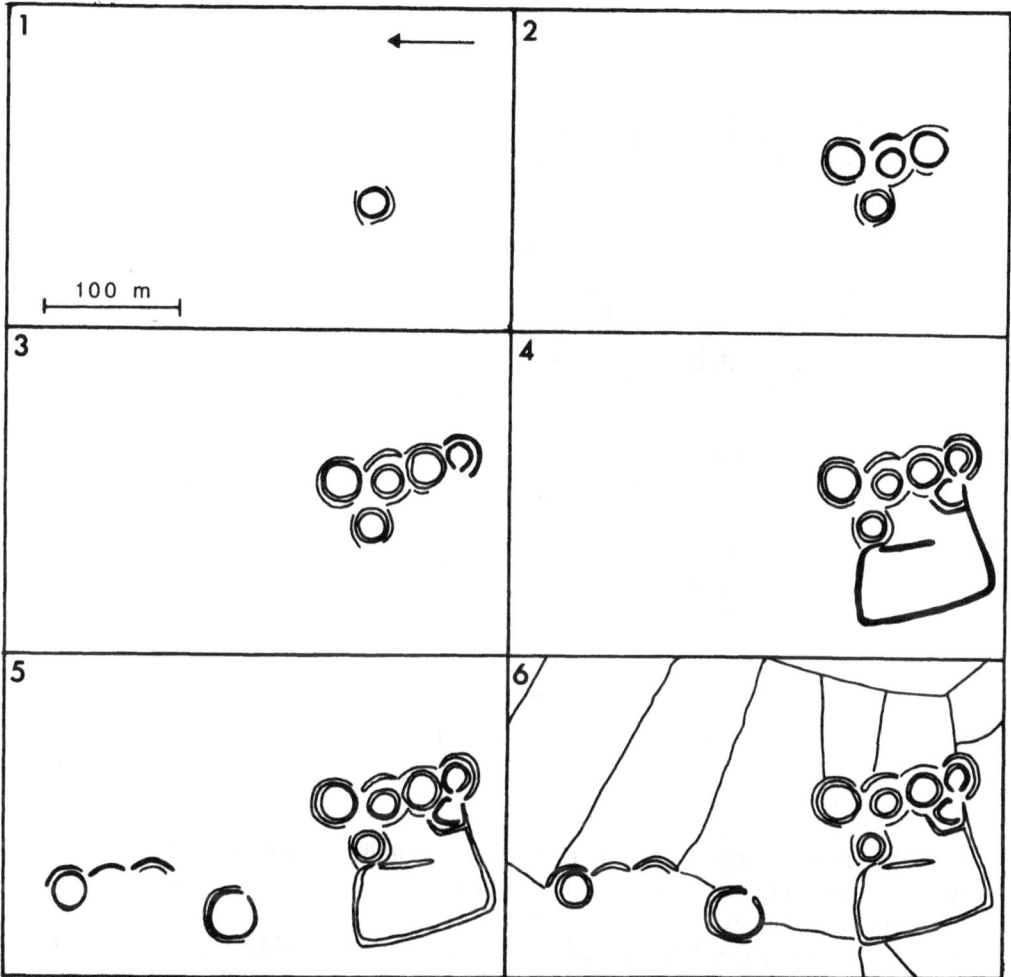

Figure 4:5   Phase plans for ring-fort complex at Cush, Co. Limerick (Ó Ríordáin 1940).

The nuclear family

There was a recognition of a particularly close tie between immediate relatives. This was called *lanamnas*, and also applied to foster-parents and foster-children, indicating how strong this relationship was considered. It is perhaps surprising that there is not more in the laws about the bonds between close relations, but this is presumably because disputes at that level would not have been settled by litigation. For this reason, the archaeological evidence is particularly important since it shows that settlement was often at the level of the nuclear family, with at most a few more distant relations present. The overwhelming evidence from archaeology is that the single dwelling for the nuclear family formed the basic modular unit in settlement.

The limited amount of dating evidence for houses in the Early Christian period has suggested to Lynn (1978) that there was a general succession from round to rectangular structures. The

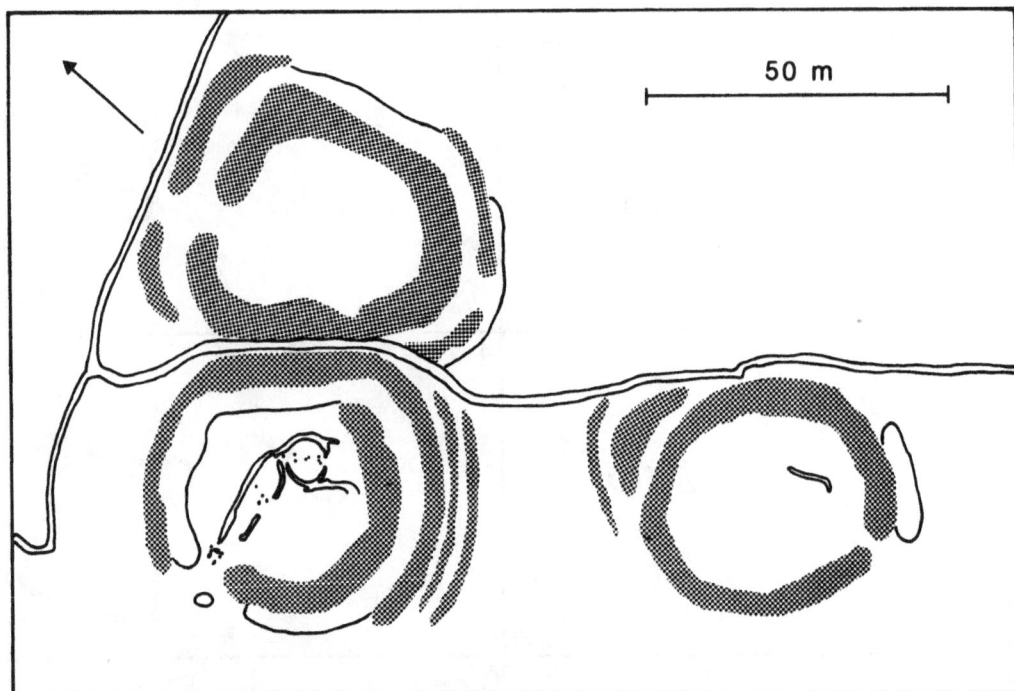

Figure 4:6   Ring-fort cluster at Ballypalady (Waterman 1972).

dating of this change is not easy, but there are some grounds for considering that in some areas rectangular structures were in use by the ninth century. Continuity in use of round stone dwellings can be recognised in some western areas, but even here, rectangular structures do appear, as at Dunbeg, Co. Kerry in the tenth century (Barry 1981). There are some early examples of possible rectangular structures, such as at Garryduff 1 (O'Kelly 1962), but the evidence is far from conclusive. For the study of social structure up to the ninth century through archaeological material, emphasis will be placed on circular buildings, together with those few rectangular ones that can be demonstrably shown to be early.

Individual unenclosed houses or pairs of conjoined structures were common features of the Early Christian landscape of Ireland, but most have since been destroyed. In the Dingle peninsula, Co. Kerry preservation of stone buildings, clochans, has been exceptionally good (Cuppage 1986), and examples from there can be used to illustrate the range of forms (Figure 4:7). In some cases, such as Ballybowler North, there is evidence that one hut was constructed first, and then a second added to it, perhaps implying a population increase or change of use.

There are many cases where conjoined houses were planned as such from the beginning, though it is not always possible to be certain without excavation. There was a limit to the size that a corbelled stone house could reach; beyond a certain diameter, so much stone was used on the roof that it became either too high or very unstable. Within the clochan building tradition, provision for a population larger than that accommodated within a single roundhouse of 6 m diameter had to be achieved through the construction of several structures. To facilitate

GLANFAHAN 1284

GLANFAHAN 1283

BALLYBOWLER NORTH

BALLYNAVENOORAGH

10 m

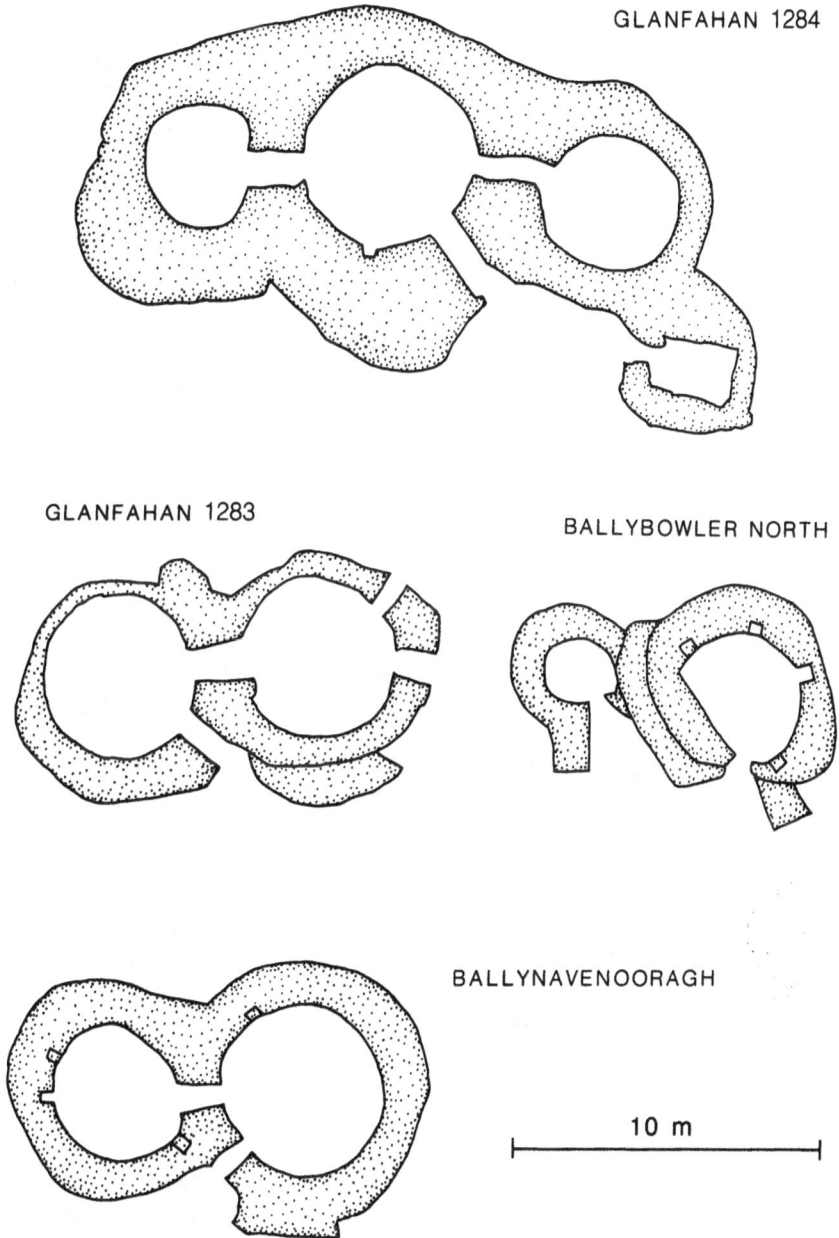

Figure 4:7 Single stone roundhouses and multiple complexes from the Dingle peninsula, Co. Kerry (Cuppage 1986).

communication, it was often decided to make the roundhouses conjoined, with a doorway between the buildings. Sometimes, as at Ballynavenooragh and Glanfahan 1284, only one house had an external door; in other cases like Glanfahan 1283, both did. These represented quite different arrangements. In the former, one building was in effect an inner, more private room dependent on the outer one, whereas in the latter each had a certain independence. There were some conjoined stone structures where there was no direct access between the two buildings, indicating a greater degree of separation that may well have been social as well as physical.

Conjoined groups of stone buildings, in the various configuration described above, also occur within ring-forts, as at Ballynavenooragh and Caher Murphy, Glanfahan (Figure 4:8). These are among the most concentrated occupations of ring-forts known from Ireland, but both surface evidence and excavation at Leacanabuaile indicate that these are multiperiod sites and the retaining of the older structures may have been partly at least due to the resilient nature of the stone remains. Sites like Reask (Figure 3:4) and eremitic monasteries such as Skellig Michael (Figure 3:3) also have hut groups that are similar to the ring-forts and open settlements and are part of the same building and settlement tradition.

Not all houses with stone footings or walls were roofed in stone. Many must have had timber roofs with thatch or wooden shingles. The use of timber rafters increased the possible roof span, and so roundhouses could be much larger in these cases. There are a few examples of conjoined timber or stone-footed buildings, such as Dressogagh, Co. Armagh (Figure 4:9), but there is strong evidence to support the theory that multiple clochans were built because of the roofing constraints. There is limited archaeological and documentary evidence for internal subdivision within some wooden buildings, and the individual clochans in a conjoined group may have been used for different purposes. As such, they may be an important source of information for the archaeologist on the use of space in the Early Christian period, but they do not represent a different tradition in the use of space, but merely a reaction to environmental factors that produced constraints on roofing methods.

Ring-forts frequently produce evidence for timber roundhouses (Lynn 1978). They usually contained only one house at any phase, though a few may have enclosed two (Figure 4:9). In a few cases the timber buildings were conjoined, producing a similar arrangement to that found in stone, but it was also possible to construct larger diameters of buildings using timber rafters rather than the constricting technology of the stone corbelling. As a result, many timber buildings were larger than stone structures. Nevertheless, the overwhelming impression given by all the archaeological evidence is that the number of people normally living within ring-forts, crannogs and individual open settlements must have been small. Lynn (1986) states that roundhouses of this period average between 6 m and 7 m diameter.

Clientship

Whilst kinship provided one structure for social relations within Early Christian Ireland, the other medium of interaction, that of clientage, was at least as important. By becoming a client an individual could receive the protection of another more powerful individual, together with loans in various forms. The lord, *flaith*, required clients in order to hold a certain status within society. In return the client had certain annual payments to make in kind, and was obliged to carry out services within proscribed limits.

Clientship had important economic as well as social implications, and these are considered more fully in Chapter 5. Here, emphasis will be placed on the social relations, though it is

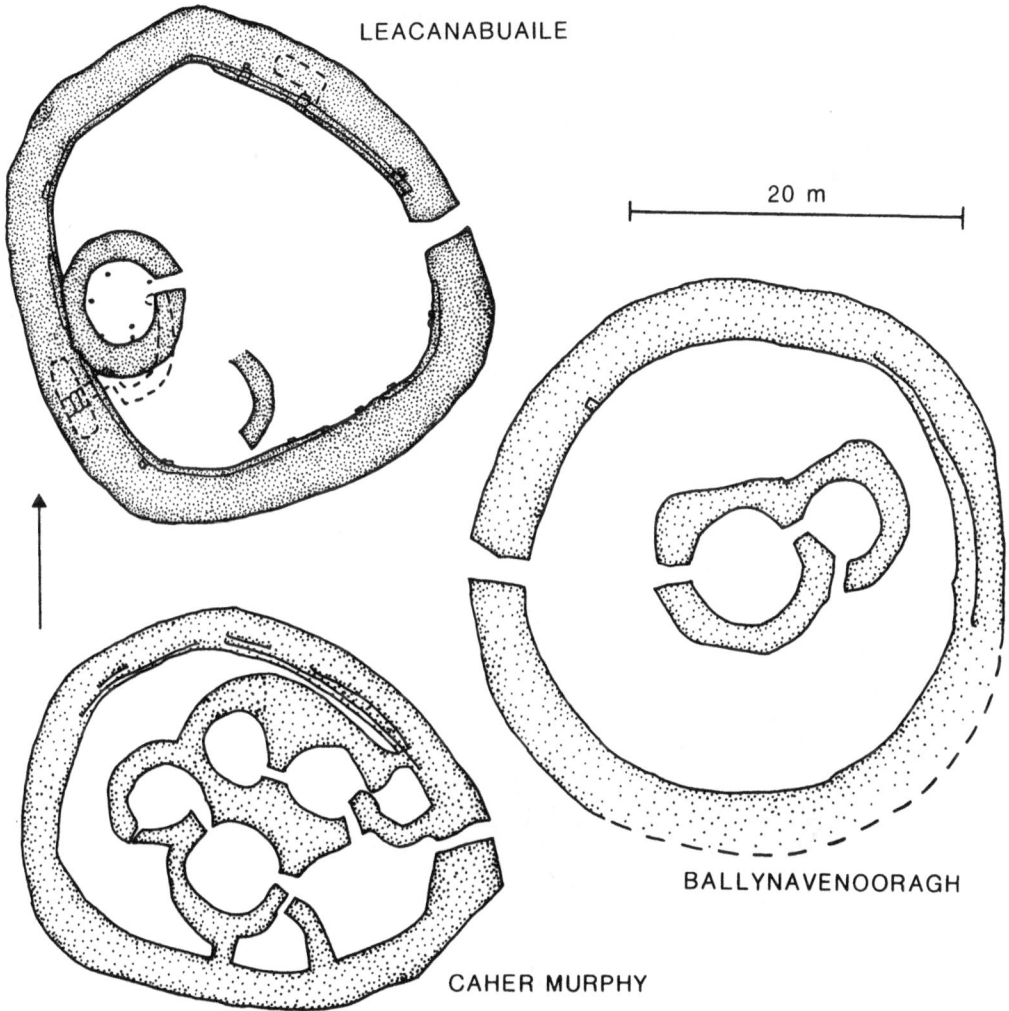

Figure 4:8 Ring-forts with multiple houses from Co. Kerry (Caher Murphy and Ballynavenooragh, Cuppage 1986; early phase of Leacanabuaile, Ó Ríordáin and Foy 1941).

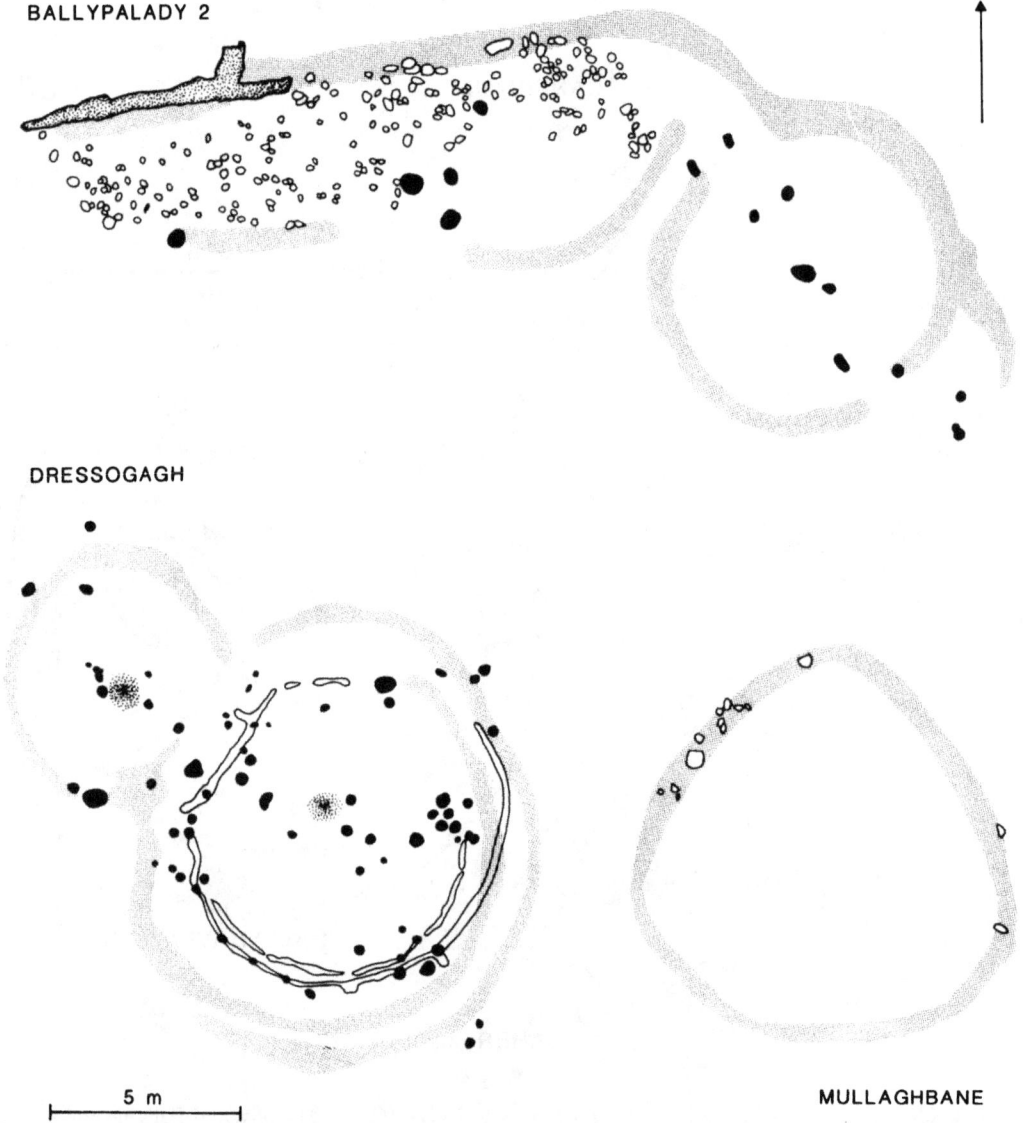

Figure 4:9   Plans of houses from excavated ring-forts (Ballypalady 2, Co. Antrim, Waterman 1972; Dressogagh, Co. Armagh, Collins 1966; Mullaghbane, Co. Tyrone, Harper 1972).

impossible to remove all economic aspects since these are inextricably part of the clientage system. The archaeological evidence for this system is slight; archaeology has so far developed only limited ways of recognising formal relationships between entities, and inter-personal social relations are particularly poorly understood. There are, nevertheless, some material remains that can be interpreted within the documented scheme, though there is not yet sufficient evidence or theory to test the system set out in the laws, and see whether it in fact worked in the same way in practice.

There were two kinds of clients, base (*dóer-chéle*) and free (*sóer-chéle*). Although permission from the *fine* had to be obtained before a member could become a free client, the client–lord relationship was essentially inter-personal, and emphasises the role of the individual within Irish society of this period. The obligations of clientage were not inherited; if either party died, the obligations continued only for a month and if they were to be renewed, fresh arrangements had to be made. Often, clientship was between kin, and the implication of the laws is that this was socially desirable. Such a strategy reduced the likelihood of conflicting interests and loyalties. On the other hand, one could choose one's lord, but not one's kin; the possibility of protecting personal interests could come higher than loyalty to kin.

Free clientship

In this relationship, the client received a fief, *rath*, and each year principal and subsidiary payments or renders had to be made. The grant seems to have normally been cattle. The principal renders were particularly severe under free clientship, and one third of the grant had to be repaid annually. After three years, when in effect the original loan had been repaid, the relationship could be continued with payments of produce to the same value, and in the seventh year there were no principal renders. For every year there were, however, additional subsidiary payments, also of agricultural produce. If the relationship were to continue beyond the seventh year, a further loan was required from the lord, and the sequence of payments was to begin all over again.

The free client also was required to carry out a number of obligations (Figure 4:10). He owed military service each year, but his main duty was to be a companion to his lord (Binchy 1941, 80). This would have been demonstrated, and the relationship cemented, through raiding and military activity, but also through that most important pursuit of the elite, that of feasting. The material culture associated with this socially vital activity could be very fine, denoting its reinforcement of essential relationships (Plate XVII). The free client was a person of note, but he had to acknowledge his respect by rising in his lord's presence. The lord was expected to defend the rights of his client in law. This would normally have involved taking part in legislation, such as providing help in obtaining distraint, the seizure of goods belonging to the accused in order to bring him to court (Binchy 1973a). There was no question of the lord taking over any of the legal rights of the client, but he was expected to give assistance and thus enable his client to defend his rights effectively. The lord was also to provide physical protection, though to what extent is not clear.

Whilst the payments to the lord were severe under free clientship, the advantage to the client was the ease with which the relationship could be terminated. All that was required was the return of the original loan. This allowed considerable flexibility on the part of the free client in ensuring allegiance to the socially and politically most useful lord. The lord could also end the

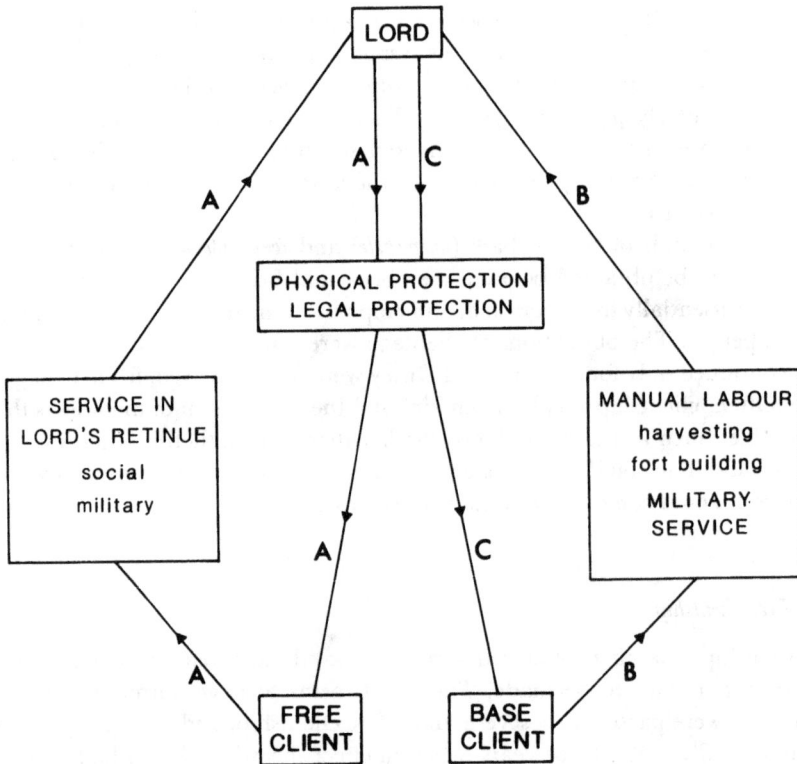

Figure 4:10 Diagram demonstrating the relationships between lord and client. *Key*: A contract limited by time and easily terminated; B contract with no time limit and difficult to terminate; C contract with no time limit and easily terminated.

relationship by returning any outstanding payments made to him, but as status was measured in part by the number of clients, a lord was less likely to wish an end to the relationship.

With the heavy economic penalties of free clientship, fiefs may often have been small, such as three cows (Mac Niocaill 1972, 60). This would have entailed an annual principal render of one cow. The free client would enter into such a relationship not for the animals which were the fief, but for the social relationship that was thereby gained. Free clients were probably themselves relatively high in the social order; Hughes (1966, 136) sees them as honoured figures to be found in the company of kings. The nobility could not be base clients (Binchy 1941, xix), so all their clientship relations had to be free. The flexibility of allegiance indeed suggests that free clients must have been at least on the fringe of the political scene. A lord would desire free clients since the outlay to obtain one could be low, and the return was high. Only the successful could expect to keep them, and so this was an important driving force for advance in political life. Success could feed on itself, leading to the rapid acquisition of free clients; alternatively, political failure would be followed by an equally rapid diminution of their numbers.

Base clientship

The relationship of base clientship entailed principal and subsidiary renders as did free clientship, but these were much smaller in quantity in relationship to the loan or fief, *taurchec*. Though still of considerable economic significance, they did not provide such a high return. The advantages to the lord were that base clients owed considerable services, and could not easily escape from their dependence (Figure 4:10). On the part of the client, there was a need for protection, and also often an economic imperative since many base clients could not effectively manage their agricultural activities without loans of capital (see Chapter 5).

Base clients were always of the freemen grades (Binchy 1941, xix) and, though of some standing in society, were clearly below the aristocracy. In undertaking base clientship, some legal as well as economic independence had to be sacrificed. Besides the payment of the loan, the lord also made over goods to the value of the client's honour-price, which entitled the lord to a fraction of the compensation due to the client in the event of injury (Binchy 1941, 97).

The base client in most cases must have been permanently tied to the lord. Whereas the lord could end the relationship by returning any payments he had received, the client had to pay dearly for freedom from his obligations. When this was to become a free man with no ties of clientship to anyone else, payment was double the original loan, plus double the renders for the year. When the client wished to transfer allegiance to another lord, the cost was even higher. Payments were calculated on the basis of not only the original loan but also the honour-price of the lord, because of the insult implicit in leaving him. These and any outstanding renders could be doubled in certain circumstances, but could be much reduced if the client was changing from one lord to another closer in kin. In general, however, escape from base clientship must have been prohibitively expensive (Mac Niocaill 1972, 62–3).

The lord's obligations have been examined by Gerriets (1983, 54–5). The *Críth Gablach* states that the lord 'defends the rights of his clients in regard to liabilities arising from contract, edict and treaty'. Many legal disputes were settled on oath, and the statement of the man with the highest status carried most weight (Binchy 1973a). Therefore, the client may well have needed the word of his lord to support litigation. In return for this, the lord received a proportion of any compensation, often one third. Gerriets (1983, 55) points out that the kin-group, the *fine*, also had a representative for the client in legal disputes. This may suggest an older custom still current even with the rise of clientship; use of one or the other might depend on the allegiances of the various parties involved, and their relative statuses. The range of issues covered by the laws, and the presence of a class of jurists in society, suggests that legal action was frequent.

Whether military force would be used to support claims is unclear, and Gerriets points out the surprising lack of reference in the laws to military equipment when defining the various grades. Archaeological evidence supports the hint that military activity was far less great for most of society than might be imagined from some of the secular tales. The laws indicate that weapons were not part of the equipment of even the *mrugfher*, a wealthy freeman.

Most settlement sites that have been excavated have not produced military equipment. No open settlement and very few ring-forts have produced swords, though a few spears are known (Figure 4:11). These, however, could be for killing cattle as mentioned in the texts. Only a few crannogs such as Lagore produced weapons. It might be argued that depositional factors have created this bias. In the muddy surroundings of the crannog it would be relatively easy for a sword to be lost by falling either through the substructure or over the surrounding palisade into the lake. In these circumstances recovery would be difficult or impossible, whereas on a dry

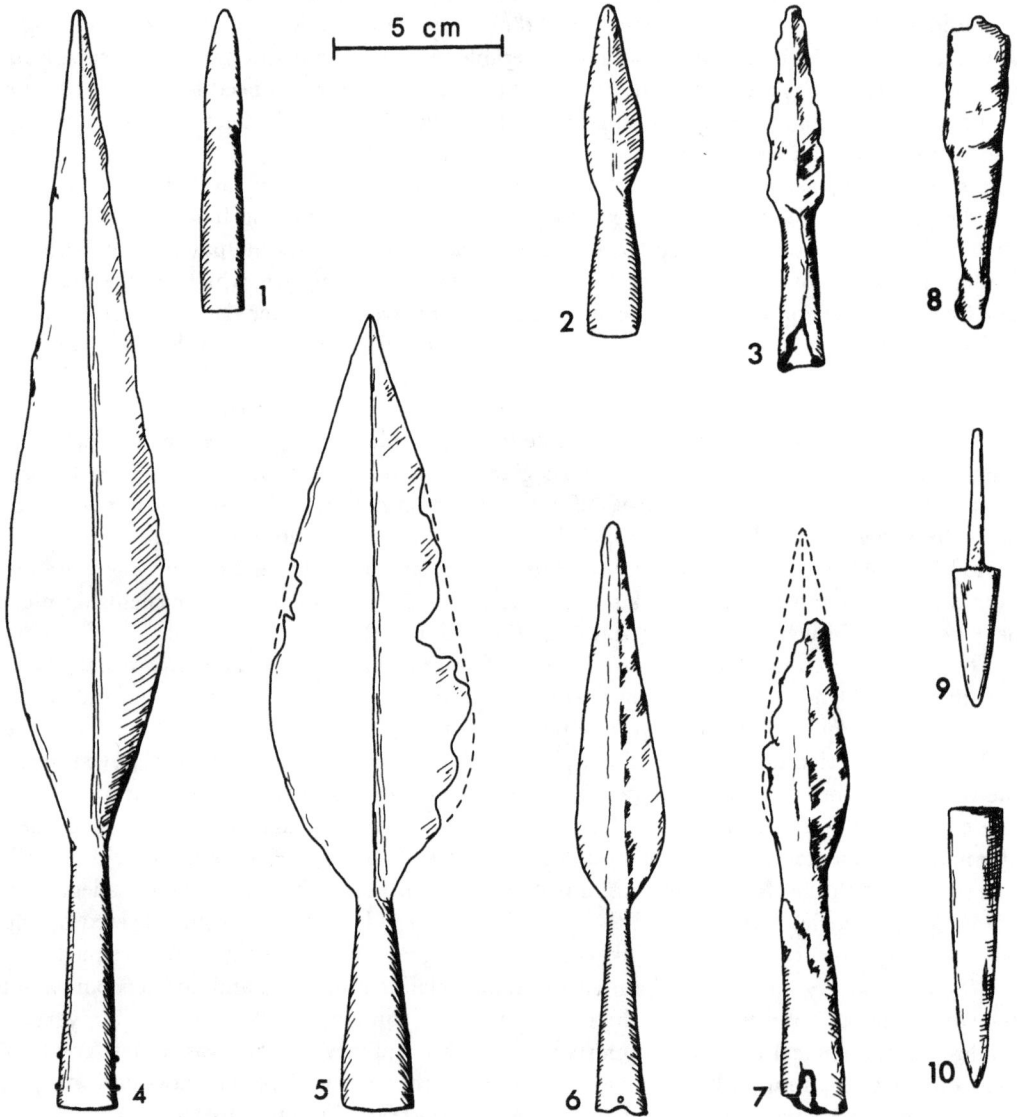

Figure 4:11   Spearheads, ferrules and butts. **1–5, 9, 10** Lagore, Co. Meath; **6–8** Garryduff 1, Co. Cork (**1–2, 4–6, 9–10** Hencken 1950, **3, 7–8** O'Kelly 1962).

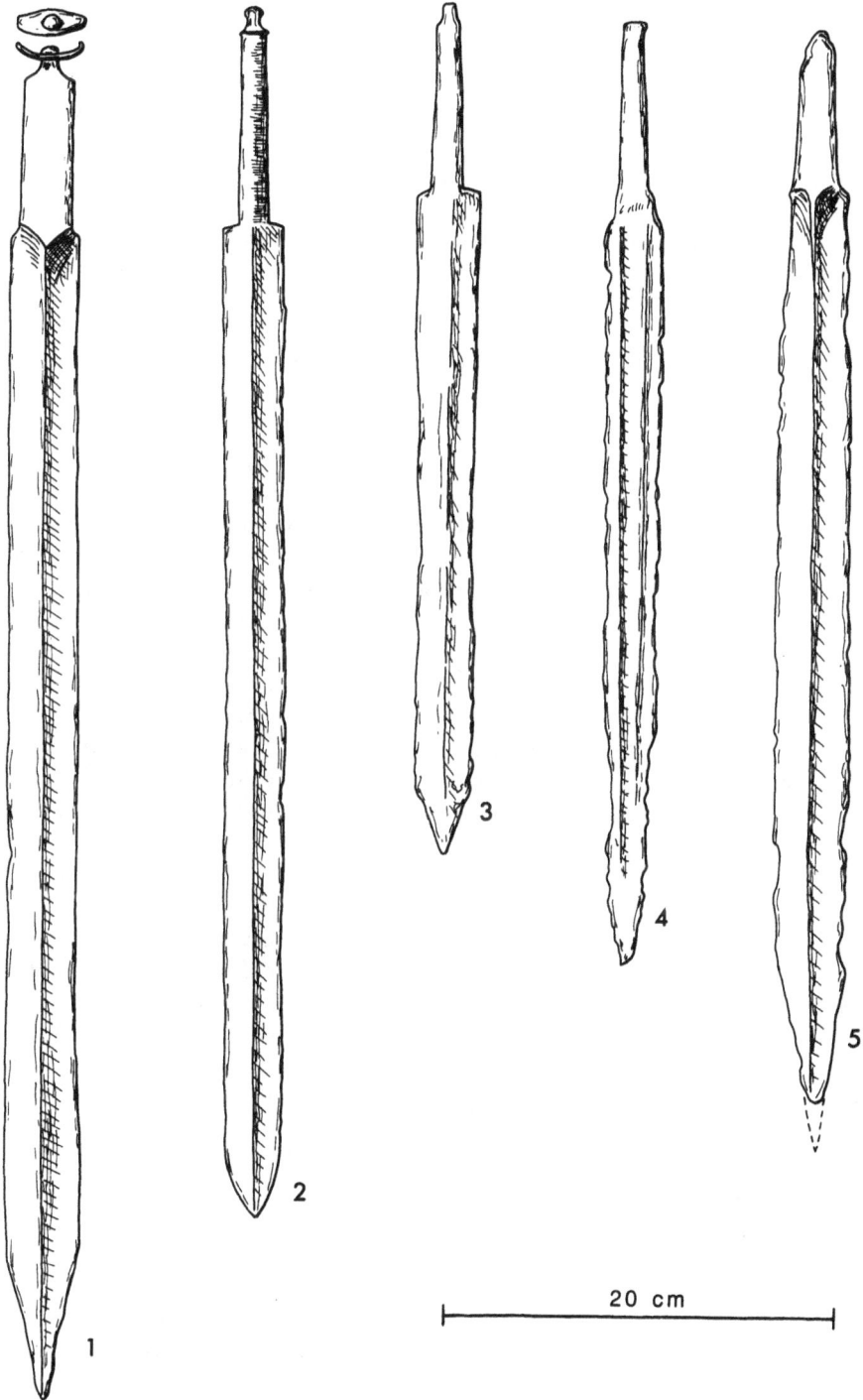

Figure 4:12   Swords from Lagore, Co. Meath, phase 1 (Hencken 1950).

land site, a sword could easily be recovered from the ground or even a ditch. The size and completeness of crannog finds suggest that depositional factors were important. This, however, does not fully explain the complete absence of military equipment from other settlements. Small items of scabbards and parts of sword hilts should be expected, and some ring-forts such as those at Carraig Aille, Co. Limerick have produced large numbers of metal objects (Ó Ríordáin 1949).

The lack of military equipment among the casual finds of this period also suggests that weapons were relatively rare. Whereas many brooches, beads and pins are to be found unprovenanced in museum collections, these contain few items of military hardware. Acquisition from all types of context – destroyed settlements, ploughing, peat cutting, river cleaning, burials – should have removed some of the depositional biases encountered on many excavated sites, but still weapons remain elusive. Therefore, although many clients were required to give military service, this must have involved the use of simple wooden staves or spears, or making do with everyday farm equipment such as spears and axes. Only the higher aristocracy and their retinues may have used specialist weapons.

It would seem that only on royal sites were weapons frequently present, and therefore available to enter the archaeological record. Lagore was almost certainly the royal site mentioned in several historical sources (Hencken 1950, Warner 1986b) and the overall assemblage of archaeological finds certainly supports the interpretation of the settlement as one of high status. It is interesting to note that Lagore has produced weapons, though few are stratigraphically shown to belong to the period before AD 800. Only one sword and a shield boss at Lagore definitely belong to phase 1, but probably many of the old finds made at the site are of this period (Figures 4:12, 7:7, 7:8).

A further indication of a relatively peaceful society comes from the fact that very few settlements have any indications of violent destruction; houses were rarely burnt down. Sometimes there must have been accidents leading to fire, so even the rare examples of burnt buildings such as the wicker circular house at Big Glebe, Co. Derry cannot be ascribed to violent activity (Lynn 1982, 167). Likewise, ring-fort gateways were not destroyed nor were their banks and ditches slighted.

The lord demanded substantial duties from the base client. Military service was expected, but far more importantly there were also manual tasks. It was these that clearly differentiated the base client from the free one, since such work was considered low status. The tasks were not very explicitly set out in the legal texts, but included service at harvest time. Another demand was apparently the building of the lord's fort, generally thought to mean the digging of the earthen bank to make an enclosure around the lord's house. The construction of a bank and ditch around a house, thus creating a ring-fort, may have been carried out by anyone; it was not a difficult exercise. But in Early Christian Irish society, with its constraining codes of behaviour and display, it is likely that such an activity was intimately connected with status. A bank and ditch or stone wall enclosure is highly likely to have carried a social message, and probably one indicating that the inhabitants had base clients.

The role of settlement enclosure may well be related to the psychological desire to define space associated with the ownership of land. It may also be related to the security of the home as opposed to the insecurity in the outside world, something easily appreciated given the various social and economic stresses that seem to have afflicted Early Christian Ireland! If the ring-fort does represent the statement of land ownership, then it suggests that it should be a symbol of those with a clear and significant land stake.

The size of the bank and the ditch varies. Typical dimensions were for a ditch 5 m wide,

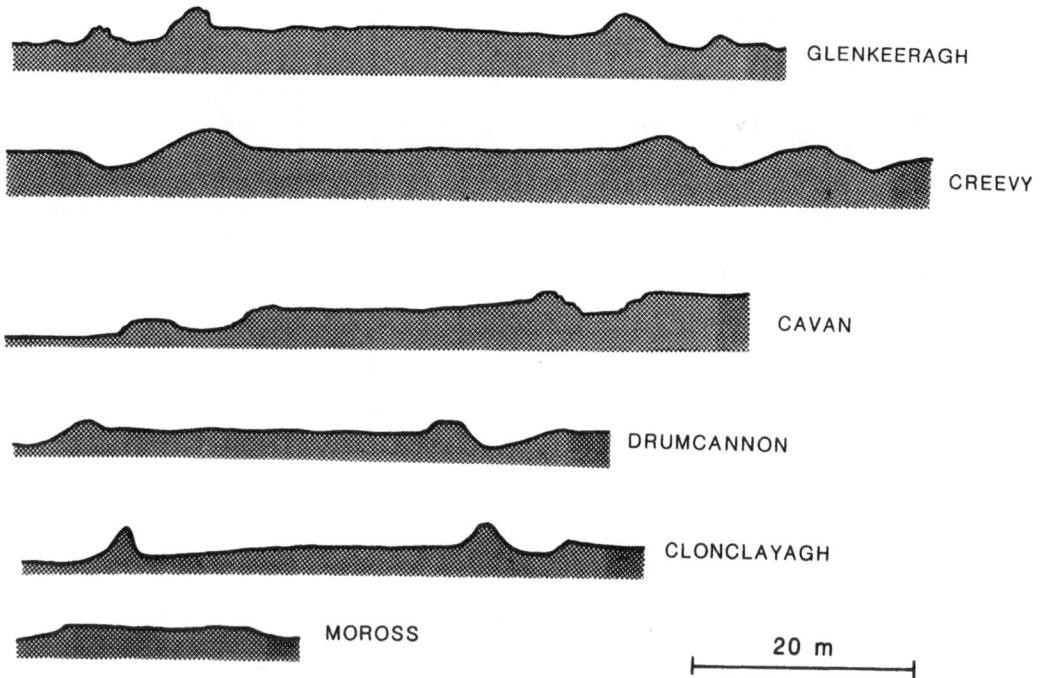

Figure 4:13   Profiles across ring-fort banks and ditches in Co. Donegal (Lacy 1983).

1.5 m deep, with a bank of similar dimensions built from the upcast (Figure 4:13). Though not insignificant, the enclosing earthworks seem to have served the most limited military function, and often had no crowning palisade. This lack of military significance is emphasised by the weakness of the straightforward entrances; outworks are almost unknown. Gateways were usually simple and were not designed for defensive strength (Figure 4:14). Even those where there is some strength in depth may have been so planned to impress rather than physically repel (Figure 4:15).

The length of occupation in ring-forts varies, but some seem to have been used for a relatively short period, perhaps to be measured in decades rather than centuries. Whatever the length of occupation, however, most sites reveal on excavation only a single phase of bank. In Co. Antrim, out of 16 ring-forts where sufficient evidence has been recovered from excavation to allow confident interpretations of the defensive sequence, only 4 have clear indications of more than one phase of enclosure bank. In neighbouring Co. Down, 12 out of 21 excavated sites produced similar evidence. This was not a pattern restricted to the north-east; of all 9 excavated ring-forts at Cush, Co. Limerick, each had only one bank phase. Once constructed, ring-fort defences were usually allowed to fall into decay; palaeobotanical evidence indicates that some became overgrown with bushes and small trees.

Ring-fort banks were therefore generally insubstantial and constructed only once. Their main purpose was to define the area around a residence, and this continued even when the bank was degraded. There were, however, cases where the defences were refurbished, sometimes more than once. There was still little indication of a military function, and some other explanation

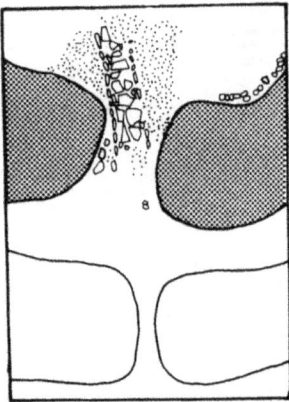
BALLYNARRY

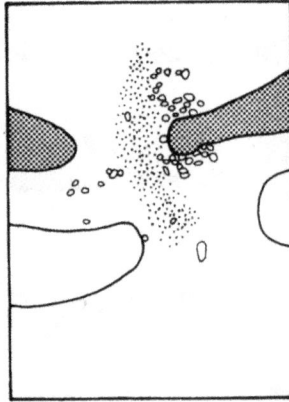
ARDCLOON

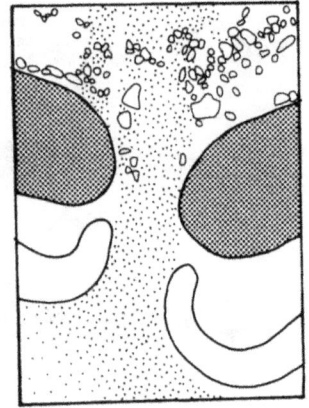
SHANE'S CASTLE

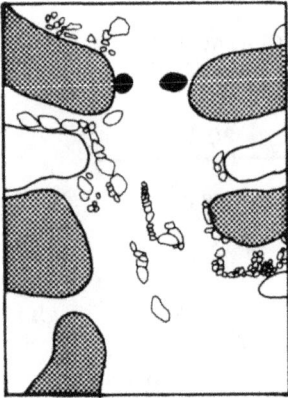
CUSH 5

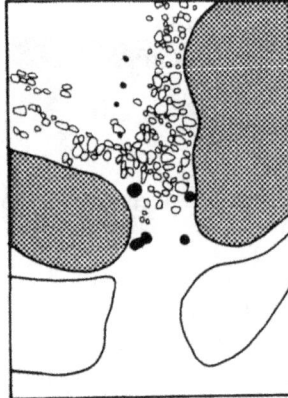
BALLYHENRY 1

FELTRIM HILL

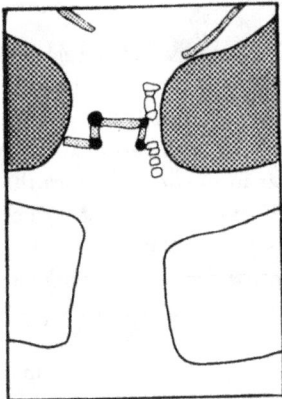
GARRYDUFF 1

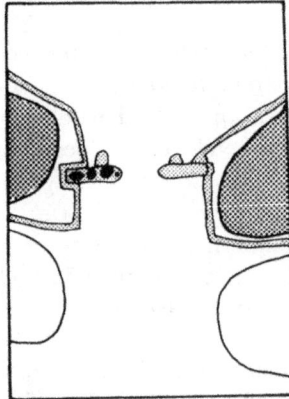
GARRYDUFF 2

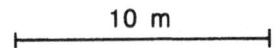
10 m

Figure 4:14 Simple ring-fort gateways. Banks shown with heavy stipple, post holes solid black, pits and slots light stipple, stones outlined (Ballynarry Rath, Co. Down, Davison 1962; Ardcloon, Co. Mayo, Rynne 1956; Shane's Castle, Co. Antrim, Warhurst 1971; Cush 5, Co. Limerick, Ó Ríordáin 1940; Ballyhenry 1, Co. Antrim, Lynn 1983b; Feltrim Hill, Co. Dublin, Hartnett and Eogan 1964; Garryduff 1 and 2, Co. Cork, O'Kelly 1962).

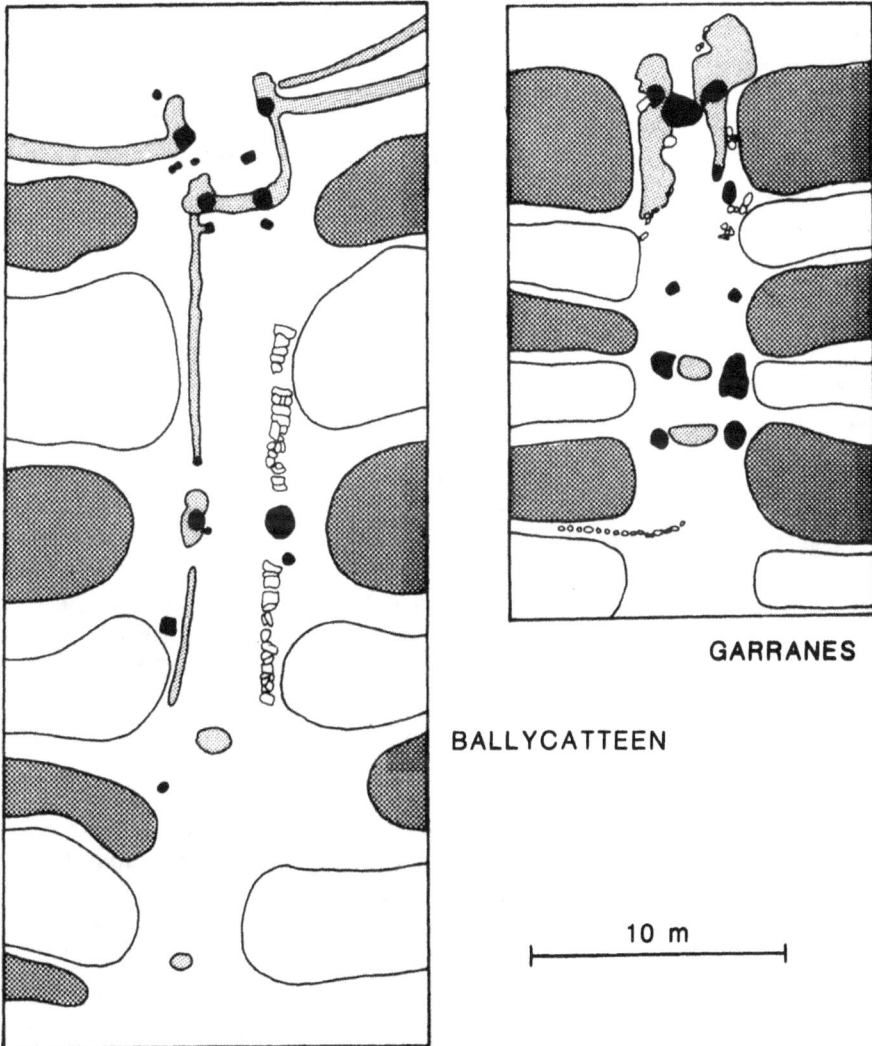

Figure 4:15 Complex ring-fort gateways. Banks shown with heavy stipple, post holes solid black, pits and slots light stipple, stones outlined (Ballycatteen, Co. Cork, Ó Ríordáin and Hartnett 1943; Garranes, Co. Cork, Ó Ríordáin 1942).

must be sought. This could lie in the social obligation of clients to build the noble's fort. The successive rebuilding of a ring-fort could indicate generations of high status occupants at the site. Certainly the ditch recutting and bank rebuilding were not merely seasonal cleaning; refurbishment was infrequent, and could represent separate generations. Ring-forts with multiple phases of bank construction have been found in the north-east (Figure 4:16), but there are few of these.

Some ring-forts have been built up over a period of time, forming a mound (Figure 4:17). Nearly all these platform ring-forts were created less by a steady accumulation of occupation debris and more by occasional phases of raising the mound by deliberate dumps of sterile material. These dumps can be considered equivalent to the re-working of the defences on other ring-forts. The platform design may have had further significance. Consistently successful families would have wished to emphasise the continuity of their power. Genealogies were created to show the pedigree of the elite; platform ring-forts may have been a similar, physical, form of statement. A high mound gave an impression of social position, one that must have been of some antiquity. In fact, this was not always the case. Some ring-forts were created from the first as platforms by scarping prominent natural features, as at Dromore, Co. Antrim (Collins 1968). This can be seen as a conscious attempt to create a visual image of pedigree, which may have been real or imaginary. At Dromore there were no rebuildings, but at many others there were further phases.

The refurbishment of ring-fort banks and ditches, or the raising of a habitation mound by the deposition of a sterile layer prior to rebuilding, was not necessary for any strictly functional reasons. Social factors were likely to have been important. At this stage of analysis it is sufficient to suggest that such rebuildings might be related to the presence of base clients. They were responsible for carrying out certain manual labour, and only the aristocracy could have base clients. The implication, therefore, is that multi-phase ring-forts were the residences of the elite. This argument will be further elaborated later in the chapter, when further evidence will be presented for the identification of social ranking from archaeological evidence.

Clientship and the church

During the sixth century, as the church gradually spread and began to own land, it was forced to become more integrated into secular society. One aspect of this was its relationship with those who worked on the land, and this included a form of clientship.

Charles-Edwards (1984) has suggested that in the earliest period, the *manach* may have been of lower status, and is linked to the *mug* or slave in secular law. In particular, the legal relationships of the *manaig* are equated with the slave. In other aspects, however, the *manach* was more like the free client. Indeed, it may be that when they entered the church family, slaves became free in the sense that they became *manaig* and so had more rights than previously. This may have originated in the earliest church authorities setting up a social structure similar to the Roman one where the *colonus* was tied to his land but was free; the *manach* may be the fifth century newly created equivalent to mirror the pattern of Christian establishments in Britain.

Despite the possible Roman influence in the status of the *manach*, in most respects he was brought within the established Irish social structure. This is most evident, of course, by the time the church was becoming more integrated with secular society anyway, and may have followed on from an earlier stage when the *manach*, modelled on the Roman *colonus*, was an aberrant category. The collective term *mainche* was equated with the *fine* or kindred, and obligations of a

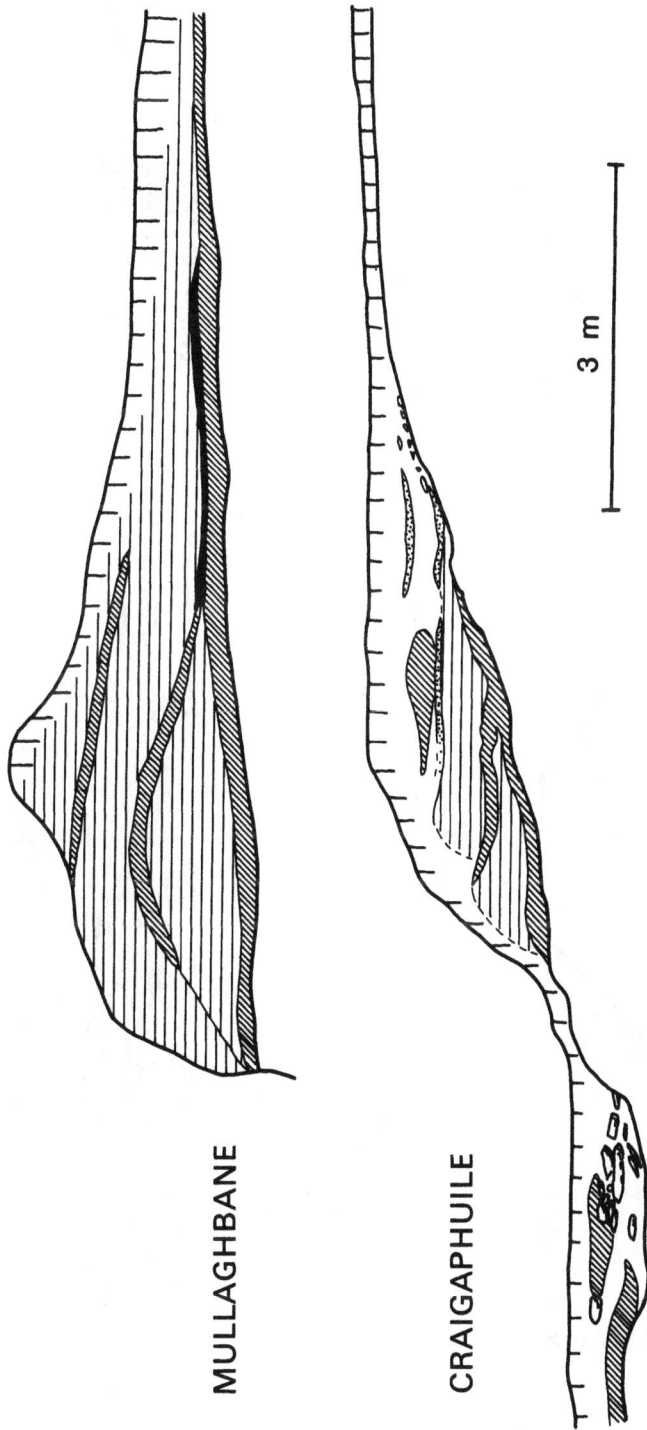

MULLAGHBANE

CRAIGAPHUILE

3 m

Figure 4:16 Sections of ring-fort banks with multiple phases (Mullaghbane, Co. Tyrone, Harper 1972; Craigaphuile, Co. Down, Collins 1959).

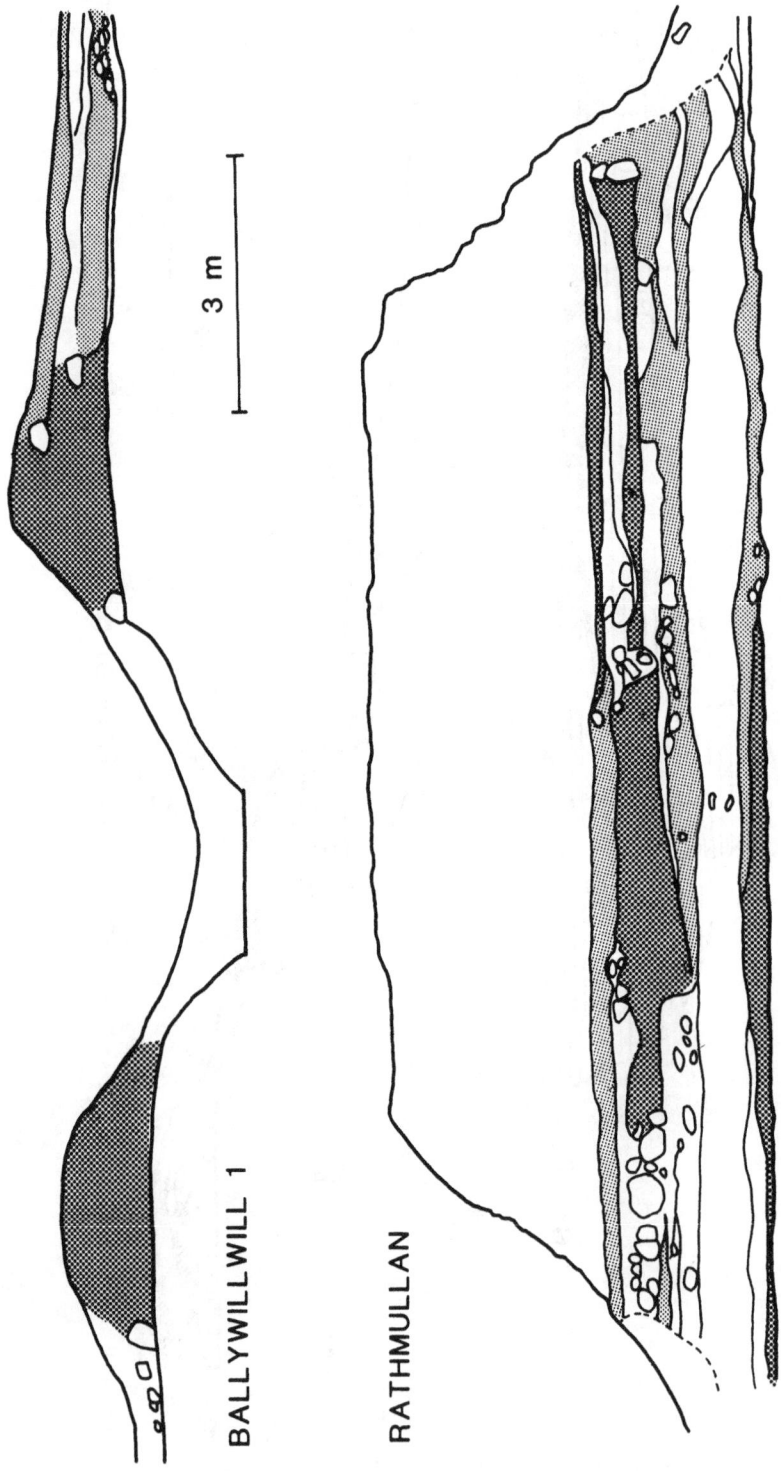

BALLYWILLWILL 1

RATHMULLAN

3 m

Figure 4:17 Sections across platform ring-forts in northern Ireland (Ballywillwill 1, Co. Antrim, Waterman and Collins 1952; Rathmullan, Co. Down, Lynn 1982).

manach were based partly on those of the slave, partly on those of the base client (Charles-Edwards 1984, 174).

Hughes (1966, 137) has shown that the secular laws such as the *Corus Bescna* saw the lay monks, *manaig*, who farmed the lands owned by the church as clients, with the abbot as lord. They were required to do certain labour services, *manchuine* (Hughes 1966, 139). It seems, however, that the relationship was more that of a kin-group, since the monks had some control over contracts made by the abbot (Hughes 1966, 137). There are also parallels in the relationship with that of man and wife in marriage (Ó Corráin 1981, 333). There seem to be many categories of people all described as *manaig*, and these ranged from the primarily agricultural workers with families to celibate ecclesiastics fully concerned with worship and contemplation. Ó Corráin (1981, 333) sees a change in the meaning of *manaig* from monk to monastic tenant during this period. Charles-Edwards (1984) points out that not only monasteries but other churches could also accept *manaig*.

Some of the *manaig* were on their own land which they inherited. In each generation, the first son was offered to the church, which educated him. This did not prevent him from in due course inheriting his share of family land, but he was treated as a free client of the church. This, as we have seen, was a position of honour, but involved some payment, notably first fruits such as the first lamb and the first calf (Ó Corráin 1981, 334). In effect, the eldest son of the family inherited the clientship (Hughes 1966, 140–1). The *manaig* of this type may well have been descendants of donors to the monastery, and so were able to inherit some rights of protection. Where church lands were some distance from the monastery or mother church, service obligations may have been converted into rent payments (Charles-Edwards 1984, 174).

In settlement terms it has been suggested that free status could be equated with dispersed settlement, and unfree with clustered (Charles-Edwards 1984, 170). This is because the sharing of land within kindreds scattered the group members onto their distinct holdings, but the servile population was tied to a lord and his land, and so clustered on it.

The individual

The hierarchical structure of society in Early Christian Ireland starts from the basis of the individual. Whatever kin-based and contractual associations might contribute to a position in society, they were insignificant without the individual's personal standing based on wealth and power. By the eighth century the various grades had become complex in the eyes of the legal commentators, though Binchy (1943, 224–5) suggests that in practice there were only three grades of the free: kings, nobles and free commoners. Nevertheless, the more detailed grading reflects the type of criteria in use to assess individual rank, and there is little doubt that in some circumstances nuances in ranking were vital.

High status individuals – the nobility

Noble grade was calculated not on property owned but on the number of clients held (Mac Neill 1923, 296 note 2). The normal fief given to clients was composed of cattle, though land and agricultural equipment could form a part. The capital distributed to clients would generally have been that inherited on the death of a noble's father. Adolescent aristocrats who had not yet inherited may have joined warlike bands, the *fianna*, which seem to have had pagan ritual associations and acted as outlaws one moment and protectors of the *túath* at another (McCone 1986).

Most of the aristocracy held base and free clients of their own, but were also free clients to more powerful lords. This chain of mutual obligations led up through the aristocracy to the king of the *túath*, the smallest political unit in Early Christian Ireland, and from thence to over-kings and ultimately, provincial kings. The lowest noble grade was the *aire désso* and the highest was *aire forgill* (Tables 4:1, 4:2).

Table 4:1 Relationships of the grades of nobility and freemen, with the equivalents in the *filid* and the church, according to the *Bretha Déin Chécht* (Binchy 1966)

Grade		Filid equivalent	Church equivalent
Ollum rig	Supreme king (province)	Master poet	Bishop
Rí ruirech	Superior king (several tribes)	Poet of 2nd grade	Priest
Rí	King (one tribe)	Poet of 3rd grade	Deacon
Aire ardd	Noble	Poet of 4th grade	Subdeacon
Aire désso	Noble		
Bóaire	Freeman		
Ócaire	Freeman		
Fer midboth	Freeman		

Table 4:2 Number of clients, by noble grade, according to the *Crith Gablach* (Mac Neill 1923, Binchy 1941)

Noble grade	No. free clients	No. base clients
Aire forgill	20	20
Aire tuise	12	15
Aire ardd	10	10
Aire désso	5	5

Aristocratic and royal families were often large. Despite church pressure, polygamy long remained popular amongst the elite, and second wives were often taken by those who could afford them if no sons were born of the first. The genealogies clearly indicate that aristocratic families must have been substantial, and estates would have been split each generation. This would have created difficulties for some sons who did not inherit sufficient capital to acquire the clients required for noble status. Indeed, the normal position, as emphasised both by Mac Niocaill (1972, 67) and Ó Corráin (1972, 44–5), was one of social decline.

Occasionally a member of the most wealthy grade of freemen became a noble, though this was not easy. The *fer fothlai* in the *Crith Gablach*, and the *flaith aithig* and *aire iter dá airig* in other tracts (Binchy 1941, 89), was a freeman in the process of becoming a noble. As Mac Neill (1923, 293) translates, 'The surplus of his cattle, of his cows, his swine, his sheep, that his own land cannot bear and that he cannot sell for land, that he himself does not need, he gives in capital to acquire clients.' By having clients, the *fer fothlai* was able to spread his assets more widely, and even develop a limited amount of political power. The *fer fothlai* could not enter a noble grade just by reaching the minimum material qualifications. Instead, he had to have twice those of the lowest noble grade, the *aire désso*, and maintain this for two further generations. Only then were the descendants made up to the noble grade. This implies a deferring tactic on the part of the elite to prevent those below them who have been economically successful rising too fast up the social scale and becoming a threat. By demanding a three generation delay, decline may have set in and the requisite conditions could not be met. A family at the level of *fer fothlai* for the three generations necessary to obtain promotion to the nobility would have had to have either been very expansive or produced few male children.

It is likely that most movement up the social scale, as indicated by the *fer fothlai* grade, must have been during the sixth and seventh centuries when there were still untapped agricultural resources that could be taken into use (see Chapter 5). It is also possible, however, that some individuals inherited large amounts of land from extinct branches of their *fine* following the plagues and famines in the later seventh and early eighth centuries.

There were other ways by which noble status could be achieved. Binchy (1941, 71) considers that the *aire échta* was a freeman who was given this noble grade in return for helping solve cases of manslaughter with a neighbouring *túath* with whom a treaty had been recently arranged. The *aire coisring* was also a freeman, but given special status as head of his kin-group and one who made arrangements with those outside it (Binchy 1941, 70). For a freeman to be given either of these positions, however, it is likely that he would have had to have been in control of considerable resources. The responsibilities of the offices would have required a household of some size to provide on the one hand the requisite entertainment for numerous guests and on the other the supervision of essential agricultural activities whilst the office holder was carrying out his duties. It is likely, therefore, that those given the rank of *aire échta* or *aire coisring* were already established figures in the social system.

It has already been suggested that the earthworks that define ring-forts were constructed by base clients as part of their service. This would carry the implication that all ring-forts were therefore the residences of the aristocracy, together with a few of the highest grade of freemen who possessed base clients. The ring-forts with several phases of defences thereby represent continued occupation by a family of high status; those that do not indicate either a short occupation of the site or a subsequent decline in status, perhaps caused by partible inheritance.

Most previous interpretations of ring-fort status have suggested that this settlement type belonged to the average freeman or above (Duignan 1944, de Paor and de Paor 1958, Proudfoot 1961). Therefore, a suggestion that it was a form used only by the elite requires detailed justification.

The number of ring-forts is uncertain, but is in the order of tens of thousands. Westropp (1902) considered there were about 30,000, based on his counts from the first edition Ordnance Survey maps. Subsequent fieldwork has vastly increased the number of known sites, and whilst some have been recognised as non-settlement features such as tree-rings (Williams 1980), the overwhelming majority are indeed ring-forts so Westropp's total has to be recognised as an underestimate. Haworth (1975), using the evidence of a 25 per cent increase on the Westropp figures in the Old Pallasgrean area of Co. Limerick (O'Dwyer 1964) and a doubling of the known sites in Co. Down in the Archaeological Survey of that county (Jope 1966), suggested that the final total could be double the 30,000 estimate. With the recent Co. Donegal survey (Lacy 1983) again showing a 100 per cent increase on the Westropp count of known sites, a total of 60,000 seems increasingly credible, and can be used as a working figure.

The very frequency of ring-forts has encouraged many to see them as a long-lasting form, with prehistoric origins (J. Raftery 1981, Caulfield 1981) or continuing into the medieval period (Barrett and Graham 1975). Detailed analysis of the dating evidence, however, suggests that all ring-forts are Early Christian (Lynn 1975, 1983). Whilst it may in time be possible to recognise phases within the period when ring-forts were mainly built, at present this is not possible. The date of construction for ring-forts runs from the sixth to the eleventh centuries – a total of 600 years – and so the settlement form was indeed a long-lived one. This imposes severe limitations on interpretation of field evidence, particularly the social implications of regional distributions.

At first sight, so great a total as 60,000 ring-forts would preclude any restriction of their use to the higher echelons of society. However, consideration of the excavated evidence demonstrates that only a small proportion of the sites would have been inhabited at any one time. Not all ring-forts were inhabited at all; despite extensive excavation, no trace of human occupation was found at Garryduff 2, Co. Cork (O'Kelly 1962) or at Shewis, Co. Armagh (Brannon 1980). Of those which were occupied, the average length of the occupation is unlikely to have been more than a century, even if more than one building phase is recognised (Lynn 1978). A few sites demonstrate a long and complex sequence, such as Gransha, Co. Down dated to the seventh–tenth centuries (Lynn 1985) and Rathmullan, Co. Down (Lynn 1982), but these are relatively rare. Therefore, for the purpose of rough calculation, it can be assumed that the non-occupied ring-forts balance the multi-period sites, and that on average ring-forts were each occupied for a century.

There must have been times when ring-forts were constructed in greater numbers than others, but if an even rate is assumed for examining the general density of settlement, then at any one time one sixth of the suggested original 60,000 ring-forts were occupied, a figure of 10,000. It has been demonstrated that each ring-fort contained little more than the nuclear family, and it is not possible to imagine that normally more than one noble grade individual, his family and entourage could have lived in each site. This would imply around 10,000 adult male members of the aristocracy in Ireland at any one time.

Documentary sources such as the laws, though extremely schematised, do give some indications of the scale of political activity for the first part of the Early Christian period. The smallest political unit was the *túath*, and it is thought that 150 existed at any one time (Byrne 1973). The figure of 10,000 ring-forts in use at a time would therefore give an average aristocratic male population of under 70 for each *túath*. Given that the king of a *túath* was expected to raise an army of 700, this would suggest an average of 10 fighting men contributed by every member of the aristocracy. The lowest grade of noble, the *aire désso*, was required to have 10 clients, whilst others were required to have up to 40. Many of these, however, were free clients and as the aristocracy were engaged in many relationships of free clientage with each other in a hierarchical pattern of social and political alliances, an average of 10 men from each adult male noble would not seem unreasonable.

With the political fragmentation into numerous small independent units, there were not only many nobles but also about 150 kings at any one time. Each *túath* was roughly the size of a barony, and indeed the boundaries of these units may represent the latest phase of the *túatha* (Byrne 1973). Comparisons can be made within a region using criteria such as site type, size, complexity and, on occasion, location. Ring-fort densities vary considerably over the country, and social as well as economic factors may have been responsible for this. For the later discussion, however, concentration will be placed on particular areas where field survey results are available (see pp. 152–8).

Middle status individuals – the freemen

Just as there were many grades of noble set out in the law tracts, so freemen were divided into a hierarchy, though these grades were based on material possessions. The *bóaire* is only briefly discussed in the *Críth Gablach*, and has a lower food-rent than in most other law tracts (a year old steer rather than a milch cow). It is likely that the major freeman grade in the *Críth Gablach* was that of the *mrugfher*, and this was the same as the *bóaire* in other texts (Binchy 1941, Gerriets 1983). His property is defined in great detail (see Chapter 5) together with penalties for damage and trespass. He was able to farm without help of others and owned his own mill. It is generally considered that this was the 'typical' freeman of the laws, though the difficulties in maintaining this position over generations must have been substantial if more than one son survived to inherit.

The *Críth Gablach* states that the *fer midboth* grade was split in two, based on age. There were few differences between minors aged 14–17 and those of 17–20, and this may be part of the schematised nature of the tract. The *fer midboth* had finished his period of fosterage with another family, and lived apart from his father in a separate dwelling (Binchy 1941, 90). The term seems to have referred to someone of *bóaire* status but yet to inherit; as a result, older men could be counted as this grade if their father had not died.

The *ócaire* was the lowest grade of adult freeman in the tract. He had some land, but not sufficient to be economically independent. As a result, he was reliant on others for further land and probably stock in order to survive. Binchy (1941, 101–2) suggests that *ócaire* means 'young', and this may be because this was a relatively new grade. It may have been added because so many freemen could not meet the property requirements of a *bóaire*.

There were social pressures to have as large a family as possible, and the rule of partible inheritance amongst all sons led to increasing fragmentation of estates. This could therefore lead to a drop in status for all descendants unless political, military or economic manoeuvring allowed some to prosper. For a period during the sixth and seventh centuries, it was possible for many to expand agriculture into areas not previously colonised, and so smaller landholdings could be augmented. There is palaeobotanical evidence for the widespread winning of farmland from upland and more frequently from areas of primary and secondary woodland (Mitchell 1976).

During the early part of the period many individuals had the chance to maintain or improve their position, and the positive, optimistic indications of rise in social position given by some of the laws may well be from this period. Presumably in the seventh century this expansion began to slow, and by the eighth century when it came to a halt, the pressure had already begun to accumulate amongst the freemen. The strict property qualifications prevented many sons from maintaining the positions of their fathers, and there was no free land available.

The creation of the *ócaire* grade was an adaptation of the social system to alleviate the strains of maintaining freeman status with an expanding population in a now filled landscape (Figure 4:18). There was great pressure to avoid losing free status; once lost, it could not be recovered. There was then only the prospect of the slide into serfdom as a *sen-cléithe*. The creation of a new, lower grade of freeman had not been the only alternative available. Another strategy, for example, would have been to lower the property qualifications necessary to become a *bóaire*. There would, however, have been great pressure from those able to maintain such a grade that their status should not be diminished by the inclusion of others with less. It was better for them to create a new, lower, grade which allowed those of *bóaire* status to maintain their ranking and meant that those with less could still be considered freemen but at a lower grade.

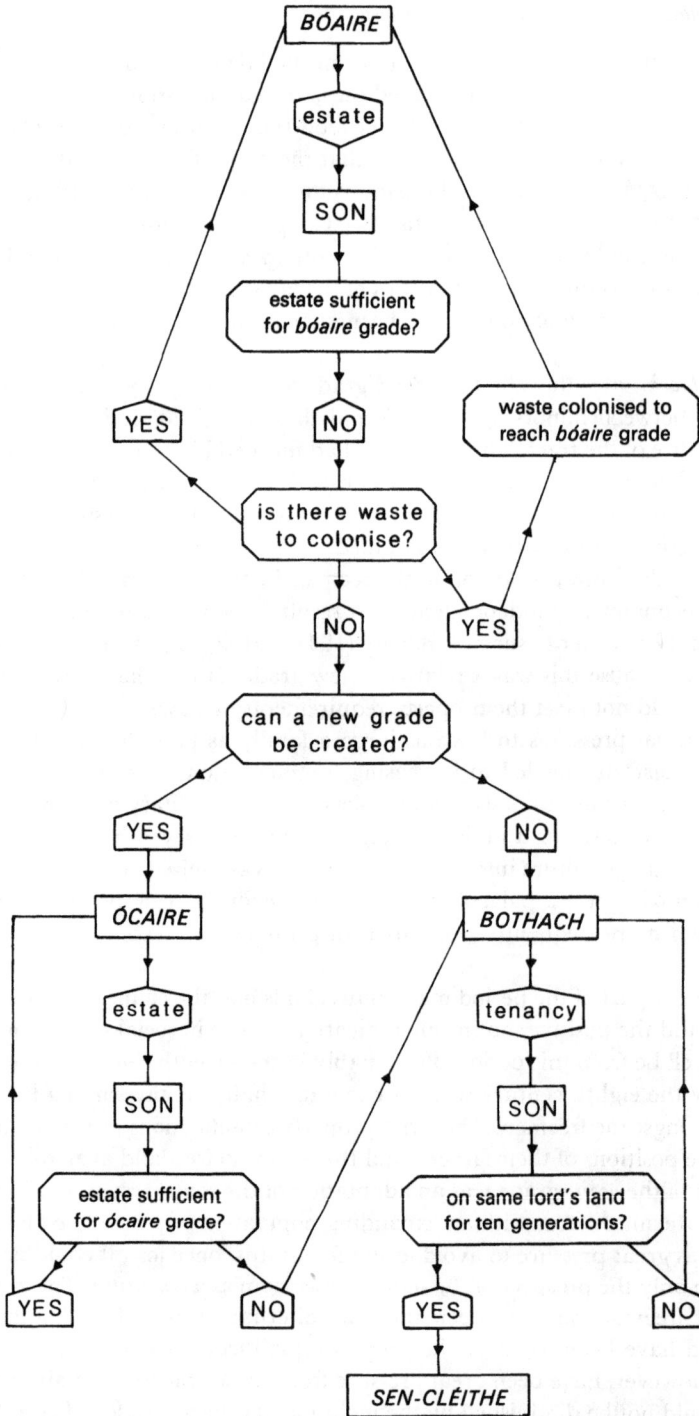

Figure 4:18   Diagram indicating the pressures leading to the creation of the *ócaire* grade.

The aristocracy would also have benefited from the creation of the *ócaire* grade, rather than let many sons of freemen fall into the unfree class. The new grade of freemen were bound to be dependent on the nobility as base clients for land and other capital for agriculture, since their inheritance was by definition small. Indeed, the *ócaire* was a most desirable grade for those who wished to be socially dominant through the acquisition of base clients. For this reason, the *ócaire* grade, once created, must have quickly become widely acceptable across Ireland since the elite in those areas that did not adapt would have had a much smaller pool of potential clients, and so would have had less social and political status. Knowledge of the new grade would have spread through those processes outlined in the discussions of peer polity interaction. Those at the top of the social hierarchy relied on a broad base; the creation of the *ócaire* not only increased the height of the pyramid, but also very considerably widened its base. It was one stage in the process of gradually increased stratification that is a major theme throughout the Early Christian period.

A ring-fort on the lower slopes of Brandon mountain, presumably the residence of a high status individual and his entourage, contains three circular stone buildings. Nearby are three pairs of conjoined roundhouses (Cuppage 1986, plate 52). Each hut pair may represent a single family, since access to one of the structures can only be gained through the other. Within one room in each dwelling complex was a small souterrain or wall passage, a typical Early Christian period feature. Souterrains suggest possession of a surplus kept under the control of the family, presumably from their own land. Whilst the unfree may have held some supplies, they are more likely to have been dependent on rations given out by the noble land owner in return for the labour on his land. Any produce from a small garden plot worked by the serf or cotter would not have required the elaborate storage facilities of a souterrain. For this reason, it is likely that these conjoined roundhouses represent the homes of freemen, though probably at a fairly low level since their proximity to each other and to the ring-fort suggests that (if contemporary) each householder must have owned little land. It is likely that they would have been base clients of the adjacent ring-fort owner, since most such relationships must have been decided on the basis of proximity.

Low status individuals – the unfree

The unfree were at the bottom of the social hierarchy, and may have been considerable in number. The written sources are, however, unconcerned with them – they were merely chattels that were occasionally mentioned alongside cattle or land.

An individual with a few material possessions but not tied to the land was the *fuidir*, considered to be of very low status. The *bothach* or crofter was similar, but may have had to perform different services. Both these grades were reliant on land and other agricultural requisites given to them by those higher in the social system in return for services. Unfortunately, these obligations are unknown but must have contributed a significant part of the labour input on larger farms, especially at ploughing and harvest. Both the *fuidir* and *bothach* were tenants-at-will who could leave their lord and smallholding in return for two thirds of their agricultural produce (Binchy 1941, 93). Hughes (1972, 51) emphasises that it must have been extremely difficult in practice for this to happen. After ten generations a *fuidir* or *bothach* became tied to the land and descended to the level of a serf, *sen-cléithe*. He was bound to the land and considered part of it. Mac Niocaill (1972, 68) mentions a case of 15 such individuals being given with land as a fosterage fee.

Slaves could be male or female, and carried out a wide range of the most menial of tasks.

Presumably slaves could be acquired through capture (though individuals of higher status would be ransomed), but many must have been hereditary slaves. Those at the lowest levels in Early Christian Irish society were clearly considered by those above to be of little or no importance. Though possibly numerically significant, they played no direct part in society and were generally involved only in menial household and agricultural activities.

Archaeologically, low status individuals are undetectable. They presumably had few possessions and those were probably perishable. Indeed, their low status in Early Christian Irish society would have been identified in a negative manner – lacking personal ornaments which, it has been suggested, belonged to the free. Some of the open hut sites found in western Ireland may have been the dwellings of the serfs and crofters, but many slaves and other servants will have lived in the houses and settlements of the freemen.

Personal adornment

Since so much of the social fabric of Early Christian Ireland was founded on an individual's status based partly on kinship and genealogy but even more on access to personal wealth, it is likely that the individual displayed his place in society by what he wore. Status may have been indicated in part at least by the very bearing and manner of an individual, but clothing and ornament would have also played a part. In various references including some of the highly schematised legal tracts, gold is associated with the very highest grades, and silver with those just below, implying that these were the most highly prized metals for brooches and pins. This is not surprising, perhaps, but is comforting to have confirmed. It is possible on the basis of metals used and the extent of specialist craftsmanship employed to place examples of metalwork of the period into a hierarchy which might in general terms be seen to reflect grading within the free grades of contemporary society, both secular and religious. The technical achievements of the pieces are discussed in Chapter 6 under the relevant crafts; here the concern is with their use once made.

Probably the simplest, cheapest and therefore lowest status pins were those made from wood and bone, particularly the fibula of the pig, which needs little or no modification for use. Wooden pins have been found on crannogs, and the bone pins have been frequently recovered in excavation from all types of site when the soils have not been too acid for bone to survive. Iron was occasionally used for a range of functional dress fasteners. Simple knobbed, disc and bifid pins were produced, together with ring-pins and penannular brooches, but they are relatively rare. Whilst Garryduff 1 produced a good range, for example, only a few came from Ballinderry 2 and Lagore, with none from Garranes (Figure 4:19). This is probably because small iron artefacts are relatively difficult to make, rather than suggesting rarity and high status. Indeed, there are very few examples of iron artefacts with any complex decoration. Enamel inlay is known on only two items, a plate from the crannog of Lagore and a strap-end from the platform ring-fort of Rathmullan (Bourke 1985). Both these are high status sites, which suggests that the enamelling of iron only occurred at important sites.

At the beginning of the period, copper-alloy pins, 'latchet' dress fasteners and simple penannular brooches elaborated with cast ornament and enamel were the main forms of personal adornment (Plates XIV–XVI). As time went on, these became more elaborate, with increased size of the brooch as a whole and the terminals in particular to allow the display of decoration (Plates XIX–XXII). There is little doubt that this development was a result of competition

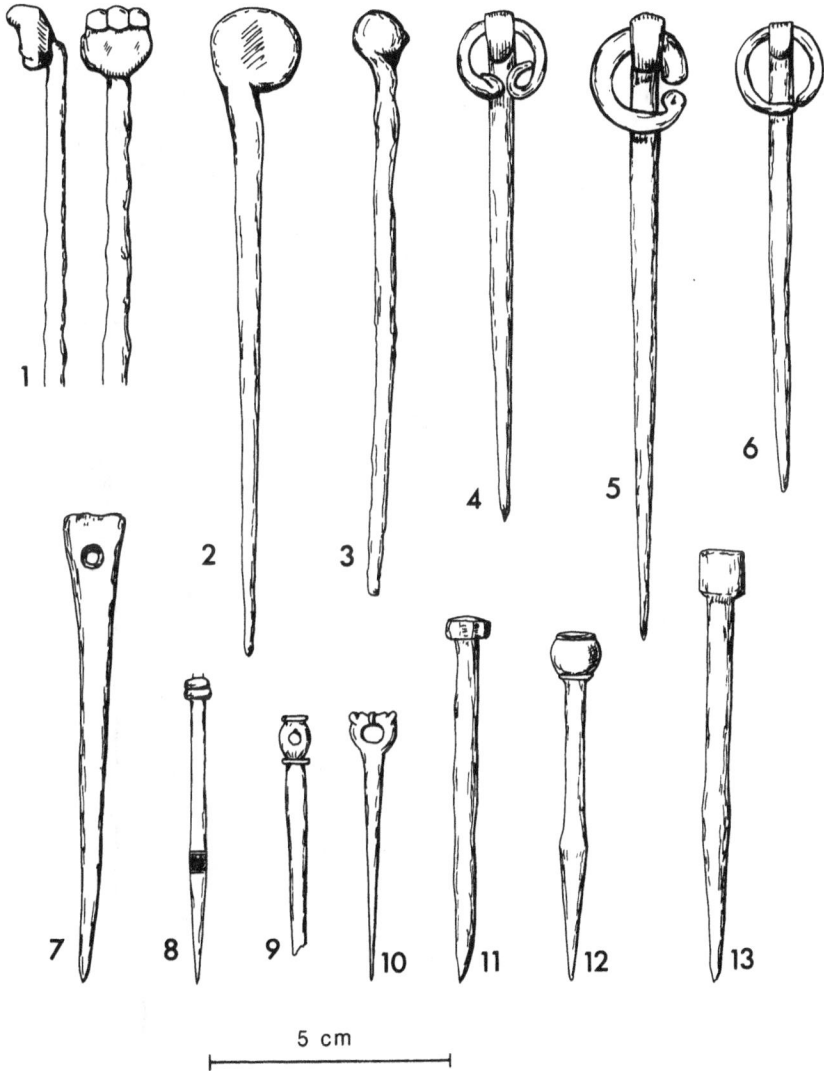

Figure 4:19 Iron and bone pins. Iron: **1** hand-pin, Carraig Aille 1, Co. Limerick; **2, 3** pins with solid heads, Carraig Aille 1, Co. Limerick; **4–6** ring-headed pins, Carraig Aille 2, Co. Limerick. Bone: **7** perforated pig scapula, Carraig Aille 2, Co. Limerick; **8–13** carved bone pins, Lagore, Co. Meath (**1–7** Ó Ríordáin 1949, **8–13** Hencken 1950).

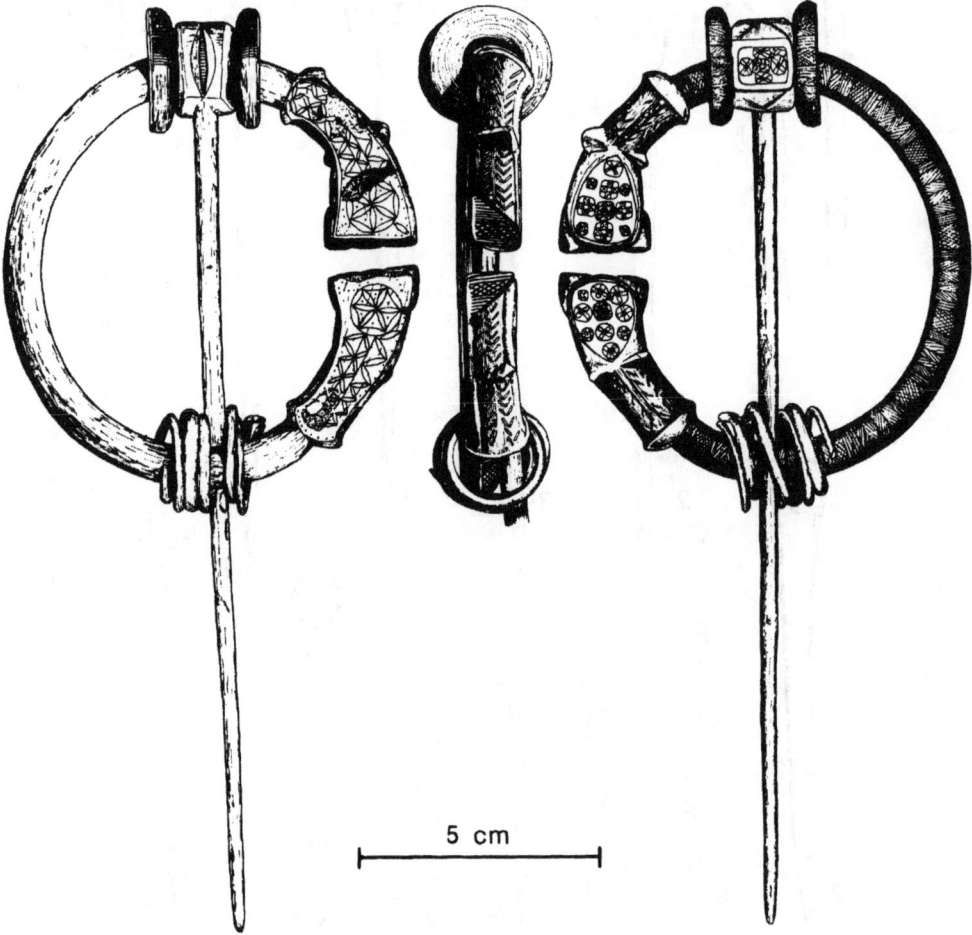

Figure 4:20   Ballinderry 2 brooch (Hencken 1942).

between those who had access to the resources necessary to employ specialist craftsmen of the highest calibre available, and culminated in products such as the Ballinderry 2 brooch (Figure 4:20). The competitive emulation through brooches seen at major gatherings or when renders and tribute were exchanged meant that, where they could be afforded, ever more complex products were created. In many cases, of course, only a lesser complexity could be afforded, and at all times throughout this period simple brooches and pins, notably the ring-headed form, were common (Figure 4:21). The dress fastener in the form of pin or brooch was the dominant item of display, although more rarely buckles were used (Plate XVIII).

In general the competition in personal adornment between the elite was based not on the use of precious metals but on the control of actual craftsmen and their abilities to use copper-alloys, enamels, glass and occasionally amber insets, together with millefiori glass. The display therefore showed not ownership of precious materials that could in themselves be converted into bullion and thus recycled, but rather more an investment of specialist craftsmen's time and artistic expression which was an irreversible investment. In this sense it was a particularly strong show of disposable wealth.

During the seventh century, silver started to be used on brooches, the beginning of a process that became much more significant in the ninth century when the bullion value of personal ornaments was the way in which status was indicated, leading to the creation of larger and heavier items over time. In the period before 800, however, this change was only just beginning, and there is still considerable decoration of the brooches even of precious metal. This can also be seen in the use of gold which is not merely plain, but presented as granulation, filigree or as decorated insets. The only gold items from excavated sites are the gold bird from Garryduff 1 (O'Kelly 1962), a mount from Moynagh Lough (Bradley 1982) and the interlace design from Lagore (Hencken 1950). All involve great artistic skills in their design and production. Gold was clearly rare, since even the elaborate Tara brooch incorporated relatively little solid gold and instead was largely made of gilt copper-alloy (Plates XXI, XXII).

A large number of sites produced a few copper-alloy items such as ring-headed pins, but brooches are much rarer. Given all the difficulties over original loss patterns, differential survival depending on soil type and recovery dependent on excavation strategies, it is not possible to quantify the relative status of all sites by their finds. Nevertheless, it is likely that the full spectrum through, from the higher echelons of society to the lower ranks, is represented.

There is little doubt that much of the craft expertise was within monasteries, and these institutions themselves engaged in competition in the production of works to the glory of God. The ownership of relics became important during the eighth century in the legitimation of power and control over other foundations. The importance of relics could be emphasised and even enhanced by their encasement in suitably sumptuous reliquaries, adorned with highly complex and symbolically significant decoration of many materials and colours (Plate XXV). The liturgical equipment could also be made to a very high standard as both the Ardagh chalice and the Derrynaflan altar set illustrate (Plates XXVII, XXIX). In addition, the fabric of churches and the permanent shrines within them could be highly decorated, as the description of the church at Kildare by Cogitosus (Connolly and Picard 1987) and finds such as the crucifixion plaque from near Athlone (Plate XXVI) and door handle from Donore (Plate XXXI) indicate.

Manuscripts are another material in which special skills and abilities could be displayed, and the increase in decoration between the sixth century *Usserianus Primus* with merely simple marks in red, such as round a cross (Figure 3:9), and the books of Durrow (Plates XXXIII, XXXIV), Dimma (Plates XXXV, XXXVI) and Kells (Plates XXXVII–XXXIX) indicates a rapid

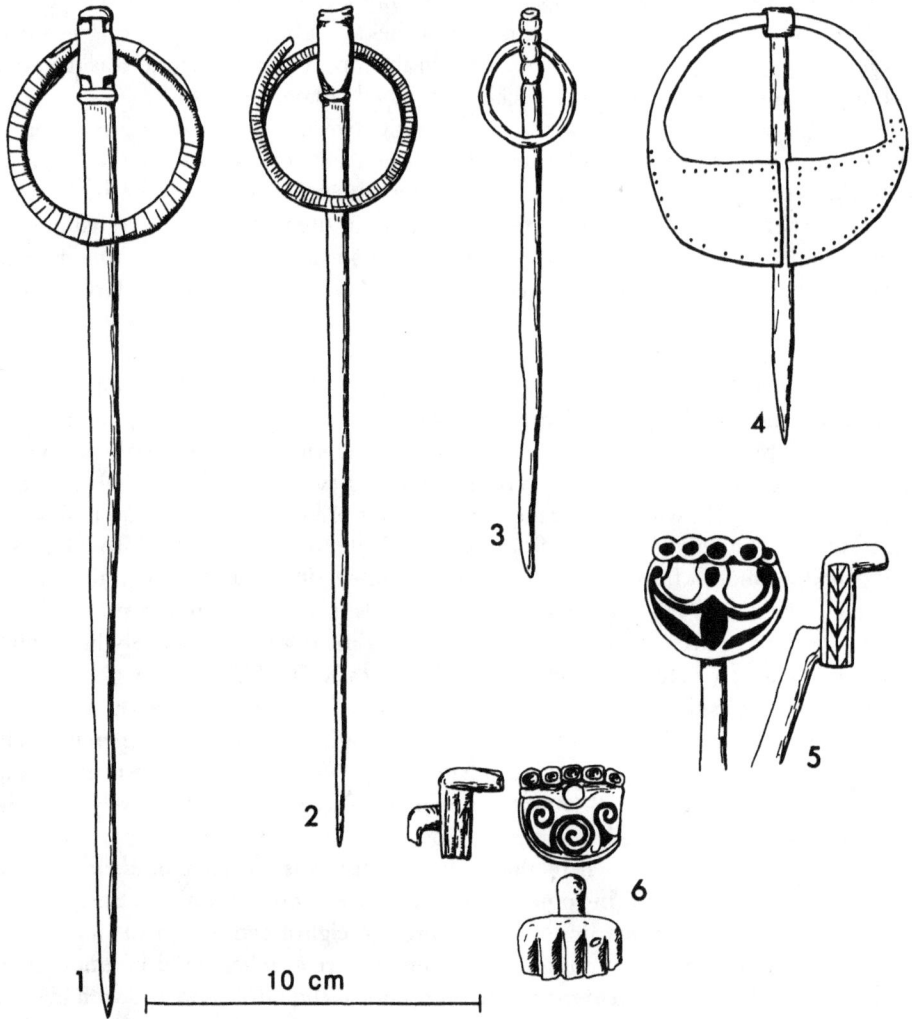

Figure 4:21   Bronze dress fasteners. **1–3** Ring-headed pins: **1** Carraig Aille 2, Co. Limerick; **2, 3** Lagore, Co. Meath. **4** Penannular brooch, Lagore, Co. Meath. **5–6** Hand-pins: **5** Carraig Aille 2, Co. Limerick; **6** Ballycatteen, Co. Cork (**1, 5** Ó Ríordáin 1949, **2–4** Hencken 1950, **6** Ó Ríordáin and Hartnett 1943).

development, inspired also by external contacts elsewhere in the Christian world (Meehan 1983). The same might also be said for developments in sculpture, particularly with regard to the standing, high cross, though that development had little more than begun by 800.

The túath

The fundamental building block of the political system in Early Christian Ireland was the *túath*, led by the king, *rí* or *rí tuaithe*. There is considerable dispute as to whether the *túath* represented a tribe (Mac Neill 1911, Byrne 1971). There was no ethnic, linguistic or cultural division, but it did represent a political unit, and one on a larger scale than that of the kin-group. Belonging to a *túath* was an important concept in Early Christian Ireland, and in that sense the *túath* can be considered a tribe. The king led the *túath*, but reported to the assembly, the *óenach*, though it does not appear to have had much power by this period.

The *túath* occupied a relatively small area, and it is thought that there were around 150 *túatha* in Ireland at any one time. They have been equated in size with the modern barony, an Irish administrative unit. As political fortunes rose and fell, individual *túatha* might grow or shrink, or even disappear and be replaced by others. *Túatha* were territories, and a member of one *túath* was not necessarily legally protected when in another. How these territories were constructed on the ground is less clear, since they were based on a combination of kinship and clientage. Each may not have had a continuous boundary within which all land belonged to the one *túath*, but may have been somewhat fragmented. Though this geographical complexity may not appeal to our ordered, map-dominated view of the world, all those in Early Christian Ireland could understand and work within the concept of a *túath*'s territory.

The fluid nature of Irish society has meant that it is archaeologically very difficult to recognise entities the size of a *túath*. In some of the peripheral areas where political units may have been stable for centuries it may be possible to recognise them. The Corco Mruad of the Burren, Co. Clare were of little importance during this period, and were under pressure from their neighbours the Corcu Baiscind and the Uí Fiachrach Aidni to the south and east. Their probable boundary on the east can be recognised by a band of unsettled territory, but on the south there is a great density of ring-forts. In this area, however, there is also a line of churches which define the boundary of the tribe (Figure 3:6). There are many motives for such locations, but whichever applies, a boundary pattern could emerge (Mytum 1982).

Another possible indicator of *túatha* may be ogham stones, particularly the earlier ones which include the word *MUCOI* followed by a remote ancestor (Jackson 1953, 137–8). Where enough are found in one area, the approximate size of a *túath* at the beginning of the period might be defined. Oghams are most common in Co. Kerry, and in the Dingle peninsula four ogham stones are known with *MUCCOI DOVINIAS* (Cuppage 1986). These indicate that Dovinia was a female ancestress claimed by the Corcu Duibne, and Byrne (1973, 166) links this with the genealogical tradition where the Hag of Beare acts as foster-mother to Corc Duibne, ancestor of the Corcu Duibne. The distribution of ogham stones carrying this inscription may therefore indicate the extent of the tribe and its *túath* in the fifth century. It would seem, however, that different tribes may have had the same name, since there are scattered inscriptions with *MUCCOI LUGUNI* and *MUCCOI MACORBO* (Figure 4:22). Therefore, the oghams with *DOVIN(IAS)* in the southern part of the Iveragh peninsula may not be part of the same *túath* as those to the north, though they may well represent distantly related groups. Later oghams only give the name of a relation (usually the father) of the deceased, and so cannot be used to indicate the extent of *túatha* in subsequent periods.

The king of the *túath* had to be physically perfect, and carry out all his duties appropriately otherwise disaster could befall the *túath* (Byrne 1973). Various taboos had also to be kept to avoid disaster, and these symbolically again protected the population and were for the common good (Dillon 1951, O'Leary 1988). Many of these aspects, together with the inauguration rites, are clearly pagan in their origins. The king continued to be an embodiment of the *túath* throughout the Early Christian period, even after conversion to Christianity. Indeed, as time went on it seems that the king acquired more power, particularly as a judge in disputes, with the slight decline of the professional legal grades and the encouragement of the church (Gerriets 1988). Competition was severe for the esteemed position of king.

There has been much discussion about succession rules and conventions (Mac Neill 1921, 114–43; Hogan 1932; Binchy 1956; Mac Niocaill 1968; Ó Corráin 1971). There were no rules of primogeniture, and most writers have considered that any adult male within the *derbfine* was eligible. Ó Corráin (1972) has suggested, however, that all families that had ancestors who had been king considered themselves possible successors. Naturally, those closest to the king both physically and by kinship were most likely to succeed. They had access to greatest resources and could manipulate alliances to create a power base, but others were entitled to attempt the throne if they could muster support. Usually the succession went to a brother or nephew of the dead king, since sons were usually too young. Byrne (1973, 36–7) points out that the result was often a foregone conclusion because there was one individual obviously more powerful than others. On the other hand, there is plenty of evidence that fighting could be involved in succession struggles, and could include forces from outside the *túath* (Hogan 1932). In this respect, then, kingship was quite different from property which passed to sons and was divided equally; in only a few exceptional cases the kingship was split or shared (Mac Niocaill 1972, 55).

The insecurity of succession to a *túath* and the wide eligibility (however defined) provided an important dynamic quality to Irish political life. Although particular close family groups built up dynastic successions of kings, these were inherently unstable and were at any time open to overthrow. Whilst the king of the *túath* may have been concerned with wider issues beyond his immediate territory, he was also concerned with maintaining his position internally, through his client system. The king was able to wield sufficient power to gain and hold office through his own kinship ties and clientship; indeed, these were in many cases synonymous since there were only very limited resources which actually went with the office of king to help in the maintenance of any administrative system. Relations who could be placed into free clientship were by definition supporters. The king also had other free clients belonging to other aristocratic families in the *túath*, and also numerous base clients. These provided a permanent income from their renders as well as a military force. They also carried out manual service including building the king's fort, and the *Críth Gablach* states: 'It is then that he is king when ramparts of base clientship surround him' (Byrne 1973, 32). The same text states that the highest grade of noble, the *aire forgill*, has 40 clients, half free and half base (Mac Neill 1923). These figures are schematic, and presumably represent some nominal minimum number; the balance between the two kinds of client is highly unlikely, and base clients must have been far more common. Presumably a king would have had more clients than this minimum for a noble.

Although clientage was a personal matter between a base client and a lord, if that lord was in turn a free client to a higher noble, a complex social network could be created. Obligations

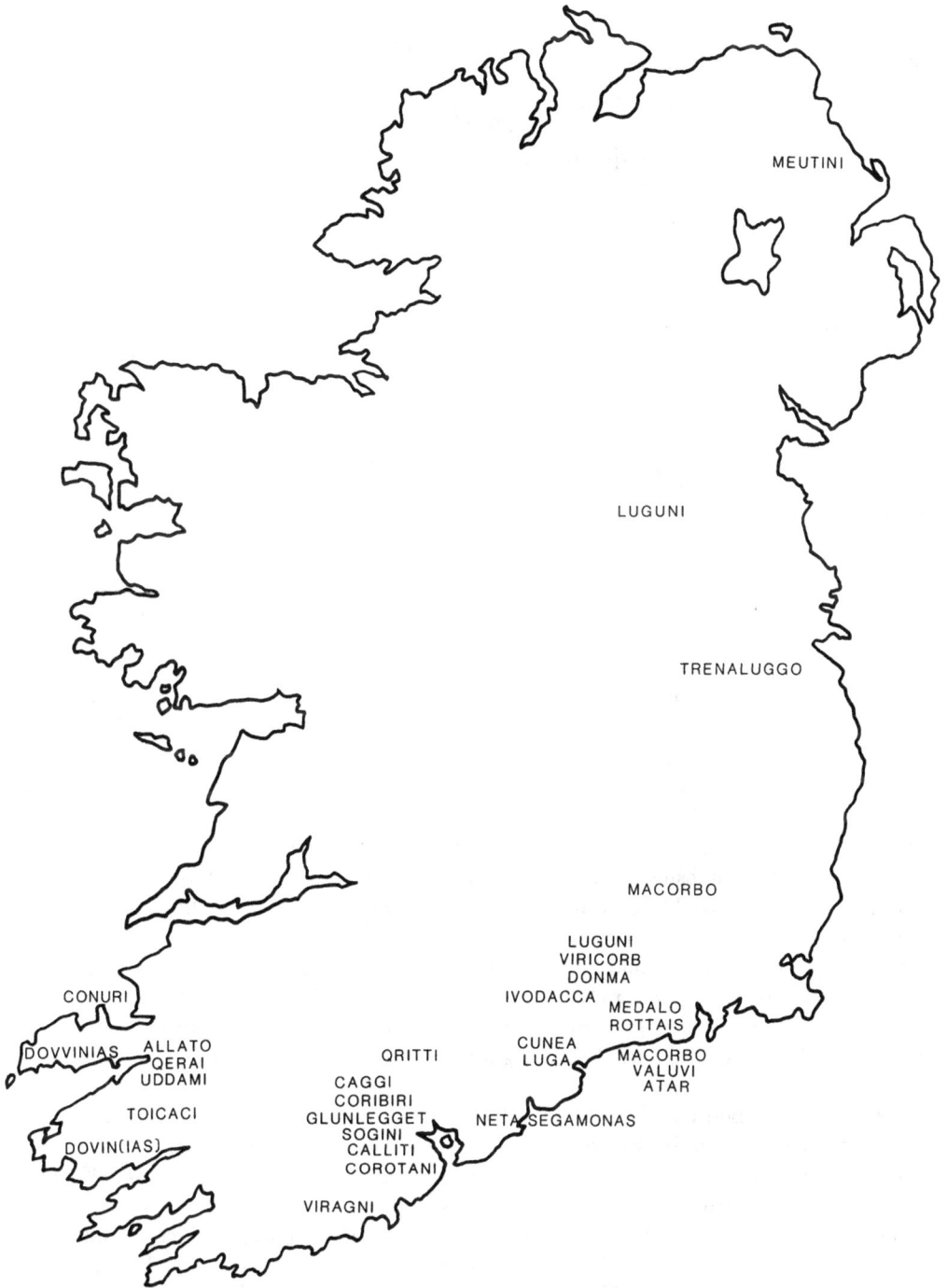

Figure 4:22   Map indicating distribution of tribal names on ogham inscriptions (Mac White 1961).

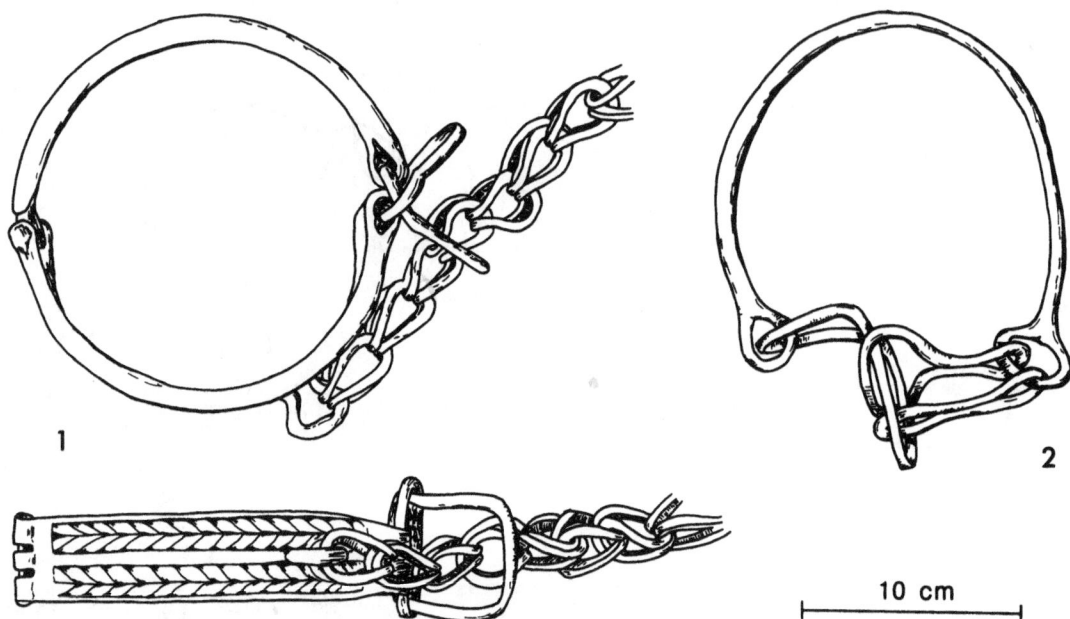

Figure 4:23 Iron chains from Lagore, Co. Meath (Hencken 1950).

due from the base client such as military service could be called on by the lord when he was asked to provide armed support. In this way, a king could command a considerable force if one was required. The *Uraicecht Bec* law tract states that the king of a *túath* was entitled to accommodation for 700 men (Mac Neill 1923), and this is the nominal number that a *túath* was able to raise.

Internal security for the king was rarely certain, and clientage alone was not sufficient. Kingroups related through fostering could be considered allies, but factions unsuccessful in getting their choice crowned would be waiting for an opportunity to overthrow the king and take the reins of power. In order to minimise risks, the king took hostages from other lineages. These were held by the king and would be put to death if rebellion occurred. The excavations at the royal site of Lagore produced a chain which was interpreted as a slave chain (Figure 4:23). Recent re-examination has suggested that it is very well made and might have been for hunting dogs (Scott 1978), but it could also be argued that it would have been appropriate for high status hostages.

The king was responsible for external relations, and might need a military force to support his claims. Most relationships were less violent, and the kings of neighbouring *túatha* usually arranged treaties so that legal disputes could be settled. The king could also himself be a free client of a more powerful king, thus ensuring greater protection.

The *túath* was a relatively small social, political and economic unit, and it could only support a limited court. Most of the king's entourage was made up of his free clients, hostages and his immediate family. When travelling about the *túath* he was entitled to accommodation and entertainment from clients, but the size of the retinue was controlled; only 12 for public business, and a mere 9 for private (Binchy 1941, 82). Given the importance of the agricultural regime, he was only allowed his judge and two free clients during 'the month of sowing' (Hughes 1972, 53). The king of the *túath*, though not involved personally in such low status activities, was not far removed from these operations and was directly dependent on their success. Cattle were needed to maintain and expand clientship relations; agricultural produce as a whole was required to maintain his court at a respectable level.

The *Críth Gablach* lists the people expected at a king's court (Byrne 1973, 33). Whilst schematic, it indicates the lifestyle that the king was expected to maintain mainly, it must be remembered, out of his personal income. Apart from the king and his wife, there were free clients, hostages, forfeited hostages in chains, a judge, mercenaries, a doorman, a steward of the base clients, envoys, guest companies, harpers, pipers, horn-players and jugglers. Perhaps there were up to 50 people present. It is perhaps surprising that few excavations have produced buildings that are large enough to hold a gathering as large as that suggested for the king of a *túath*; perhaps on festive occasions, conditions were rather cramped.

There are various archaeological traits that can be taken to represent high status sites, but not necessarily specifically royal ones. Given the limited and unsophisticated bureaucracy, the lack of centralised control of resources and the absence of elaborate paraphernalia of office, the recognition of actual royal sites on material culture evidence alone is impossible. Warner (1988) has suggested some general archaeological correlates for royal sites, but considers that in the final analysis documentary evidence may be necessary. However, those sites which were clearly high in the social and economic hierarchy can be suggested as at least potential royal sites. In occasional cases there is clear documentary evidence which supports the site identification, but often any association with royal families and events in the Annals is tentative. The archaeological evidence that is adduced for high status is the form of the site, presence of long distance trade goods, numerous high quality artefacts, and evidence of craft activities associated with the production of such goods.

The form of ring-fort sites has already been discussed as an indicator of high status. Long-occupied platform ring-forts and those with two or three concentric rings of banks and ditches are most likely to have been of greater than average importance. It would also seem that crannogs would belong to this higher status category, as would those stone-built forts with high quality masonry facings and interior terraces with steps.

Imported pottery from the eastern Mediterranean and the western seaboard of Europe has been considered by many to be high status, simply because of the long distance over which it had travelled. The same appears to be the case for glass vessels, which originated from the Continent and may have come via Britain. Whether it was the vessel itself, the original contents or merely the external relations represented by the goods which were so desirable is not of great concern here (for further discussion see Chapter 7). However, there is some evidence that the imported containers could themselves be viewed as of high status (Mytum 1986b).

The locally produced high quality goods that would be most likely to be associated with high status, possibly royal, sites are those containing gold and silver. The documentary sources, admittedly extremely schematic, associate the highest grades of both sexes with personal adornment in such materials. Unfortunately the value of such goods meant that they were rarely lost and not recovered on settlements, and most of the impressive items of this period have not been found in association with occupation sites.

The craft activities most usually identifiable archaeologically which can be ascribed to high status patronage, and therefore may have taken place at such sites, consist of the working of non-ferrous metals and glass. Evidence can be in the form of slags, moulds, crucibles, motif-pieces and unfinished goods (see Chapter 6).

Using the various criteria, several excavated sites can be identified as high status, and some of these may be royal; in the cases of Knowth, Clogher and Lagore there is strong documentary evidence to support the royal links, with less reliable attribution claimed for Garranes. Whilst many other sites, notably ring-forts, have produced evidence for one or two of the categories, most do not show sufficient range of evidence to place them at the high status level. There was a complex hierarchy of people and their habitations, but fortunes fluctuated rapidly over time. The archaeological record probably only identifies the homes of families that were consistently successful over a period of time.

The chronologically earliest site in this category is probably Garranes, where evidence in the form of imported A and B wares indicates that occupation was already under way in the sixth century. The presence of the later imported pottery, E ware of the eighth century, suggests a considerable length of occupation. Throughout this period there was craft activity including the working of bronze and glass; very large numbers of crucibles, both complete and in fragments, were found on the site. This is a trivallate ring-fort of impressive appearance with elaborate entrance (Figure 4:15), though no coherent internal buildings could be recognised. Another trivallate site in the same area is Ballycatteen, which was occupied only in the seventh and eighth centuries (Figure 4:24).

Some of the apparently high status ring-forts were only univallate, as is the case at Garryduff 1. The presence of a fine filigree gold bird ornament from period I emphasises the site's importance, and supports the evidence of the craft activities and E ware. It is also interesting to note the two small standing stones within the enclosure. O'Kelly (1962, 27) considers that they may have been put down as markers in the laying out of the site, but they may have been there before the ring-fort and could be associated with ritual activity. Standing stones are known to have been part of royal inauguration ceremonies, and ring-forts occur on pagan ritual sites to emphasise associations with the land and ancestors and thus reinforce the authority of the king. This can be seen at Tara, and excavated examples include Clogher and Knowth (see below).

Knowth is a case where the re-use of an earlier sacred site also could be combined with the impression of a platform ring-fort, as at Gransha (Lynn 1985). Unfortunately only interim reports are available for both these sites, but clearly the range of activities at both suggests patronage and long distance contacts over some period. The petty kings at Knowth, Cnogba in the Annals, were distantly related to those at Lagore and controlled north Brega. They ruled from the site from the eighth century onwards, but it was in the preceding century that the dynasty had been at its most powerful; the taking over of the earlier sacred site may have even been part of a not fully successful strategy to re-create their fading influence by association with a potent ancient centre; there was a resurgence, but not until the tenth century. Until the full publication of the site and its finds, however, it is not possible to discuss the artefactual assemblage and structural sequence associated with this royal site in the period up to 800.

An important site which has received considerable excavation but has yet to be published in full is Clogher, *Clochar*. Nevertheless, there are several valuable summaries available which allow some assessment of the site (Warner 1979a, 1988). A univallate ring-fort formed the main residence of the kings of the Uí Cremthainn, one of the tribes of Airgialla. The ring-fort had a counterscarp bank which respected an existing mound, and to the south was a ring-barrow.

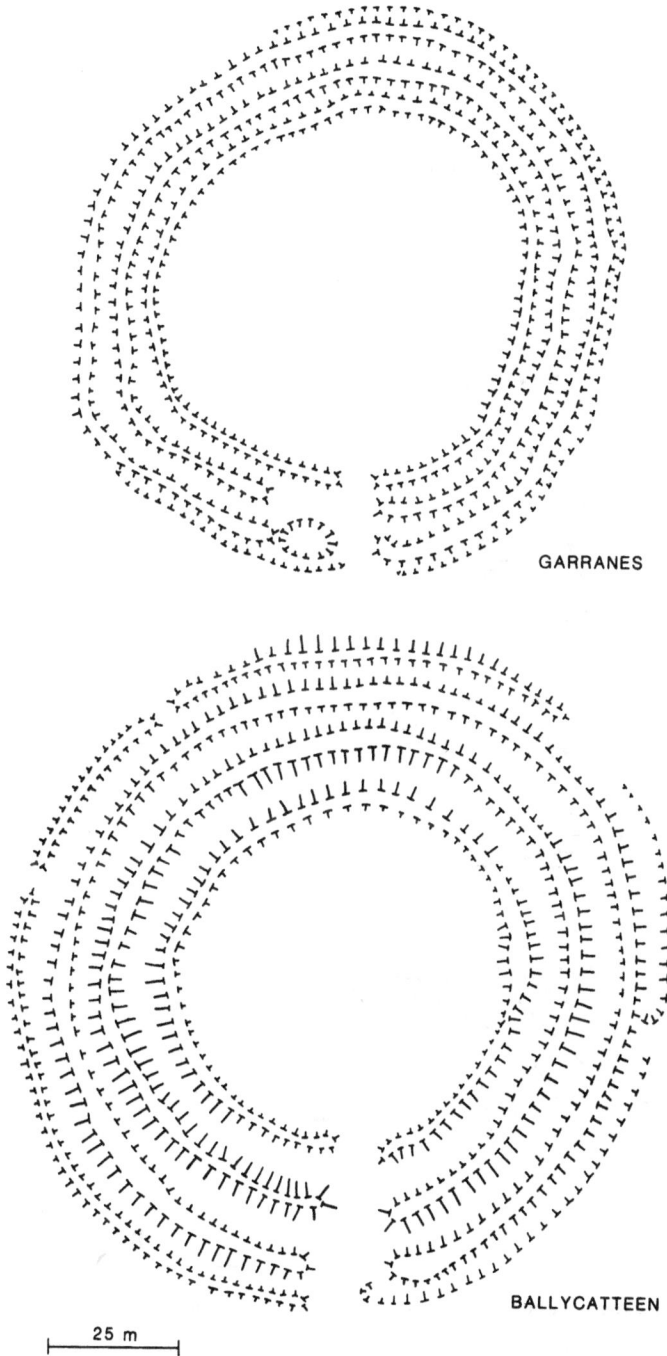

GARRANES

BALLYCATTEEN

25 m

Figure 4:24 Trivallate ring-forts in Co. Cork (Garranes, Ó Ríordáin 1942; Ballycatteen, Ó Ríordáin and Hartnett 1943).

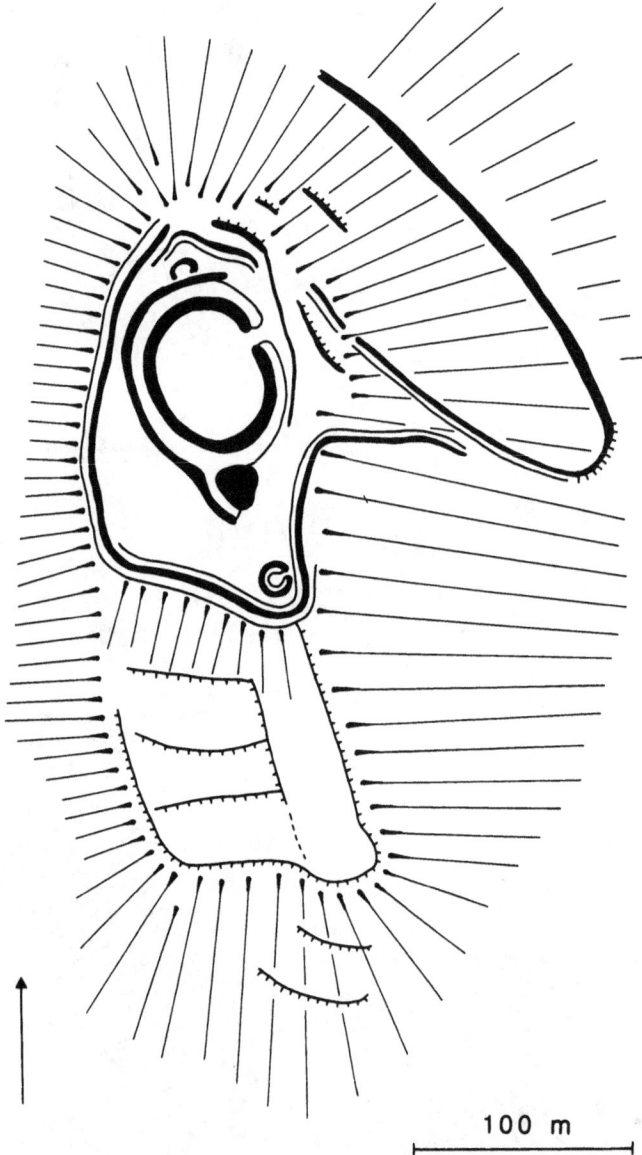

Figure 4:25   Plan of the Clogher hillfort, Co. Tyrone (Warner 1988).

The whole complex was set within a hillfort (Figure 4:25). The excavations have produced considerable evidence of metalworking, and the site has yielded a range of imported pottery. It was probably an important focus for regional trade and exchange, though this may have been also undertaken by the monastic site lying only a couple of hundred metres to the north. The association of royal site and nearby monastery or early church site is repeated frequently, suggesting on the one hand royal patronage of the church and on the other Christian support for the elite.

The crannogs of Ballinderry 2 and Lagore both have the advantage of good contexts for deposition and preservation. The relative richness of the sites is to a point due to these factors, but even so the evidence from both is sufficient to point to high status residences.

Ballinderry 2 was a small crannog which produced a fine range of bronze artefacts of which the large zoomorphic brooch was the most spectacular (Figure 4:20), and suggests high status occupants (Hencken 1942). This is further supported by the presence of E ware and craft activity including the working of non-ferrous metals, bone and leather. Though occupied for a relatively short time, perhaps under two hundred years centring on the eighth century, the crannog was of importance during that time (Figure 4:26).

The material from Lagore is of an order unparalleled at any other secular site in Ireland, and would on any grounds be considered a royal site (Figure 4:27). The documentary evidence (Price 1950) for this can now not be seriously open to doubt, though the value of the Annalistic evidence in dating structural phases can be largely discounted; the artefactual evidence now strongly supports a beginning for the occupation in the seventh or even early eighth century (Warner 1986b). Lagore, *Loch Gabair* in the Annals, is first mentioned in 785 when its king, Maeldúin mac Fergusa, died. It seems that the kings who used the site ruled south Brega, and sometimes are recorded under that title; no king at this time would in any case have spent a large part of his time at one central place. Most of the kings that are recorded seem to have been subordinate kings, rulers of a single *túath*, even though sometimes they were in alliance with very powerful figures on the regional and national political scene. The kings of Lagore were drawn from the Clann Chernaigh Sotail, part of the powerful southern Uí Neill. The kings of south Brega first appear in the Annals in 718, but their ancestors included Diarmait Ruanaid, high king *c.* 653 to 664. Another high king, Fogartach, died in 723, and his grandson, Maeldúin who died in 785, is the first named king of Lagore though of course the site could have been occupied earlier.

It may be that the changes in relative wealth during the occupation at Lagore could be related to the political fortunes of the kings of south Brega. Phase 1a on the site, with a small range of craft debris and a few fine artefacts including a gold filigree ornament, may represent a period when the family was developing its power base, and the phase 1b massive expansion of craft activity and the presence of imported pottery belong to that of the high kingship of Fogartach itself. It is in this phase also that there was the highest proportion of cattle eaten (Table 5:1), presumably largely received in the forms of render, tribute and booty. The subsequent phases, though still clearly high status, do not compare in the extent of craft activity or range of artefacts and ecofacts with that of 1b, and represent the relative decline into minor kingship of the site's occupants during the rest of the eighth, the ninth and little more than the first half of the tenth centuries. The king of south Brega may always have had more power, or at least influence, than many because it was within his *túath* that the great centre of Tara lay (see below). Bearing in mind the importance of military power and protection offered by a king, it is worthy of note that Lagore has produced a wide range of swords, spears and even

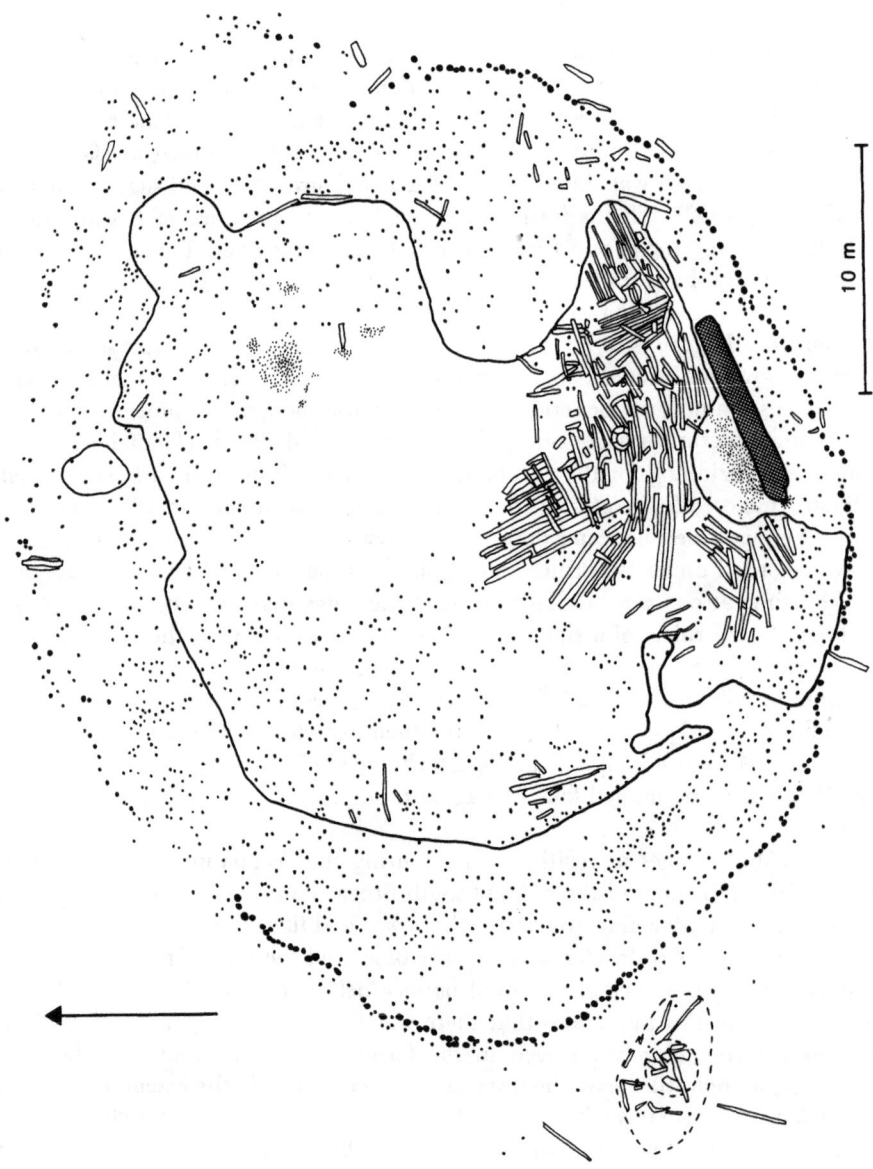

Figure 4:26 Ballinderry 2 crannog, Co. Offaly (Hencken 1942).

Figure 4:27 Lagore crannog, Co. Meath (Hencken 1950).

shield bosses (Figures 4:12, 7:6, 7:7) which suggests an interest in military protection over a long period of time.

It is also possible to examine *túatha* at a general level, looking at overall distributions of sites in a region, and the proportions of ring-forts of various sizes and extent of defining banks and ditches.

The County of Donegal, despite its limited areas of agriculturally productive land, contained several *túatha* (Cenél nEnnae, Cenél Luigdech and Cenél mBogaine) in the sixth century, though two further groups, the Cenél Conaill in the fertile valley of the river Foyle and the Cenél nEogaiin in Inishowen, already present in the sixth century, came to dominate the region (Lacy 1983). The latter also expanded to the south and east and became a major political force in the Uí Neill expansion.

The total number of known ring-forts, including destroyed examples, is 686 according to recent detailed survey work (Figure 4:28). The main concentrations are in the Foyle valley and in the south-west on pockets of high quality soils (Barrett 1980). There are also significant scatters along the north coast and in Inishowen. The varying density of forts does not indicate the relative political status of the local ruling elites.

The barony of Ikerrin, Co. Tipperary has a total of 206 ring-forts known (Figure 4:29; Stout 1984). During the Early Christian period this area was the approximate territory of the Éli Tuaiscirt (Ó Corráin 1972, 4). If this study area can be taken to represent the equivalent of an ancient political unit, the *túath*, then the 206 ring-forts within it would suggest an average of 34 sites in use each century. This would be adequate for the aristocracy, though if anything the number seems low. There are a few crannogs known from the low lying marsh and bog areas in the centre of the barony which might slightly increase the number of aristocratic sites. Moreover, in the south-east in particular, platform ring-forts are numerous, perhaps indicating frequent continuity of site occupation in that area.

If the size and number of surrounding banks and ditches might indicate relative ranking within the ring-forts and thereby the nobility, then it would be expected that there would be fewer larger sites, and more of these would be bivallate. This is the case in Ikerrin, where 18 of the 111 typical ring-forts were bivallate, and as size increases a higher percentage are bivallate (Table 4:3).

There are also indications that the platform ring-forts may represent the more successful aristocratic groups. There are no small ring-forts of this type, and 25 per cent are over 35 m in diameter. Furthermore, there seem to be two traditions of platform ring-fort represented which are geographically, and perhaps socially, distinct. In the far south-east of the study area are found many of the platform ring-forts, indeed more there than in the whole of the rest of the barony. Within this small and distinct area all the larger examples are found, though bivallation is less common. This may indicate a preference here for a larger size of platform rather than additional outer works. It has been suggested that platform ring-forts were built in this area because of the low lying nature of the ground (Stout 1984, 26). Whilst this may have been a factor in this type being popular in the area, it does not explain the use of platforms on only larger sites. There were 17 other ring-forts that were not of this form (and notably not one of them was bivallate) and so a simple environmental explanation cannot be sufficient. It may be that the choice between bivallation and raising a mound was a family tradition, or may have indicated subtleties of ranking within the nobility.

The Dingle peninsula is renowned for the large number of archaeological sites preserved there. The rocky terrain means that many ring-forts are of stone, and 55 of these cashels are

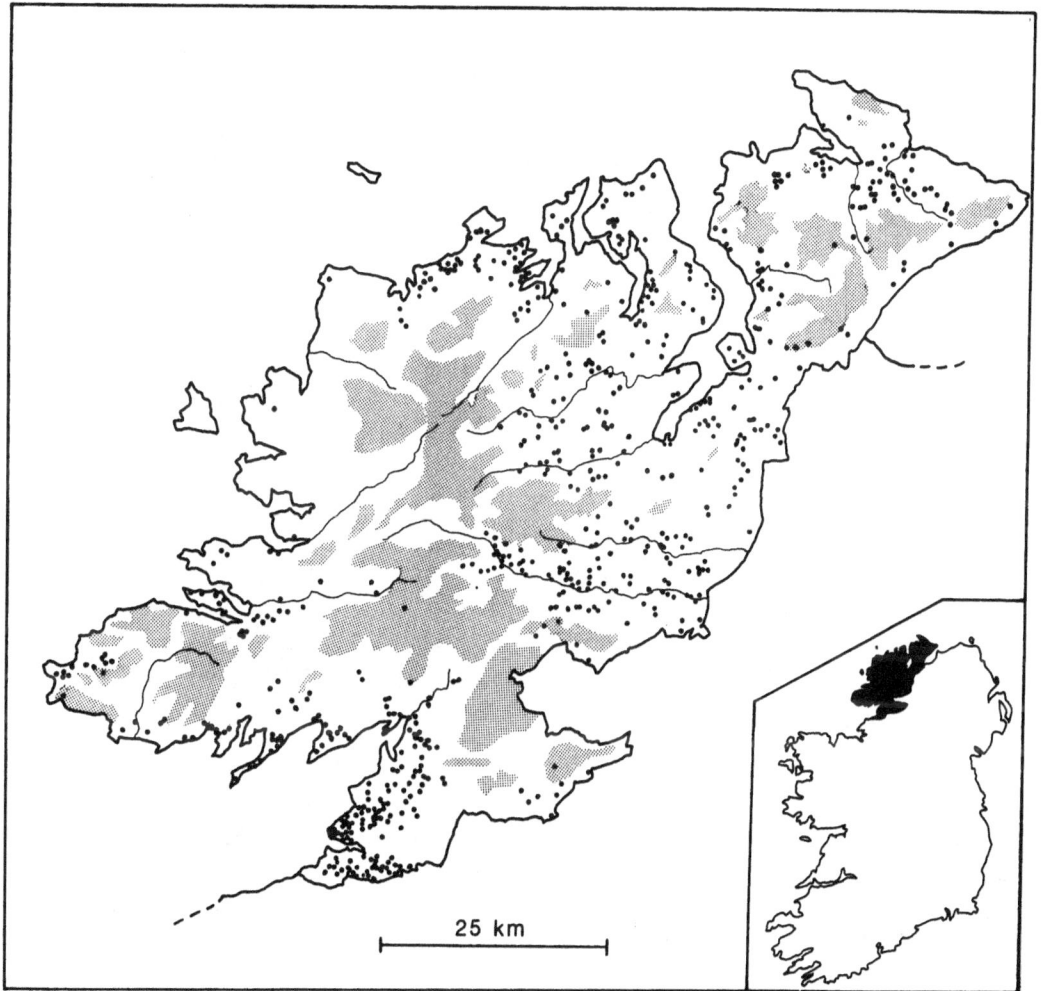

Figure 4:28 Distribution of known ring-forts (including those of stone and those known only from cropmarks) in Co. Donegal (Lacy 1983).

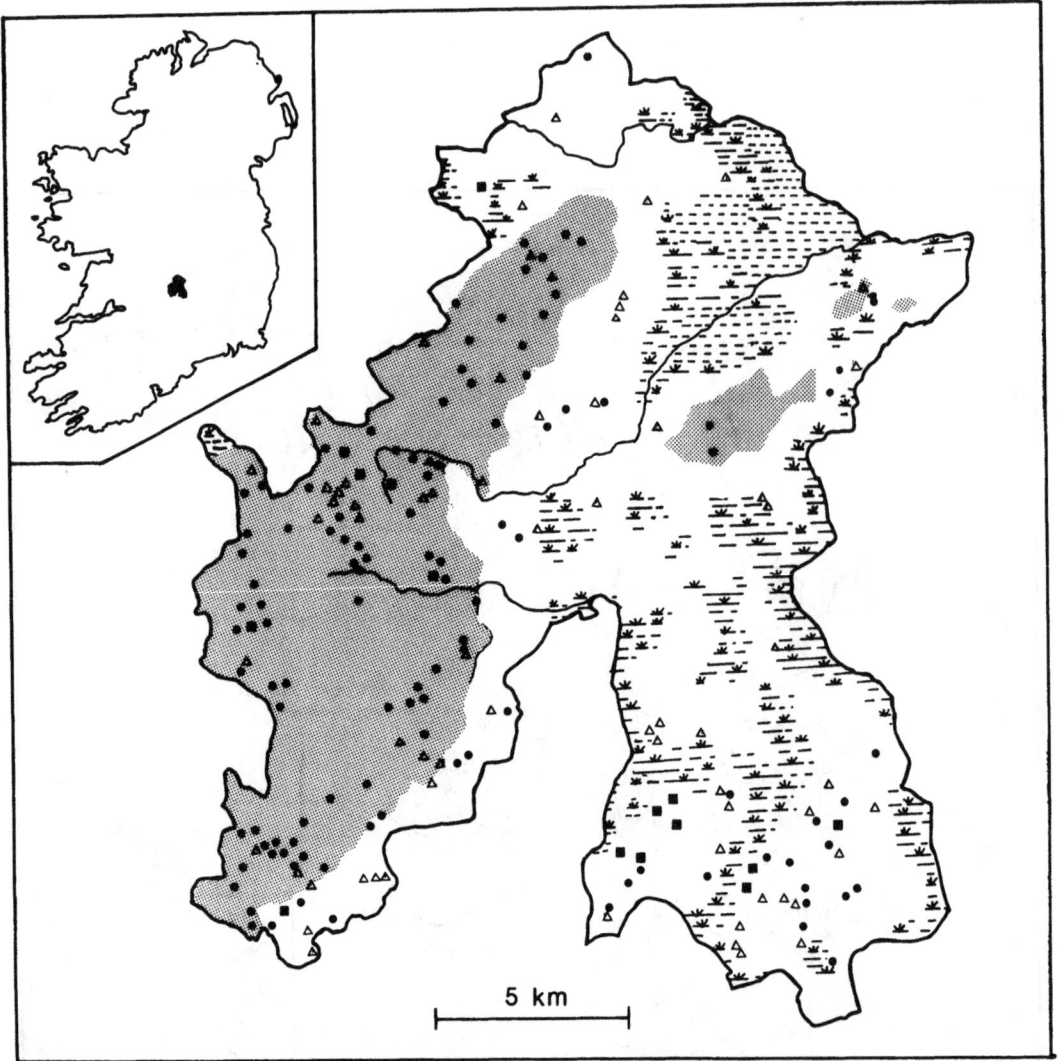

Figure 4:29 Distribution of known ring-forts in Ikerrin, Co. Tipperary. Platform ring-forts shown by squares, destroyed sites by open triangles (Stout 1984).

known in the Dingle, together with 400 of earth or earth and stone ring-forts (Figure 4:30; Cuppage 1986). The peninsula consisted of about half of the territory of the Corco Duibne, and so the number of sites seems excessive, since it would suggest a total for the whole *túath* of perhaps 900 ring-forts, 150 occupied at a time. How can this be explained if these sites were only the homes of the nobility?

It is possible that there were many aristocratic families in this region, but there could be other explanations. In some of the western and upland areas transhumance was an important economic strategy, and this involved duplication of sites. This might have been the case in the Dingle, as it was in the more consolidated upland areas such as the Burren, Co. Clare. Alternatively, it might suggest different strategies by sons on inheritance. In the more fertile

Table 4:3 Distribution, by size and number of banks, of ring-forts in study areas (derived from Stout 1984, Cuppage 1986)

Internal diameter	Normal ring-forts		Platform ring-forts		Total
	Univallate	Bivallate	Univallate	Bivallate	
Barony of Ikerrin – whole area					
<25 m	27	3	0	0	30
25–35 m	51	7	8	4	70
>35 m	15	8	3	1	27
Total	93	18	11	5	127
Barony of Ikerrin – south-east only					
<25 m	5	0	0	0	5
25–35 m	8	0	4	1	13
>35 m	4	0	3	1	8
Total	17	0	7	2	26

areas, concentration of settlement was possible, but this might not have been economically desirable in the more peripheral regions such as the Dingle. This may have encouraged creation of new, dispersed sites rather than continued use, or re-use, of old sites. This pressure would have particularly applied to the less successful nobility. It is therefore worth considering whether the potential royal sites also are numerous, or whether these seem to exist in more predictable numbers.

When the bivallate or platform ring-forts are examined in the Dingle, it is clear that they accommodated only a very small proportion of the population, which suggests that they may have been for those of royal or near-royal status (Table 4:4). Only 30 ring-forts were bivallate, with just one multivallate and no platform types. These 31 represent under 8 per cent of the total, and even if as many were located in the other part of the *túath* across the bay to the south, making a total of only around 60 very important sites, this would represent only 6 in any century. Multivallate cashels are rare in any part of Ireland (just one example was noted in the peninsula) but it may be that the more substantial univallate examples with particularly fine masonry and elaborate stepped ramparts and intramural passages and chambers were the equivalent of the multivallate ring-fort. Such forts are widely found in the west of Ireland, though are not very common. Doon Fort, Co. Donegal is an example of such a site (Figure

Table 4:4 Distribution by numbers of banks of earthen ring-forts and stone cashels in the Dingle peninsula (derived from Cuppage 1986)

	Ring-forts			Cashels		
	Univallate	Bivallate	Multivallate	Univallate	Bivallate	Multivallate
Extant	223	30	1	54	1	0
Destroyed	142	4	0	0	0	0
Total	365	34	1	54	1	0

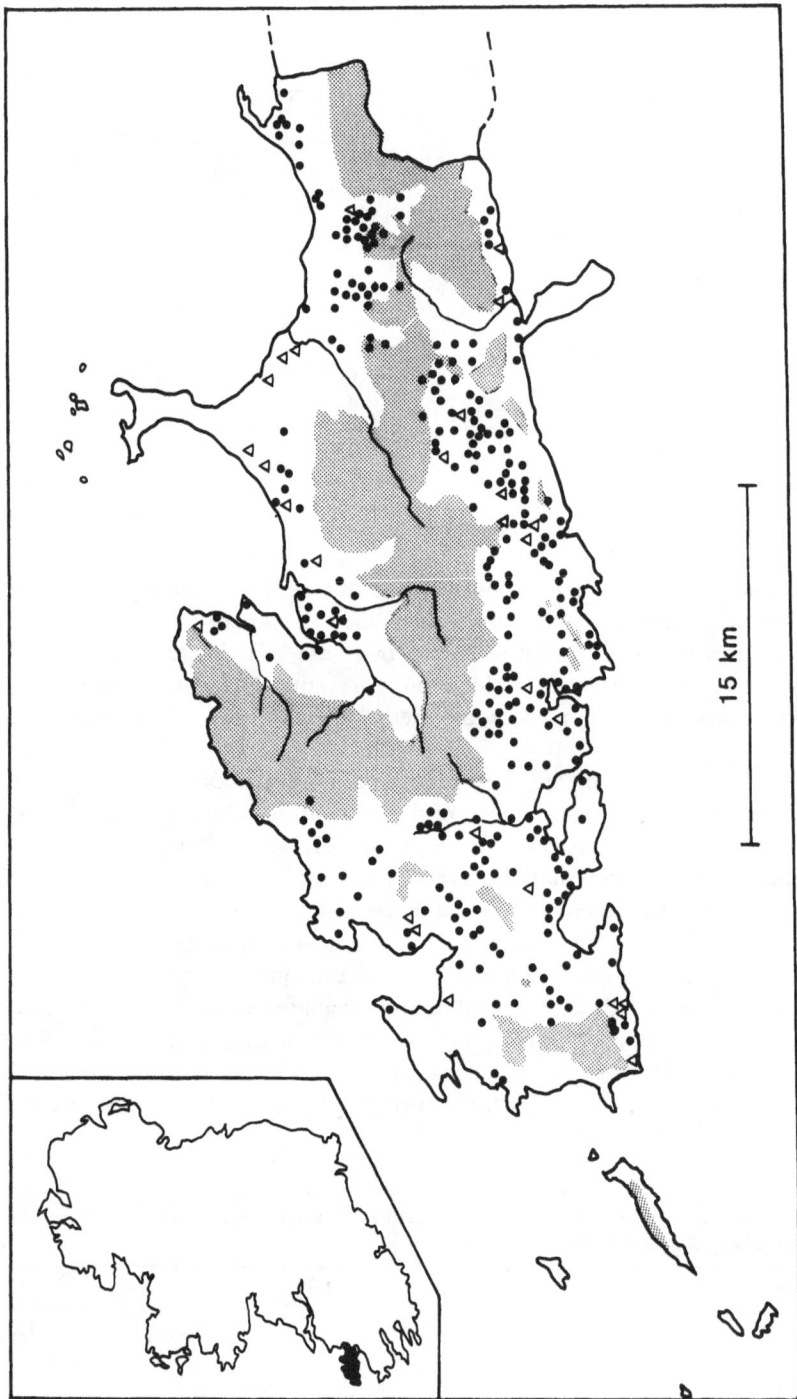

Figure 4.30 Distribution of known ring-forts (including those of stone and those known only from cropmarks) in the Dingle peninsula, Co. Kerry. Destroyed sites shown by open triangles (Cuppage 1986).

15 km

4:31). If the circuit wall of such stone forts stood to some height, the dominant effect would have been like that of a platform ring-fort.

Stone cashels may have been refurbished by successive generations of base clients but this would leave little archaeological trace. Even the partial reconstruction in the nineteenth century on some of the sites then taken into state care cannot now be differentiated from ancient work, and if rebuilds were originally carried out similarly, they would be undetectable. It is likely, therefore, that some elite residences were in the cashels, but the numbers cannot now be easily demonstrated.

The combined archaeological and historical evidence does not suggest that ring-forts could have been the homes of the substantial farmers. If that had been so, the individual *túatha* would have been severely limited in their choice of kings, since few nobles could have been supported by the freemen in each. There could have been only a handful of noble households in any *túath* if each had 10 or more clients who themselves lived in ring-forts. The barony of Ikerrin could have supported only 3 aristocratic households at a time, and even the densely distributed Dingle would have had only 7, and therefore perhaps 14 in total from the Corco Duibne. In such circumstances there would have been practically never any dispute over the kingship since most of the small number of potential candidates would have been excluded on the basis of age, let alone ability or inclination, yet the documentary sources constantly refer to struggle between a number of major contenders.

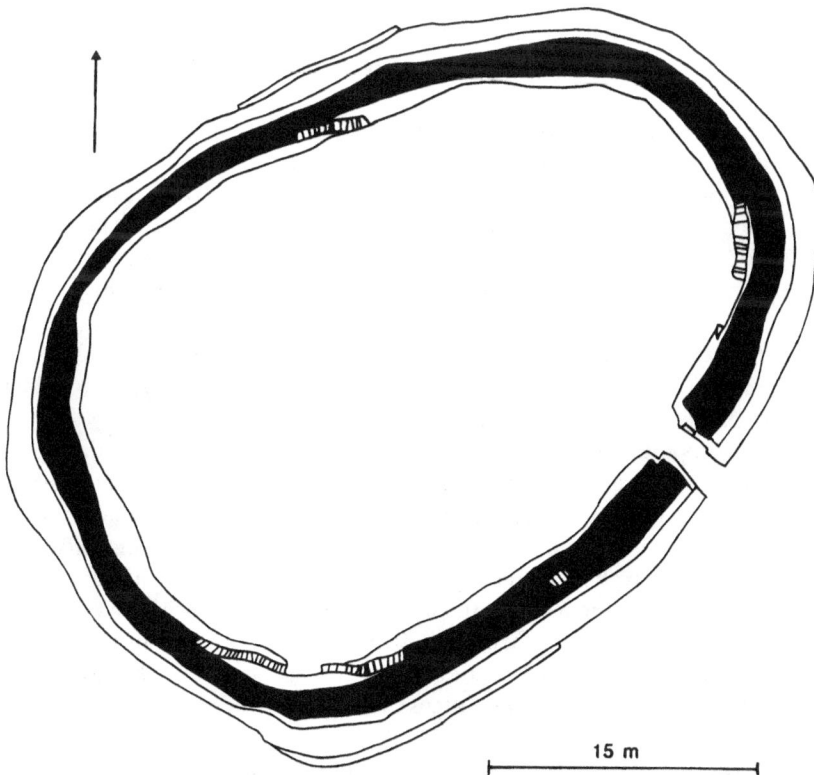

Figure 4:31   Stone ring-fort with stepped interior walls, 'Doon Fort', Drumboghill, Co. Donegal (Lacy 1983).

The association of ring-forts with the colonisation of previously marginal areas can be convincingly demonstrated. As the nobility were not directly involved with agriculture, it might be expected that the ring-fort distribution would not therefore reflect this agricultural revolution if such sites belonged to the elite. This, however, would be incorrect. Some land may have not been owned by any kin-group at the beginning of the Early Christian period, but certainly all land, however used, would have been quickly claimed. The legal tracts on fencing indicate that by the eighth century divisions were erected in forests, and not just in the intensely managed woodland (Ó Corráin 1983). Upland was used for communal grazing, and even though much of the terrain may have been under-used still in the sixth century, it would have had an owner, often a kin-group. Colonisation, therefore, could only have been effective with the support of the elite. This may have involved aristocratic support for the division of communal land among the *fine*, but could also have included the taking of land, if necessary by force. The sons of the aristocracy who would otherwise have had too small a share of the inheritance to be viable at the social level they desired could increase status by claiming marginal land and giving this out to base clients. Therefore, the ring-forts indicate the elite domination of the agricultural expansion. Clearly, some freemen could rise socially in this situation, as the *fer fothlai* grade indicates, but it is highly unlikely that the elite would miss the opportunity to gain economic and social advantage from agricultural expansion. Indeed, the density of ring-forts in the marginal land suggests that just as the whole population could expand with the increased production from the new areas, so the numbers of nobility also increased. Indeed, it has been argued that the idea of the ring-fort came as part of the economic expansion, and was an integral part of the material culture package that came with the ideological change associated with Christianity.

The documentary sources give some indications of how the successful elite manipulated the political situation to ensure that such expansion was possible. An aristocratic father was to a certain extent responsible for planning the future of his sons by ensuring strong political support. This could be achieved by fostering, by which children were sent away from home at the age of 7 until 17 for boys and 14 for girls (Mac Niocaill 1972, 59). The foster-parents were paid a fee for this, they treated the child as their own, and it played with their own younger children. Friendships and alliances built up in this way were as strong as kinship ties. Though freemen also carried out fostering, it had a special political value for the aristocracy. Careful placing of sons with different powerful lords could ensure backing for them when they were older, allowing them to be free clients of the influential higher aristocracy and royalty.

With powerful support, the elite could take 'sword land' from others with impunity. Up to some time in the seventh century, land could often be taken that was under-used and, whilst there may have been conflict, this was not often extensive. Once the landscape was full, however, successful aristocratic groups could only continue to establish their increasing offspring by taking away land already intensively exploited by weaker groups. This pressure for expansion at the expense of others was also supported by the freemen lower in the social scale since they in turn had sons who required new land to farm. The *ócaire* grade was created in an attempt to reduce some of the tensions in the freemen grades, as discussed above, but this could only act as a temporary palliative. Competition was intense at all levels of society, particularly with the pressure of population increase.

Competition can often lead to display and the use of material remains to legitimise and reinforce a position. The bivallate and platform ring-forts and the elaborate cashels may be examples of settlement forms which displayed prestige. But status belonged only in part to families; as individuals carried personalised rank, this was more effectively demonstrated through personal adornment.

The province

Although the king of a *túath*, the *rí benn*, was a figure of power within his territory, this did not make him secure. Whilst *túatha* arranged treaties amongst themselves, it was also necessary to have recourse to higher powers in the event of trouble. Just as a noble might become a free client of the king, so a king could arrange a contract (to be agreed by the *túath*) with an over-king, *rí buiden*. The name means 'king of bands' because the over-king had two or three other kings under him, and so was able to muster several bands each consisting of the 700 men each *túath* was expected to raise.

Only in crises such as war did the over-king have any direct powers over *túatha* other than the one for which he was himself king. After defeat in battle or an attack of plague, the over-king could call an assembly of several *túatha* to make arrangements that would prevent chaos resulting. This is an interesting case of an underlying, nascent power structure which was not normally imposed but could be activated in circumstances where the social and political systems were threatened with collapse. For most of the time, decisions could be made and resources found to carry them out at the level of the *túath*; only in emergencies did the over-king become a relevant decision-maker, able to overrule local interests for the wider benefit. It was probably also only in such obvious circumstances of difficulty that the kings of the *túatha* would accept the authority of the over-king.

An over-king might wish to align himself with the king of over-kings, *rí ruirech*. There are various other names for this grade, but these are the provincial kings which for the period to AD 800 can be considered the ultimate powers in Early Christian Ireland. Ireland was supposedly divided into five fifths: Munster, Leinster, Connaught, Mide and Ulster. The last of these had by the fifth century been reduced to a relatively minor unit in the extreme north-east, and as political fortunes changed, so did the composition and number of fifths. The generalised political map of Ireland at around AD 800 can be seen in Figure 4:32.

The provincial kings did not have more control over any individual *túath* than did an over-king. Examination of Figure 4:33 shows how the provincial king, A, was also over-king A of a group of *túatha*, one of which was his own *túath*. Only there was his rule direct. Elsewhere, control by the over-king was only through the sub-kings (E, I ,M) to the individual kings (B–O) by a system of personal relations. Whilst payments were expected in goods and services, interference in local affairs was difficult, and institutional change could not be enforced. The bureaucracy was extremely small, and information flow limited. Indeed, many subject groups were not of certain loyalty, either because of their support for rival potential over-kings, or because of their feelings of independence. The provincial king was therefore in charge of a geographically large area, but with a correspondingly diffuse control compared with the king of a *túath*.

In order to cement the personal relations between the various grades of kings, tribute was paid by the lesser kings and gifts received by them. Byrne (1973, 44) emphasises the similarity between this and clientship. There is a reliable source for the kingdom of Cashel, the *Frithfholaid* texts, which sets out the arrangements and wording very much in terms like those of free clientage. Payment to sub-kings was in *cumala* every seven years, just as a free client would have received, and it was called the same word, *rath*, as the fief in clientship. Although this text may

Figure 4:32   The major political powers in Ireland about AD 800 (Byrne 1973).

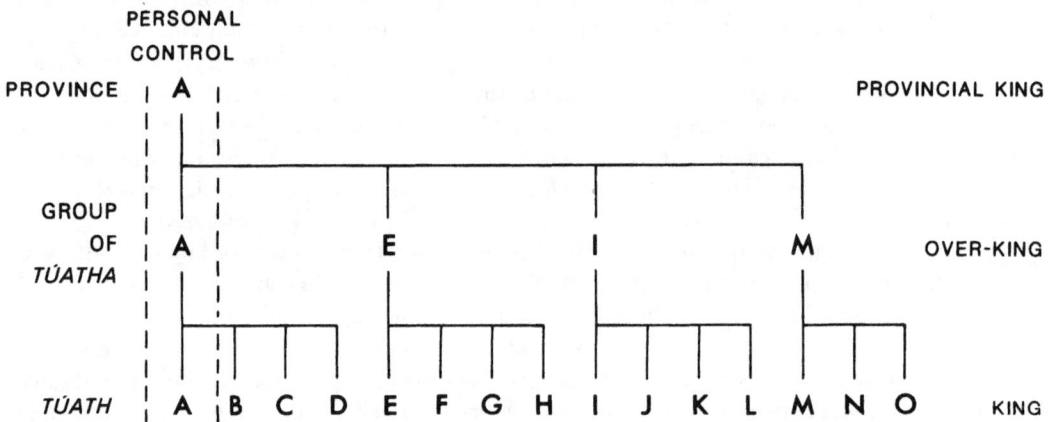

Figure 4:33   Diagram showing the relationships between over-kings and lesser kings.

be ninth century in date, it is likely that it represents the type of obligations that were expected in the sixth and seventh centuries.

The authority of the over-king was a personal one, and would have had little direct correlation with material remains that would be archaeologically recognisable. There were few major power centres that remained such for any length of time; there were central people rather than central places. Some of the royal centres discussed in the last section were, at times, the homes of over-kings at least but this was a temporary change in degree rather than kind. One of the few ways in which the provincial power base can be recognised archaeologically is by examination of the major inauguration sites which provided the setting for some at least of the political activity. The major centres, unlike the inauguration sites for the single *túatha*, generally provided a ritual focus and agglomeration of structures commensurate with the large numbers of people of all grades who would have gathered there.

According to literary sources, Rathcroghan was the most important ritual site within Connaught. The archaeological evidence, recently surveyed by Waddell (1983) and Herity (1983, 1984, 1987), would support this view, and indicates a ritual significance that stretched far back beyond the Early Christian period. The area of interest is spread over many hectares, with two foci at Carnfree and Rathcroghan, Rath Cruachan, itself (Figure 4:34). There are Bronze Age barrows and standing stones, with probably later banked avenues and large enclosures, followed in turn by Iron Age ring-barrows in a range of forms. The numerous ring-forts and an unusual density of church sites form a still later, Early Christian, layer of settlement on a multi-period palimpsest. However, it is highly likely that many of the early sites retained or regained importance at later dates, emphasising the continuing ritual and political significance of this area within Connaught as a whole.

The Rathcroghan mound is a massive Iron Age ring-barrow set on the highest point in the whole area, but within the Early Christian period could have served as an inauguration mound or even for a settlement, as at Knowth. Herity (1983, 130) considers that it is an unusually large ring-barrow, and points out that at both centres of ritual activity, there are no ring-forts, though in the areas nearby they are common. Ring-barrows are unusually numerous at Carnfree and Rathcroghan, and suggest a focus or ritual in the late Iron Age which continued on into the Early Christian period.

Herity (1987) identified 134 ring-forts within his study area. One of the most important is the now destroyed triple banked Cashelmanannan. An unusually large enclosure can be found at Rathra with two banks and three ditches, an unusual arrangement for a ring-fort. Inside is a low mound and circular embanked platform which could be of any date, but the presence of a souterrain certainly shows Early Christian activity and may support identification as a ring-fort. Herity (1987, 137) suggests that it may have had a ritual purpose. The same may have been the case with the univallate enclosure at Oweynagat which was recorded in 1864 by Samuel Ferguson but has since been largely destroyed. It contained burials and a souterrain in which, re-used as lintel stones, are two of the few ogham inscriptions from Connaught.

Of particular interest for the ritual and political importance of the Rathcroghan area is the location of several church sites, often set in patches of land not densely settled by ring-forts. This suggests that each had a surrounding estate given to it, and some at least may have been very early foundations. The church at Carns is located by a concentration of earlier ritual monuments at the Carnfree complex, and Kilnanooan is similarly positioned for the Rathcroghan group. Both may be associated with the Christianising of the royal inaugurations, and an assertion of the new faith over the pagan belief system. It is also significant that the early church site of

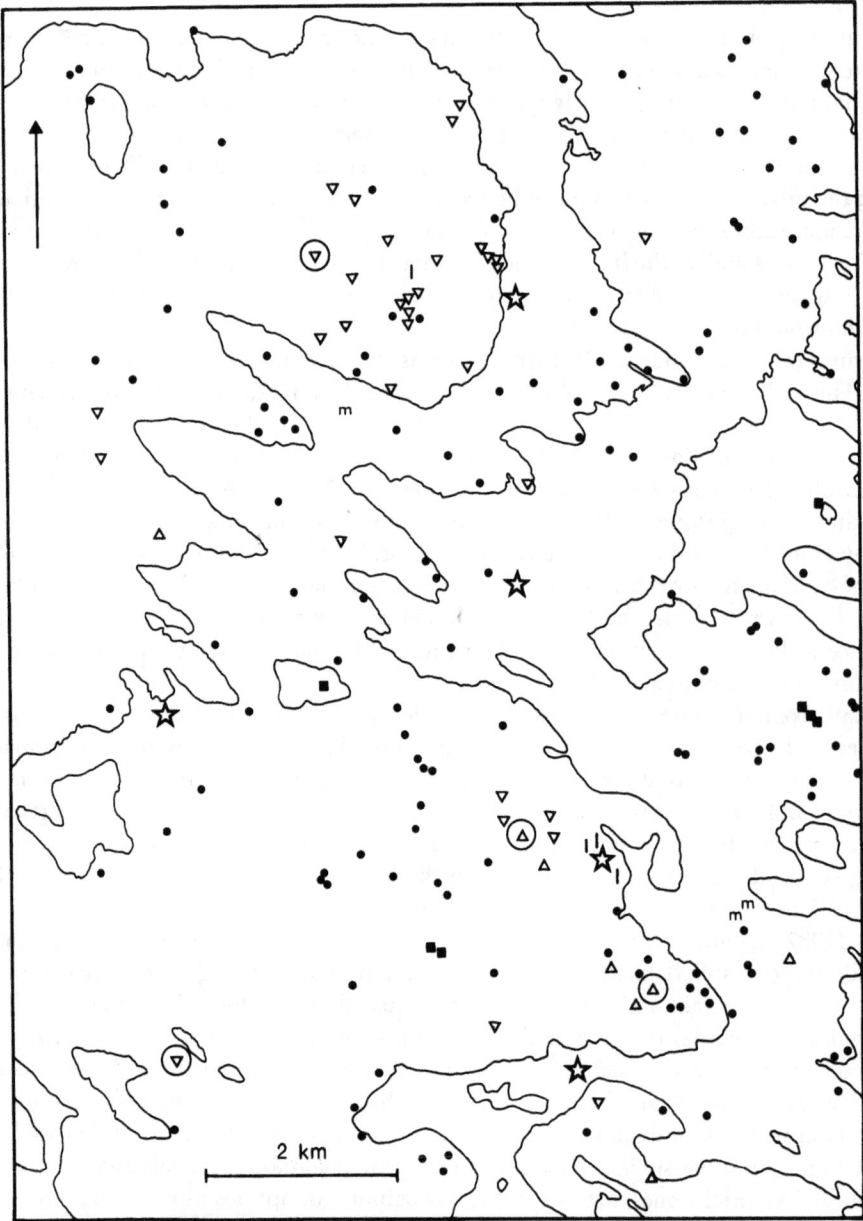

Figure 4:34   Map of the Rathcroghan area, Co. Roscommon (Herity 1987).

Baslick, *baslecc* from the Latin *basilica sanctorum*, lies only a short distance to the south-west of Rathcroghan. Doherty (1984a) considers that this church was the centre of fifth century evangelisation in Connaught. It did not remain a centre of ecclesiatical power because it belonged to the Ciarraige Aí who were during the seventh century dominated by the expanding Uí Briúin dynasty. Baslick was supposedly the burial site of the Uí Briúin king Ragallach in 649 (Byrne 1973, 246); the choice of burial there after assassination by the local population may in fact have been a symbol of Uí Briúin domination, a reality fully achieved during the following century.

The other major inauguration site for which extensive remains survive is that of Tara (Figure 4:35, Plate VI). Much has been written about this site from the beginnings of Irish archaeology (Petrie 1839, Macalister 1931) and attempts have been made to identify structures on the ground with those mentioned in texts of various dates, though not always with great success or accuracy (Byrne 1973, 56). Surprisingly little work has been carried out recently; Ó Riordáin (1954b) provides a brief outline, though his unexpected death curtailed the excavation programme which he had begun on the site. Recent aerial photography by Swan (1978) has augmented the sites known at Tara, some of which were known from the earlier descriptions and plans. Only two of the features are probably Early Christian in date, namely the conjoined ring-forts of Teach Cormaic (Cormac's House) and Forradh (Royal Seat). The trivallate enclosure, Rath na Seanadh (Rath of the Synods) seems to have been an earlier site and was not a ring-fort. It was partially excavated by Ó Riordáin (1954b, 25–6) and has a sequence stretching back to the late Iron Age, though no full report has appeared. Most of the structures at Tara are, as at Rathcroghan, earlier monuments which had accumulated over millennia of ceremony. Probably of earlier date is the Teach Miodhchuarta (Banquet Hall), in line with which the Rath of the Synods was placed. Iron Age ring-barrows still survive as earthworks on the slopes of the hill to the north-west, and many of the features identified by Swan (1978) may be others. Various standing stones are also Iron Age, the most important being the Lia Fáil of significance in the inauguration of kings (see below) and one with a carved figure. Presumably late Bronze Age in origin is the hillfort of Rath na Riogh which encloses the ring-fort pair on the summit of the hill; the smaller Rath Laoghaire immediately to the south and Rath Meave on the next hill may be of similar date. The earliest monument is Dumha na Ngiall (Mound of the Hostages) which has been excavated and shown to be a neolithic passage grave re-used in the Bronze Age (Herity 1974).

The title of king of Tara, and its associations with control or at least pre-eminence throughout Ireland, became significant in the ninth century as the Uí Neill dynasty became dominant though it is mentioned from the seventh century (Byrne 1973, 254). It is unclear when inauguration may have ceased, but it was probably before the ninth century. It is a case where the early church suppressed the rites and the site because of its deep-seated pagan associations, rather than taking them over as was the case at so many other ritual centres. Despite this discontinuity in ritual, a few descriptions survive from the eighth and ninth centuries that may contain some reliable information. They suggest that various stones played a part in the ritual, two opening up to let the king on his chariot pass, the Lia Fáil screeching against the axle to proclaim the rightful king. The phallic significance of standing stones in Celtic ritual has been widely demonstrated, and makes these comments credible. It may be that the Banquet Hall was used in the ceremony, though there are other routeways which focus on the complex which may have also played a part in ritual, though at what date is not known.

It can be seen that a range of features, often of prehistoric date, form part of the complexes

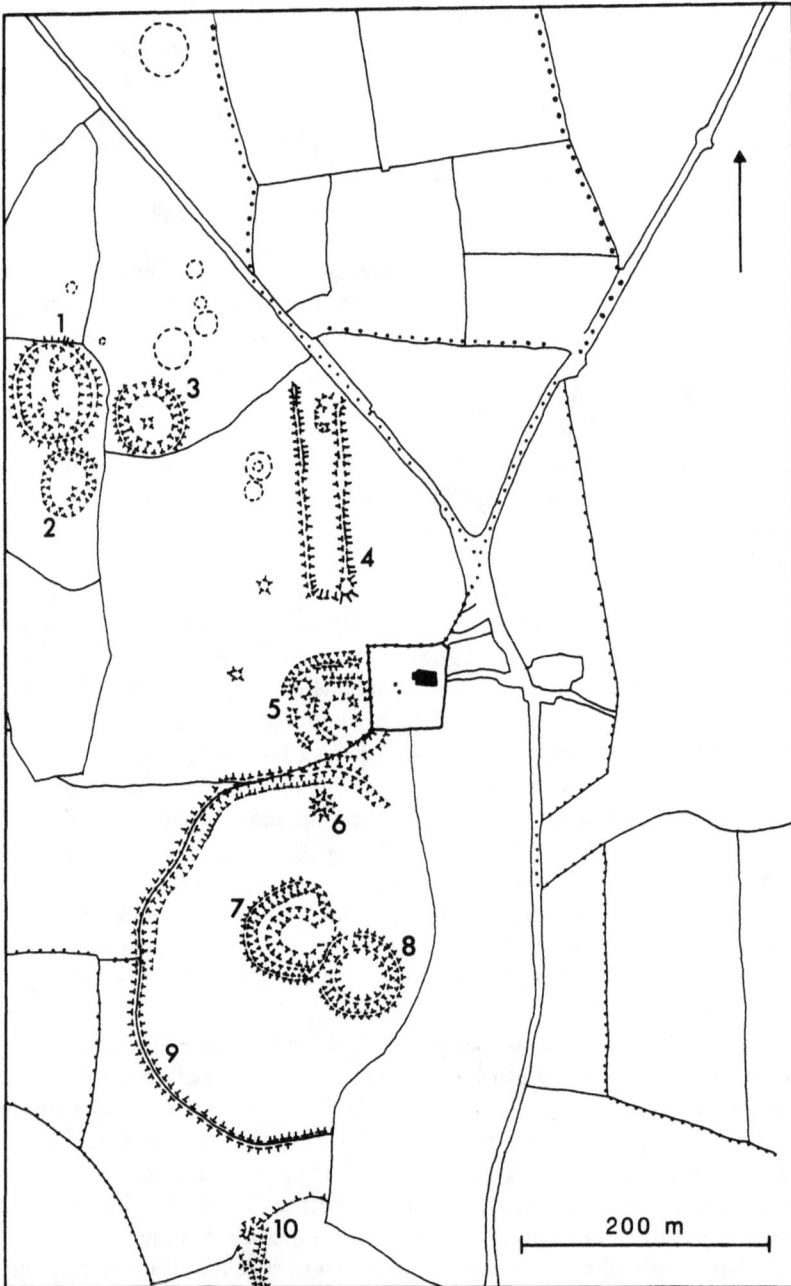

Figure 4:35 Map of complex of monuments at Tara, Co. Meath. **1** Claoin Fhearta (north); **2** Claoin Fhearta (south); **3** Rath Grainne; **4** Teach Moidhchuarta; **5** Rath na Seanaid; **6** Dumha na Ngaill; **7** Teach Cormaic; **8** Forradh; **9** Rath na Riogh; **10** Rath Laoghaire (Ó Ríordáin 1954b).

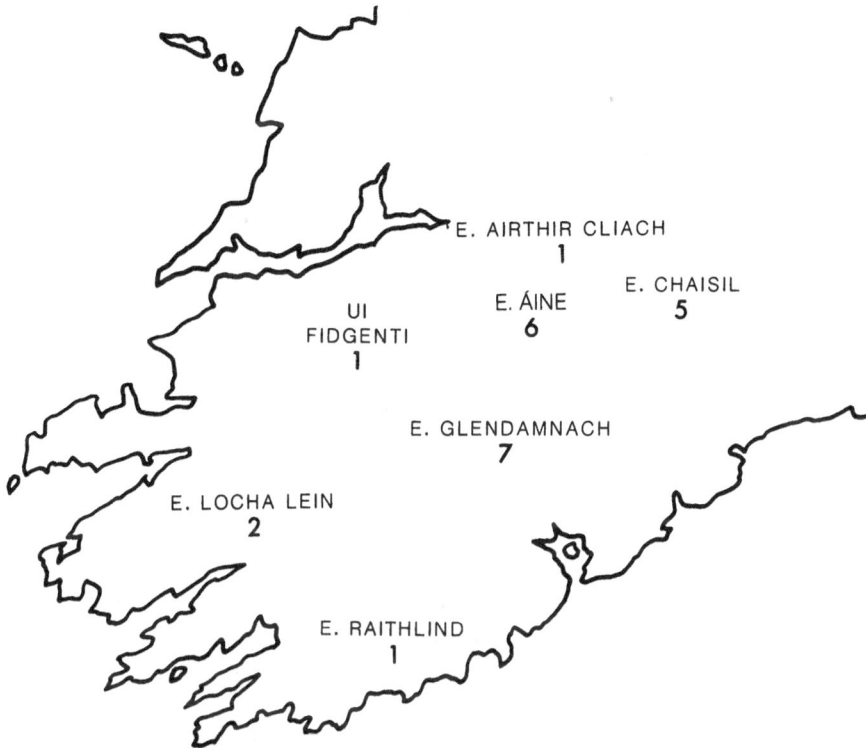

Figure 4:36 Map of Munster showing the dynasties from which the provincial kings had come, and the numbers from each (Byrne 1973).

used at provincial royal and inauguration sites. Not all are necessarily present at any one site, but several of the various elements – megalithic tombs, Bronze Age barrows, embanked linear earthworks, large enclosures (including hillforts) and ring-barrows – formed a focus to which was added the ring-fort. Nearby royal habitations or inauguration sites can be found early churches, indicating the Christianising of the power foci. The association of power with ancient forces has been widely demonstrated, and can be seen not only on other royal Irish sites such as Knowth and Anglo-Saxon palaces like Millfield (Bradley 1987), but also at major ecclesiastical centres such as Armagh near Emain Macha and Old Kilcullen near Dun Ailinne.

Although the picture of complex succession rules and fluid political alliances at any one moment is correct, it is possible over the long term to see a certain stability in the political power base at the provincial level. Cashel, a dramatic rock outcrop on the flat plain of Co. Tipperary, was associated with the kingship of the province of Munster (Plate V). Byrne (1973) has listed the provincial kings of Cashel, and if these are plotted out according to their dynastic base, it is clear where within Munster the real power lay (Figure 4:36). The Éoganacht dynasties of Glendamnach, Áine and Chaisil dominated the provincial power politics throughout the seventh and eighth centuries. The longer-term view therefore demonstrates a picture of greater stability than the short-term personal rivalries would indicate. Yet it is this structural level of analysis which allows the recognition of the important social trends through the period, and the beginnings of centralisation of power in a few highly successful dynasties.

5
The subsistence economy

Introduction

Many archaeological studies have recognised the subsistence economy as a vital element in past societies, and have considered that it is particularly suitable for archaeological analysis. Cunliffe (1978a) devoted considerable space to subsistence in his synthesis of the British Iron Age.

There have been criticisms of the use of the term subsistence, since no society operates with merely a subsistence economy; all produce a surplus which is manipulated economically and socially. However, the term subsistence economy is used here in the same way that Cunliffe and many others have used it, meaning the primary production and processing of the agricultural economy. Much of this was necessary for basic subsistence, and as such is part of the fundamental underpinning of Early Christian Ireland, but it is also true that there was always some form of surplus which was used for social ends. As shall be seen, the difference between subsistence base and a surplus for social use was not necessarily clearly recognised, since social pressures were so strong; a surplus above the basic needs for physical survival was not a desirable luxury but essential to maintain position in society. Failure to maintain social position could be just as physically dangerous as lack of foodstuffs; therefore surplus to fulfil social obligations above basic subsistence needs was required, and this should be considered as part of the subsistence economy.

The use of systems analysis on subsistence strategies has a long history in archaeology. Many studies have taken an ecological stance and have been related to hunter-gatherer societies (Schrire 1972, D. H. Thomas 1972) or simple agriculturalists still reliant on wild foods for part of the year (Ford 1977). Often, however, the lack of archaeological, or historical, data concerning economic priorities and social organisation has forced scholars to take a stance that assumes an extremely simple, maximising position for past societies. From numerous ethnographic studies, it is clear that such assumptions cannot be made, and for this reason many archaeologists are dismissive of the ecological approach, and the value of a systemic analysis of the subsistence economy to explain stability and change (Hodder 1986).

Where there are historical sources to provide some sort of social framework and recognised economic priorities, then detailed analysis on a much firmer basis is possible. An ecological study of Iron Age Norway used archaeological and topographical data from the Valldalen valley combined with historical sources from Iceland (Odner 1972). This model has some extremely interesting features, several of which can be paralleled in Early Christian Irish society and economy. As data becomes available it should be possible to undertake simulation studies to see how the subsistence economy operated, and what level of surplus production could have been achieved (Cooter 1984).

In the case of Early Christian Ireland we are fortunate in having a relatively large number of contemporary documents of several types which can give some clues as to the priorities and aims of those involved in the subsistence economy. Within the primarily rural and agrarian society of Ireland there can be no doubt of its significance, providing a link between the environment and the society which operated within it.

Studies of the subsistence economy in Early Christian Ireland have not been numerous, and often they cover very specific aspects; these are referred to in detail under various headings throughout the chapter. The first synthesis of agriculture was that of Duignan (1944), and a more generalised outline was later provided by de Paor and de Paor (1958). In recent years, more historical syntheses have appeared, notably Ó Corráin (1972). The complexity of the society and economy is consistently emphasised through all these studies, and historical and archaeological data are combined. In this regard this chapter continues the tradition already set, but within a defined theoretical position, using systems analysis within a processualist framework.

The environment

Subsistence strategies are dependent on cultural factors, which are of especial interest to the archaeologist, but also on the physical framework within which human groups had to operate. It is therefore necessary to examine the climate and physical geography as the background to the cultural changes that took place. The choices made both were affected by the environment and in turn affected it. Many early systemic approaches which sought to understand cultural change invoked climatic change as the prime mover (Hill 1977). There is no evidence to suggest that climatic change was a major factor in the initiation of developments in Early Christian Ireland, although it may have had an impact in the choices open to some, especially in marginal areas.

Ireland is an island with a range of landforms that provide a rich mosaic of environmental zones. Before the Early Christian period, these had already been significantly modified by man (Aalen 1978), and this process continued during the first millennium AD. Despite this human interference, however, the constraints of geology, topography and climate provided a framework that can be readily identified today, and which provided some regional diversity in subsistence strategies.

Climate

The location of Ireland at the western edge of Europe has given it a characteristically mild yet wet climate. It seems that the climate may have been slightly colder than it is at present, but bathed in the relatively warm North Atlantic Drift, and surrounded by water, Ireland has always experienced limited extremes of heat and cold (HMSO 1952). This has very important implications for the agricultural regime. Frost occurs frequently during the winter in central and eastern Ireland, but is rare in the west. Spring starts earliest in the south-west, and takes three weeks to spread to the north-east. Of course, topography plays a major part in temperatures, but even so these general trends can be recognised. The beginning of the grass growth is a crucial factor in the pastoral economy, and parts of western Ireland clearly had a much longer growing season than parts of the east and north. The average January sea-level temperatures for most coastal counties from Mayo to Wexford do not fall below 42°F, the critical temperature for plant growth. Clearly the presence of long autumns where grazing can take place helps to explain the limited provision for fodder in Early Christian Ireland, though this clearly led to difficulties in cases where too many animals were kept for the winter grass supplies available.

Precipitation is heavy over much of Ireland, and is combined with low evaporation rates (Orme 1970). The upland areas are particularly wet, with over 80 inches per year in some parts of the west, but even the lowlands generally receive 30–50 inches each year. At Lough Neagh rainfall exceeds evaporation even in the four summer months. Because of the high temperatures throughout the year, there is relatively little snow. Only inland parts of the north-east have over 17 days per year when snow falls; much of the south-west has fewer than 5. In most cases this does not settle and causes problems for animals, but of course there are exceptions, and deep snow and drifts can prevent grazing for considerable lengths of time. These disastrous winters are noted in the Annals, but it may be salutary to realise that several of these sources are northern, and may reflect severe and even catastrophic conditions in perhaps far less than a quarter of the island. Snow clearly could be a problem, but a rare one. In general, the Irish climate allowed a long grass growing season, and so grazing was possible through the autumn, and it was only in the New Year that the real effects of winter were felt. The coming of spring was clearly a much-anticipated event, as can be told from the numerous poems eulogising spring (Jackson 1951). February and March must have been the hardest months to endure. If there was any worsening of the climate it would have been in the lateness of the spring and any consequent loss of over-wintered animals would have been the most significant problem which needed to be faced.

Whilst the climate may have been ideal for the growth of grass, there were consequent difficulties in the production of other crops, notably cereals. The rainfall and temperatures might promote crop growth, but ripening is a major difficulty with the frequently overcast skies. As May and June are usually the sunniest months, this creates a problem for the ripening of cereals in the late summer. Many crops must have been harvested green, and the more resilient oats and barley would have been more reliable than the socially more desirable wheat crops. It is likely that there were considerable regional differences in cereal variety production over the island, with most wheat in the south-east, and greater yields of barley and oats in the north and west. How important specialisation may have been, and whether this promoted any internal exchange of cereals, it is not as yet possible to say.

Topography and soils

Most areas of Ireland are covered by glacial deposits that have, combined with the climate, influenced the types of soils that have developed. This has produced a complex mosaic of soil types that afford great variation in potential for both pastoral and arable production. These soils have been mapped in detail for several parts of the country (including Finch and Ryan 1966, Finch 1971), and some of these areas have been analysed by archaeologists to recognise patterns of land use in the Early Christian period (Proudfoot 1951; Fahy 1969; Barrett 1972, 1980). It is clear that soils played a crucial role in the diverse development of the landscape, and this can be examined archaeologically.

The most productive soils in Ireland are the brown earths, having good drainage characteristics and a well developed structure. They can be relatively poor in nutrients, but manuring can remedy this. Brown podzolics are similar in their ranges of use, but require greater management to ensure high productivity. Grey-brown podzolics are also general purpose soils, though some are heavier and better suited to pasture. Rendzina soils are free-draining and occur in parts of western Ireland where this is a particularly favourable feature given the high rainfall. They are important because of their wide use range. Modified grey-brown podzolics are also well drained, and frequently used for arable. In some cases, drainage can be too easy and drought conditions arise. Many poorly drained areas have developed gley soils that are heavy in texture yet weak in structure. As a result, they are susceptible to over-grazing and need careful management to prevent this and produce the high grass yield of which they are capable. Podzols are poor soils with drainage problems and are only of use for extensive grazing; a similar use is all that can be expected from the various skeletal soils.

The variation in land use potential of the soils in Ireland can provide a background framework on which to set the settlement and consequent land use patterns. Whilst the social system outlined in Chapter 4 constrained selective economic activity, it did not prevent it. Within the social system there was opportunity and incentive to maximise production, and that had to be achieved within the given local topographic constraints. This led to various strategies being employed which archaeology is best placed to study, though it is first necessary to examine how land was defined and held in Early Christian Ireland, as this tenurial system was the one through which all agricultural strategies had to be enacted.

Land

From the arrangement of settlements and field systems in the landscape it is possible for the archaeologist to infer something of landholding and tenurial arrangements, but in the case of Early Christian Ireland there is a large body of historical material which can provide a more detailed outline. This documentary evidence is crucial for understanding one of the main cultural changes that took place during the period AD 500–800.

There is no doubt that the Irish were aware of varying land qualities and potential, within the limits of their technology. The *Tír Cumaile* lists various qualities of land: uncultivable and cultivable, the latter being subdivided into first-class, upland or cultivable by labour (Mac Niocaill 1971). Other features including woodland, water, access by cattle track or road, or a mill site all enhanced its value. The most valuable land was that which could be used for high quality pasture and tillage. Therefore the relative value of land was much the same as would be the case today, although the various classes of soils may have been differently rated than by modern criteria. For example, soils with naturally high nutrients were more valued before chemical fertilisers, and soils with rocky outcrops that would now prevent mechanised production were more highly valued when plough teams could more easily avoid these. The evidence from the documentation means that it is possible for site distributions and finds from excavations to be used in elucidating the exploitation of the landscape in general terms, and to recognise changes through time.

With the advent of Christianity and the development of the church as a force in Irish society, the concept of personal inheritable property, rather than a share of kin-land, began to take hold (see Chapter 3). It was not an immediate change, and took place gradually and at different rates in different parts of the country. Not until later in the sixth century does it appear that the church was becoming a recognisable major force, and was being accommodated into the fabric of society. By this time, though adapting to fit into the indigenous social system, the church was disseminating a number of concepts which had a profound effect on ideology, as described in Chapter 2. The most important of these were the concept of the individual (individual salvation is stressed in Christianity, though there still remained some vestigial concept of kin responsibility), and that of individual rights. Combined with this was the presence for the first time in Irish society of an institution. The main difference that this brought was that whatever was given to the institution remained in its possession forever. Unlike an individual kin member, the church never died, and land given to it could not be redistributed. The effect of this was that the church constantly absorbed resources and grew, rather than running through cycles of birth, acquisition and death followed by redistribution.

The concept of permanent ownership, to be passed on directly to one or more heirs in the secular context, was a change brought about indirectly by the church. As ecclesiastical institutions were seen to grow in wealth and power by acquisition, the secular authorities recognised the benefits of such a system, and began to increase their own control over their assets. The development of private ownership was the result of increased control, formalising this tenurially. This was a crucial development that had far-reaching implications, and it is necessary to spend some time examining the process of change in land-owning patterns through time. Fortunately, several scholars have studied this problem, notably Mac Neill (1923), Binchy (1971), Charles-Edwards (1972a, 1972b) and Ó Corráin (1972). The summary below is dependent on their work; the general trend to greater ownership of land has been recognised, but as yet some of the further implications of this have not been realised.

The shift to an emphasis on personal property in the tenurial pattern can be clearly seen in the changes in the structure of common farming outlined by Charles-Edwards (1972a, 61–4). This shift can be seen in a number of tracts; some such as *Bechbretha* and *Coibnes Uisci Thairidne* are basically early, whilst *Comingaire* and *Bretha Comaithchesa* are late, though containing many early features.

In the early phase, perhaps at the beginning of the seventh century, farming in common was still largely shared between members of the *derbfine* old enough to be entitled to their equal share of the communal property, *fintiu*. This group was called the *comaithches*, and it organised not only joint ploughing but also pasturage. Open common land was grazed during the summer, and belonged to the whole *túath*, the wider social and political unit under the control of a king. Other pasture was enclosed, and consisted of that for summer use, *athlumpaire*, *athbronnad*, and that important element reserved for winter grazing, *etham díguin*. The arable seems to have been open, with various scattered strips owned by each member of the *comaithches*, and it must have been grazed jointly after harvest.

Trespass was a legal infringement in all periods, but was treated differently in each. At an early date, animal trespass was the fault of the herdsman responsible for the joint herd on unenclosed land. The man responsible had to pay compensation in sacks of grain, unless the transgression was across the boundary of the *fintiu*, into the land of another *derbfine*. Then, the penalty was more severe and involved compensatory seizure of that man's pasture for a year. Clearly, penalties within the shared property were quite different from those outside.

In the later phase, perhaps by the eighth century according to Hughes (1972, 51), the *gelfine* had become the basis of inheritance. Land was now assumed to be enclosed and individually owned, and co-operation was not necessarily between kinsmen. The partnership was now called *comingaire*, and each man contributed an area of pasture that belonged to him. That enclosure must have been far more extensive, and included more than just winter pasture, is clear from references to piglets and lambs. There also seems to have been a change in the payment of fines, making them more substantial. There was now a fine in the form of sacks of grain, as well as temporary confiscation of grazing land. Trespass beyond the land used by the *comingaire* was now a much more serious offence.

The dating of the changes in ownership is not easy, and they must have been gradual. Probably relatively little was privately owned by the early seventh century, but from then on the pace of acquisition accelerated. Ó Corráin (1972, 49) notes that many early monasteries incorporate the placename element *dísert*, meaning waste land, thus suggesting their location on peripheral, unused land and also, by inference, the presence of considerable areas of such land. He also suggests that *cluain* may mean pasture won from the forest, implying further expansion. The exploitation of waste and forest in the seventh and eighth centuries suggests that it was possible to reclaim and so own land previously not held by any kin-group, and it may have been this peripheral land that was first owned by individuals. This would be most feasible since it would not involve direct competition with those having vested interests in the kin-group, and also would be based on emulation of the monasteries.

The distribution of ring-forts suggests that they may be associated with colonisation; it has already been pointed out in Chapter 2 that the enclosed nature of the settlement implies a concept of ownership and territoriality, and their locations within the landscape can be interpreted as part of a programme of entrepreneurial expansion brought about by the personal benefits of investment in the immediately less tractable lands. When these were held as marginal common land, incentives for improvement were not present; as some of these lands became available for personal ownership, it was possible for such investment to allow larger agricultural surplus and the increased social status that went with this.

Ring-forts are distributed widely in Ireland, and in some areas a surprising number can be found on relatively heavy soils (Proudfoot 1961). This can be seen clearly in eastern Co. Limerick (Figure 5:1). Around Lough Gur, many areas of lighter soils had long been settled, such as around Lough Gur itself where neolithic settlements and ritual monuments have been excavated (Ó Ríordáin 1951, 1954a). Early Christian settlement is relatively dense here, as one would expect, with a crannog in the margins of the Lough, several ring-forts including Carraig Aille 1 and 2, and open settlements like The Spectacles. To the west, in the rolling country leading down to the Maigue river, much of the land was heavier and needed some drainage. This land was probably left as managed woodland or waste whilst the lighter and more easily cultivated, though less fertile, soils were owned by the kin-group and were used as arable and enclosed winter pasture. The heavier soils have numerous ring-forts sited on them, and these probably reflect a major phase of colonisation from the seventh century onwards. Once cleared, the heavy soils would have required some further investment in drainage but would have been ideal summer pasture, with high natural nutrient levels and with drainage the problems of maintaining soil structure could have often been alleviated (Finch and Ryan 1966, 119).

The location of monasteries at peripheral locations has been noted by many scholars (Ó Riain 1972, Herity 1984), and recent discussion has focused on the range of reasons for this (Mytum 1982). From the subsistence viewpoint, marginal land was often under-utilised in the first few

EAST LIMERICK soil suitability classes and sites

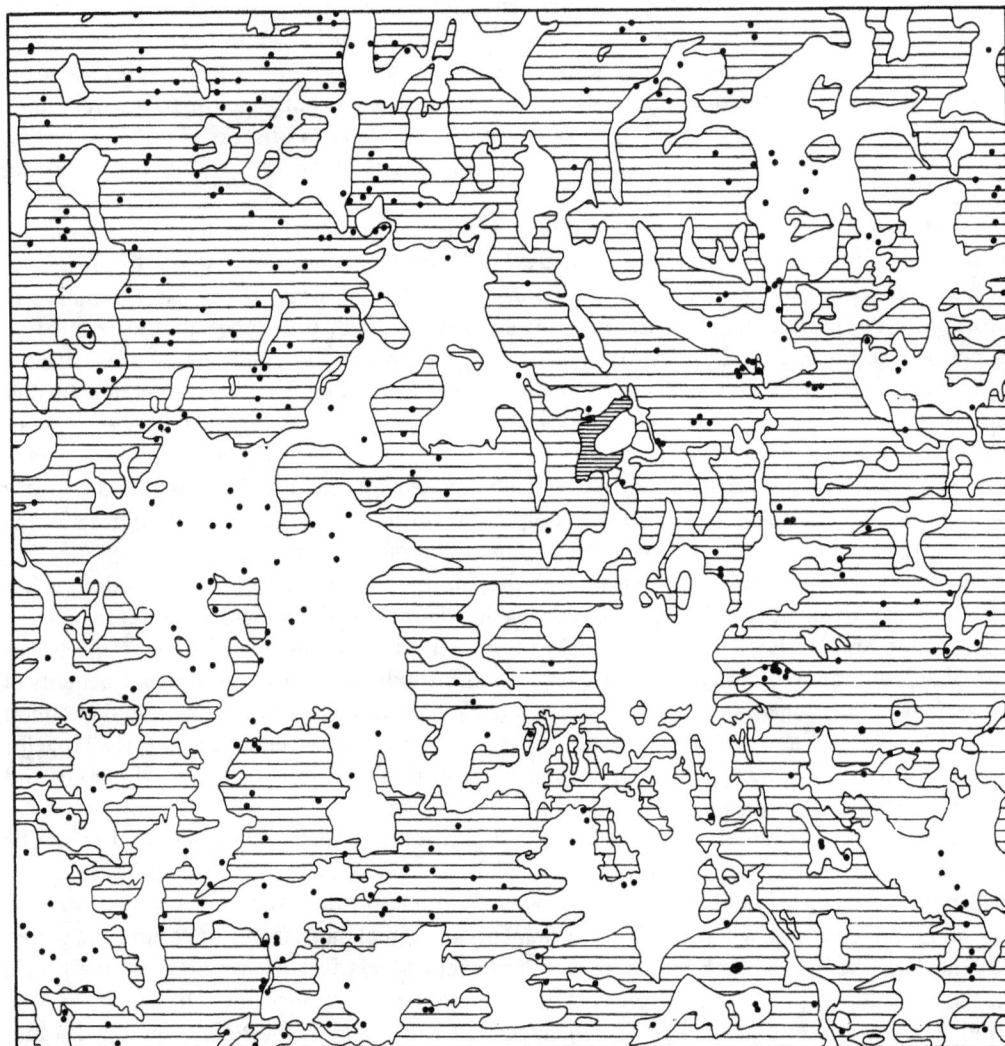

Figure 5:1   Distribution of ring-forts on soils of varying quality in East Limerick. *Key*: A wide land use potential; B, C medium land use potential; D, E limited land use potential (source for soils: An Foras Talúntais).

centuries of the Early Christian period, and so donation to the church would not have been a great loss. Indeed, the foundation of a church in such an area often would have promoted its exploitation and so could have had a positive benefit on the founders who may have retained some controls and rights over the church. In most respects church and monastic estates functioned in the same ways as secular ones, with similar patterns of tenure, technology and range of products.

As land shifted from kin-group ownership and communal farming to a situation where the individual cultivated his own fields or worked them in combination with others of his choosing, there must have been a considerable increase in the amounts of enclosed land. The archaeological evidence for this is surprisingly limited, though in a few areas there are extensive field remains. It is worth first examining the documentary evidence for fences summarised by Buchanan (1973) and recently re-assessed by Ó Corráin (1983). Four main forms of fence can be distinguished: the ditch and bank, *clas*; the stone wall, *cora*; a timber fence, *dairime*; and finally the post and wattle fence, *felmad*. It seems that these types all remained in use for most if not all the Early Christian period, and only the first two would be recognisable as surface remains. The arable was enclosed using the permanent banks and walls, whilst pasture was divided by wattles and the forest by fences made from the readily available timber. The forest that was enclosed must have mainly been managed woodland used for coppicing and panage for pigs.

Archaeological evidence for the various fences is patchy. The only site where a visible field system has been extensively excavated is at Cush, where the banks and ditches fit perfectly into the description of the *clas* (Figure 5:2). The U-shaped ditch was 3 feet deep, as defined in the text, and though the surviving bank was only 18 inches high, it must have originally been higher. The simple dump construction, like that used on the ring-forts, would have involved simple spade digging, followed by routine ditch cleaning in subsequent years. Such work would have been carried out by low status individuals, though the final responsibility for maintaining property boundaries rested firmly on the land owner himself, as the law tracts clearly demonstrate (Binchy 1971).

The overall field systems may have been relatively static, and it is possible that large fields were used by those farming in common, though they may have worked together within a number of smaller defined plots. Partition caused by joint inheritance must have tended to lead to gradual fragmentation of property. It is perhaps under such circumstances that ring-forts could be built over existing fields, as was the case at Lisduggan North, Co. Cork (Twohig 1990). Here, banks and ditches suggest part of the infield was abandoned in favour of a new settlement, caused by either partition or settlement shift.

At The Spectacles, Lough Gur, each house was set in a small field, defined by earth and stone boundaries (Figure 5:3). The large north-western wall was made of rubble and earth with rough facings of stone over 3 m apart. A similar though smaller wall only about 1 m wide ran along most of the terrace, and it must have originally complemented a wall of the same proportions dividing the field containing House A from that to the south-east. At a later phase, however, this dividing wall was doubled in width, hiding one set of facing in the body of the bank. At this stage the entrance through the wall was blocked, and the oval timber House B was constructed. This may suggest a subdivision of ownership, with the two fields being controlled originally from House A. These were then divided, and House B constructed in the second field. The most southerly bank in the complex was made only of earth with no stone revetment, whilst another field bank with a single revetment was found further up the hillslope to the east, possibly part of a wider field system associated with the settlement. The various stone-faced banks do

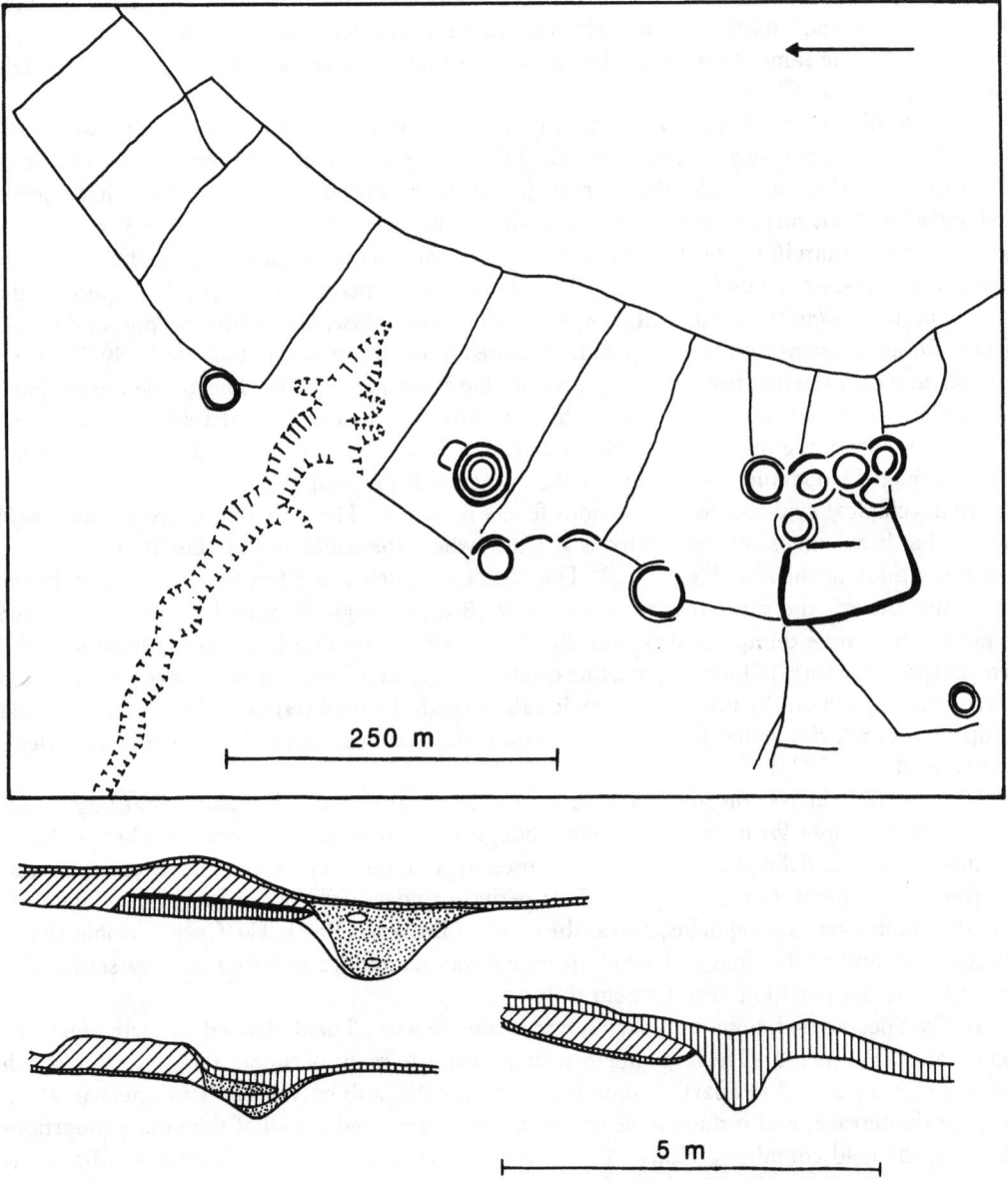

Figure 5:2   Field system at Cush, Co. Limerick. Upper: plan of site. Lower: cross-sections across field boundaries (Ó Ríordáin 1940).

not fit exactly into any of the documented categories, though they may well be versions of the stone wall, *cora*. At Twomile Stone, Co. Donegal, excavation across one of the walls of the field system associated with ring-forts and open houses indicated a rough construction of stone (Davies 1942). The excavator considered that this was the base for an earthen bank, but it could have been all that remained of a rough stone wall.

Field systems where they survive tend to consist of large numbers of small, irregular fields, apparently added in a haphazard manner. Aerial photography by St Joseph has revealed these systems in upland areas of the Burren, Co. Clare and in Co. Roscommon (Norman and St Joseph 1969; plates II, IV). The association with ring-forts suggests that these patterns may be Early Christian in date, though some could be many centuries later. Work in the Burren (Dillon 1983) suggests that when many of the field boundaries were built on the flat limestone plateaux the ground cover was similar to that of today, but around depressions filled with brown earths there was some evidence for erosion subsequent to wall construction. This might reflect greater intensity of use in these relatively limited areas of fertile soil, possibly leading to further diminution in their size. Only further work will provide more precise dating and interpretation.

The pattern of ring-forts set in a field system associated with open settlements was known for many years from the isolated example at Twomile Stone, Co. Donegal (Figure 4:1). A flat plateau was divided round the edge into small rectangular fields, with larger rectangular and irregular fields in the centre of the upland mass. A stone ring-fort was linked to the system, though its relationship to a spinal droveway was unclear. A second ring-fort lay to the east, on the northern plateau edge, and was associated with a small enclosure. Nearby lay several stone houses of which one, house g, produced on excavation some pottery that is probably to be taken to be souterrain ware, and so Early Christian in date.

Recent fieldwork on the edge of the Antrim plateau has revealed a series of further field systems associated with Early Christian settlements (Williams 1983). Though they are on marginal land beyond the edge of present cultivation, several of the sites preserve what was probably a common arrangement of fields around centrally placed farms (Figure 5:4). Ring-forts have been found in several cases with sub-circular or pear-shaped enclosures adjoining them. These may be the greens noted so commonly in the texts, where sheep were grazed and hurley played. Running off these enclosures are further banks which must have defined the other fields of the farms, presumably the intensively cultivated arable. In some cases there are several ring-forts present, as at Ballynashee, and these may be the sort of farms that would have acted in common. In other cases, the ring-fort is on its own, as at Carnlea, or with small roundhouses presumably of the dependent farm workers, as at Dunnyvadden.

Around the shores of Lough Gur there are several important field systems that survive relatively intact. Because of the long period of intense land use in this area it is not easy to assign an Early Christian date to many, but the system at Knockfennel on the north-west side of the Lough is likely to be of this date (Figure 5:5). A scarp runs parallel with the present Lough shore, and a series of rectangular fields were laid out between it and the old shore line. To the west was a ring-fort, onto which the field boundaries join. To the north of the ring-fort and between it and the scarp were small enclosures used for stock or vegetable plots. Above the scarp, a modern field boundary probably marks the western side of a droveway with its eastern boundary still surviving as an earthwork. The droveway heads inland, with fields running off it and back to the top of the scarp above the Lough. A second ring-fort lies within the field complex, and is respected by it. The presence of the ring-forts supports an Early Christian date for the whole field pattern.

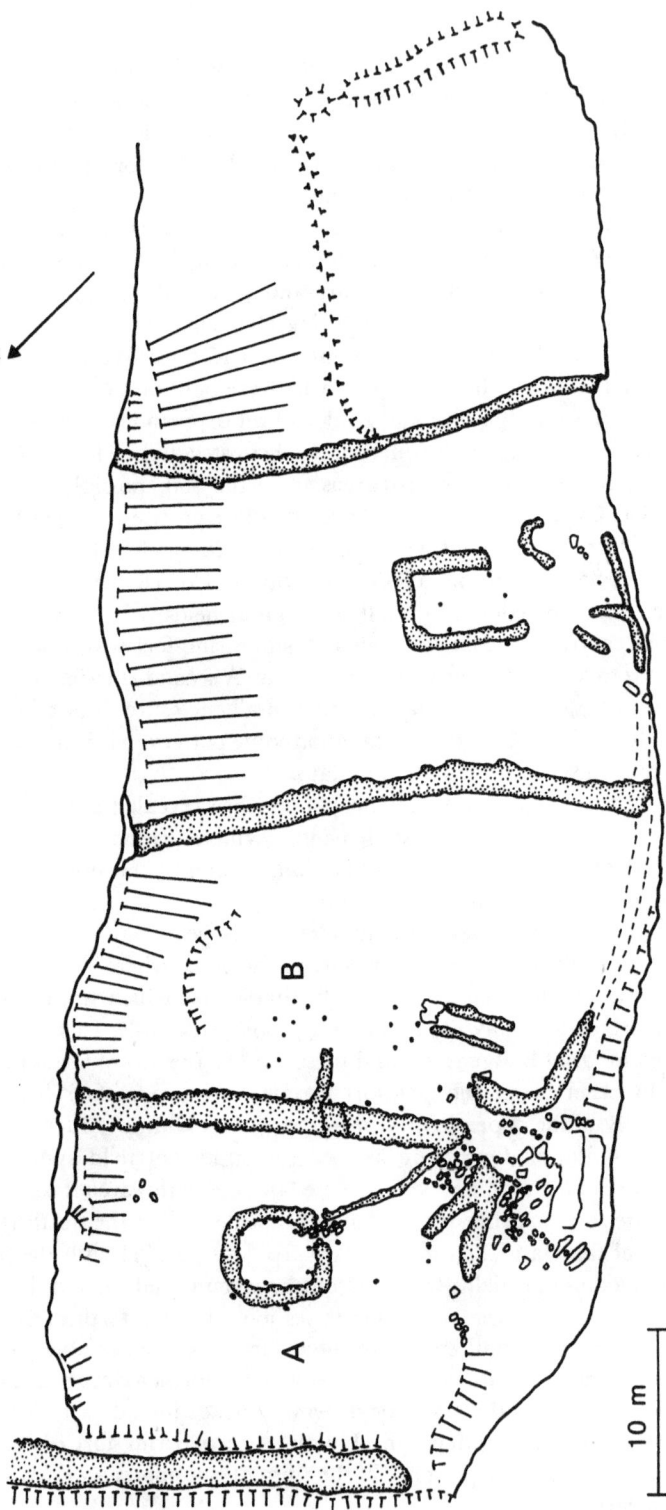

Figure 5:3 Open settlements at The Spectacles, Lough Gur, Co. Limerick (Ó Ríordáin 1949).

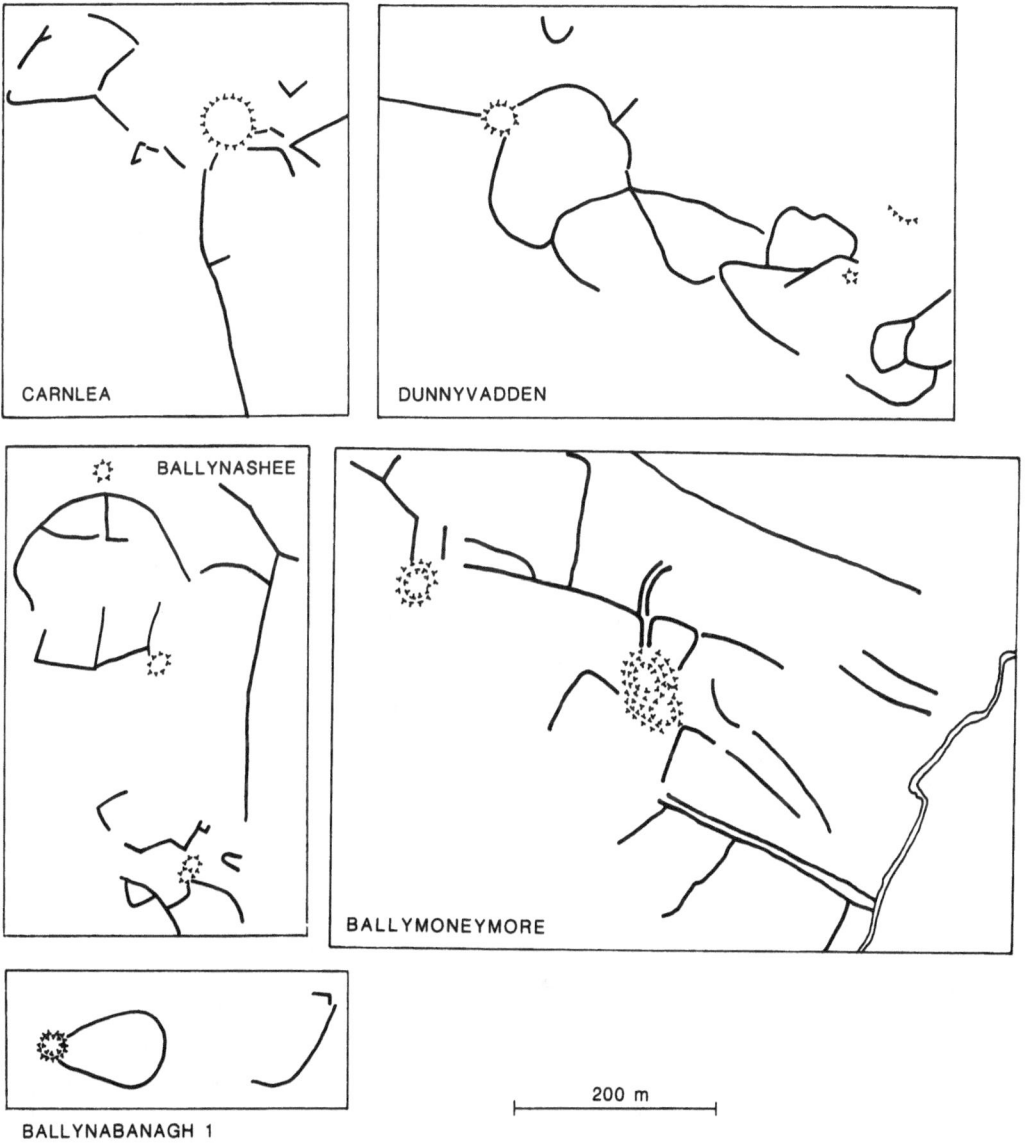

CARNLEA

DUNNYVADDEN

BALLYNASHEE

BALLYMONEYMORE

BALLYNABANAGH 1

200 m

Figure 5:4   Field systems in Co. Antrim (Williams 1983).

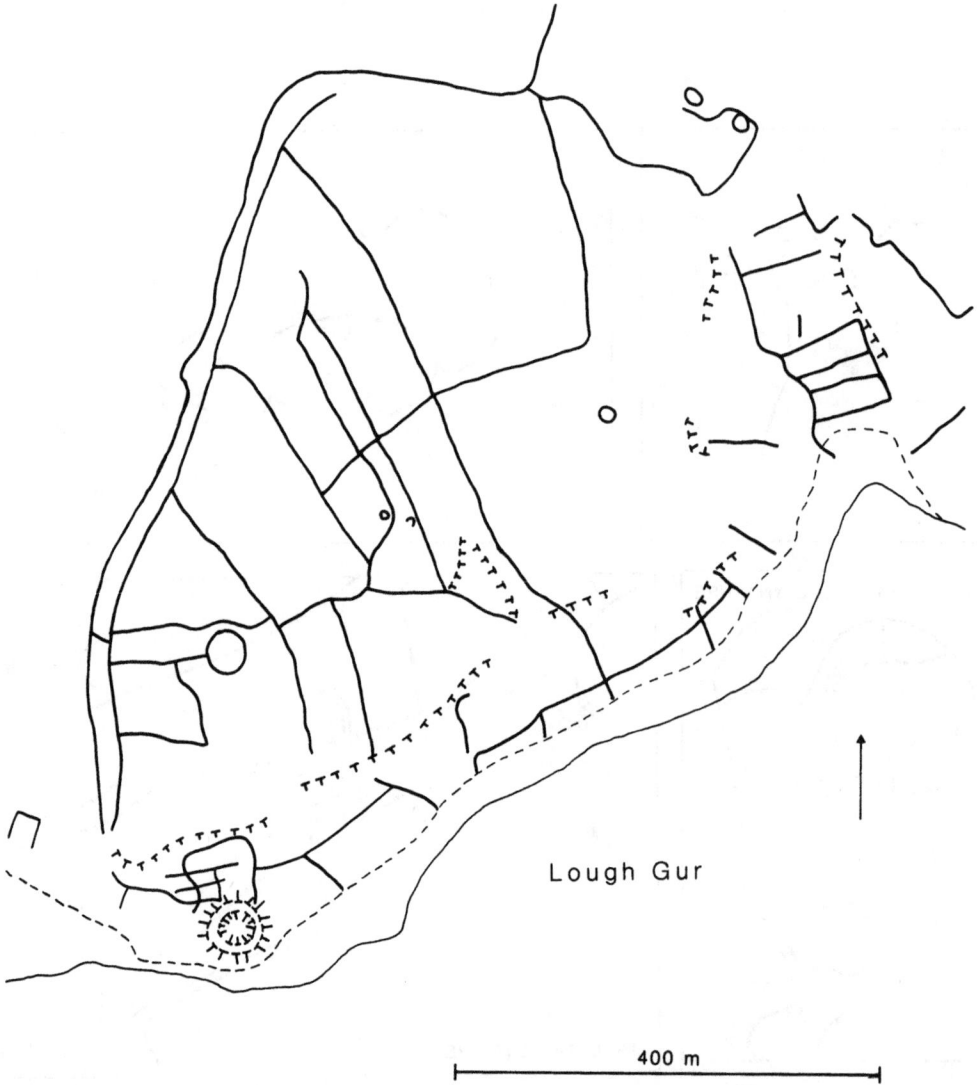

Figure 5:5 Field systems around Lough Gur, Co. Limerick (O'Kelly unpublished).

Norman and St Joseph (1969) illustrate several lowland sites with dependent enclosures visible as cropmarks, and subsequent aerial photography in many parts of the country has revealed fragmentary arrangements of enclosures around ring-forts. Rarely, however, are extensive and coherent field systems evident, and the dating of all such cropmark data is anyway extremely difficult (Barrett 1982, 1983).

   The most famous example of a field system associated with conjoined ring-forts is that of Cush (Figure 5:2). This settlement complex on the hillslopes of Slieve Reagh overlooking the Limerick plain is contained within a string of rectangular fields running along the contours. They tend to be long and thin, running down the hillslope, though those at the northern end are more

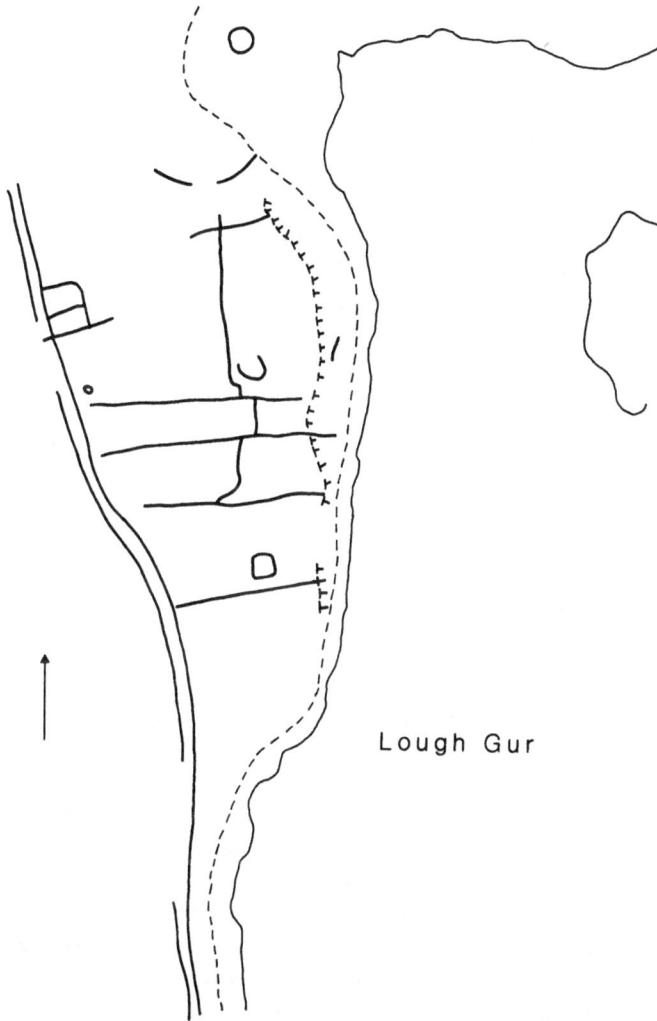

Lough Gur

Figure 5:5 *continued*

square in plan. Overall, the ring-forts lay downhill of the fields, and presumably further fields demarcated by wooden fences lay still further down the slope. Beyond the visible fields must have lain the rough grazing, just as it does today, and presumably held in common. The fields marked by banks must have been under cultivation at least occasionally since ridge and furrow have been seen within them (Fowler 1966). However, their elevation suggests that they may have only been occasionally under arable, and were normally pasture. The complex at Cush has probably survived only because of its marginal location.

Field systems do not occur only with ring-forts. In Co. Antrim, survey followed by excavation at Ballyutoag indicates a large oval enclosure containing numerous houses occupied in the Early Christian period. Adjoining the settlement enclosure were several fields, curvilinear in shape, later subdivided by straight banks (Figure 4:4). A possible trackway led off to the north. The

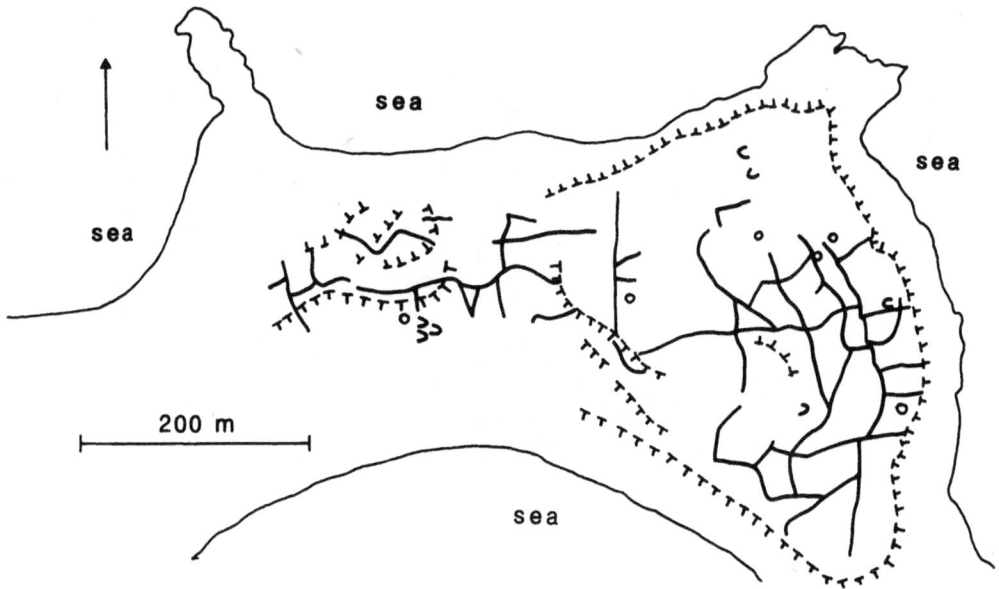

Figure 5:6   Field system on Beginish, Co. Kerry (O'Kelly 1956).

excavated upland site of Lissachiggel which produced important evidence of cereals (Davies 1939) has been re-interpreted as a similar enclosed settlement rather than a cashel (Williams 1983, 239). Such enclosures may also have been common in the lowlands, and one at Killylane lying about half a kilometre from a church site consists of a small enclosure with a second appended, and a large oval enclosure to the west. These may well be related to the oval settlements recognised from aerial photography and cartographic study over much of Ireland, though particularly common in the central lowlands (Swan 1983, 275) and the south-west (Hurley 1982). Many may be ecclesiastical, but this may not be true of them all, though it is possible that they could be related to the church, possibly tenurially, as discussed in Chapter 3. A settlement that has recently been attributed to an ecclesiastical owner is that of Beginish, Co. Kerry (O'Kelly 1956). Ó Corráin (1981, 340) has suggested that the settlement may be an outfarm of the nearby ecclesiastical site of Church Island. The field system consisted of small rectangular fields on the eastern part of the island, subdivided by some irregular walls which gave way to a more fragmented pattern to the west. Some stone dwellings lay in the fields, but most were scattered over an open area to the north and were associated with small structures that may have served as animal shelters (Figure 5:6).

Field systems are also known to be associated solely with unenclosed settlements. At Killelan West, group 1, Co. Kerry, Henry (1957) found a series of small round stone structures, including a conjoined pair, with field walls joining them by running along the contours. The system included a droveway which ran along the edge of a scarp and led to the main complex of buildings.

Despite the examples of field systems that survive around upland areas and are being discovered from some lowland sites through aerial photography, the number and extent of the systems are very small compared with Iron Age and Romano–British landscapes in eastern

England (Whimster 1989). They are comparable, however, with what is known of western Britain over the same period and reflect a pattern where presumably much of the land was not marked out in ways that leave any archaeological trace. We are therefore uncertain as to how typical those that do survive may be of the original landscape demarcated in other ways.

Animals

Domestic animals, primarily cattle but also pigs and sheep, were important animals in the Early Christian period. Cattle and sheep were both more valued for their secondary products – milk and traction in the case of the former and wool and milk in the case of the latter – than for their carcasses. In contrast, the pig was only of economic benefit when dead. All animals are well represented in the archaeological record and in the literary sources, so their general economic role can be assessed. It is not possible, however, to recognise many regional special-isations in the keeping of particular animals. Few settlements have produced sufficient faunal remains for detailed analysis, and only those excavated in recent years have been published in a way that gives a firm basis for discussion. Likewise, changes through time are not easy to distinguish, though a few slight trends are beginning to emerge.

Cattle

Cattle are with few exceptions the most numerous animal remains on Early Christian sites. Recent work by McCormick (1983) has elegantly demonstrated that, though the meat of cattle must have been very much predominant, the faunal remains support an interpretation of a primarily dairying economy. At all sites where samples were large enough, the greater number of cattle killed were juvenile. These represent the surplus animals produced to ensure continuing lactation, but not needed for herd regeneration. Most, by inference, were young males. In contrast, where the mature beasts could be sexed, a predominance of females was noted; these would be the old dairy cattle killed off when they reached the end of their productive lives.

Written sources provide much information on the economic aspects of cattle production. These have been frequently quoted, particularly by O'Loan (1965) and Lucas (1958a). Cattle were kept in herds which were managed by professional herdsmen, presumably of low status, and young boys who had to prevent calves returning to their mothers. There were various fines for letting cattle stray, or for taking down a section of fence and letting them graze on another's land (Plummer 1928, 116). Those involved in co-tenancy took turns at watching the communal herds (Plummer 1923b, 117), and it seems that dogs were used to control the animals. The main threats mentioned were wolves, swamps and animals fighting, though presumably cattle raiding was also a major, though less common danger (Lucas 1958a).

At night cattle were frequently placed within enclosures, sometimes disused ring-forts (Plummer 1928, 116–17). Probably some animals were kept in ring-forts in front of the house occupied by the humans, as suggested by the trampling by cattle at Ballymacash (Jope 1981). However, Lynn (pers. comm.) considers that the frequent discovery during excavation of finely laminated layers within ring-forts suggests that they had not been subjected to the trampling of animals; this would imply that such sites were not heavily used for stock enclosures.

The various enclosures where animals were held during the legal process of distraint (Binchy 1973a, 1973b) may have been all physically similar, though they had different names. There is

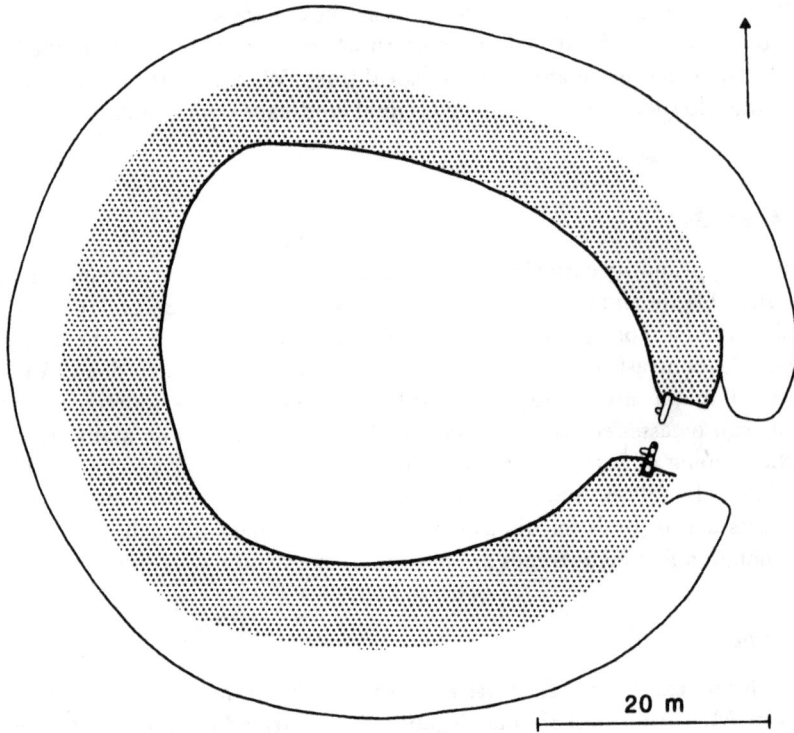

Figure 5:7   Garryduff 2, Co. Cork (O'Kelly 1962).

some archaeological evidence for the use of abandoned ring-forts for animals, such as Castle Skreen 1 with its pond (Dickinson and Waterman 1960), but often it is unclear whether this was carried out within the Early Christian period or later.

The ring-fort of Garryduff 2 has been interpreted as a possible cattle enclosure (O'Kelly 1962). This impressive ring-fort measured 38 m by 31 m internally and was defended by a ditch and internal bank (Figure 5:7). A stone revetment ran round its inner edge, and linked up with a partial timber blocking and gate at the entrance; there was no evidence of any human occupation. It would have been an ideal overnight cattle enclosure, and could have contained a large number of beasts. It was adjacent to the wealthy ring-fort settlement of Garryduff 1 and, if related to it, suggests that the owner may have maintained a large herd which he wished to keep secure. Other cases of adjacent or conjoined ring-forts show evidence of occupation in both enclosures, though it is not normally possible to demonstrate that this was strictly contemporary.

The feeding of cattle was essential to ensure growth and maintain milk production. The most common, of course, was pasture, and this occurred as both enclosed and open land. The *nochtmachaire* (bare plain) has been interpreted by Ó Corráin (1983) as the arable, which could be grazed when the crops had been harvested. Most time was probably spent in the *lethmachaire* (half-plain) which could be interpreted as outfield, divided up by *felmad*, post and wattle fencing.

This was made of posts hammered into the ground, linked by wattling and topped by blackthorn. Though substantial, this sort of fencing could have been easily dismantled and re-arranged as necessary, and would have been appropriate in the efficient management of pasture for cattle. It was essential, particularly in the damp Irish climate, to ensure that ground was not over-grazed or poached (trampled and the soil structure destroyed). Such a threat was particularly real on the gley soils on flat and gently sloping areas.

It was always important for cattle to have access to water, and Ó Corráin (1983) points out that the *gelestar*, summer cattle pond, was enclosed by post and wattle fencing so that the surrounding arable land could be protected from the beasts belonging to the group of farmers who all had a share in the pond. Away from the arable, access to water must have been rarely a problem, except in some limestone areas such as the Burren and parts of Roscommon and Limerick. Erosion of some brown earths has been noted in depressions of the Burren (Dillon 1983), and this may have been caused by the herds grazing on the upland plateaux coming down to the limited sources of surface water found in these low lying areas.

More distant regions could also be used for cattle pasture. There is sufficient evidence to suggest that booleying, transhumance, was a frequently applied strategy, particularly in regions with large blocks of upland and lowland. There seems strong evidence for this activity in the Burren, Co. Clare where movement upwards in winter was appropriate, though in other areas this generally occurred in the summer. In some regions, such as Co. Antrim, this led to the creation of upland settlements of distinct form (Williams 1983) but in many others the typical ring-forts predominate. Although upland pastures may have been exploited these did not always entail the distinct division of the community as is normal with transhumance. When adjacent mountain slopes were grazed, as was frequently the case in the more dissected parts of the country such as south-west Co. Cork, then most of the population could remain in the lowland, and the cattle be moved up and down slope as required, and even daily if necessary. It was during the summer that most milk was produced and there was considerable pressure to turn a large part of this surplus into a storable and transportable form. If animals could be brought down to the farms for milking rather than having to carry the milk back or process it on the hillsides, this would clearly reduce the amount of human effort and equipment that were required.

Cattle did not only rely on grass for food. There is no evidence that hay was ever grown and cut for winter fodder, and despite the long growing season for grass in Ireland with its mild Atlantic climate, there were many months when the grass would contain little of value. Of particular concern were the times when the snow fell and even the winter grass was not available. The Annals occasionally mention the devastating effects of the snow. These are no doubt only the random recording of regionally devastating freak weather conditions, and cannot be used to extrapolate climatic trends with any confidence. However, they do emphasise that the Irish do not seem to have been able to effect a strategy which would allow for significant storage of animal foodstuffs. This may well be because of the drive for maximising numbers, even at the expense of risking bad weather over winter. The provision of fodder for large numbers of animals would have been too great a drain on resources, but it does appear that some supplies were available and these were presumably reserved for the most important of the breeding stock. The *Feast of Bricriu* mentions heather and twig tops as fodder not of the best quality, but presumably frequently given (Henderson 1899, 9). In contrast to the fodder so far described, the *Feast of Bricriu* describes corn as part of the diet of a prime cow (Henderson 1899, 9). An arable surplus may have been at least partly required, therefore, to act as a winter feed for the most important animals. It was probably also used as fodder for animals enclosed whilst held on distraint (Plummer 1923a, 35).

Most cattle ranged free, but some were hobbled or kept in pens. These may well have been the cows yielding the most milk which could be cosseted and given preferential treatment. They were also close at hand for milking. Milking was undertaken by women, and usually in the presence of calves since these were supposed to encourage a high milk yield (Lucas 1958a).

Herds mainly consisted of female beasts, though there were the young bullocks growing to maturity before being butchered; faunal evidence suggests that many were over-wintered once to increase their size. Other males were either selected as breeding stock, or castrated and trained as traction animals. The length of training necessary to bring an oxen up to a sufficient standard is very great, and many could not afford the time or the resources to maintain a full team. This is discussed in relation to agriculture below, but it should be remembered that the oxen formed part of the animal stock. They were of considerable value, but would have consumed large amounts of fodder. The structure of the herd would have been carefully regulated (Figure 5:8) to produce a sufficient number of meat and traction animals whilst maximising the number of milch cows. They produced the secondary milk products and offspring to be also consumed or manipulated in socially important economic transactions.

Milk could be consumed fresh, *lemlacht*, or in a thickened form, *bainne clabair*, or thickened, soured and skimmed, *draumce* (Ó Corráin 1972, 56). Alternatively, it could be processed into butter or cheese (O Sé 1948, 1949). Ó Corráin states (1972, 55) that lightly salted butter was the most popular, and that the heavily salted form, *gruiten*, was considered bitter. Sometimes butter was flavoured with onions (Lucas 1960, 32). The storage of butter may have been purely in houses and outbuildings, but the underground chambers of souterrains may have been used. These were certainly cool and of even temperature, though access was not easy and most were not designed for large scale storage. Numerous examples of bog butter have been found during peat cutting, and the storage of butter containers in bogs was certainly common from the medieval times onwards. Some may date from the Early Christian period, but the scale of butter storage in this manner is unclear; most of course would have been subsequently recovered. It certainly would have been an ideal way of storing supplies either in a secret place against a time of crisis, or near to the upland booleys where so much of the dairy produce must have been made in regions with substantial blocks of upland. Rather than carry all the newly made butter back to the farm, some may have been left in the bogs in a particularly good year.

Cheeses were extremely varied, and quite in contrast to the limited cheese available in early modern Ireland (Evans 1954). Lucas (1960) made a careful search of the Early Christian literature, and found reference to a wide range of soft and hard cheeses. A form of curd or cottage cheese, *gruth*, was widely available and this could also be pressed into *fáiscre grotha*. A soft, sweet cheese was *maethal*, made into very large discs, probably over 2 feet across. There was also a hard cheese, *tanag*, which was dry and pressed, presumably in a mould. Ó Corráin (1972, 56) considers that *táth* was a cooked cheese from sour milk curds, whilst *mulchán* came from buttermilk curds. Other cheeses such as *grus* and *millsen* have still yet to be identified. The presence of regional varieties is likely, but not certain.

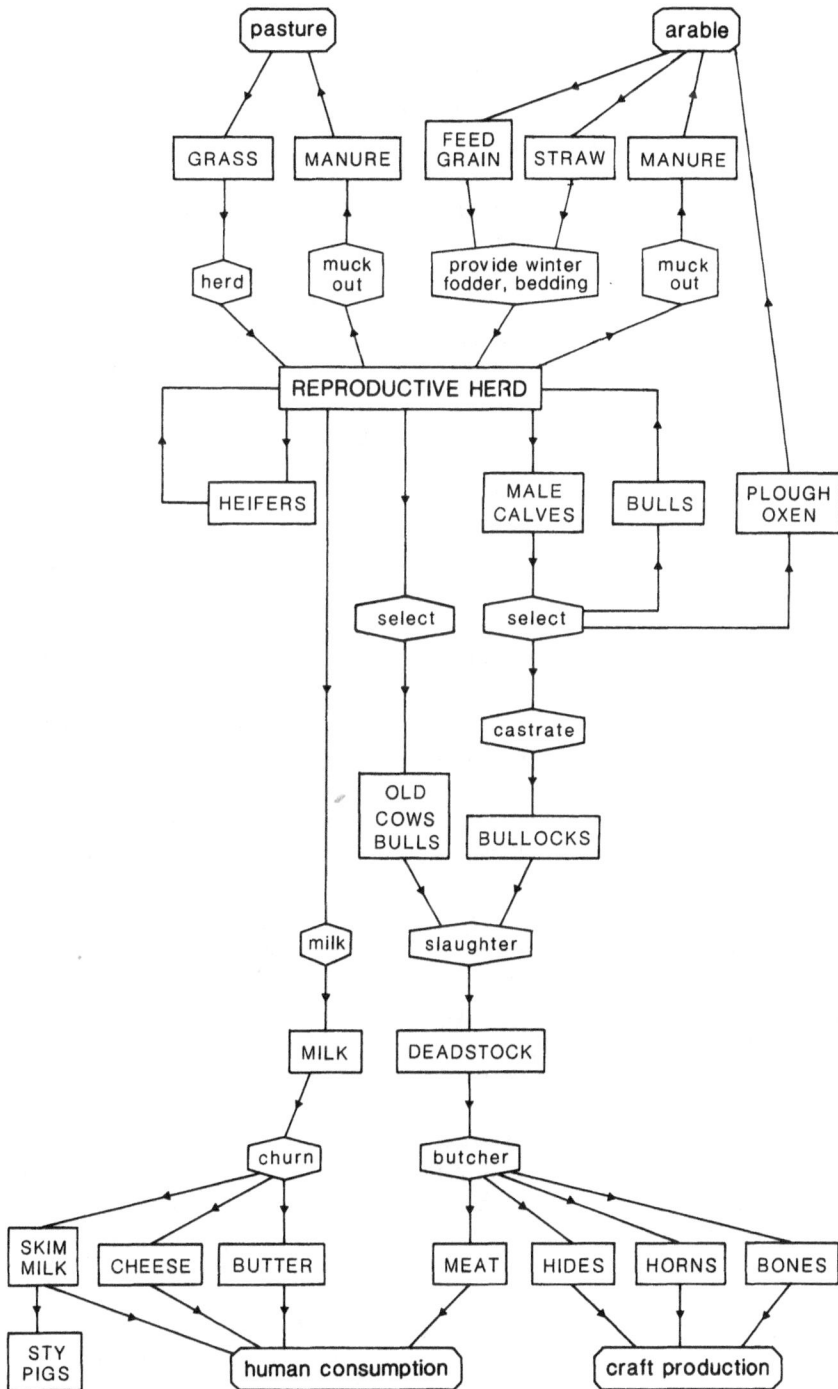

Figure 5:8   Cattle: production and consumption.

Sheep

Sheep were far less important economically than cattle, but still contributed significantly. They were small breeds, generally with two horns but some had four (Stelfox 1942, 71). The overall evidence from the faunal remains suggested to Jope (1953) that the sheep of Early Christian Ireland were very similar in size and build to the Soay breed. It is interesting to note in this regard that at a later date Giraldus Cambrensis claimed that most were black (most Soays are coloured), but white sheep were far from unknown (Plummer 1968, 55). It is only possible to differentiate between sheep and goats by a few anatomical variations, but at Armagh where these were specifically considered, no goat was identified (Higgins 1984). However, some of the textiles from Lagore may have been made of goat hair (Start 1950).

Sheep tend to be the least common of the main domesticates in site faunal assemblages, though Proudfoot (1961) claimed that there may have been more sheep than appear archaeologically since they were kept for wool and not necessarily for meat. It is indeed possible that, as with present upland sheep farming, many died on the hills, but this may also have applied to other animals. It is interesting to note that the one exception to low numbers is that of Larrybane promontory fort, Co. Antrim (Proudfoot and Wilson 1962). Sited on the chalk, this settlement would have been positioned in a naturally desirable sheep grazing area and, though cattle predominated, sheep were clearly a major part of the economy. This does hint at some regional and topographical specialisation within the farming regime. In phase 1 at Rathmullan, Co. Down there was also a large proportion of sheep killed, but this was not repeated in later phases (Collins 1982).

It is likely that each ewe produced only one lamb a year, and losses may have been heavy. Most males were castrated, and it is these wethers that were the beasts used in the payment of social obligations. This presumably meant that herds were mainly female, with a few rams and a number of castrates awaiting butchery (Figure 5:9). All sheep could of course produce wool, and so had some continuing value. If sufficiently large bone assemblages are found in excavation, it will be possible to check these assumptions.

Professional shepherds looked after flocks with the help of dogs, though women were also often responsible for the sheep. Flocks presumably ranged far and wide, even in winter. Though sheep folds may have been used, the lack of fodder meant that generally sheep ran loose all year, and as a result losses could be heavy, as indicated in the Annals. Sheep were also found on the lowland near settlements, and there are frequent references to sheep on the green around the ring-fort. These animals were constantly near the settlement, and by grazing on the green, they provided short turf suitable for playing sports such as hurling. They were also easily available for killing at short notice if unexpected visitors of rank arrived.

The flock on the ring-fort green may have provided milk for human consumption. Though of far less importance than cows' milk, sheep milk was drunk (Plummer 1968, 56). Shepherds no doubt consumed milk from the herds under their care, and it may have been usually available to those of lower rank whilst the less bitter cows' milk was retained by those of higher status. It could also be used in a porridge.

The wool from Soay sheep can be plucked rather than sheared; there are sets of iron shears from a number of sites which may have been used for sheep, but could have been used for cutting cloth rather than fleeces (Figure 5:10). The amount produced by each sheep would have been small by modern standards, and flocks would have had to have been large for a reasonable scale of production. The craft production of textiles was an important female activity,

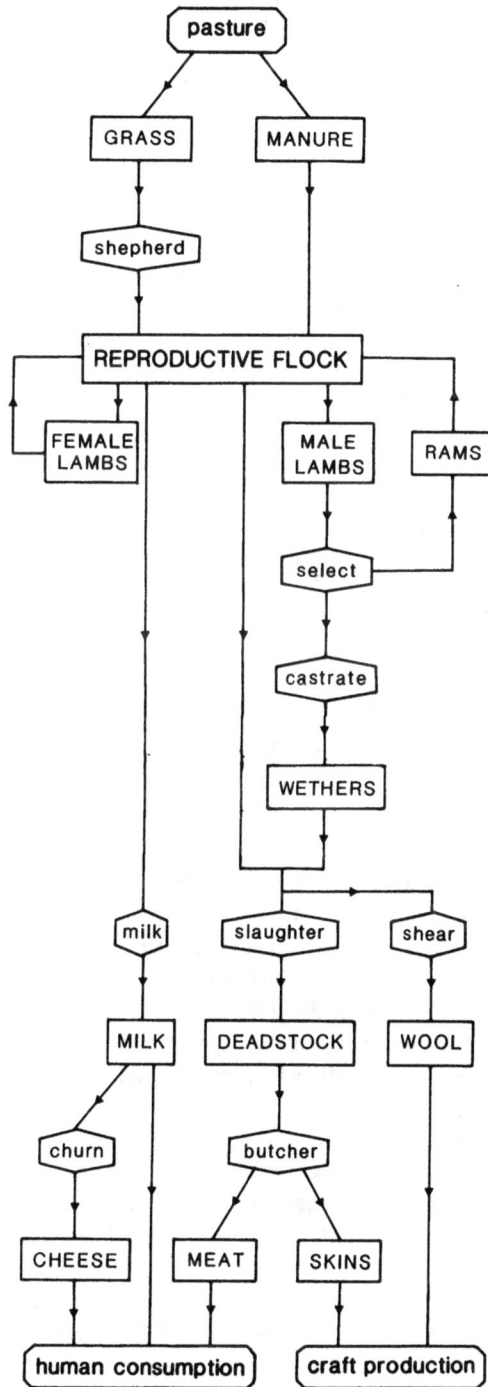

Figure 5:9 Sheep: production and consumption.

discussed at length in Chapter 6. Another important by-product from sheep was that of their skins after being killed. These were of particular value in the monastic setting for the production of fine vellum, and this may have been a major market for young male lambs which would not have had an equivalent in the secular sphere.

Pigs

Pigs were active, lithe and relatively slim breeds, though they could be fattened up with special care (Figure 5:11). They were kept for meat which could be eaten fresh, salted or smoked into bacon. Pigs were relatively fast-breeding, and though litters may have only been annual events, they were of up to 12 piglets (Plummer 1968, 115). Pigs were relatively fast-growing, and could produce meat quickly. Animals were kept for 2 or 3 years before slaughter according to the documentary sources (Ó'Loan 1965, 173) and also to the faunal remains from Rathmullan (Collins 1982). However, the faunal evidence from Balliderry 2 and other sites suggests that most pigs were slaughtered whilst immature, and some were very young (Stelfox 1942, 71), as was the case at Armagh (Higgins 1984).

Pigs were let free in open country and woodland to live off the natural vegetation, notably mast (the Annals note particularly bountiful years in this regard). Such animals must have been half-wild and breeding control must have been negligible, though swineherds are mentioned. They were presumably culled periodically but there must have been a relatively low return, though for little effort. Some excavated settlements have yielded surprisingly low pig frequencies in the faunal assemblages, and this is presumably related to the absence of woodland pigs. Downland grazing around Larrybane was probably clear of forest cover, and so feral pig herds must have been absent. Such a situation may have also been the case around the lake containing Lagore, though this seems less likely. The few pigs that were present at these sites probably came from the sty.

In contrast to the low-intensity forest pigs, the sty animals were intensively reared. They may have spent all their time penned up, or could have been let loose during the day on common land (Plummer 1968, 109). Piglets were only covered by the rules of joint pasturing from 1st August each year according to the *Comingaire* tract (Charles-Edwards 1972a, 63). Pigs may have been used to turn over the soil, and pig manure was an important by-product. Those pigs kept in sties were fed up on milk and grain. Such beasts would have grown relatively quickly and would have been available for slaughter if fresh pork was required. During the summer and early autumn pigs could have been fattened up on surplus production, then killed and stored for the winter.

Pigs may have been most important as a form of food storage for the seasons when fresh supplies were extremely limited and hunger was a very real threat. At Rathmullan, most of the pigs were slaughtered at the same age suggesting a periodic cull (Collins 1982). This may have been an autumn killing of feral pigs after they had been fattened on mast or sty pigs fattened up on surplus milk over the summer. The types of bone present indicate that carcasses were then processed into smoked or salted hams and consumed elsewhere. This may suggest that Rathmullan was a central processing centre for pigs, especially in phase 2 of the occupation.

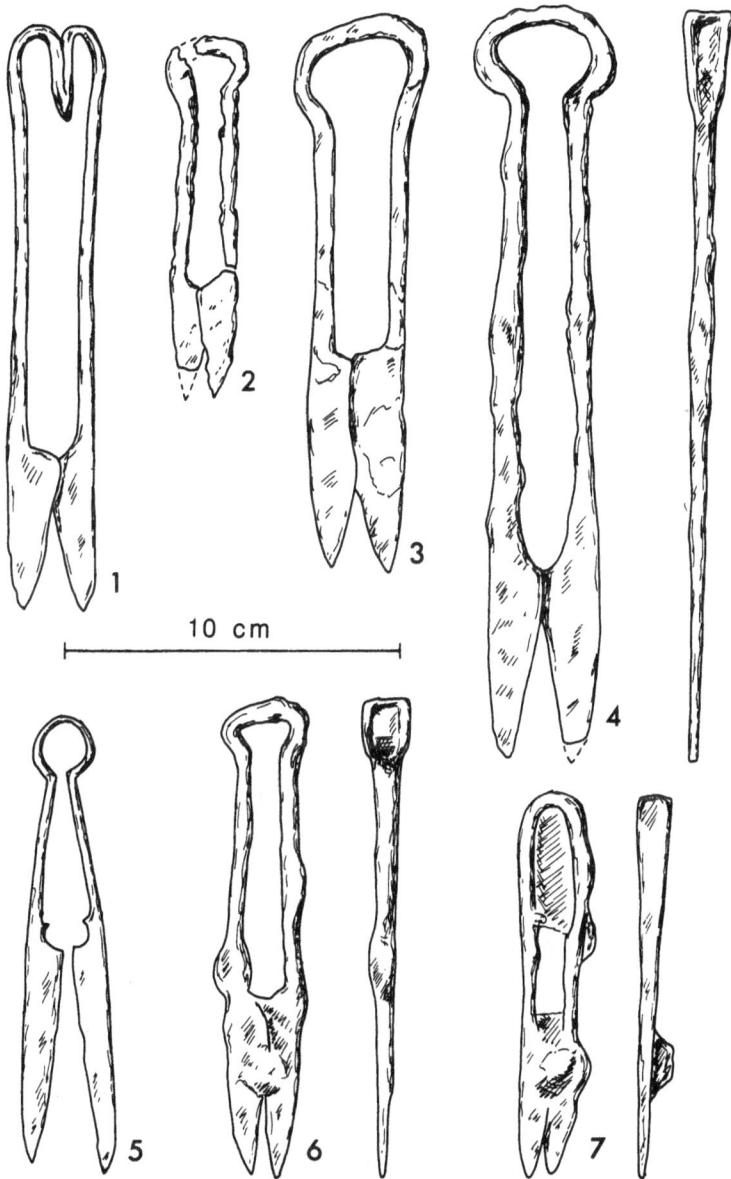

Figure 5:10 Shears from excavated sites. **1, 5** Lagore, Co. Meath; **2** Killederdadrum, Co. Tipperary; **3** Garranes, Co. Cork; **4, 6, 7** Garryduff 1, Co. Cork (**1, 5** Hencken 1950, **2** Manning 1984, **3** Ó Ríordáin 1942, **4, 6, 7** O'Kelly 1962).

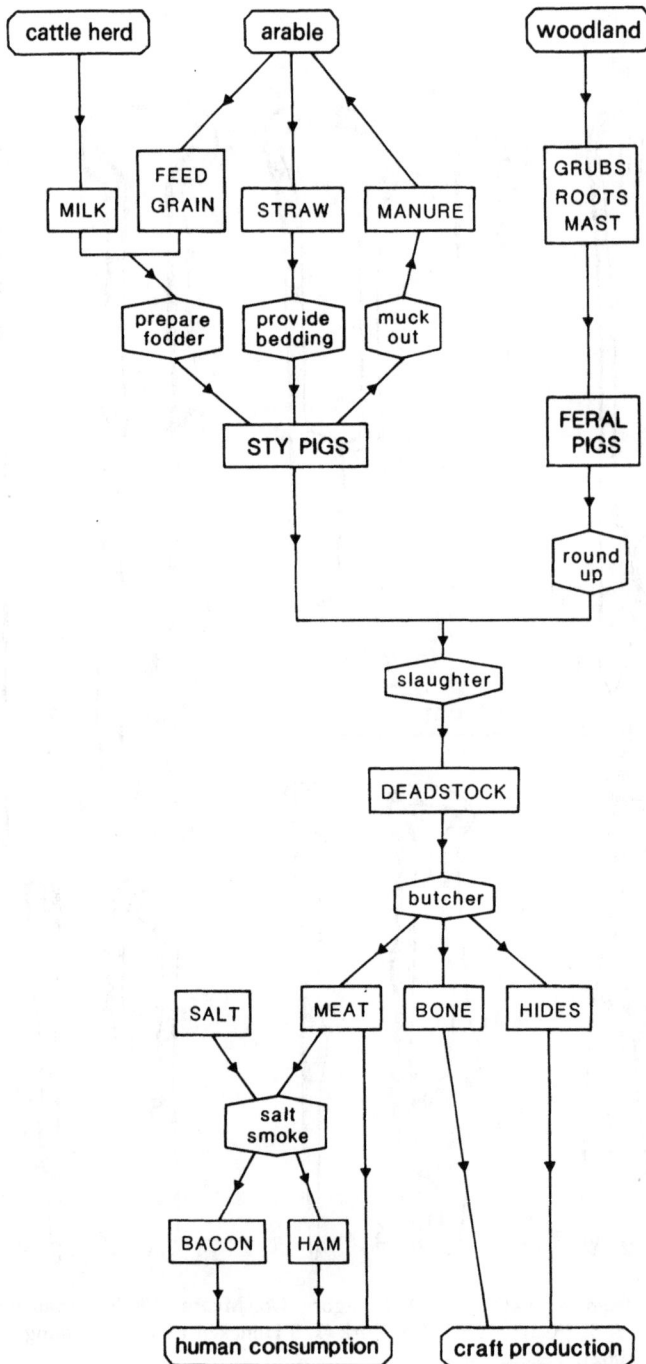

Figure 5:11   Pigs: production and consumption.

Arable

Cattle may have been socially the most important agricultural product, but arable farming probably contributed at least as much in dietary terms as pastoral activities. The largest scale activities were devoted to cereal production (Figure 5:12), but a wide range of other crops are known from documentary sources. There seems to have been a very considerable range of crops, but most must have been garden-grown in small quantities and with small sized, semi-wild varieties.

Cereals

Until recently, only a few cereals have been identified archaeologically, but flotation has now become common on excavations in Ireland, and so carbonised grains are now being recovered from many sites, mainly due to the work of Monk (1986). Only a few sites have produced wheat, including straw from Lagore (Hencken 1950, 242). Documentary evidence suggests that wheat was the most appreciated cereal, with red and white varieties being grown (Duignan 1944, 140), and the archaeological evidence supports its rarity. Archaeological evidence suggests that barley, particularly the six row type, was the most commonly grown cereal, though Lucas (1960, 11) considers that oats were most common. It may be that the enclosed settlements from which most samples have come were those consuming the better quality barley, and that oats were mainly consumed by the lower grades of society. The law tracts have an obsession with grading everything, but it may be of significance that kings consumed stirabout of wheaten meal and the sons of chieftains ate barley meal, whilst those of lower grades had oatmeal (Lucas 1960, 13). Oats are found widely, with the common cultivated, wild and bristle pointed oat known; rye has also been recovered from a few sites.

Fields of any size were ploughed prior to planting, though the only evidence for ridges resulting from this were noted at Cush by Fowler (1966). The mouldboard must have been part of the plough to produce such ridges that at other sites have either been ploughed flat or been hidden under later cultivation rigs. No mouldboards have survived as they would have been of wood, but iron coulters which were set at the front of the plough to cut the sod have been found (Figure 5:13). Two from Ballinderry 1 and Lagore are very similar in size and shape, with shanks about 7 inches long. Duignan (1944, 136) considers that they are from low, wheel-less but heavy ploughs. A more recent discovery at White Fort, Co. Down was larger and heavier, with a length of 22 inches, of which 9 inches was the blade (Waterman 1956). This is possibly large enough to have come from a wheeled plough, though this is not certain.

Duignan (1944, 136) also notes that several iron plough tips or shares have been recovered from excavations, and others, presumably Early Christian in date, have been found as casual finds. These ploughshares are light and roughly triangular in shape. A double-flanged, heavier triangular form which Duignan considered also to be early has been shown by Brady (1988) to be a post-medieval type. These were smaller and less pointed, but this may be because the lighter soils around Lough Gur would not have required such a heavy plough tip. Alternatively, they may have been quite worn; experiments have shown that everyday wear can be quite considerable on iron plough tips.

Plough teams were of oxen, occasionally two or six, but more usually four (Plummer 1968). Lucas has made a special study of ploughing arrangements, and these could be complicated. This was because the full set of equipment necessary was too great for many individuals to own,

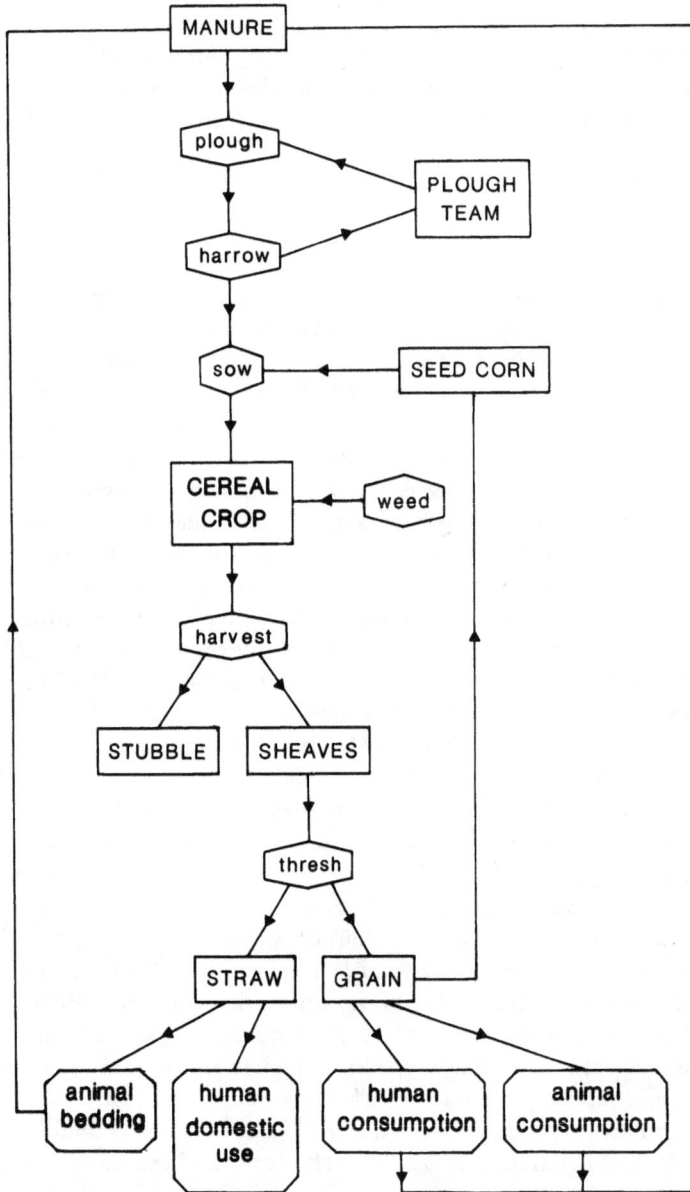

Figure 5:12   Arable: production and consumption.

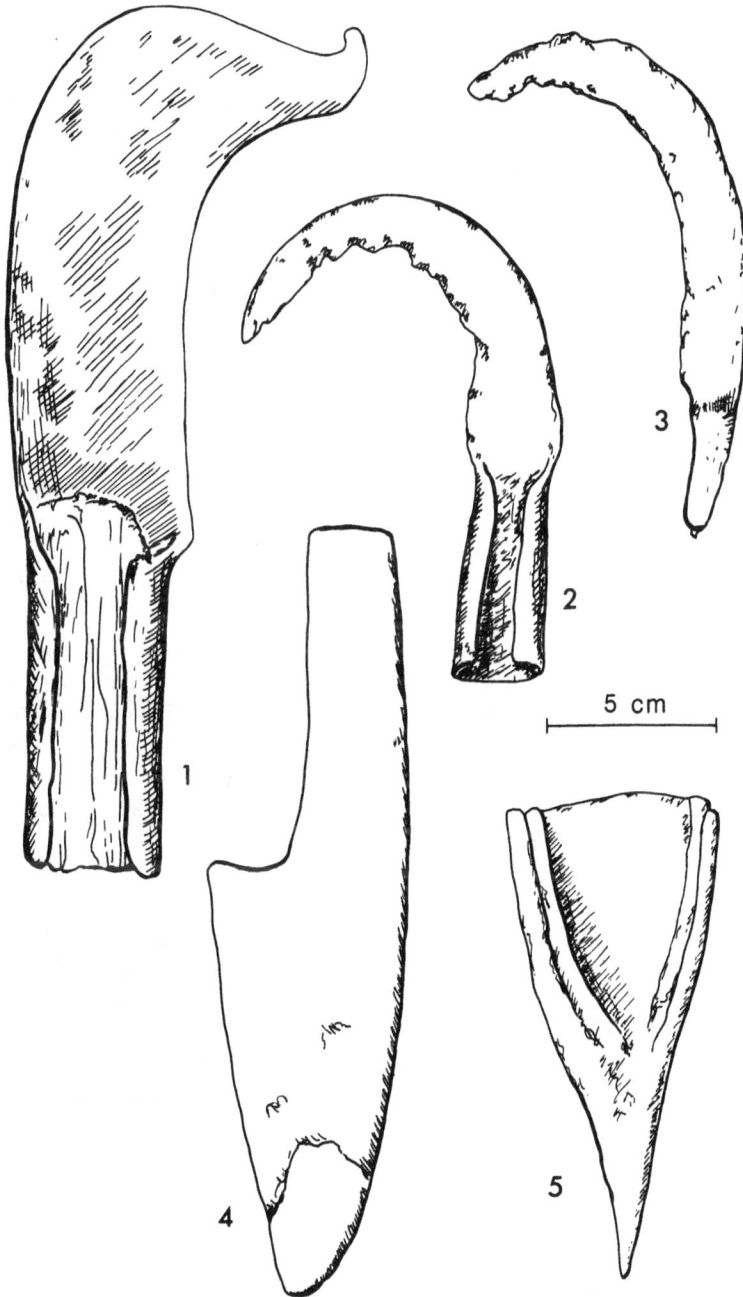

Figure 5:13 Selection of agricultural implements from Lagore, Co. Meath. **1** Billhook; **2, 3** sickles; **4** plough coulter; **5** plough sock (Hencken 1950).

so that groups of farmers would together contribute a plough team with tackle. This has led to considerable detail being set down in law tracts to ensure equality. The *ócaire* of the *Críth Gablach* had a fourth share in a plough, and provided an ox, the ploughshare, goad and halter (Mac Neill 1923, 289; Binchy 1941). The other partners would also contribute an ox each, together with other equipment. Lucas (1968) suggests that the second might provide the coulter, the third the wooden frame of the plough and the fourth the yokes. Each pair of oxen would have been provided with a yoke, and the outer, forward one would have been the most substantial and took most strain. An example from Erriff, Co. Mayo may have been such a yoke, the other surviving examples being lighter and probably all were inner yokes. Fenton (1969) suggests that the pairs of oxen would not have been directly behind each other but would have overlapped, with the strongest at the front. Each animal would have been trained for its specific position in the team, and this would have been a long and time consuming business.

Only one crop was grown on the land each year, with ploughing carried out in the spring. Ó Corráin (1972, 51–2) notes that there are references to harrows drawn by horses. It is unusual to find any mention of horses involved with agricultural activities; they were normally too valuable a status symbol to be used on such menial tasks. Sowing seems to have been broadcast, though references to the activity are few; there is little indication of crop management whilst it was growing. Only when excavated seed remains are available will it be clear whether weeding was carried out at any stage in the growth of the crop.

Harvesting took place in the autumn, and small sickles were used. Early Christian examples are all small, and Duignan (1944, 140) considers that they must have been used to reap the crop near the ear. Two types have been identified (Figure 5:13). Lagore crannog has produced an example with an incomplete socket and a rivet hole. The second form is tanged, and examples have come again from Lagore and also Garryduff 1. Reynolds (1979) considers that during the British Iron Age grain may have been harvested by hand, picking the ears of grain off the stems without the use of any tools. He considers that the small sickle-like objects would have been used for cutting coppiced woodland and hedges. This may have been the case in Early Christian Ireland, but as yet the evidence is equivocal.

The straw that was left standing after the grain harvest could be collected separately for fodder or thatch. Alternatively, some may have been harvested with the stalks, as there are references to corn in ricks (Plummer 1968, 127). Straw could be ploughed back into the ground (Ó Corráin 1972, 52), or it may have been left for animals to graze, their manure also providing some nutrients. The law tracts make it clear that the value of manure was well recognised, and it was collected in the folds and pounds used to house stock overnight. The wheat straw at Lagore may have been used as bedding for animals (Hencken 1950, 242).

Once harvested, the grain needed to be processed, and the threshing and winnowing were carried out at the farm. They were low status activities, as were most concerned with arable farming. They seem to have taken place in association with corn drying. Much grain was dried in kilns, and the documentary references to this are frequent. One form had a wooden circular frame onto which the cereal, still in ears, was laid (Morris 1973). The larger examples were of some size and must have been used by more than one household (Binchy 1973a, 55). There is some archaeological evidence for kilns, though all are small. The best example is from Letterkeen, Co. Mayo (Ó Ríordáin and Mac Dermott 1952), but another was found at the unpublished excavation of Ballymacash. A stone structure at Uisneach previously thought to be a cist was re-interpreted as an oven by Proudfoot (1961, 108), though the excavation and publication were of a quality to render any assessment difficult. An oven at Garranes (Ó Ríordáin 1942) may have had an agricultural purpose, but with the evidence for metalworking at the site, it may have had other functions.

Reynolds and Langley (1980) have questioned the value of drying corn in Romano–British contexts, though they recognise the value of this activity for barley in the production of malt. The production of malt in the Early Christian period was certainly a major activity, as evidenced by the literary references. Indeed, brewing was an activity carried out on most farms, and was of great social importance (Binchy 1981). In the extremely damp Irish climate, however, other cereals may also have had to be dried prior to storage. Certainly, experiments have shown the value of dry grain in milling (Monk 1981, 217). If damp, the grains clog the surface of the querns, and the effort required to produce a quantity of flour is many times greater than that with dry cereal (Curwen 1938, 151–2). Small quantities could be dried by an open fire, but larger quantities required a kiln. Indeed, it may be that substantial kilns should be seen as a necessary complement to the water-powered mills. In the *Críth Gablach* the *ócaire* is stated as having a share in a kiln, a mill and a barn, implying that all three structures were functionally related. As yet these structures have not been archaeologically recognised in a single landscape, and indeed most structures away from ring-forts are still very poorly understood.

There is little archaeological evidence for cereal storage. There are no four-post structures that can be convincingly called granaries, and the arrangement of four post holes recognised by Piggott (1940) at Cush 1 could be for any sort of structure. Ring-forts and crannogs do not contain structures that have any distinguishing features which suggest a storage role, though many buildings could and perhaps did have grain stored in them. Sacks, baskets and boxes may have been used, and some may have been placed in the underground souterrains as well as on the floor and roof space of buildings. There must, however, have been other repositories of grain since production was on a scale that must have warranted some other arrangements. These may have included the barns mentioned in the law tracts, and they may not have been found archaeologically because of their location at a distance from the ring-forts. However, they would have required protection, and most grain storage must have been in secure locations of some kind.

Ethnographic evidence suggests that till very recent times much grain was stored in Ireland in straw rope granaries (Lucas 1958b, 1959). These structures, *an fhóir*, were set on a furze or brushwood base, and consisted of a coil of straw rope. As the walls were built up, grain was poured in, and after a few feet the coil was turned in ever decreasing circles, producing a conical roof. Despite being made of the most perishable of materials, it was apparently an effective barrier to both vermin and weather. It may have been very common in Early Christian Ireland, though there is no definite mention of this form of structure in the literature. A straw rope granary would not leave any direct archaeological trace, though it may be possible to infer presence of some structures by clear gaps in the arrangement of buildings in an enclosure. Straw rope granaries would clearly need protection from animals searching for food, particularly in the winter months.

Grain was probably stored at monasteries because they had considerable room within their enclosures and were relatively safe from raiding, at least in the early part of the period. Lucas (1967) has shown that monasteries were repositories for all sorts of secular wealth, and that was one of the reasons they became popular targets for attack as time wore on, though they appear to have quickly recovered from raids. However dangerous a monastery may have been, it may well have been safer than a secular site. Monasteries appear to have taken on this banking function which cost them little, and allowed them considerable power and prestige, as well as an income in the form of tithes. Unfortunately, large scale excavations at major monasteries have been few and poorly published. This is an area where the future holds great archaeological promise.

Grain could be stored on or off the ear, and was kept for seed corn and animal and human consumption. Not even all human consumption was of ground grain, as mixtures such as stirabout involved the use of whole grains. Nevertheless, milling was an important activity. On many excavations small hand-worked rotary querns have been found, indicating the scale of much grain processing (Figure 5:14). Such a method was relatively slow and labour intensive, and was, like so many other arable associated activities, low status. The documentary sources indicate that it was an activity suitable for a slave girl, though the daughter of an *ócaire* was expected to learn how to use a quern from her foster-parent (Hughes 1972, 25). As Christianity spread, there were laws to prevent milling on a Sunday, the penalty for which included breaking the querns (Hamlin 1981). Many stones broke as they wore thin, but this provides one context in which viable stones could be destroyed. Another context was when legislation was introduced forbidding the use of hand querns, thus forcing all (legal) milling to be carried out at water mills.

The presence of rotary querns on settlements suggests the widespread small scale processing of grain, even at sites such as Lackan and Letterkeen where grain could not be grown in the vicinity (Proudfoot 1961). Given the importance of bread, however, it is surprising that a few sites do not produce querns at all, and this may be because of the development during the Early Christian period of the water-powered mill.

The archaeological evidence for the horizontal water mill in Early Christian Ireland was first studied at length by Lucas (1953). By collecting a large number of scattered references to previous casual finds, and discussing these together with several well preserved examples that he had been able to examine, the form and structure of the mills was clearly defined.

The water wheel on Irish mills was small, only about 3 feet in diameter. This has been demonstrated by the famous early find from Moycraig (McAdam 1856, 6) and more recent discoveries at Killinchy and Drumard (Figure 5:15). The individual blades are spoon-shaped, and some may have had an artificial twist in them (Lucas 1955, 107). Horizontal mills were still in use in Ireland during the nineteenth century, so dating of mills found by accident was always problematical. It was likely that most were Early Christian, and that their use died out only to be re-introduced in relatively recent times from the Outer Isles of Scotland, but this could not be easily proved. To this end, programmes of dating these mills by Carbon 14 and dendrochronology have been carried out (Baillie 1985). It is now clear that no high medieval examples are known. Some mills were constructed as early as the second quarter of the seventh century, with another phase of building which began in the late eighth century and continued through into the tenth century. Mac Eoin (1981) has pointed out that mills must have been common by the beginning of the eighth century as their full or part ownership was one of the indicators of status according to the *Críth Gablach*.

There has now been considerable historical work on the law tracts and contemporary stories that relate to milling (Curwen 1944, Lucas 1953, Mac Eoin 1981). The mill was one of the most, if not the most, technologically complex pieces of equipment in use in Early Christian Ireland, but the detailed analysis of the various elements given in one law tract means that the various elements recognised archaeologically can be linked with the contemporary terminology (Mac Eoin 1981).

Both documentary and archaeological work has until recently been undertaken on the

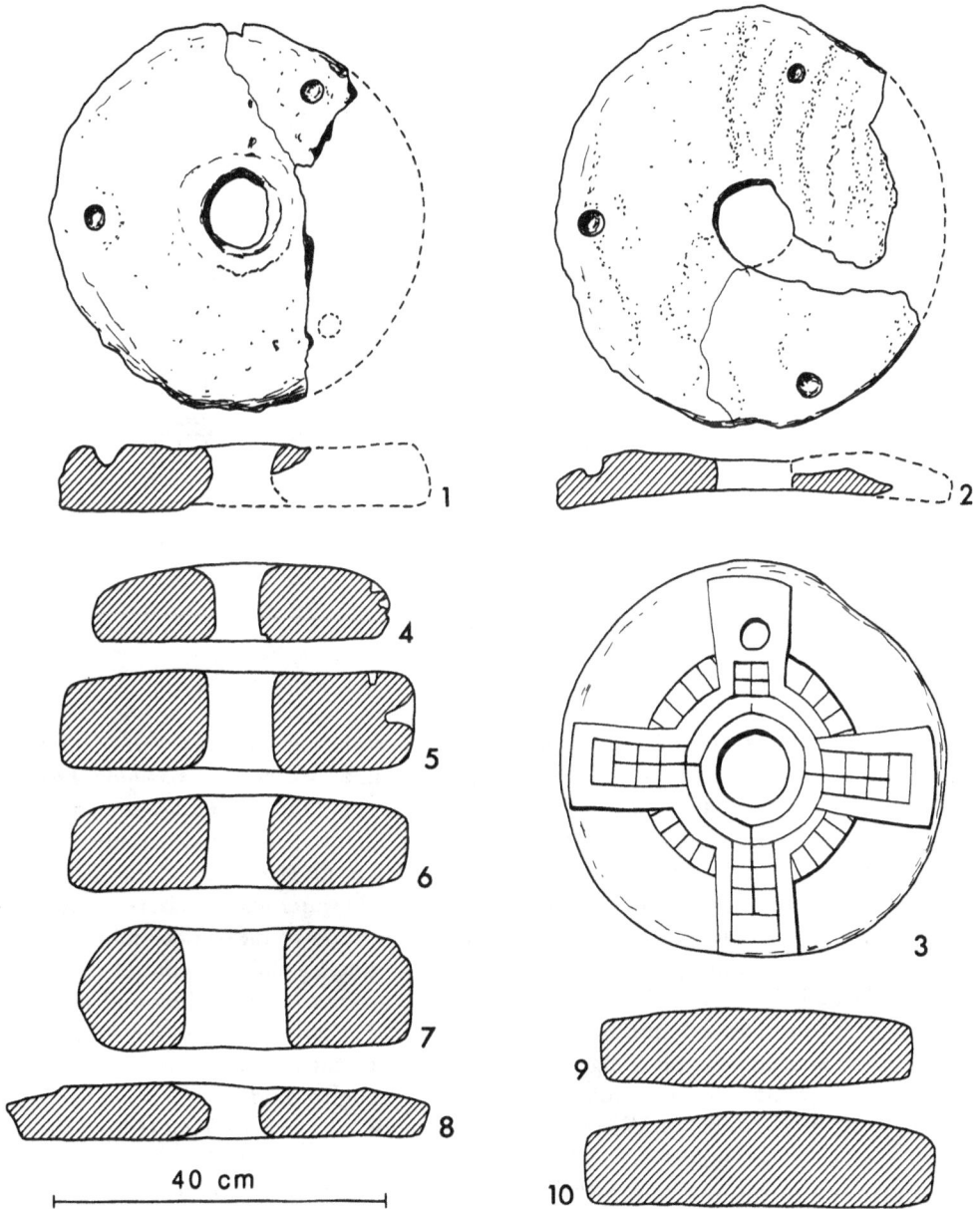

Figure 5:14 Rotary querns. Upper stones: **1, 2** Reask, Co. Kerry; **3** unprovenanced; **4–8** Cush, Co. Limerick. Lower stones: **9, 10** Cush, Co. Limerick (**1, 2** Fanning 1981, **3** Power 1939, **4–10** Ó Ríordáin 1940).

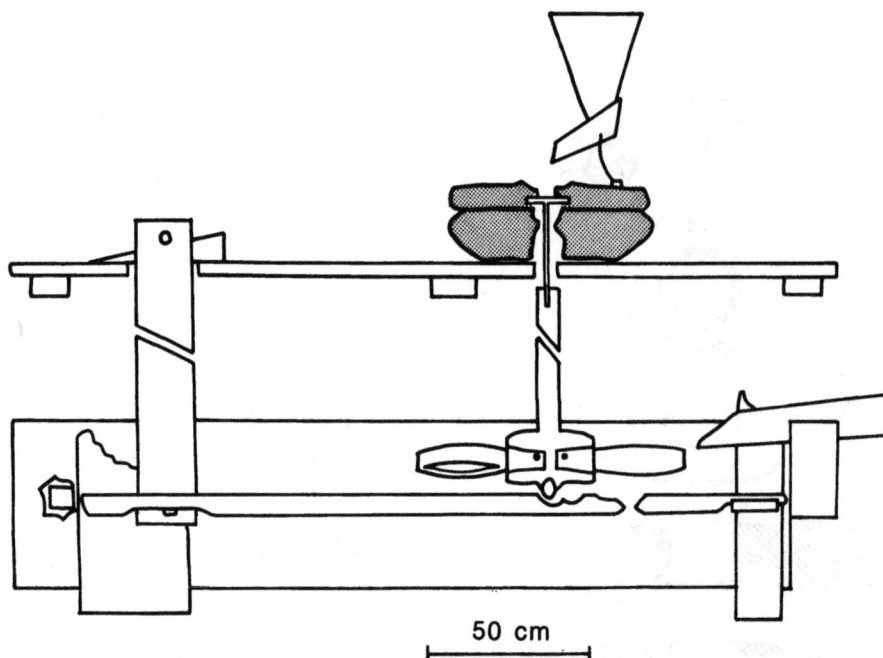

50 cm

Figure 5:15 Cross-section of a horizontal mill (Baillie 1975).

assumption that all mills were of the horizontal type. Whilst the vast majority were of this form, Rynne (1989a, 1989b) has identified a vertical wheeled mill at Morett, Co. Laoighis. This was a well preserved understructure described in detail by Lucas (1953). The dam was a triangular boarded area, edged with massive beams which would in turn have carried timber walling forming the sides of the dam. The water was funnelled down this channel, and into the trough below. A large balk of timber lay at right angles to the flow of water and to this were fixed both the dam structure and the trough, thus preventing dislocation of the various mill elements. Above it was another beam with a slot for timber walling and a sluice to control the flow of water into the mill. The trough itself was supported on two transverse timbers and was hewn from a single timber. This led into the wheelhouse, similar in construction to the dam but less well made; the flooring was planking and stone, but not neatly laid. Lucas had thought a horizontal wheel would have been housed here, but the trough would have been ineffective in this regard, but ideally suited for directing force to an under-shot wheel. Timber from the mill has now been dendrochronologically dated to AD 770. A mill at Little Island, Co. Cork has also been shown to have had a vertical wheel, and is dated even earlier, to AD 630, showing that both forms were being used in Ireland from about the same time.

The use of mills had an important social as well as economic function. Once the legislation preventing the use of hand mills was in force, the mill owner could control access to the milling equipment, and so to one of the important stages in the agricultural cycle. It is interesting that all the free grades of society had to own at least a share in a mill, thus ensuring their freedom from this dependence. The lower grades of unfree tenants were, even if they owned some land of their own, required to make use of a secular or monastic mill, no doubt at a considerable charge.

Fruit and vegetables

Most other crops were probably grown in small plots, often near the settlement. Archaeological evidence for the plots is not great, but some enclosures are likely candidates. The open houses at The Spectacles were located on a natural terrace overlooking Lough Gur in Co. Limerick (Ó Ríordáin 1949). They were set in small yards or plots that may have grown vegetables. The small fields around the southern group of ring-forts at Cush may have served a similar purpose, as might those adjacent to the ring-fort by the shores of Lough Gur (Figures 5:2–5:5).

The hand tools needed for horticulture contrast with the heavy capital equipment necessary for arable farming (Figure 5:16). Spades were simple but effective tools, and iron tips have been found at Ballinderry 1 and Lagore. There were some flanged iron objects which Duignan (1944) considered were shares but they may in fact have been spades; a similar though unstratified item from Uisneach was identified as an iron spade. Small fields and garden plots were probably dug with spades rather than any attempt to plough in confined areas. A composite wooden spade type has been recognised from a range of waterlogged contexts (Morris 1973), and appears to be an indigenous form (Bradley 1982).

Almost all evidence for garden crops comes from documents, since few produce seeds that survive; the one exception is that of flax, used for the production of linen. Monk (1986) considers that flax was probably produced on quite a large scale. Woad was also a popular and highly valued crop (Mac Niocaill 1971, 83), being an important dye used in the textile industry. Vegetables provided variety to the diet, but must always have been a small part of it. Ó Corráin (1972) lists several varieties, notably an onion, *cainenn*, and the leek, *foltchep*, which were commonly mentioned in texts. Celery and tap-rooted vegetables were grown in ridges, and peas and probably kale were also cultivated.

Fruit was certainly eaten, but most was probably collected from the wild and in relatively small quantities; apple is the only fruit tree which appears to have been intensively cultivated. Mention of orchards occurs usually in monastic contexts, but Lucas (1960, 38) notes that in the secular laws tenants who moved could be compensated for apple trees they had planted.

Woodland and moorland

It is likely that even in the late Iron Age part of the woodland was managed; the wooden trackways of that period (Raftery 1987) that have been found running across bogs suggest the ability to acquire large quantities of suitable timber at one time. In the Early Christian period when the landscape began to become more intensively used, the control of timber must have grown in importance. Because of various phases of clearance since the neolithic, there was probably little original wildwood left by AD 500, the forest being that of secondary woodland in various stages of maturity.

In the fifth and sixth centuries, and probably still in the seventh, there were areas which were still under-utilised and were available for clearance and conversion to agriculture. However, stands of trees must have been maintained to provide structural timber, and it is highly likely that coppicing was widely practised. Because of post-medieval clearances (McCracken 1971), early woodland landscapes do not survive in Ireland as they do occasionally in Britain (Rackham

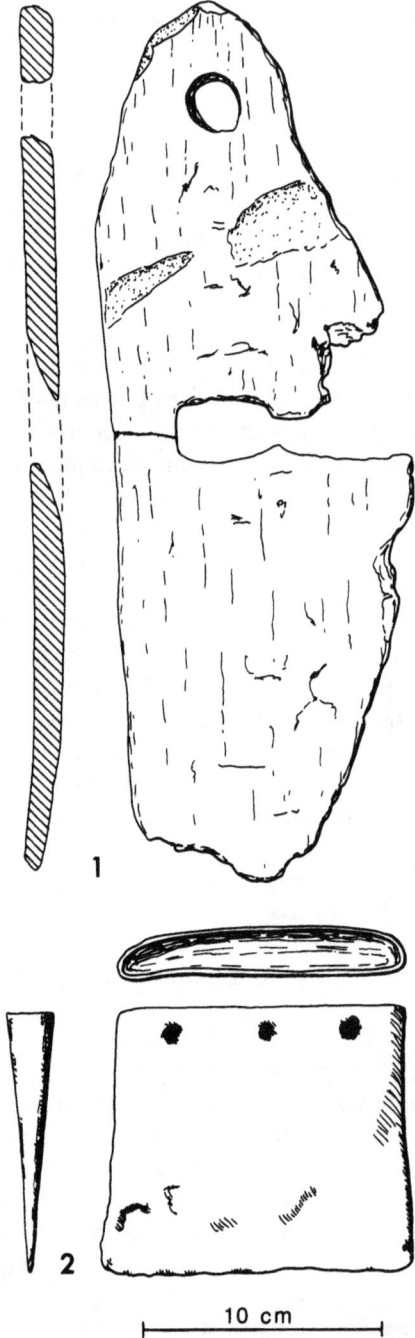

Figure 5:16 **1** Wooden spade from Moynagh Lough, Co. Meath; **2** iron spade tip from Ballinderry 2, Co. Offaly (**1** Bradley 1982, **2** Hencken 1942).

1980), but the Irish pattern must have been essentially similar. By having a system of wood-pasture, it was possible to graze cattle as well as the feral pigs, and at the same time provide timber. The presence of some trees on land did not prevent it being categorised as high quality according to the law tracts. The large quantities of wattles necessary for hurdle fences and buildings would have come from coppiced trees whilst larger timbers could come from selected trees left to grow to suitable sizes. The thinnings and fallen branches would provide firewood, as would the debris from hedge cutting.

The economic importance of trees was clearly recognised, and the properties of the different species were well understood, as can be seen in the tree list which forms part of the eighth century *Bretha Comaithchesa* (Kelly 1976). A couple of examples will suffice to illustrate this. The oak was recognised as valuable because of its acorns, and also there are compensations to be paid for taking parts or the whole of the tree for timber. Bark was used for tanning leather, but the scars could be healed by the application of a covering made up from clay, cow dung and milk. The hazel was valued for its nuts and its rods – the coppiced wattles that were very suitable for fences and walls of buildings.

Marginal land such as moor was also of economic importance. The use of peat for fuel is well attested in the documentary sources, and archaeologically at sites such as Reask, Co. Kerry where the hearths of the stone roundhouses of the Early Christian period produced prehistoric Carbon 14 dates since they dated when the plants which formed the peat had died, not the date of the burning of the peat (Fanning 1981). Iron panning in the bogs was also exploited (see Chapter 6). Other marginal areas were utilised also. Bracken may have been burnt to produce potash necessary to bleach linen (Kelly 1976, 120). Furze also had a range of uses such as fodder, dyes and fuel in later periods (Lucas 1960) and the fact that it was given a value in the Early Christian period suggests that some at least of these were already appreciated then.

Honey was extremely important as the only real form of sweetener and was used in cooking and in the production of mead. Beeswax was used to make candles. There is no archaeological evidence for honey, but the *Bechbretha* law tract covers this subject in elaborate detail (Charles-Edwards and Kelly 1983) and it is also mentioned in numerous other sources.

Fishing and strandlooping

There is surprisingly little documentary evidence for fishing either inland or at sea. The archaeological evidence is also very slight, but this is mainly because of the difficulty in recovering fish bones from deposits unless rigorous sieving is undertaken. A few fish bones were found at Lagore, which suggests the possibility of inland fishing. At Oughtymore, Co. Derry, a shell midden in sand dunes showed the full potential of detailed analysis (Mallory and Woodman 1984). A number of eel and cod bones were recovered, together with a smaller number of flatfish such as plaice or flounder, salmon or salmon trout and possibly haddock. None would have required deep sea fishing techniques and all could have been netted in or near the Lough Foyle estuary.

Shellfish are not necessarily a very important dietary element, but more archaeologically visible. At Oughtymore, and nearby inland sites such as Park and Potters Caves, winkles and cockles were the most common shellfish exploited, with mussels of some significance. Although the sand dune site was close to the sea, rocky areas where such shellfish could be collected were at some distance from the settlement. Rathmullan, under a mile from the sea, also produced mussels and some limpets.

A small amount of whalebone has been found in excavations at Rathmullan, but this must have come from a beached whale; one is mentioned in the *Annals of the Four Masters* in 739 (Lynn 1982, 154).

Salt was used in the preservation of food, but how this was produced is unknown. As yet no briquetage has been identified on settlements, nor have any evaporation pans or boiling hearths been found. However, this had remained a gap in the British archaeological record until fieldwork was carried out in appropriate areas (de Brisay and Evans 1975).

The system at work

The various elements of the agricultural system have been described, and it is now possible to examine how they worked together as a whole, maintaining a state of equilibrium overall. The model can examine the subsistence production, processing, storage and consumption as a cyclical and largely unchanging phenomenon throughout the period under discussion. There were, however, two important trends which developed during this period, the most notable being that of expansion, with far greater numbers of people producing greater quantities of subsistence goods. Whilst this led to significant changes in the social and exchange systems, within the subsistence system itself it had little impact. The other important trend was that of increasing violence which threatened the reliability of agricultural production and storage. Here there was more influence on subsistence strategies, with secure storage becoming increasingly vital. These changes, however, had most impact after AD 800, and so are not greatly discussed here.

There may have been some changes in the relative importance of animal species, and animal products compared with arable ones, but this is difficult to recognise with the relatively few well dated and sufficiently large assemblages of environmental data as yet available. The few sites with substantial faunal remains divided by periods or phases are shown in Table 5:1. Comparison is difficult because of the different criteria by which the figures have been derived but the importance of cattle is clear in all these sites. The smaller percentages at Rathmullan may be due to better collection of smaller bones during the excavation, but there must have been regional variations in animal husbandry patterns. Moreover, status and economic significance would have affected consumption patterns and sites of different types (crannogs versus ring-forts for example) may have had different bone disposal strategies. The sites show no general trends through time and are too dispersed to allow recognition of regional economies. Cereal remains are so limited that even changes on a single site cannot be readily identified.

The decision-making groups in society were not directly involved in the day-to-day running of agriculture, and their main concern was that the system should produce as large a surplus of cattle as possible in order to be able to participate in the social and political manipulations which dominated Early Christian Ireland. This was the desire that created the specific demand, and mere subsistence (in whatever form) was not enough. Nevertheless, the vagaries of farming are never insignificant, the more so in a system where the control of the environment was extremely limited and technology was not advanced to allow for elaborate storage. The agricultural system therefore had to be flexible within its overall aims, and there were numerous ways by which stress could be alleviated.

Table 5:1   Percentages of cattle, pig and sheep bones from Early Christian period settlements (Lynn 1982)

Site and reference	Cattle	Pig	Sheep/ goat
Carraig Aille I and II (Ó Ríordáin 1949), 6 tons	'up to 90%'		
Boho (Proudfoot 1953), 223 bones identified	67	20	7.6
Ballyfounder, primary levels (Waterman 1958), 235 bones	57.9	26.8	12.3
Shaneen Park (Proudfoot 1958)	85	14	1
Lough Faughan Crannog (Collins 1955)			
Upper habitation (misc.) 419 bones	64.8	27	7.9
Habitation, 537 bones	65	22.5	9.5
Structural levels, 192 bones	56.5	24	16
Lagore Crannog (Hencken 1950), percentages based on no. of skulls (total 959)			
Outside palisade	67.5	17.5	15
Period III	84.6	15.4	–
Period II	46.4	33.9	19.6
Period IB	70.5	14.4	15.1
Period IA	61.4	12.5	26.1
Rathmullan			
Souterrain fill (177 bones identified)	42.4	27.1	21.5
Phases 3, 4 (542 bones identified)	51	30	9
Phase 2 (1619 bones identified)	56	23	16
Phase 1 (478 bones identified)	41.4	9.6	42.7

Note   Figures are based on the total number of bones identified unless otherwise stated.

The annual cycle

The arable and pastoral systems were, though distinct, inextricably linked. Not only were both carried out over the same landscape, with some conflicting interests, they also relied on each other for their very operation. Both were also highly dependent on the yearly cycle of production.

The spring ploughing involved the use of oxen, a product of the pastoral economy, as was much of the manure spread on the ground. After the crop was sown, it was tended and grew, finally being harvested in autumn. In the meantime, the herds had begun to feed on the spring grass, gave birth to a new generation and, during the summer, were able to grow fat on the lush grazing. The length and intensity of the growing season were critical for success during the coming winter, and every source of grass, from mountain top to water meadow, was exploited to the full. The legal tracts show that animals could be in close proximity to crops, and that trespass and illegal grazing took place. There was also fine control of pastures, with permanent and temporary fencing in use.

Animals were vital in the Early Christian economy of Ireland because they could turn a plentiful resource – grass – into one fit for human consumption. This was particularly important in the wetter western areas where arable farming, though still important, could not fulfil the same role that it could in parts of the east. Fields and open, common land were grazed and the summer milk foods, 'white meats', were produced in great quantity. Many were consumed immediately, letting humans as well as the fattening pigs build up stores that could be burnt off during the winter. Others were preserved in the form of butter and cheese for later consumption or exchange.

In many respects the autumn was the most crucial time. The length of the grass growing season could dictate how fat and strong animals would become, how long they would continue to produce milk and how quickly the stored foodstuffs could remain untouched. At this point, grazing of stubble was used to supplement animal diet, and fattening could continue. Supplies were limited, however, and there were constraints. For humans there was a gradual change from summer foods to winter ones, including meat. Pigs that had been fattened and killed earlier in the year were available smoked and salted; sheep and cattle were now culled. The long, cold winter of attrition had begun. Gradually supplies dwindled during the cold months. Animals let out during the day scratched what little they could from the low-nutrient pastures, supplemented in their diet by twigs, heather and straw. They were also, if of sufficient value, allowed grain fodder. Men and animals often went hungry and, no doubt, this related to position on the social and economic scale. The desire to own as many cattle as possible promoted large herds, herds that could be supported easily with careful management during the plentiful summer months when grazing was abundant, but which were impossible to maintain in good condition through the winter. This put a strain on the whole system, and the prize cattle were real competition for human grain supplies during this time. The suffering was, however, considered worthwhile, particularly by those decision-makers who suffered least but benefited most from the system.

Considerable variations did occur to the system, causing forces of negative feedback to come into operation. The relationship between herd size and arable production was clear. If crop yields were low, then there was to be relatively little for animal fodder. Therefore, slaughtering probably took place earlier in the autumn and absolute herd size was reduced. In contrast, with a higher than average grain surplus, more animals could be over-wintered. The same might also be true if winter came late, and grazing continued to the end of the year. This adjustment of animal populations was a relatively straightforward business and, though there was room for expansion of herd size after all social obligations had been fulfilled, the carrying capacity of the land prevented ever-growing herds.

Major disasters were also possible. The Annals frequently mention mass starvation of animals and humans, particularly when snow had fallen. Such comments cannot be taken to indicate climatic trends but should be seen as selectively recorded local disasters, examples of more widespread sporadic crises. Most beasts were at a low point by late winter, and any cessation of grazing could place them in jeopardy. Fodder supplies would by then be low, with herds dispersed and relatively inaccessible in their attempts to find some nourishment. Such substantial losses would have been very serious for those holding animals in clientage, though providing some of the herd survived, rejuvenation up to previous levels could be achieved in relatively few years. Of equal or even greater seriousness were cattle diseases. These are also mentioned in the Annals, and again suggest a weakened animal population under stress through excessive numbers. The tendency for pastoralist groups to over-extend their herds is well attested throughout the world, and the natural constraints to balance the system frequently came into operation. Poor weather and disease may well be related, though one could occur without the other.

Checks and balances therefore kept the agricultural system in equilibrium. Sufficient grain was grown to provide enough surplus for human consumption, with some left for animal fodder.

The extensive grazing areas remaining could, at least in the summer, provide more than enough grass. However large the herds grew, they could only be maintained at that level if the winter supplies were sufficient; this was the critical factor in determining carrying capacity. The annual cycle prevented growth in the overall total, though individuals could increase their stake at the expense of others. This is discussed elsewhere, but here we are concerned with the working of the system as a whole.

Agriculture was run as efficiently as was possible within the technology and tenurial framework. However, these actually provided several substantial constraints on production. The most obvious is the poor system of storage, another is the tenurial system. It was not in the interests of the elite to change these arrangements, however, since they derived their power from the control they exercised over the storage (often monasteries) and the land tenure (generally secular groups). It was also the case that no group had sufficient power to carry out effective changes. The social system, already outlined in Chapter 4, prevented the development of centralised control which might have allowed directional change.

The control of the agricultural system was one of the main ways by which the elite maintained its position. It is worthwhile examining the main ways this was done, and how these controls provided the negative feedback that prevented change. Where innovation was undertaken, this was only to strengthen the existing framework, and so did not threaten but in fact strengthened the status quo.

Articulation of subsistence goods

The social relations based on kinship and clientage have been discussed at length in Chapter 4, but these had important economic implications which can be considered separately. Decision-making in Early Christian Ireland involved a balancing of social and economic objectives, but as so much of social status related to the maintenance of a certain material wealth, the generation of that through subsistence activities was vital. It is possible to consider on the one hand the distribution and manipulation of capital which were essential to allow production to take place, and on the other to assess the flows of produce between those who lent and borrowed the capital. This is largely derived from legal tracts, but there is some archaeological evidence that can be compared with these schematised frameworks.

Throughout the following discussion it is assumed that there was no political unrest with cattle raiding and the taking of land. In fact raiding became increasingly widespread as time went on. Most groups would have roughly balanced gains and losses from raiding, which did not greatly diminish the total livestock pool for Ireland as a whole. These forms of redistribution were, however, major factors in the growth of certain dynastic elements at the expense of others. The potential growth outlined below through clientage and investment in the land formed the background expansion of the total subsistence base (and human population which it supported) which fuelled the social developments outlined in the previous chapter. Success of certain political groups overlay this long-term process of expansion in the subsistence base, but was only marginally related to it in that there was a greater amount of resources to manipulate as time went on.

There were occasional natural disasters such as bad winters and cattle murrain which could deplete stocks. This was, for Ireland as a whole, more significant than the mere redistribution by raiding. Such disasters, however, appear to have been relatively rare and may only have led to limited and temporary adjustment of mutual obligations for several subsequent years until a level of equilibrium at a satisfactory stocking level could be once more achieved. The various regulations laid out in the law tracts were schematic; they may have been relaxed in times of crisis. There must likewise have been adjustment during and after the plagues which struck the human population. It is difficult to calculate the scale of dislocation, but certainly many important figures succumbed according to the written sources. Nevertheless, it is perhaps too easy to invoke such random impacts as the cause of major economic changes. There does not seem to have been a plague which could be considered to have struck on the same scale as the later Black Death. Human populations could recover from plague in the same way that cattle could recover from murrain.

The most important item of capital in agriculture is land. As has already been outlined, control of this was largely communal at the beginning of the Early Christian period, but gradually more and more land began to be held by individuals. Whilst land was redistributed from a large pool, fluctuations in family size would have had little effect, but this was of vital importance once land was owned and subdivided on the death of the father. Moreover, as the population rose, the amount of land per capita decreased and land became a valuable commodity in itself. The population increase and the consequent problems in maintaining free status led, as has been demonstrated, to the creation of the ócaire grade below that of the bóaire, and it is significant that it is this grade that sometimes had to take its base clientship payment in land.

It is likely that much of the land that fell into private ownership from an early date was that which was free from traditional obligations, in other words newly colonised areas. These were open to manipulation in different ways and were probably most heavily structured according to clientage principles. As kin-groups lost control of ancient communal lands, these too would have been available for manipulation. As time passed, a greater amount of land was held by the elite, who parcelled it out, along with animal stock, seed corn and any necessary equipment, to tenants who entered into a range of base clientship relationships dependent on their status.

The law tracts discuss most of the clientship in terms of cattle, and this emphasises their social as well as economic importance. Cattle were a measure of wealth, and the attraction of the clientship obligations was that they gave a chance for the efficient (and lucky) farmer to expand his herd at a greater rate than the payments made to the lord, and thus improve his own position.

By using the work of Mac Niocaill (1981) and Gerriets (1983) it is possible to produce a model showing the manipulation of cattle in clientage and the range of agricultural produce given in return. Concentration here is paid to base clientship since free clients seem to have received only token numbers of animals and probably only paid small amounts of renders and so are of social rather than economic significance.

The exact amounts lent out and received back in the *Críth Gablach* and the *Cáin Aigillne* law tracts are similar but not identical, and are of course somewhat schematised. Nevertheless, they provide a useful framework for analysis. The value of the amounts given out by the lord varied depending on the status of the recipient, and the renders in return were not in proportion. The *Críth Gablach* and *Cáin Aigillne* differ in details, but the general structure of loans and payments is clear (Table 5:2). Thus, there is clearly a social element here rather than just an economic one and those lower down the social scale paid more dearly for their clientship. All, however, paid agricultural produce and this must have been an important mechanism in the redistribution of subsistence goods.

Using the number of clients of various grades that are needed to attain a certain noble grade,

Table 5:2 Payments made between client and lord according to the *Crith Gablach* and *Cáin Aigillne* (Gerriets 1983)

Rank		Séoit turchluide		Taurchrecc		Bés	Fosair	
Crith Gablach	Cáin Aigillne	Crith Gablach	Cáin Aigillne	Crith Gablach	Cáin Aigillne	Both texts	Crith Gablach	Cáin Aigillne
2nd *fer midboth* = *oenchiniud*	*Oenchiniud*	1-year-old calf	(not given)	5 *séoit* = 4 cows	6 heifers or 3 cows	Wether	12 loaves, an *ól* of butter, an *ól* of 3 kinds of milk, a handful of leeks	Bacon of 2 finger breadths, 2 sacks of malt, ⅓ sack of wheat, 1 handful of candles
Ócaire	*Fer midboth*	3 *séoit*	(not given)	8 cows = 10 *séoit*	12 *séoit*	Male calf in its first year	Bacon 1 finger breadth thick, 3 sacks of malt, ½ sack of kiln-dried wheat	Bacon 3 finger breadths thick, 3 sacks of malt, ½ sack of wheat, 1 handful of candles
Bóaire	*Ócaire*	5 *séoit*	3 *séoit*	12 cows = 15 *séoit*	16 *séoit*	1-year-old male calf	Summer and winter food	Bacon of 3 finger breadths, 3 sacks of malt, ½ sack of wheat, 2 handfuls of candles
Mrugfher	*Bóaire*	6 *séoit*	(not given)	2 *cumala* 20 cows = 25 *séoit*	30 *séoit*	Cow	Summer and winter food	Bacon 1 hand thick, ½ a bacon, fat from the rear third of a cow, fat of an entire year-old male calf, fat of an entire wether, 1 calf of 1 sack, 1 calf of 2 sacks, 1 calf of 4 sacks, 1 pig of 9 fists long, 8 sacks of malt, 1 sack of hardened wheat, 3 handfuls of candles, 1 cauldron of curds and butter, 24 loaves of bread, 2 handfuls of garlic, 2 handfuls of leeks

Forms of payment

Table 5:3 Capital in cattle needed to obtain requisite numbers of the various categories of clients, by noble grade, according to the *Críth Gablach* (Binchy 1941, Mac Niocaill 1981)

Noble grade	Mrugfher	Bóaire	Ócaire	Total
Aire forgill	120	96	99	315
Aire tuise	96	80	66	242
Aire ardd	48	48	55	151
Aire désso	24	16	33	73

it is possible to draw up a chart of the total resources needed in loan capital and subsequent returns by grade (Table 5.3). Considerable total loans are involved, though if much of those to the *ócaire* grades were in land rather than cattle, the number of beasts necessary would have been considerably reduced.

Clientship relations lasted for seven years, and renders were paid on all but the last. If the clientship relationship were to be maintained after this time, a further loan was required from the lord. The income derived from the loans was a mixed collection of items necessary for subsistence; they were not only related to cattle. When it is remembered that the *aire forgill* grade of noble had 20 clients, 5 of whom were of the *mrugfer* grade and returning considerable quantities of renders, the total income would have been large. It is unclear as to how extensive were the agricultural interests of such nobles; it is likely that much of their capital was in fact invested to produce not only the economic return but also the social prestige. The renders, therefore, would have been essential for the maintenance of the noble household.

The noble also managed, though not personally, lands of his own. The exploitation of these may well have been dominated by cattle. The surpluses of beasts which were thus produced could be used to replace those whose obligations had terminated after seven years and if possible increase the number of clients.

Although the social benefits of maintaining clients are easily demonstrated, what were the economic advantages? Surely in economic terms it would have been better for a rich man to maintain all the stock himself, and keep all the surplus. The manipulation of stock through clientage did reduce income, and some rich individuals did not engage in clientship, but remained outside the system; they are poorly documented because they do not figure prominently in the surviving legislation. However, there were some important short-term and long-term economic advantages with clientship. The short-term advantages were the diversity of renders paid to the lord. These were valuable in that one resource was lent out – cattle – but various animal and arable products were income. This spread the risks of failure in any one product and ensured a steady supply. There could also be occasional windfalls of income, since the lord kept part of any payments made with reference to successful legal claims made by any of his clients. The long-term advantages were also concerned with spreading risk, since the lord's beasts were physically scattered about the landscape under clientship, and so the chance of cattle murrain or losses through raiding causing major dislocation of income was further reduced. It also meant that the lord's herd could keep increasing in size even if his (albeit extensive) estates could not cope with the additional beasts. If there had not been a system of clientship, his acreage of grazing would have been a major constraint. With the loan out of animals that could not otherwise have been supported, the lord could receive back the various renders.

In economic terms the clientship system can be seen to offer all parties an opportunity for betterment. The clients had capital that, with good fortune, could grow and allow their own standing to rise. Likewise the lord could manipulate greater amounts of capital than would have been possible on his own estates, and also spread the risks of losses over a wider area. In a society where the manipulation of capital was otherwise difficult, clientship provided a finance system that allowed the poorer entrepreneur to develop his own farm (perhaps taken in forest clearance) by the loan of capital whilst it allowed the aristocracy to make continued surpluses which they could not otherwise have supported. Whilst this may have often been in cattle, it may have been in a wide range of farm equipment or seed corn.

Arable farming was, despite its low status, far more capital-intensive in terms of equipment than pastoral farming. The plough was, for many farmers, an item that had to be shared; the *ócaire* owned a quarter of the equipment. For others, not in such an arrangement and unable to provide one out of their own resources, the ploughing of land was difficult and involved a subordinate relationship with another. Payment had to be made for the ploughing to be done, and those who owned the plough could determine what that charge would be. It was inevitably a high economic and social price that had to be paid. It would seem that even small items of agricultural equipment may have been obtained as part of the package of resources received through base clientage; the law tracts mention the loan of an axe and billhook (Mac Niocaill 1981).

The storage of grain has left little archaeological trace. Even if straw rope granaries, *an fhóir*, were in use, there seems to have been insufficient space for large grain supplies in ring-forts and crannogs. The large oval or circular monastic enclosures, however, were clearly in contrast to the secular settlements and could house many granaries. This use of the monastic enclosure and its sacred protective power was only possible with the creation of economic and social relationships between the secular and religious groups. In return for the payments of tithes, the secular population could enter into a relationship which provided spiritual support but also, of more importance in this context, the protection for surpluses. Both groups benefited from this arrangement, but particularly the church which was in fact having to do relatively little for its part. The aristocracy often prevented any conflict of interest by founding or taking over a monastery and manning it by their own kin, thus keeping both sides of the contract under familial control.

6
Technology and craft activity

Introduction

The use of technology to produce a wide range of material culture items was an important activity in Early Christian Ireland. Whilst there had been limited craft specialisation and production during the early Iron Age, the relatively rare finds of material culture from the period indicate craft activity at a stagnant level, limited in the main to the production of personal equipment for the elite. In the Early Christian period there was, however, a major change to larger scale production of everyday objects and, though most settlements sites still have a relatively limited surviving artefactual assemblage, the range of material goods was much greater than before. The paucity of finds on many excavated Early Christian sites can be related to depositional and post-depositional factors, and the few settlements with appropriate deposits such as crannogs produce large quantities of material and indicate a rich material culture assemblage.

Craft activity implies some form of specialisation, and from the quality of many surviving artefacts and from documentary sources it is clear that the range of specialists that could be found in Early Christian Ireland was considerable. This is not to deny that individuals could practise more than one craft, or combine it with farming or landholding. The picture was, not surprisingly, complex. Not all craftsmen of a certain speciality were of the same ability or status. Craftsmen were given status in the law tracts depending on their craft and, in some cases, their competence.

The change to greater production, and the alteration in the organisation of craft activity, is one that has received relatively little interest for Early Christian Ireland. There has been considerable attention paid to the artefacts themselves, and to the techniques of production, but not to the organisation of the crafts at a higher level. Evidence for such an analysis can be drawn from the form and distribution of artefacts, from the association of artefacts and production debris with settlements and from documentary references to craftsmen and their activities. Some outline can thus be drawn, though the lack of detailed published studies, apart from the notable exception of motif-pieces (Plates XII, XIII) by O'Meadhra (1979, 1987), hinders detailed discussion.

210

Production of all material goods in the period to 800 can be seen to be at most at the level of small schools of craftsmen. Some artefacts were made by those who needed them, and this applies particularly to simple objects of stone, bone and wood. The vast majority of items, however, were made by specialist craftsmen. It is the organisation of these craftsmen that is less clear, and it probably varied through both time and space, and by craft. Where these variations can be discerned they are discussed in detail under the appropriate craft.

Some activities were primarily the work of women, notably textiles. The spinning of yarn, its dyeing and subsequent weaving all took place within the domestic context, though different women may have had special expertise in various stages of the work. There were also status variations; high quality embroidery was an activity of aristocratic women. The archaeological evidence suggests that inhabitants at many sites (but far from all) were engaged in spinning, but the other stages of textile production are less visible.

Relatively little is known archaeologically or from documentary sources about the working of other perishable materials such as wood, leather and bone, but what little can be discerned would imply that they were unlike textiles, and were predominantly male preserves to be broadly compared with metalworking activities for which much more evidence survives.

Metalworking can be separated in documentary sources between working with iron, and working with other materials, notably precious metals, copper-alloys and, on archaeological evidence, glass. The working of iron and other sources must sometimes have been co-ordinated, since composite artefacts are known, but this could still have involved the co-operation of two craftsmen with distinct areas of expertise. The ironworker needed to work at higher temperatures, with larger quantities and for a wide range of clients. In contrast the worker of non-ferrous metals used small quantities of materials with a high labour input; he was mainly producing decorative items, even if most also had a functional aspect such as clothes-fastener or receptacle.

It is also likely that the ironworker and non-ferrous craftsman organised their work in different ways. Whilst there is evidence from many sites of small quantities of iron slag, suggesting limited ironworking, this was probably repair work and not primary manufacture; some may even have been done by the normal inhabitants of the settlements. A specialist smelting, and possible later working, site has been identified at Ballyvourney, and this can be usefully compared with the law tract descriptions of the smith's forge. It would appear, therefore, that the ironworker was often permanently established even if he may have made visits to scattered sites for limited repair work and recycling of scrap.

The incidence of significant amounts of non-ferrous metalworking debris is more widespread than that of ironworking, and suggests that craftsmen in such activities were more peripatetic during this period. A wide range of sites have produced archaeological evidence: ring-forts, promontory forts, crannogs, monasteries. Whilst some sites such as Garryduff 1 may have been the permanent residences of craftsmen (and such individuals could be of high status according to the law tracts), most are clearly not. The craftsmen in these cases therefore appear to have been itinerant, though perhaps having a base at which some work could have been done. Peripatetic craftsman might also be suggested by the archaeological evidence for the production process whereby creation of artefacts in advance does not seem to have been common, but rather each artefact was a unique and specific creation made to order. Detailed study of superficially similar high status artefacts and repeated elements in composite objects shows that they are very rarely identical and so normally not made from the same mould bearing decoration (O'Meadhra 1987, 138).

It is almost certain, however, that less complex and lower status objects were produced in quantity. Ring- and stick-pins and ring-brooches may have been mass-produced in clay impressed with lead dies. Glass beads and bangles would have easily been manufactured in considerable numbers, as would the lathe-turned lignite or jet armlets which are frequent casual losses on settlements.

The position of the (at least partly) itinerant craftsman in society can be discerned from the law tracts which accept that such individuals are protected beyond their own *túath*. This was in contrast to the clearly sedentary smith who was able to act as a focus for legal pronouncements within the society.

For metalworking and most other crafts it would appear that secular manufacturing units consisted of only one craftsman, with perhaps assistants and apprentices, as mentioned in the *Uraicecht Bec* (Mac Neill 1923, 278). Training may have been given during fosterage. There is no evidence that groups of secular craftsmen, each specialising in a particular stage of processing or in related crafts, lived and worked together. This prevented large scale mass production on the one hand and ensured the individuality of high status items on the other. As ecclesiastical establishments grew in wealth and power they were able to support larger groups of craftsmen than had even the most powerful secular individuals. This may merely have been because the ecclesiastical institutions could, because of their greater and more stable wealth, support such activities. It also reflects, however, a different attitude to material culture, and the desire to use highly decorated items both to an ideological end – the greater glory of God – and a sociopolitical one – the emphasis of monastic power in society. The investment in craft activity was not limited to those crafts already developing in the secular sphere but additionally included manuscript production and sculpture in stone. That ability in such trades was held in high esteem can be seen from the number of powerful clerics who were themselves craftsmen.

Whilst larger monasteries certainly supported a number of craftsmen, it is unclear still how many of any one speciality there might have been, and whether all were more or less permanently assigned to one house. Hughes (1972) suggests that there were many involved in a scriptorium, others such as Cramp (1967) suspect that there were few. There is some evidence here, however, of specialisation; the more decorative elements of the manuscripts seem to have been often produced by different individuals. For example, several scribes and yet other illuminators have been identified for the Book of Kells, though one individual may have done some of each (Henry 1974, 211–12). The archaeological evidence is so partial that, even when workshops can be suggested on the basis of a number of stylistically similar items, it is not possible to assess the number of individuals involved in their production. Thus the size of the Clonmacnois school of grave slab sculptors cannot be estimated, though it probably consisted of more than one individual at any one time.

There is evidence by the eighth century that designers and producers within monasteries may not have been the same people, suggesting a more complex arrangement. The evidence for this comes from the Ardagh and Derrynaflan chalices where in both cases the complexity of design was considerable and in places outstripped the skills of the makers. The complex symbolic meanings also suggested in these and other intricate items might indicate a more educated background for the designers than might have been expected for craftsmen. It is unclear, however, how many craftsmen within the ecclesiastical milieu were well educated; it may be that this was the case and that both intellectual and practical skills developed hand in hand.

Changes through time are now becoming apparent in craft production, mainly through the study of finished artefacts and motif-pieces; as yet other production evidence from sites is limited, though the excavations at Clogher and Moynagh Lough crannog are clearly going to be important. There is a trend from AD 500 to 800 towards greater size and complexity of artefacts at the higher end of the social scale. In the earliest phases of the Early Christian period the predominant market appears to have been secular, but by the end of the period the ecclesiastical demands and controls were beginning to become more dominant.

In the rest of this chapter, groups of crafts are examined in turn, in each case considering the production system with the necessary inputs and outputs. Within this framework, the craft activity as such, and the demand for the output produced, is placed in a systemic social and economic framework. Particular emphasis is placed on both the organisation of the activities at the various stages of production, and the degree of specialisation.

Non-ferrous metals and glass

Much of the working of non-ferrous metals and glass was carried out by the same individuals. As the processes required were complex, and many of the final products extremely fine, there can be little doubt that highly trained specialists were involved. The same craftsman used related technologies and tools for gold, silver, copper-alloy and glass, and indeed many products were composite artefacts made from more than one of these.

Copper-alloy

The working of copper-alloy was a craft that was well developed in the Iron Age. It meant, however, specialising in the production of a limited range of artefacts for the elite, particularly those associated with military and equestrian activities. Although some minor personal ornaments such as brooches and pins were produced, these were not the most important output. In the Early Christian period, it was these small items for a much wider clientele that became dominant.

The processes of working non-ferrous metals and glass each can both be seen as separate subsystems (Figure 6:1) with a number of distinct stages. Each requires personal skills and resources, and also a range of materials and equipment, some of which can be detected archaeologically. It is thus possible to identify particular activities and centres of production.

Evidence for the organisation of copper-alloy production in Early Christian Ireland suggests relatively little working of copper with major emphasis on the re-working of existing artefacts. Only at Lagore has copper pyrites ore been recovered from excavation, and even there merely two fragments were found. There was no direct evidence for smelting at the site, but calcium carbonate was found within the crannog that could have been used as a flux. The slags from Lough Faughan crannog have been analysed, and they indicate strong circumstantial evidence for smelting according to Tylecote (1986, 26), and the presence of sulphides on crucibles suggests melting in hearths that had already been used for smelting copper sulphide ores (Tylecote 1986, 101). Numerous areas in Ireland have copper deposits, but the only tin known from the country is from the Wicklow gold deposits (Jackson 1978).

No tin or copper ingots of the period have been found in Ireland, though they are known in copper-alloy. The initial ingots produced from smelting may have been plano-convex like the Romano–British examples produced in north Wales, formed by being left to cool in the bottom of the furnace. The subsequent ingots are much smaller, and represent a further stage in the

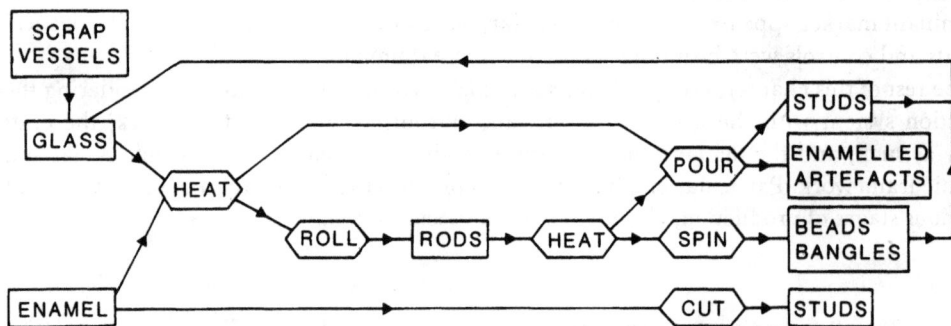

ARCHAEOLOGICAL EVIDENCE

SCRAP GLASS	CRUCIBLES	IRON TRAYS	GLASS RODS	CRUCIBLES	MOULDS	FINISHED ARTEFACTS
	TUYERES			TUYERES	GLASS DROPLETS	
ENAMEL BLOCKS	IRON PANS			IRON PANS		

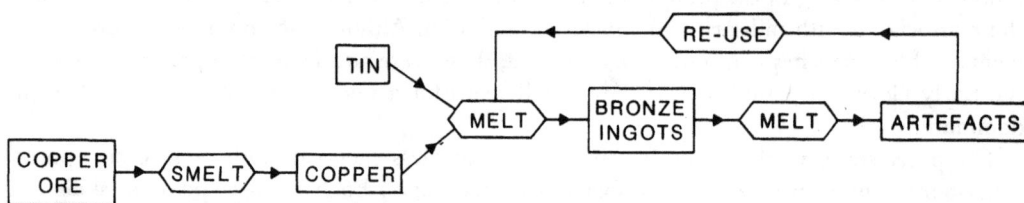

ARCHAEOLOGICAL EVIDENCE

MINES	FURNACES	INGOTS	CRUCIBLES	INGOTS	CRUCIBLES	FINISHED ARTEFACTS
ORE	SLAG		TUYERES		TUYERES	
	TUYERES		MOULDS		MOULDS	
			SCRAP BRONZE		DIES	

Figure 6:1 Diagrams showing production processes and archaeological evidence for these. *Above*: glass. *Below*: copper, tin and copper-alloy (bronze).

production and distribution process. Analysis of a crucible from Lough Rea, Co. Galway indicated an alloy of copper, tin and zinc had been melted, and the presence of zinc suggests the re-use of Romano–British material that was partly made of brass from Roman coins, or from coins themselves. A Romano–British brooch fragment was found amongst other copper-alloy scrap at Clogher (Warner in Youngs 1989), though this has yet to be analysed. The introduction of zinc to increase the strength of objects must have come from the Roman world since it is not found in Ireland; more zinc was used in wrought work than in cast.

The presence of nickel on the crucibles from Lough Rea and Lagore in amounts far greater than in Romano–British artefacts indicates that the copper used must have been from indigenous Irish deposits in which the trace element was already present. The Lough Faughan slags indicate that a bronze alloy of copper, tin and lead was produced, and other analyses indicate the use of simple tin bronzes. Craddock (1989) points out that most Irish metalwork was, on the basis of limited analysis so far, made from native copper; this was then alloyed with addition of often over 10 per cent tin (Oddy 1983). The use of local raw materials or the recycling of artefacts made from these appears to have been normal, perhaps with imported tin from south-west Britain. Sometimes imported brass, or a copper-alloy including brass, was also melted to increase the strength of artefacts by the addition of zinc.

Recycling of copper-alloy was extremely important. Many sites with evidence of bronze working produce assemblages of broken items that could be taken to represent collections awaiting re-processing. Complete objects may have been lost by their owners, but where there are many broken and fragmentary pieces this strongly suggests a copper-alloy worker's stock.

One of the most frequent and informative forms of evidence for working in copper-alloy is the presence of crucibles on a settlement (Figure 6:2). Tylecote (1976, 19) has produced a typology which includes most of the forms found in Ireland and, though this may indicate some transfer of ideas and techniques from other areas where such forms were in use, most are so simple that such assumptions would be misplaced. The most common form has been found at several early sites such as Garranes and Garryduff 1, and is triangular in shape with a deep pointed bottom. In some cases no residue could be identified, though some have definitely been shown to have been used for copper-alloy working (Moss 1927). Glazes in a range of colours including reds, greens and greys have suggested to some excavators that glass must have been worked, but such effects are produced whilst melting copper-alloys. Covered crucibles are also known, one from Garryduff 1 having a vertical lug which could be held to aid the pouring of the contents; it was similar to one from Dinas Powys except that it was more triangular in shape. A single example from Ballinderry 1 had a simple pinched cover and a horizontal pinched lug opposite the pouring hole. They are also known from Armagh. Since the covered examples have lugs, the open forms must have been gripped on the lip, presumably midway along one side, and the melted metal poured out over the opposing corner. The triangular crucibles could not have stood up unsupported, and at Nendrum shaped stone stands were found which had been used to support them in the fire.

There are also numerous examples from some sites of circular round bottomed crucibles which are shallower than the triangular forms. They have been noted at a range of secular and religious sites with other kinds of metal- and glass-working evidence. At Garranes this form was almost exclusively in stone rather than the fine clay usually used for triangular crucibles. Some circular crucibles have horizontal or vertical lugs to aid manoeuvring with tongs. D-shaped crucibles are not common from Early Christian Ireland, but were present at the monastic site of Nendrum, and might have had some of the easier handling qualities of the triangular forms.

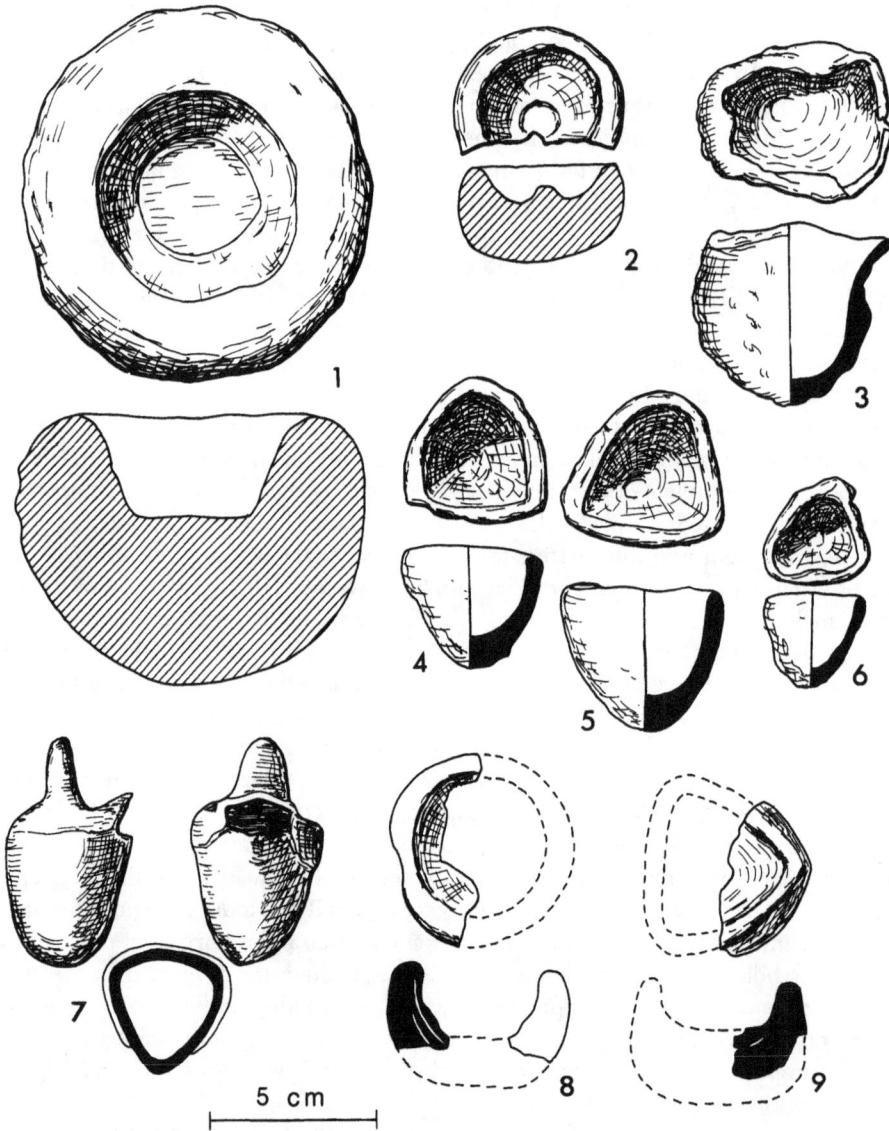

Figure 6:2   Crucibles. Garranes: **1, 2** stone; **3–6** clay. Garryduff 1: **7–9** clay (**1–6** Ó Ríordáin 1942, **7–9** O'Kelly 1962).

Two unusual crucibles were noted at Lagore. One was provided with three legs, the other was bag-shaped and resembled Roman examples (Tylecote 1976, Bachmann 1976). Whether the latter indicates the immediate origin for the round bottomed crucible forms is unclear. The triangular forms are similar to those used in Iron Age Britain and which continued in use through the Roman period in the western areas of the province.

Stone crucibles would have been more durable than ceramic ones, but the latter were also re-used. To improve their effectiveness they were re-lined, with up to three additional thin linings of clay on examples at Dalkey Island. Experimental work suggests that clay crucibles may have been ground up and re-used as temper in the production of new ones since the clay was so fine. If this was the case, then the presence of few examples in an excavation might indicate extensive crucible recycling rather than only limited bronze-working activity on the site.

The triangular crucibles were placed within the fire and heated, whilst the flat bottomed circular forms appear from the limited areas of glazing to have been heated by a direct blast of air from above (O'Kelly 1962, 97). Whether these two techniques were used for different products is uncertain. Tylecote (1986, 99) points out that the crucibles tend to be very small in volume, and so would have cooled very quickly, making pouring difficult. However, they would have contained sufficient metal required for a single brooch or mount.

Moulds of stone or clay provide considerable information on the production of artefacts, whether of copper-alloy, silver or even gold. Not only do they suggest the manufacture of goods at a site, but the shapes in the moulds indicate the range of items produced. Partly finished artefacts are not generally found, perhaps implying that most items were made to order individually from the smelting stage onwards, rather than being made up from an already moulded blank.

The most frequent shape of mould in stone is that of the ingot. The form is standard, finger-shaped with a plano-convex section (Figure 6:3). Relatively few copper-alloy ingots have been found, though silver examples are known from later hoards and the moulds have been found on secular and ecclesiastical sites. One copper-alloy fragment from Garranes exactly fitted a mould from the same site and must have been made in it. Sometimes more than one ingot mould can be found on the same stone; at Garranes, up to four were noted on the longer faces of stone fragments. No analysis has been undertaken of the volume of these moulds to ascertain whether any system of weights may have been in use for these ingots. If this were the case this could have significant implications for exchange systems and the wider economy beyond that of metalworking. Even if not of exact weights, ingots were convenient objects of value which could be used in exchange.

Clay moulds include more complex two-piece forms, though some were flat and used to make impressed blanks from which finished artefacts could be hammered. Curved and annular shapes were particularly common for items such as penannular brooches and the the heads of ring-brooches and -pins. Many others have no obvious function, but must have been parts of complex composite metal artefacts or various mounts and fittings for clothing and furniture. Stevenson (1974) suggests that these moulds could have been for the production of lead blanks that could then be carved in detail to provide the decorative detail necessary to make a two-piece mould for casting in silver or copper-alloy. Lead examples of decorated rings for brooch-pins have been found at Moylarg crannog and Dooey, and two-piece moulds have come from the latter site. Open clay moulds were also made using patterns or dies, and Moynagh Lough crannog has now produced a range of flat moulds some of which have impressed designs. One was for a

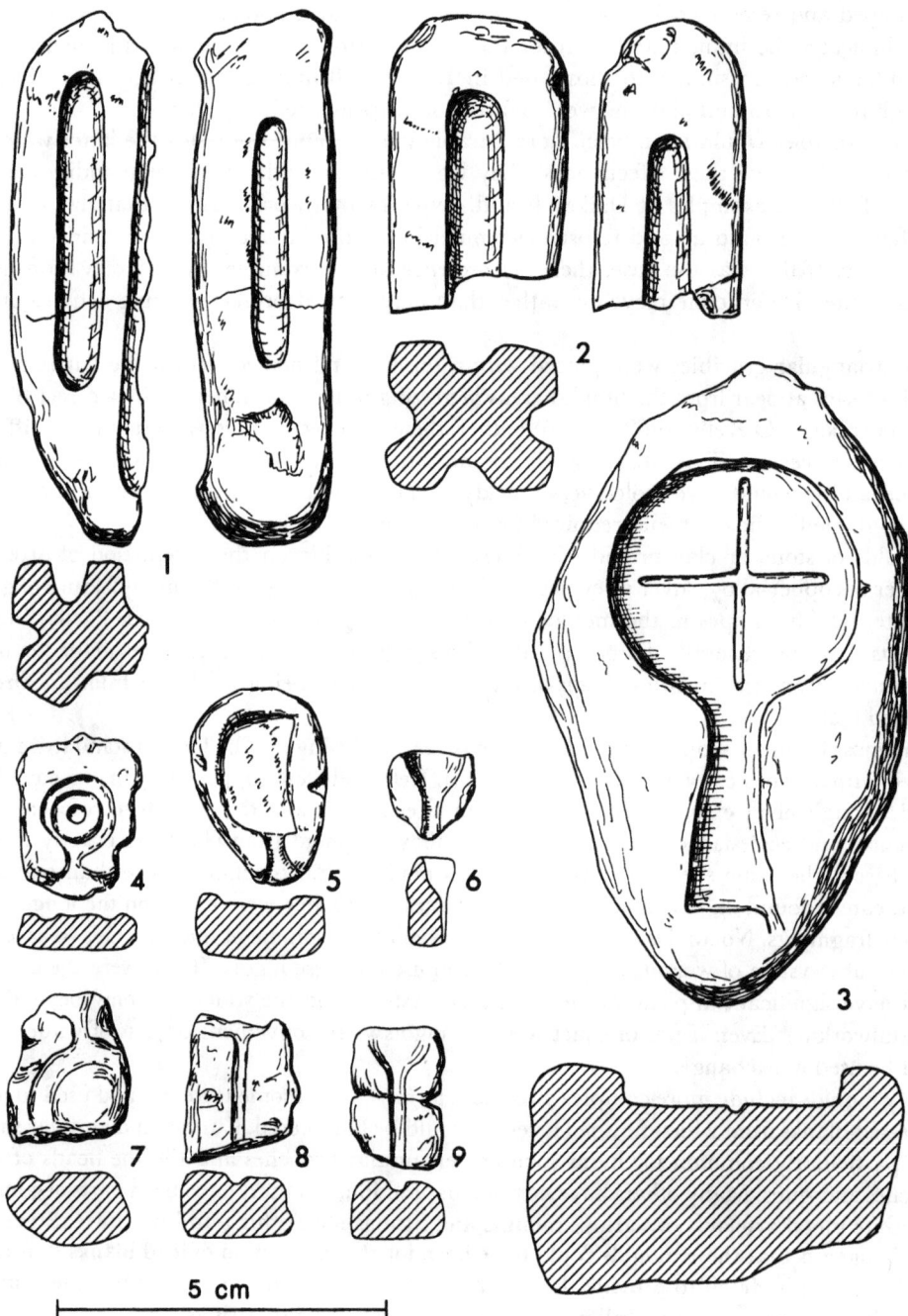

Figure 6:3 Moulds from Garranes, Co. Cork. Stone: **1, 2** for ingots; **3** for artefact with raised cross design. Clay: **4–9** (Ó Ríordáin 1942).

stud with ribbon interlace which is similar to those used on house shrines and saddle fittings (Bradley in Youngs 1989, 182–3).

All final shaping and the detail of decoration were added after casting, though this stage has left few archaeological remains. An exception is the waster of a terminal from a zoomorphic penannular brooch found at Clogher which, if perfect, would have needed decoration which may have included millefiori decoration (Warner in Youngs 1989, 198). Even artefacts made from moulds formed round the same original die would not look identical once the necessary filing and polishing had taken place. Moreover, the addition of inscribed designs or enamels and studs could allow for individualism. Nevertheless, the use of lead dies allowed for a relatively rapid production of the smaller artefacts such as pins and brooch-pins. Two almost identical brooches found separately in the river Bann were probably made from moulds formed using the same die (Warner in Youngs 1989), but even here details on their pins differ. Some tools such as awls may have been used for final finishing, and these have been recovered in some numbers from Garranes and Garryduff.

Gold

Some gold may have come from native Irish sources, notably from panning in rivers, but importation is also likely; the Roman gold coins at Newgrange certainly indicate that this was the case in the latter part of the Irish Iron Age. There is no evidence surviving for the use of gold in Early Christian Ireland before the seventh century and even from this date the amount of gold available was clearly very restricted. Only small quantities are used on even the most sumptuous of objects, either in small panels or as gilding. The process of mercury-gilding may have been employed, for example on silver, though the mercury necessary may have had to be imported.

A small amount of evidence for the working of precious metals has been discovered. At Clogher, a tiny crucible has been found with a bead of gold on the interior. From the same site has come a piece of sandstone which was used for polishing gold, probably gold leaf on wood or leather (Warner in Youngs 1989, 209–10). Three finds of gold artefacts have been retrieved from sites having metalworking activities. A filigree panel from Lagore, possibly an experimental item (Ryan in Youngs 1989), can be compared with the tiny bird in gold from Garryduff 1 (O'Kelly 1962) and new discoveries of a small panel and a wire fragment from Moynagh Lough (Bradley 1982).

Artefacts themselves give much information on the techniques employed in manufacture. Gold and silver were rarely used on their own, but in combination and with glass, enamel and bronze. The precious metals were used only on the more elaborate artefacts. The amount of workmanship, its quality and the use of rare materials are all highly correlated, and this must relate to access to resources and so reflect the social and economic standing of the patron. Thus, study of technology and craft can allow a scale of ranking to be devised that may be applied to artefacts and, by implication, their owners (see Chapter 4). The recycling of gold and silver, however, has led to a very limited array of finds, especially from excavations. Many of the finds, even single items, may have been hidden and never recovered by their owners rather than casual losses.

Filigree work on gold has recently been intensively studied by Whitfield (1987). The gold wire and granules were fixed to gold foil back-plates, and it was these that were affixed to the artefact to be decorated. Round wire was made from block-twisting, whereby a gold rod was twisted and rolled out into a thin strand. This could then be made into beaded wire by being pressed with a grooved tool. Wires could also be twisted together to make a more dramatic decorative effect. The granules of gold were mainly used to give emphasis to details of the design, such as on the Derrynaflan paten (Plate XXIX), but were also applied singly and surrounded by gold wire. There is evidence both from the details of the techniques and in the motifs used that some inspiration came from Anglo-Saxon England and, perhaps to a lesser extent, the Merovingian world. Nevertheless, the Irish craftsmen themselves developed their own techniques, particularly in the area of three-dimensional effects. The discovery of the Derrynaflan hoard has greatly increased the repertoire of known designs using filigree (Ryan 1987), and has also provided a splendid example of gold foil panels with die-stamped designs used on the eighth century paten.

The documentary evidence for gold-working augments and confirms the archaeological evidence for high status use (Scott 1981). There is some evidence for purification and alloying of gold to produce the appropriate degree of refinement and colour. There are also descriptions of composite artefacts which imply how gold was used, and a complex vocabulary suggestive of a well developed oral method of describing in detail the materials, production techniques and finished goods.

Silver and lead

Two hoards of late Roman silver are known from Ireland, and later Anglo-Saxon coinage may have been a source of supply, but analyses suggest that the Irish craftsmen had access to a separate, pure source of silver to which they added some copper (Craddock 1989); this was as much as 30 per cent in the case of the Derrynaflan chalice and paten. Whether the silver was imported or came from within Ireland cannot as yet be ascertained. Wherever the original metal may have come from, Irish craftsmen must have spent most time re-working precious metals into new artefacts. There is no evidence of conspicuous consumption through the deposition of rich accompaniments to burials, even of pagans, and there are no votive hoards in bogs or rivers at this period. Most casual finds have been single objects, although a few larger ecclesiastical hoards such as that from Ardagh have been discovered, probably buried in times of trouble and never recovered.

Silver was increasingly used on finer objects during the Early Christian period, and whilst the greatest demand was after 800, there are a few earlier items (Ryan 1981). The small silver proto-hand-pin and a silver-plated hand-pin both from Castletown, Co. Meath, are perhaps of the sixth century (Ryan in Youngs 1989, 25). Despite these survivals, the number of silver artefacts surviving from the fifth to seventh centuries in Ireland is not great. Whilst this may be because much was re-worked into later artefacts, quantities were probably small for much of the period compared with those circulating in Scotland as indicated by the contemporary Pictish silver hoards. This hypothesis can be supported by the fact that the total quantity of silver bullion used in these early objects was also very small. In the eighth century, however, quantities increased and silver became the dominant material as the production of polychrome artefacts reached its height of elaboration. These works of consummate skill were both ecclesiastical and secular, and shared the same range of techniques including the use of woven or knitted wire, trichonopoly, in silver or gold.

Surviving ecclesiastical artefacts of the highest quality are the Ardagh chalice and Derrynaflan paten which Ryan (1985, 20) has tentatively assigned to the same north Munster workshop.

Indeed, Rynne (1987, 89) has gone even further by suggesting that the Ardagh chalice and the Derrynaflan paten and strainer may have been originally made together as a set in the first third of the eighth century. The bowl and conical foot of the chalice and the plate of the paten were polished on a lathe, and the latter was assembled from components as indicated by engraved letters and symbols. However, this does not mean that the craftsmen were necessarily well educated. The letter forms on the Ardagh chalice inscription can be compared with those decorative majuscules in the Lindisfarne Gospels, but as two of the Apostles' names have been portrayed in the nominative rather than the genitive, it may be that the craftsman was not well versed in Latin.

The Tara brooch is perhaps the most famous artefact surviving from Early Christian Ireland, and is probably eighth century in date, although its exact chronological position is, as with most Irish artefacts, a matter of considerable debate (Ryan 1987). This silver pseudo-penannular brooch is decorated on both sides, the front dominated by filigree (Plate XXI), the back by gilt imitation chip-carved ornament (Plate XXII). The overall impression is of gold with multicoloured glass and amber studs, and only on the pin and the knitted wire is the silver surface extensive.

In silver-working as well as gold, there is evidence of foreign influences. The lightly incised band round the Ardagh chalice had a background picked out with a pattern of small punched dots, a technique with parallels in Merovingian metalwork.

Covering copper-alloy objects with silver or an imitation (such as tin) was common from the fifth century onwards (O'Meadhra 1987, 35), and numerous brooches treated in this way have been found. The technique was used even on the magnificent Ballinderry 2 brooch, suggesting that the imitation of silver was not only practised by the less affluent who could not afford it, so reflecting a real limitation of supply.

Lead was not commonly used in Early Christian Ireland, though a small amount of ore was found at Ardcloon, Co. Mayo. It had a few specific purposes within metalworking, such as with the production of dies already discussed, and was also used inside the terminals of some silver brooches. A few minor artefacts are known in lead, the most frequently found being spindle whorls. A lead ring was found at Garranes (Ó Ríordáin 1942, 102), and a spinning top at Ballycatteen (Ó Ríordáin and Hartnett 1943, 27).

Glass

There is no evidence that glass was produced in Ireland during the Early Christian period, and it is likely that all the glass artefacts were made from imported glass. When this scrap was re-worked it was into beads, bangles and studs; no glass vessels were manufactured in Ireland, though they were used. It is therefore not easy to tell whether a collection of fragments of vessel represent the remains of broken vessels that had been in use, or already broken pieces imported specifically for re-working. However, a poorly provenanced block of red enamel and a recently excavated piece in yellow from Moynagh Lough (Youngs 1989, 201) suggest that it may have been practice to import much of the glass in this form. Given the rarity of glass, it is likely that vessels broken in Ireland would also have been recycled.

In the Iron Age glass beads were popular in Ireland, but were mainly small blue annular examples. Many of the forms and designs in use in the Early Christian period in Ireland were those popular earlier in Britain (Guido 1978). For this reason, the dating of unstratified beads is extremely difficult but, as with so many aspects of material culture during this period, seems to reflect contact with partly Romanised areas of Britain from the fifth century onwards.

Enamel was frequently used on metal objects, normally bronze though two iron objects are known, a plaque from Lagore and a strap-end from Rathmullan, Co. Down (Bourke 1985). Enamelling was part of the metalworking tradition continuing out of the Iron Age, and was particularly popular on even high status objects in the period up to the late seventh century on items such as the Ballinderry 2 brooch (Figure 4:20). The enamel was applied to recessed areas, usually scored to provide some grip (Plate XX). Sometimes enamel was used in combination with millefiori studs, or was set in cells, influenced no doubt by Germanic cloisonné jewellery. This technique can be seen on a range of artefacts including the Lough Gara buckle which, in its form, has links with Merovingian buckles (Plate XVIII). Red was by far the most popular colour, but yellow was used from the later seventh century and green is also found.

The processes of glass-working are relatively simple, the skill coming in the manipulation of the viscous glass. The use of glass rods easily allowed the required amounts to be melted or broken off and used in the manufacture of artefacts. They have been found at several sites with extensive evidence of glass-working such as at Lagore and Moynagh Lough (Figure 6:4). Thin rods of glass of varying colours could be fused together to form a millefiori rod, which could be round or square in section. This could be cut into small plaques for application as decoration. Popular colour combinations were blue and white, and black and yellow (Henry 1965, 96), and designs tend to be marigold/sunburst or chequerboard patterns. Simple glass rods have been found at Garranes, and millefiori examples have come from that site and also Lagore and Armagh. The last site has also produced two-colour twisted rods in blues, whites and yellows. It is possible that these, and perhaps also the millefiori, were imported already made (Webster in Youngs 1989, 203–4).

Equipment associated with glass-working has been found at several sites. At Garranes, a bronze tube was used to hold a rod firmly, so that sections could be cut off it even when it was very short, thus allowing limited wastage (Figure 6:4). An iron plate from Armagh found with glass-working debris may have been used to heat glass or as a surface on which the rods could be rolled (Webster in Youngs 1989, 204). A more common find is that of small iron pans, and these may have also been used for heating glass (Figure 6:5). Crucibles would have been used in the heating of glass, and evidence of melting glass has also been indicated at Garryduff 1 by the presence of small droplets of the material.

Beads (Figure 6:6) were made by winding viscous glass one at a time (Sleen 1967, 22–3). The most common beads were simple annular forms and the most popular colour was blue, with green, white or yellow also common; other colours occurred rarely. A few melon beads are known, and these must have been made in moulds; they resemble Roman examples. Some beads were multicoloured, with different trails of glass introduced during the winding, or with the insertion of droplets of different coloured glass whilst the surface of the bead was still viscous; no particular colour combinations seem dominant. Even more complex multicolour beads also occur occasionally, and these consist of inserted droplets and millefiori segments, and applied strands, some of which were themselves made of two very thin twisted strands of different colours. Some of the forms can be paralleled in Iron Age British contexts, but are clearly later in date in Ireland. Beads are found as casual single losses on most settlement sites, so little is known about how many were on a string, or what combinations were worn. It is surprising that there is so little reference in the contemporary literature to glass beads or bangles, but they may not have been worn by the higher status women, and so were not considered worth recording.

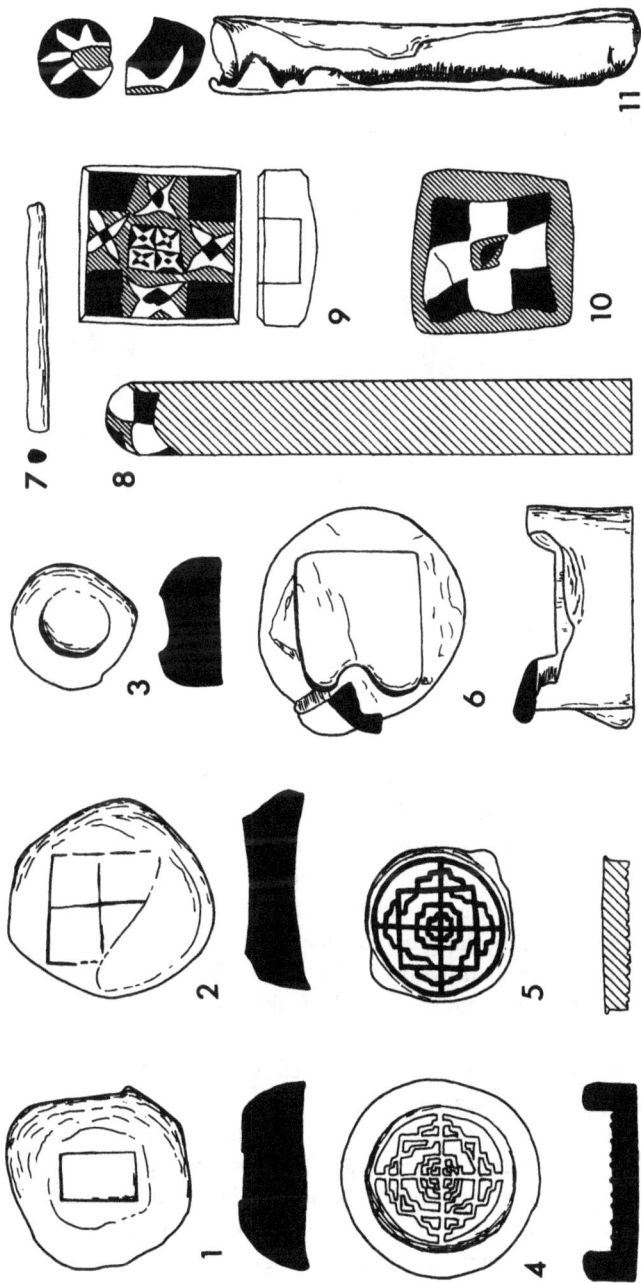

Figure 6·4 Glass-working debris. Finds from Lagore, Co. Meath: **1–6, 6** moulds; **5** green glass stud found in mould **4; 7** blue glass rod. Finds from Garranes: **8** millefiori rod; **9** millefiori stud; **10** cross-section enlarged; **11** millefiori rod with bronze tube to hold it. Various scales (**1–7** Hencken 1950, **8–11** Ó Ríordáin 1942).

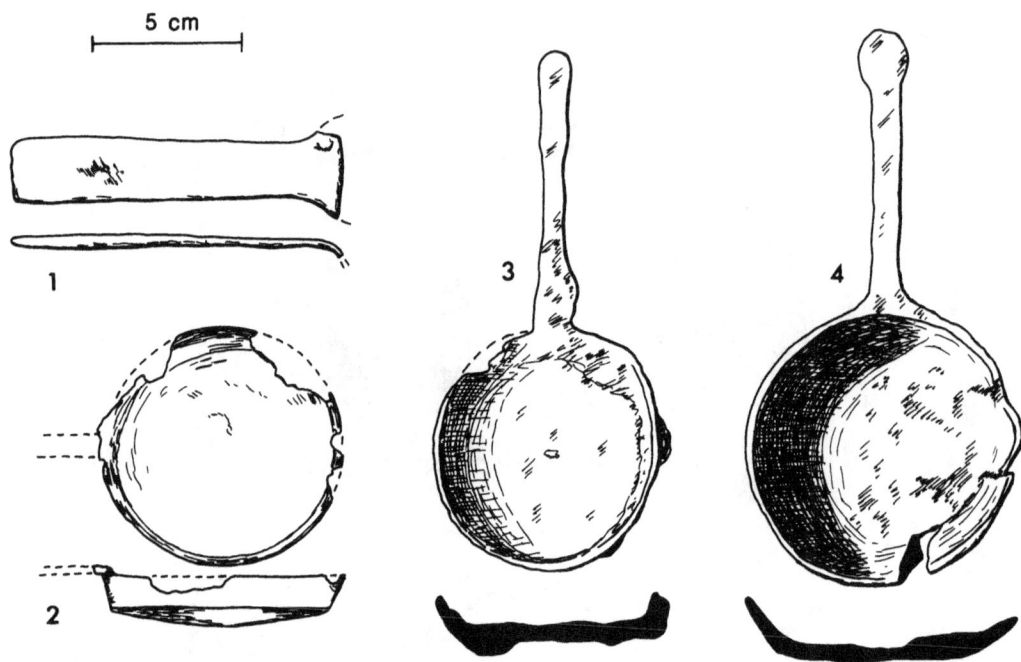

Figure 6:5 Iron pans possibly used for heating glass. **1–2** Ballinderry 2, Co. Offaly; **3, 4** Garryduff 1, Co. Cork (**1, 2** Hencken 1942, **3, 4** O'Kelly 1962).

The glass bangles or armlets are similar in form and function to shale, lignite and jet examples (see below), and come in a similar range of sizes. They closely resemble Romano–British forms which were extremely popular on native sites in northern Britain (Kilbride-Jones 1938). They were usually D-shaped in cross-section, and were made of several rods of the same colour fused together, with decorative trails or droplets of glass pushed into the exterior surface whilst it was still viscous, after which a final smoothing could take place. The colour scheme was normally that of a blue ring with dots or trails in white, unlike the earlier British examples where white and green were most common base colours, and where there was a greater variation of applied colours.

It is probably significant that the Irish bangles tended towards a standardised colour scheme whilst other contemporary glass artefacts occurred in a much wider range of colours and forms. The dark colour of the glass may have been meant to simulate the blue-grey colour of polished lignite, though with the inlaid white patterning, the glass examples would have appeared distinctive and so they cannot be considered imitations. Glass bangles are less common than stone examples but this may at least in part be because of recycling of glass. Bangles may have carried a special meaning; perhaps women of a certain age or marital status wore them.

Glass studs were used on jewellery and also on larger items such as chalices. The studs could be cut off the glass rods, often with minimal further treatment; this activity seems to have been carried out at both Garranes and Lagore. Also, some enamel was too hard to be used in a viscous state and was cut up and affixed to complex artefacts as studs. Alternatively, glass could

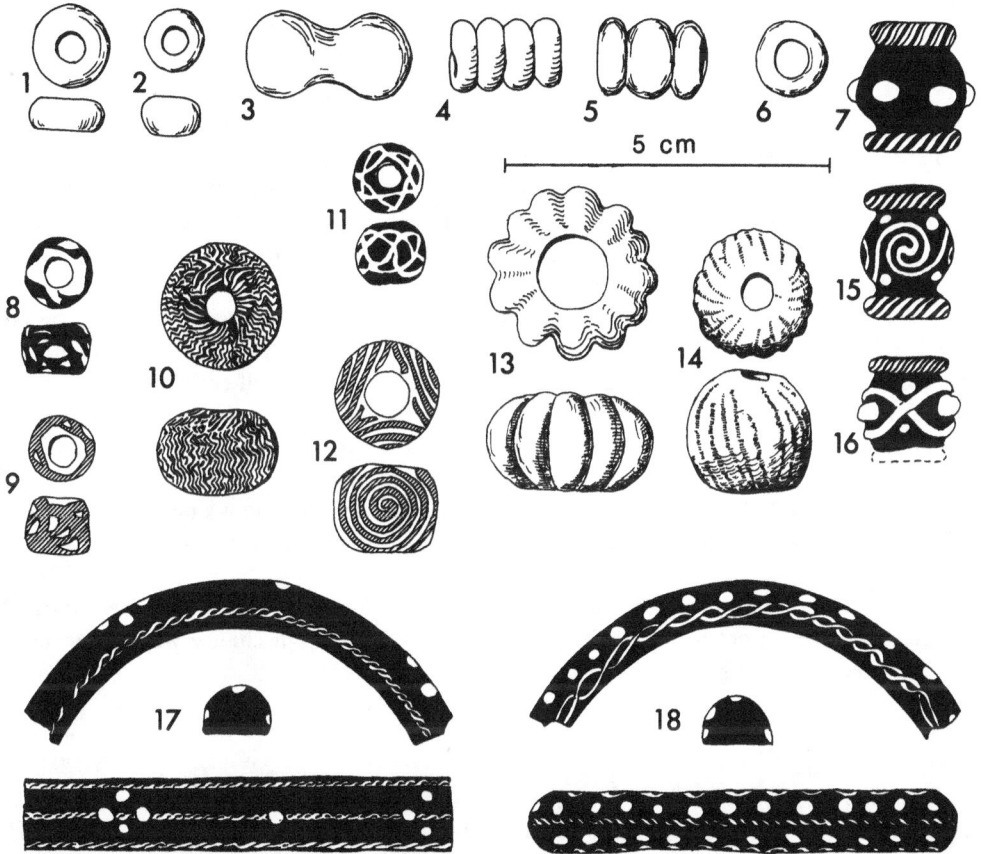

Figure 6:6 Glass beads and armlets. Ballinderry 2: **1, 2** annular beads; **3** dumbell bead; **13, 14** melon beads. Lagore: **4, 5** segmented beads; **7, 11, 12, 15** polychrome beads; **17, 18** armlets. Carraig Aille 1: **16** polychrome bead. Carraig Aille 2: **6** annular bead; **8, 10** polychrome beads. The Spectacles: **9** polychrome bead (**1–3, 13, 14** Hencken 1942, **4–12, 15–18** Ó Ríordáin 1949).

be poured into a clay mould which had been impressed with a patrix of a suitable design. The best evidence for this method comes from the earliest occupation at Lagore where a stud was found still in its mould (Figure 6:4). The raised geometric pattern in the base of the clay mould produced a pattern on the stud. Similarly designed studs can be paralleled from penannular brooches and a shrine mount. At Garryduff 1 a glass stud was excavated where the stamp (here with a sunken design) had been applied lightly, withdrawn, rotated and pressed in again with greater pressure; the stud may have been made at the site. The only possible stamp or patrix for impressing glass stud moulds is a bronze disc from Dooey identified by O'Meadhra (1987, 140).

Moulded studs by their method of manufacture could have a three-dimensional surface but were necessarily monochrome, unless recessed areas were filled with enamel to give a smooth surface and a polychrome effect. A stud from Deer Park Farms has gold wire set in it (Lynn 1989), as do some on the Ardagh chalice. It was also possible to produce pseudo-cloison moulded studs if a silver grille were placed in the mould. The result could be monochrome, as with the blue examples on the Ardagh chalice, or polychrome if only some voids were filled with one colour of glass, the others being filled with a different colour after the first had solidified. This style of stud occurring in the combination of red and blue has been noted by Henry (1965, 95–6) on the Ardagh chalice, Moylough belt shrine and Ékero crozier, all ecclesiastical products, and the Tara brooch which might likewise have been made for a cleric. The more recent Darrynaflan chalice and paten both have polychrome settings of this type (Ryan 1983). It would seem that the polychrome studs belong to items produced during the eighth and ninth centuries (Ryan 1987, 72). Genuine cloisonné work, where semi-precious stones or glass are set in metal cells, is rare in Ireland, though it does occur during this period on the base of the Ardagh chalice.

The use of amber became a dominant theme in the ninth century, but it was used sparingly in earlier centuries. It occurs on the Tara brooch and the Ardagh chalice where, because of malachite used in the glue, it appears green.

Motif-pieces

O'Meadhra (1979, 1987) has been carrying out a detailed and exhaustive study of the various motif-pieces from Irish contexts, some of which can be dated before 800 (Plates XII, XIII). Most of the designs found on stone or bone are sketches of motifs presumably made in the process of work on a commission, but they may also have been stored as a repertoire of designs. Some may have been actually used in the manufacturing process to make moulds or be impressed by sheet metal or leather.

The importance of the motif-pieces is that many have been found in excavation and so can provide a chronological and locational framework. They indicate designs under consideration if not actual production at certain sites, and can thereby imply the cultural and artistic milieu in which the craftsman was working. Whilst some designs can be paralleled with finished artefacts, this is not possible within the same site. The designs produced are generally interlace patterns or animal ornament, but at the monastic site of Nendrum, letters have also been found.

Workshops and distribution of products

Organisation of production is still unclear, although several sites have yielded considerable evidence of craft activity, usually across a range of media. Several crucial questions remain to be answered: on the one hand were such sites the permanent workshops of craftsmen or merely periodically visited, and on the other were the craftsmen the owners of such settlements or were they present in the retinue or as visitors to the aristocracy who supported them? Craftsmen could be of high standing according to the law tracts, and within the ecclesiastical hierarchy several leaders were described as such. It is possible that the roles could in some cases be conflated, but it is uncertain how archaeology can at present further unravel this difficulty.

In the matter of distribution of artefacts, the combination of excavated evidence and chance finds can give some indications. Unfortunately many of the older provenances are too vague for this purpose, but some patterns become clear. The most significant is the widespread use of techniques and motifs over the whole of Ireland and indeed the west and north of Britain. This suggests three modes of transfer of information, all of which were probably important. The first was the movement of craftsmen, the second that of artefacts within exchange networks and the third the movement of owners with their possessions. In the last two cases, the arrival of new artefacts, techniques and motifs within the general milieu could quickly be absorbed and adapted according to the skills of the relevant craftsmen. The desire on the part of the consumers – the aristocratic patrons and ecclesiastical institutions – to maintain displays in current fashions and at as high a standard as they could afford ensured continued re-working of possessions. Many complex artefacts such as shrines show evidence of adaptation through time, though simpler objects were probably recycled. Competitive emulation was a powerful dynamic in the stylistic developments within the Celtic world.

Only a few artefacts are sufficiently similar to suggest production from a single workshop, bearing in mind the rapid spread of motifs and techniques. Zoomorphic penannular brooches are mainly found in the Irish midlands and north, and the only certain production centre so far recognised is that of Clogher. Kilbride-Jones's Group D was made there, and the distribution shows a dense concentration in the immediate vicinity, with a few others more scattered. This might be a distribution expected from a production centre serving a local market, with a few brooches from this travelling much further through either migration of individual wearers or gift exchange of brooches. The local distribution may itself have been in the form of gifts by the king who was based at Clogher, or it may have been a commercial relationship between the craftsman and the aristocracy of the region. Other zoomorphic penannular brooch forms may also imply regional centres, but the distributions are more diffuse or the sample is too small (Figure 6:7).

Changes through time

There are clear changes in style of artefacts manufactured from the fifth to the eighth century, but of greater importance in the context of craft production were developments in techniques.

Artefacts belonging to the fifth, sixth and early seventh centuries are almost exclusively bronze with decoration in enamels and millefiori glass. The most commonly found artefacts are hand-pins, simple ring-headed pins, 'latchet' dress-fasteners and penannular brooches. There were only a few silver objects although some were tinned to create a silvery effect. Cast decoration was employed, particularly on penannular brooches. Relatively little metalwork had Christian

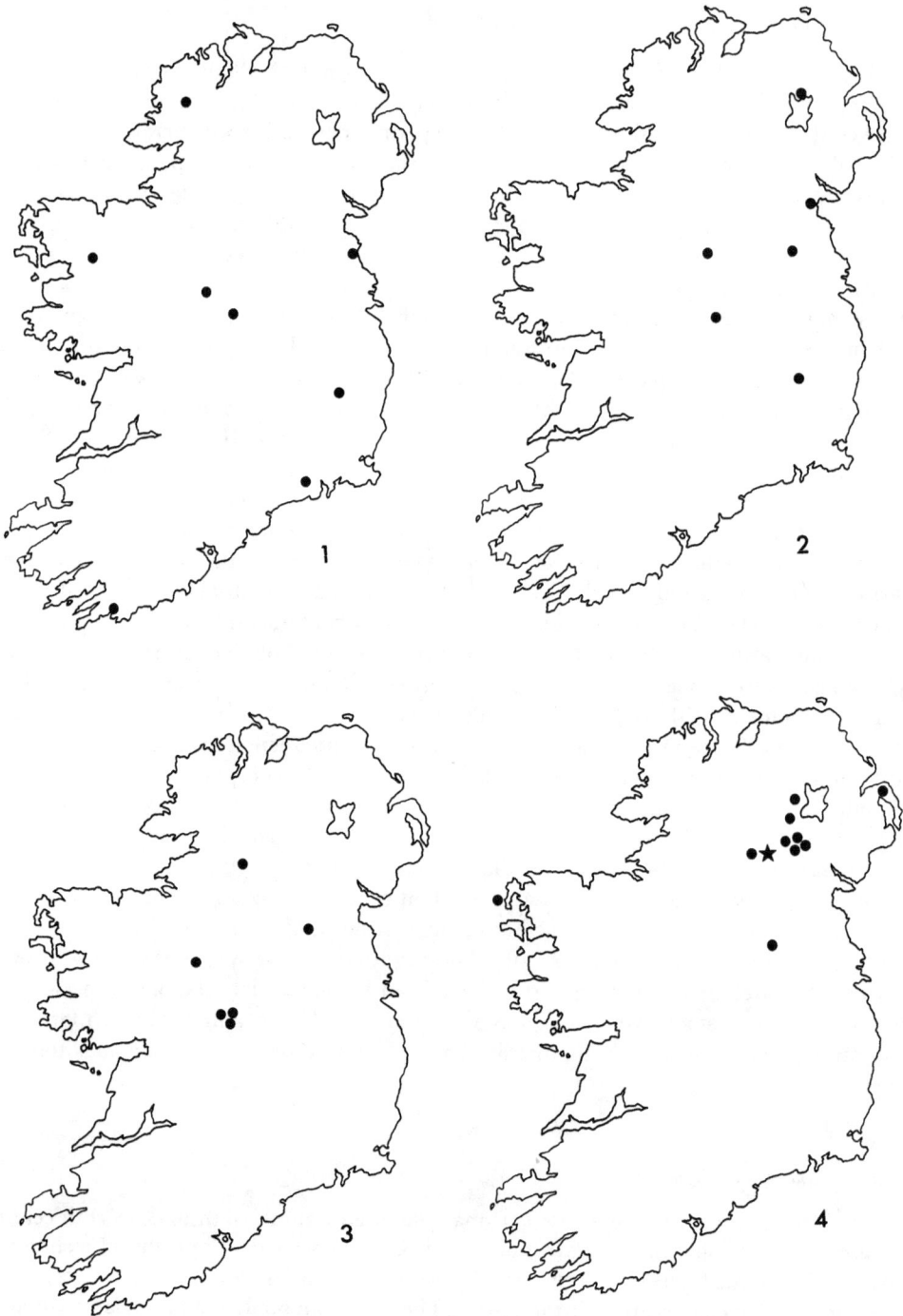

Figure 6:7 Distribution of penannular brooch types defined by Kilbride-Jones (1980). **1** A_2; **2** B_1; **3** B_2; **4** D, manufactured at Clogher, Co. Tyrone.

symbolism, apart from Maltese crosses on type C3 zoomorphic penannular brooches (Plate XIX), although Ó Floinn (in Youngs 1989, 32) suggests that the palmettes on C4 type brooches may represent *flabella*. Moreover, the millefiori studs used in such jewellery and on other artefacts often in cruciform and marigold designs may also have a Christian significance. Other designs are derived from the La Tène repertoire.

In the later seventh century and particularly during the eighth century a wide range of techniques were utilised on artefacts. Two main strands of change are of significance. The first development was the construction of complex artefacts involving many elements, in a range of materials and colours. It is from this time that gold appears and silver increases in quantity, and polychrome glass studs begin to be used. Amber and mica are also present, though in small quantities. The second development was the inclusion of many external stylistic elements. The La Tène design elements gradually go out of fashion, in their final forms merging into Germanic animal styles. Rynne (1987) has identified Salins style II bird heads complementing the indigenous triskele in the Lagore belt buckle. Cast chip-carved ornament and the use of enamels in imitation of cloisonné inspired by Anglo-Saxon or Continental metalwork became common. Many design elements came from Christian iconography, and were mainly used on ecclesiastical items such as the Derrynaflan paten where some of its filigree panels can be compared with manuscript art or sculpture.

The causes of these changes were complex and are mainly due to social and ideological developments discussed in Chapters 3 and 4. Nevertheless, changes in the details of the motifs and techniques must relate to the craft industry itself. The workshops must have had widespread contacts which, with the skill of the craftsmen, allowed inspiration and development of indigenous Irish styles.

Ironworking

In the Early Christian period there was a real expansion in the use of iron, and the quantity found on some domestic sites is considerable. Just as many parts of Britain only appear to have used iron for a wide range of artefacts from the Romano–British period, the same seems to have been the case in Ireland from the fifth or sixth century onwards. Prior to this, the techniques of ironworking and the uses to which this new resource could be put were restricted by the elite in order to maintain its position. In the Early Christian period this changed, and the individual was able to exploit local iron resources and so increase both agricultural and craft production.

The processes for obtaining and working iron are set out in Figure 6:8, and indicate two main stages, each of which leaves different debris. The first stage involves the initial extraction of ore and its preliminary processing. The second stage involves the working of iron ingots or the re-working of existing artefacts.

The most important supply of iron in Early Christian Ireland probably came from bog iron, which could have been discovered during the cutting of peat for domestic fuel. The analyses of slags suggest this source for ironworking possibly at Cush, Co. Limerick and more certainly at Mullaghbane, Co. Tyrone. Bog iron can be a renewable resource, and Tylecote (1986, 125) suggests that as deposition is a continuous process it can re-form with a thickness of up to 10 cm in 30 years. This would give areas where bog iron formed a long-term continuing value. Extraction of bog iron would leave no archaeological trace since later peat growth or peat cutting would obscure all field evidence of the activity. However, analysis of bog iron can

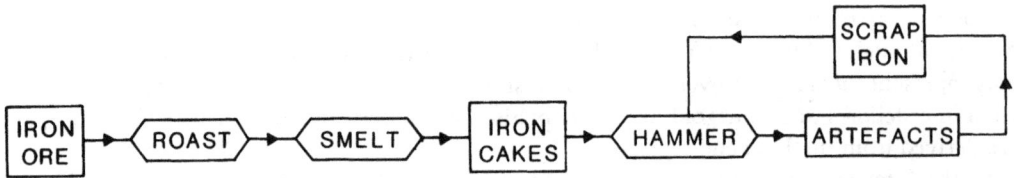

ARCHAEOLOGICAL EVIDENCE

| IRON ORE | HEARTHS | FURNACES TUYERES SLAG FURNACE BOTTOMS | IRON BLOOM | ANVIL TONGS SLAG HAMMER SCALE | ARTEFACTS BROKEN ARTEFACTS |

Figure 6:8 Diagram showing the processes involved in iron production, and the archaeological evidence for these.

indicate unusual features. Bog iron from near the major ironworking site of Ballyvourney, discussed at length below, contained a high manganese content which would be expected to show in the slags from the site. Knowledge of the use of bog iron may have come from western Britain where such sources may well have been important through the Iron Age and Romano–British period.

Iron ore was also quarried, probably from surface outcrops. At Garryduff 1 low grade ore was found that was available locally from outcrops of Yellow Sandstone or Lower Limestone Shale. Processing such ores would have been harder than bog iron, but this was probably not available near Garryduff, and it suggests that iron production normally relied on locally available sources of ore. This was not always the case, however. Iron smelting at Church Island, Co. Kerry was on an island with no fuel or ore source, and both must have been brought from the mainland at some effort. Since this was probably part of a monastic estate, the resources may have come from other church property or were payment of rents or tithes from the local population. The church may have acted as a centre of metalworking expertise in the area, and so was sent the raw materials from the mainland. It is likely that ready made charcoal was sent to the island, and the iron would have been from one of the many bogs in this area, which were also exploited for fuel, as evidenced by the excavations at Reask (Fanning 1981).

Documentary evidence gives some valuable information about mining. Mines were probably common, and the laws state that the use of another person's mine not surprisingly attracted a fine. Mining on unclaimed land was acceptable, and it is likely that the only land that would have been in that category was inhospitable upland; this suggests that these mines would have been for bog iron. Cliffs were also important sources, presumably because here the iron-rich outcrops could be located and easily excavated.

The ore may have been roasted to break it up into smaller pieces, which aids smelting and can drive off carbon dioxide or water and sulphur. Some of the slag at Lagore, however, does not appear to have been very effectively roasted since it still contained ferrous sulphides from sulphur in the ore (Tylecote 1986, 188).

The technology used for iron smelting in Early Christian Ireland was not complex, and involved those methods used in Britain during the Iron Age and which continued in use in peripheral areas during the Roman period. The smelting took place using small bowl or low-shaft furnaces of very simple forms. The excavated remains from Irish sites could be from either type of furnace since they are identical in form below the ground, but an Iron Age example excavated at West Brandon, Co. Durham had collapsed (Jobey 1962), allowing preservation of some of the superstructure. This has now been interpreted as a low-shaft furnace rather than a bowl form (Tylecote 1986, 133). It is therefore possible that the Irish examples may have been low-shaft furnaces rather than merely bowl forms.

Each bowl furnace consisted of a small pit in which the charcoal and ore were placed. Bellows were inserted into the furnace to provide a flow of oxygen through the charcoal which was placed near the tuyère, with the iron ore on the opposite side of the furnace. The ends of the bellows were covered in clay nozzles, tuyères (Figure 6:9). In the case of low-shaft furnaces, clay sides were built up above the ground and the charcoal and iron ore were mixed or placed in alternating layers. There was no provision in either case for tapping the slag which formed in the hollow of the furnace and solidified with the charcoal into a furnace bottom. These furnace bottoms were therefore waste from the iron smelting process, the useful iron being a bloom on the upper surface of these bottoms, and removed subsequently. Iron smelting sites can be identified by the presence of furnace bottoms and also fragments of tuyères and the pits in which the smelting took place. The viability of this method of smelting has been verified by ethnographic studies and by experimental work (Wynne and Tylecote 1958). The experimental work of O'Kelly (1961) suggested that very small quantities of usable iron – perhaps only one pound – were produced from each smelt, which took 4–6 hours of working the bellows to complete. O'Kelly also considers that there were many failed smelts because of the difficulty in judging the timing and temperature inside the furnace. However, this may reflect the lack of practice and expertise on the part of the experimenters since ethnographic evidence suggests that even with simple methods great expertise can apply, and consistent if small scale production is achieved.

If low-shaft furnaces were the design sometimes used during the Early Christian period, as suggested by Tylecote, then yields from these furnaces would have been higher than proposed by O'Kelly. Tylecote (1986, 134) considers that furnace bottoms less than 20 cm in diameter are unlikely to have come from bowl furnaces because the yield would have been so low, and so probably represent the use of shaft furnaces; many Irish examples are below this diameter. However, the chemical composition of the Garryduff 1 slags did not match those produced experimentally by O'Kelly in a shaft furnace, but did match those from the bowl form. It is not clear, however, whether the low-shaft form might have produced results comparable with the archaeological data, and the original form of the Irish examples still seems unclear. Excavations at Lislea, Co. Cork have revealed a furnace from which slag could be tapped, but this is not yet dated (Scott 1983). Tap-slag from Armagh may also indicate the use of more sophisticated shaft furnaces.

Ballyvourney, Co. Cork was an isolated stone-built roundhouse 6 m in diameter with a stone-lined drain leading out from the building (Figure 6:10). Inside the structure there were numerous furnaces placed near the walls and both inside and outside were found many furnace bottoms. Unfortunately the description of these does not give enough detail to allow further discussion

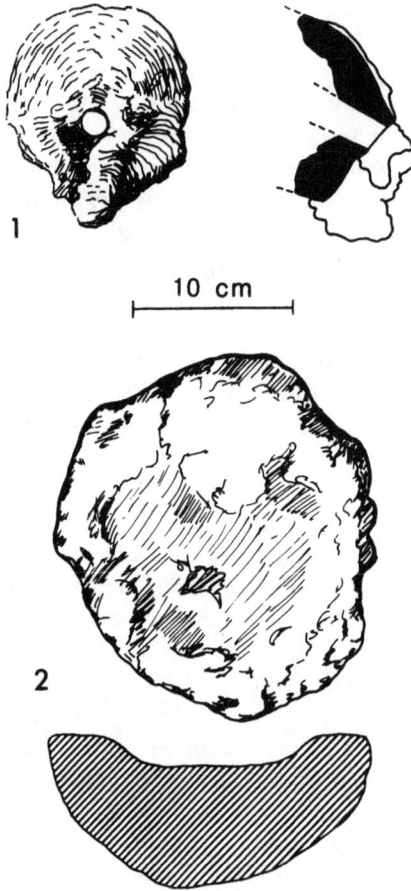

10 cm

Figure 6:9 **1** Tuyère from Garryduff 1, Co. Cork; **2** furnace bottom from Cahercommaun, Co. Clare (**1** O'Kelly 1962, **2** Hencken 1938).

of the furnace types, though the excavator assumed that they were of the bowl form. A stone anvil from the site would have been used in the removal of the iron bloom from the upper surface of the furnace bottoms, but there was no evidence from the site to suggest the form into which this raw material was worked. There can be no doubt that Ballyvourney represents a specialist production site and indicates that such activity sites existed between the more familiar settlement pattern of ring-forts and crannogs.

The only other major production centre yet identified was in a hillfort ditch at Clogher (Warner 1988), though it has yet to be fully published. Here both smelting and smithing were practised, but this appears to have been in the open with at best some form of insubstantial wattle shelter.

The ring-forts and crannogs also show some evidence of ironwork, though in the vast majority of cases only for the subsequent stage of blacksmithing. At Garryduff 1 six pits were found, each

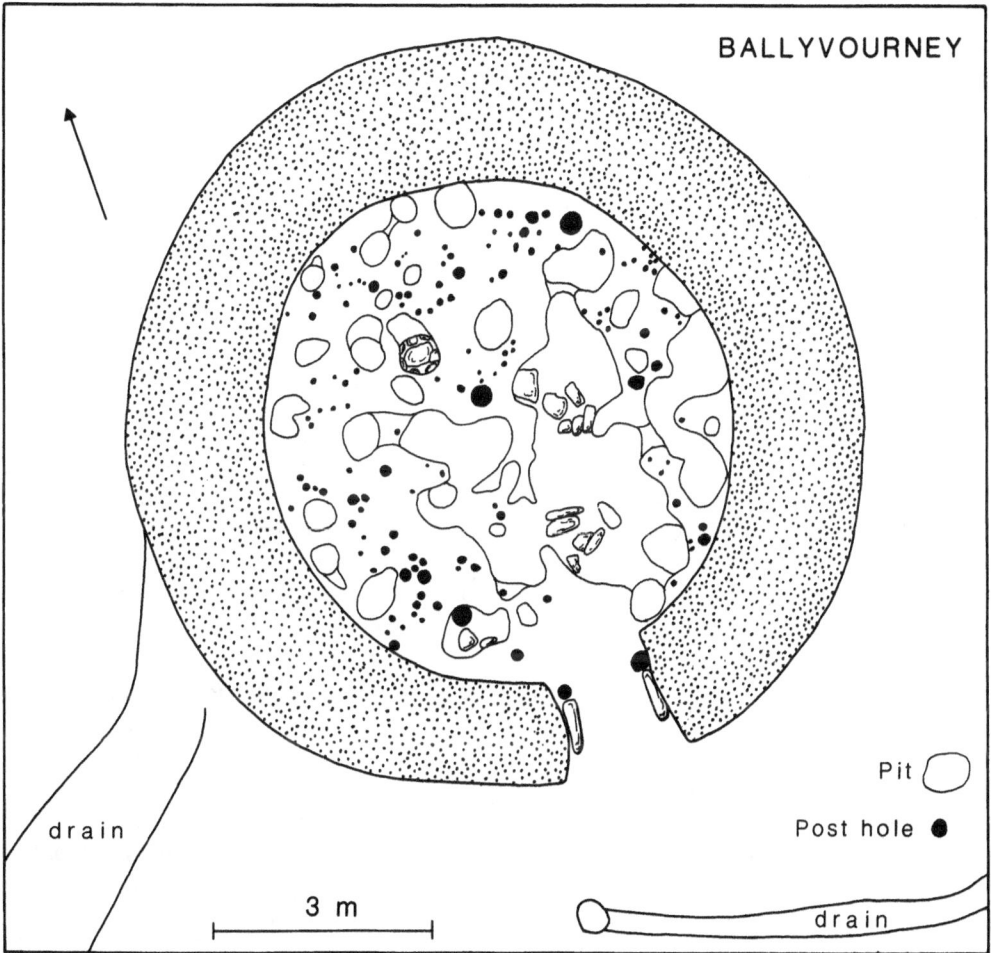

Figure 6:10   Ballyvourney ironworking site, Co. Cork (O'Kelly 1952).

lined with clay, and some still with slag in the bottom. Lagore crannog has yielded furnace bottoms, and the slags from Ballycatteen and Ardcloon suggest smelting. At Lissue slag and furnace debris were recovered, together with an iron bar which may have been the basic form into which iron was hammered if no artefacts were immediately manufactured.

Documentary evidence suggests that iron was traded in the form of 'bolts', which may have been iron bars like that from Lissue, or other shapes hammered from each smelt. Since iron was on occasion paid in tribute, there may have been a standard form in which this was delivered. The amount produced from a single smelt would have been a convenient quantity for re-working by blacksmiths into artefacts, and would have been easily transportable. Unfortunately, such units of raw material have not been found on settlement sites, even where extensive remains of smithing have been found.

Smithing activity can be adduced from many sites by the presence of small amounts of slag, probably produced during the re-working of the iron bars into finished goods. There would no doubt also have been repairs to iron tools, though few have shown signs of this. Much iron must have been re-worked into new goods. The hearths used for smithing can appear like domestic hearths, and it may be that some of the external hearths, so frequent on ring-forts, may have had this type of craft function.

The documentary evidence such as the law tracts indicates that there were specialist forges where ironworking took place (Scott 1983). The frequently found remains at settlement sites may indicate the occasional visit of craftsmen to carry out repairs or major jobs which needed to be done on the spot. Most anvils of the period were small examples that could be made firm by being hammered into a large block of wood. No ironworking example has been found but a smaller version presumably used for finer metalwork was found at Garryduff 1. The portable anvil and other tools could have been carried round to settlements with relative ease, and the small external hearths needed for smithing would not necessarily appear different to domestic examples.

The documents certainly indicate a centralised craft activity, with the forge acting as a focus of social life in the community and a recognised status for the smith. Each *túath* had one head blacksmith who was a major figure in the local community and at whose forge legal notices were proclaimed. The implications certainly are of permanent smithies to which the work was brought rather than itinerant craftsmen setting up shop in or near other settlements.

Scott (1983) has carried out detailed analysis of a legal tract on blacksmithing and from this has been able to reconstruct a detailed arrangement of the forge and the working practices carried on there. Of particular interest here is that more than one and up to even four smiths may have worked together hammering a single item, suggesting production teams of some size. Even so, these probably included apprentices and do not suggest production above a craft level. Scott also explains the reference to damage to livestock being due to smithing in the open air; this would fit not only the Clogher evidence but also the smaller scale activities at many other sites.

Archaeological evidence for smithing, apart from the finds of slag, consists of a few ironworking tools. Anvils of stone have been found at Ballyvourney and Clogher, both with much other smithing debris. Iron tongs very similar in form to Roman types (Manning 1976) were recovered from Garranes, where both pinched and out-turned jaw forms were found (Figure 6:11). The latter would have been particularly suited to holding an object firm whilst it was hammered. Punches, spikes and wedges may have been used by the blacksmith but had other possible functions.

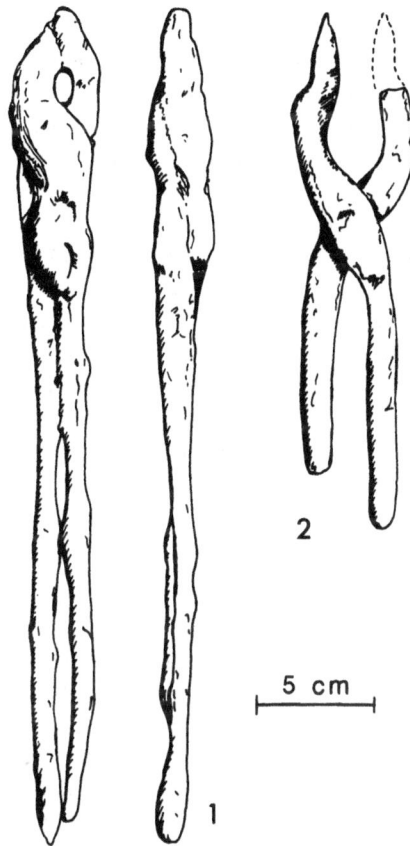

Figure 6:11 Iron tongs from Garranes, Co. Cork (Ó Ríordáin 1942).

Iron production was not highly centralised, but may have been more organised than many crafts. The documentary evidence suggests that mining was an activity carried out by the owner of the land, as part of the overall exploitation of the landscape, and as a supplement to farming. Where bog iron was concerned, extraction could have taken place as part of the seasonal cutting of peat for fuel. Smelting of the ore took place at some settlement sites and at special purpose centres such as Ballyvourney. This latter site may also have been a smithy, and both processes were certainly being carried out together at Clogher. The legal texts, however, discuss smithies in terms of secondary activity rather than primary smelting and this may have been the norm. Smithing was carried out at specialist centres and, on a small scale, at settlements. It may be that many people knew something of ironworking and could carry out simple repairs, just as many farmers do today, but that expertise in the more complex formation of artefacts, and edge-hardening and riveting, could only be carried out by full time specialists. Monasteries also were active in the working of iron from outlying estates, as at Church Island and within the monastery enclosures at Armagh.

Stone

The working of stone in Ireland can be separated into several broad categories. Whilst some stoneworking was probably carried out by farmers, much was probably produced by full or part time craftsmen. The legal texts suggest full time workers, and significant expertise was necessary for even some of the apparently simple items of material culture. Moreover the use of raw materials obtained from some distance suggests greater organisation than would have been the case with small scale self-sufficient production.

The production of small, portable objects includes functional and decorative items, but can be contrasted strongly with the production of grave slabs and crosses. The latter were only supported by the monasteries, whilst the former had secular and ecclesiastical patrons alike. The final category, stonemasons, was again mainly supported by the church, though secular settlements are sometimes of stone, and other structures such as bridges may, as implied from the literature, have sometimes been of stone also. Each of these three forms of stoneworking needs to be considered separately though it may have been at times the same craftsmen working at different levels of complexity and scale.

Smaller artefacts

A wide range of artefacts were made of stone in Early Christian Ireland (Figure 6:12), but most required relatively little skill and must have been made by anybody as required. Other artefacts are of sufficient complexity to suggest some specialisation, whilst the rock types often indicate trade or exchange of raw materials or finished objects. The detailed sourcing of stone has not been well developed in Ireland for artefacts of this period, but holds great potential.

Simple artefacts include the perforated stones found on many sites. Some may have been thatch weights, particularly the largest examples, whilst others remain inexplicable; some are small enough to have been spindle whorls. Examples in a range of shapes are well represented on settlement sites. These objects were probably not produced by specialists since they are so simple and quick to make. They can be considered as expedient artefacts, made as and when required for a specific task and not necessarily retained for further use. Partially finished examples have been found on settlements (Figure 6:12), often discarded because the perforations on each side of the discs were not correctly aligned.

Despite the extensive use of metals, there is evidence that flint blades and scrapers were produced. None are very well made, but they have been found at over half of the ring-fort settlements even if in most cases in small quantities (Harper 1974, 37–9).

Most spindle whorls were made of locally available stones, and the form has in part at least depended on the qualities of the raw material. Flat, thin whorls are common in easily split sedimentary or metamorphic rocks, whilst the thicker, more rounded examples are of less fissile rock. The shaping of the stone would rarely have presented any difficulties, and the perforations are normally made by drilling from each side, producing a V-shaped hole. The objects would have been smoothed off using a soft rock or sand as an abrasive. Some spindle whorls are of non-local materials, and were probably traded or exchanged as finished objects. Documentary evidence shows that spinning was a female activity, and it may be that non-local spindle whorls indicate movement of women on marriage, as suggested by Clarke (1972) for the Iron Age at Glastonbury. There are surprisingly few unfinished artefacts that can be clearly identified as spindle whorls so the organisation of production is unclear.

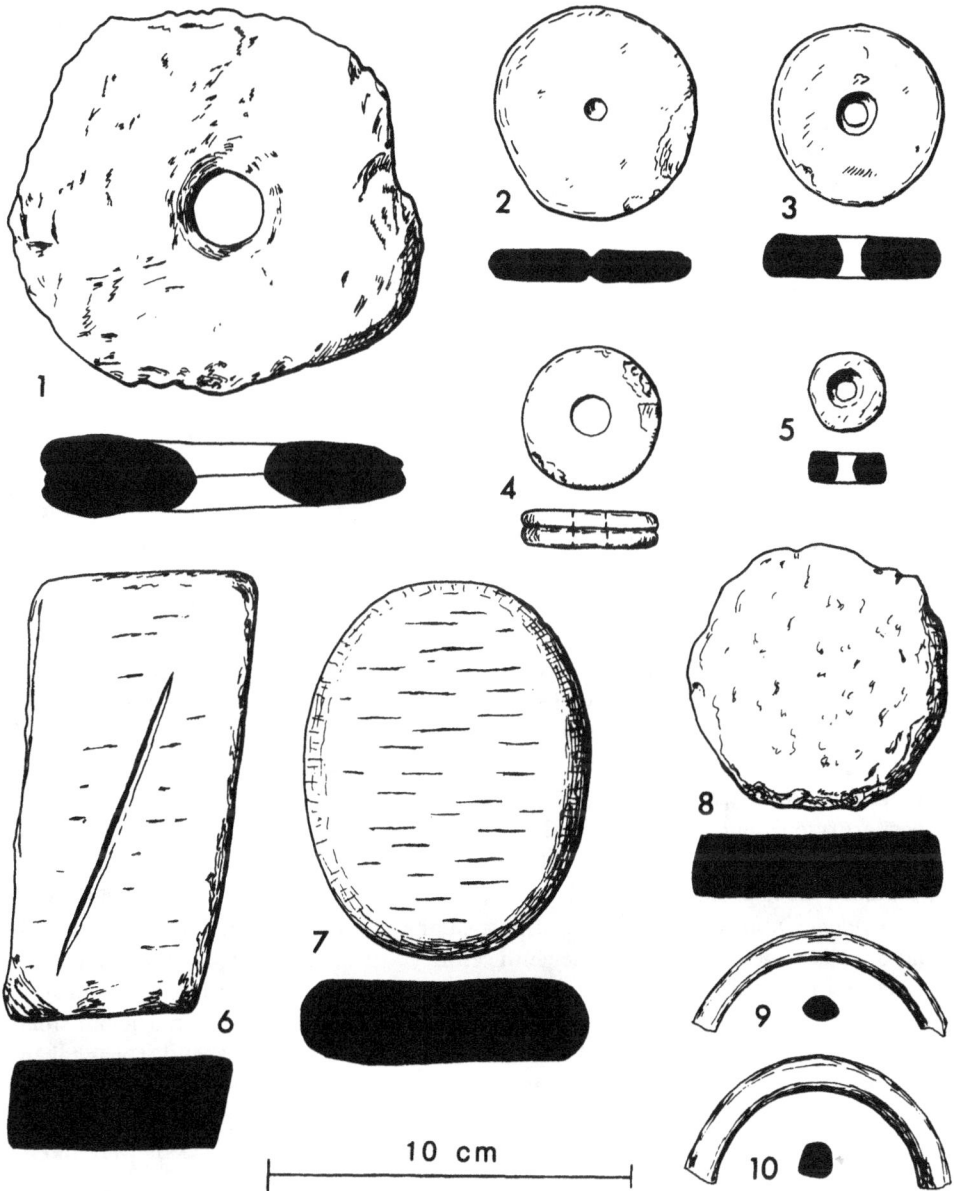

Figure 6:12 Stone artefacts. Cush, Co. Limerick: **1** perforated stone; **6, 7** whetstones; **8** disc. Carraig Aille 2: **2** unfinished perforated disc; **3, 4** spindle whorls; **5** bead; **9, 10** jet or shale armlets (**1, 6–8** Ó Ríordáin 1940, **2–5, 9, 10** Ó Ríordáin 1949).

The variations in spindle whorl shape, and particularly the weight, must also relate to the thickness of thread to be spun, and research on British Iron Age spindle whorls suggests that careful consideration was given to the type of whorl used for particular purposes. Those making the whorls must therefore have had to produce them to particular sizes. Some spindle whorls are decorated with incised patterns, but these are relatively rare and are always quite crude.

Whetstones are commonly found on sites but most are not shaped to a very great degree (Figure 6:12). The choice of rock was of one which was fine-grained, but rarely are these exotic materials; some are re-used moulds or other stone artefacts. Smaller examples are well made and would have been produced by craftsmen. These are rectangular in cross-section, and have a small perforation near the top end for suspension from a belt. The elegant shape of these sometimes tiny whetstones and the carefully produced perforations drilled from both sides made them attractive possessions and fine examples of craftwork.

Stone lamps are occasionally found in excavations, such as that from the ring-fort at Crossna-creevy in a seventh or eighth century context (Harper 1974). The rock source was probably in the Mourne mountains. Similar lamps have been recovered from Iron Age sites in north Britain, and some casual finds in Ireland have been assigned to this period. Other Early Christian stone lamps, such as those from Garryduff 1, are plain.

Personal ornaments are also found of stone, such as beads, but the most important lithic resource used for decorative items was jet, or shale, similar in appearance to jet. The most common jet or shale product was the small armlet identical in shape and size to glass examples. Its exact purpose is often unclear, since some have a very small internal diameter. Whilst they may have been worn by children, it is also possible that the smaller armlets may have really been used in women's hair. The normal form is D-shaped in cross-section, and is cut on a lathe from a disc. The waste products have been found at several ring-forts. At Armagh, a lignite bracelet was decorated with a fret pattern paralleled on a clay mould from the same site. That there were lignite discs in the deposits suggests manufacture of bracelets, with the former being polished and perforated.

Querns are often found on settlement sites, but unfortunately very little work has been carried out on the rock types. An exception, still to be published, is the work of Jope on the Mourne granite industry, the products of which have been found on several north-eastern sites. Documentary evidence also suggests the use of particular rock sources, with the increased value of the land on which they lay. The later seventh century Life of Saint Brigit includes a description of a search in the mountains for a suitable rock which was then carved into shape in situ and, after some difficulty, transported down the hill (Thomas 1971a, 210). This particular stone was not a small hand quern, but one to be fitted into a water-driven mill, and it was taken in a roughed-out state to the mill where it was trimmed to fit against the other millstone already present (Connolly and Picard 1987, 25). Water millstones required particular care since the wear on these was much greater than on hand mills, and suitable rock beds were often very limited.

During the Early Christian period, nearly all querns were rotary types, though saddle querns have been found at a few sites, most notably Cahercommaun (Hencken 1938, 58). The rotary querns are of three main forms (Figure 5:14). There are some that are small and relatively thick, and others which are slightly greater in diameter and flat; both these forms were hand querns, unlike the larger, flat examples that were used in water mills.

The thick rotary querns are somewhat reminiscent of the Iron Age beehive types, and occur at only a few sites. They were in a considerable majority at Cush, though flat forms were also present; they were between 30 cm and 38 cm in diameter and made of sandstone or conglomerate available on the hill above the settlement (Ó Ríordáin 1940). Another thick example of similar size, in Mourne granite, came from the make-up for the house platform at White Fort, Drumaroad, Co. Down (Waterman 1956).

The flat form of quern is the one normally found at this period. They generally vary in size from 35 cm to 50 cm. Frequently the upper stones have perforations for the insertion of a wooden handle, but occasionally, as at Letterkeen (Ó Ríordáin and Mac Dermott 1952) and Inishkea North (Henry 1952), both in Co. Mayo, they have been carved with protruding stone handles. Another feature, perhaps in later examples, is the provision of a raised collar round the central perforation. Sometimes a rind of wood or iron was housed between the stones to allow controlled variation in the coarseness of the flour. Occasionally the surface of the upper quernstones have been decorated, such as that with semi-circular panels from Carrigillihy (O'Kelly 1951) or the circular sinkings on two examples from White Fort, Drumaroad. An unprovenanced but decorated example was identified by Power (1939) as having liturgical symbolism (Figure 5:14).

Manufacture of querns is a skilled process, not only in the selection of raw materials but also in producing matching stones with neatly fitting grinding surfaces and making these at the correct angle to give time for the grain to be ground into flour. Also, the carving of the raised ridge round the central perforation, and handle hole or even decoration, made the artefact a complex product. Production of querns has been identified at several sites, but never on a large scale. At the ring-fort of Holywood, Co. Down a sandstone example was discarded after a hole had been drilled from one side and then just started on the other (Proudfoot 1959). A single unfinished example was noted at Lagore, and evidence of production has been found at Moynagh Lough crannog.

On the introduction of water-powered mills, only the more resilient materials were usable, and it was possible to use larger stones. However, one of the few dated examples of millstones is that from Drumard (Baillie 1975, 1979) where the late eighth century example was only 55 cm in diameter. At this stage there can be little doubt that the millstones were produced and supplied by relatively few specialists, but perhaps not from centralised production centres; the Drumard example came from a local rock source (Preston in Baillie 1975, 32).

Grave slabs and crosses

One of the most numerous categories of stone products from the period are the grave slabs found at many monastic sites (Figure 3:21), though the overwhelming majority come from a small number of centres. How far this is due to accidents of survival is unclear, but the concentrations at Clonmacnois, Inishcaltra and other sites of the Irish midlands suggest an underlying regional emphasis. Despite the pioneering work of Crawford (1912, 1913, 1916), Macalister (1909) and Lionard (1961) little large scale work has been done on geographical distributions. Greatest emphasis has been placed, as has been common with all carved material, on stylistic and art-historical analyses. Nevertheless, some trends have been discerned. Only the earliest grave slabs belong to the period under discussion, the real floruit coming in the ninth century. However, from the dated examples that have been suggested by Lionard (1961, 157–69) it would appear that a range of forms was produced from early in the sequence.

The rock used for the slabs was sometimes local material, even when not very suitable. The Glendalough cemetery contains both granite and mica-schist slabs. Both rocks present difficulties in carving, the former being very hard and the latter tending to flake; the result was a relatively impoverished repertoire of decoration. At Clonmacnois, however, coal measure sandstone from south Co. Clare was brought to the site, presumably by boat along the river Shannon. This provided a fine-grained surface that could carry the detailed carving which the extremely skilled craftsmen at the monastery could produce.

The slabs were not finished in the same way at all sites. Those at Clonmacnois were left as irregular rectangles, and no attempt was made to provide straight edges and clearly defined corners. In contrast, the Inishcaltra slabs were well shaped and usually rectangular, though others tapered towards the base and may have been influenced by Continental trends (Lionard 1961, 148). The slabs were designed as parts of cist graves. Examples still in situ at Inishcaltra and Glendalough show that many were recumbent, covering the cist, but others were upright, forming in part a side of the cist. Some Glendalough examples had a small socket cut in the slab or the cist sides to allow insertion of the base of a small upright marker.

Most designs were carved to some depth into the slabs, though patterns were found lightly incised onto the surface. Some of these were clearly produced using a compass, and it is likely that most designs were laid out by incisions first. On some rocks, the more crude method of pocking was employed in the production of design; this can be seen at Gallen where the other methods are also present.

Whilst it may be expected that the memorial slabs were the everyday products of the craftsmen at monasteries such as Clonmacnois, it would be expected that the high crosses would have been an enjoyable diversion for these men. Lionard, however, suggests that the high crosses were made by different craftsmen. This is based on the repertoire of motifs chosen for the slabs and crosses (Lionard 1961, 145). The techniques also vary, but he concedes that this was because of the medium and intention of the different monuments. But surely this might also have been the case with the decorative motifs? The absence of spirals and the great rarity of animal ornament might relate to the symbolic meanings of such designs and their appropriate uses in certain contexts. Their absence in one genre and presence in another does not indicate different craftsmen, only different purpose. And there is little doubt that the high crosses had many more purposes – and meanings – than the simple memorial slabs.

The evidence from the slabs suggests that each of the major monasteries had its own school of craftsmen. Whether these were full time specialists is uncertain, but at many monasteries they must have carried out other duties because the death rate was not sufficiently high to provide continuous work. Clonmacnois may have had full time specialists, particularly if the slabs from other sites which clearly show influence from this centre were made by the same individuals. Lionard notes 12 sites within a radius of about 25 miles which have slabs that may have been made either at Clonmacnois, or by craftsmen based there. This may represent the sphere of direct influence of the workshop. Other schools may have had similar catchment areas but the differential survival and recovery of slabs in other regions mean that these are not so easy to recognise. The similarity of the designs at Maghera, Raholp and Saul with those at Nendrum may be lesser evidence for another regional centre, and the various sites on the Aran islands may have been similarly served by a school based at one of the monasteries.

Much other early sculptured stone, such as inscribed crosses and ogham inscriptions, is not sufficiently diagnostic to have been defined as yet into schools. A wide range of techniques including pecking and inscribing have been used, but these normally relate to rock types. Some of the finer examples must have been made by skilled individuals who may have been full time craftsmen but not necessarily only in stone.

Architectural stonework

Much of the secular stonework used in the construction of ring-fort revetments, whether of the banks, gateways or ditch terminals, would have required no more skill than that of agricultural workers adept at drystone work for field walling. Nevertheless, there is plenty of archaeological evidence of the skilled use of stone in building in secular as well as ecclesiastical contexts. This is mostly visible after 800 but the origins are clearly visible before this.

Whilst some clochans are crudely constructed, others are fine examples of workmanship and show careful selection and shaping of the slabs used to form the walls and corbelled roofs. Whilst many of the best preserved examples are on monastic sites, others are known from ring-forts in the west. The survey of the Dingle peninsula indicates a frequency of clochans (Cuppage 1986) which suggests that there would have been sufficient demand for specialist builders, both to construct and repair them. However, the dating of such structures is notoriously difficult, and the majority at least belong to the later part of the Early Christian period not under discussion here.

Some cashels are of such fine drystone construction it is difficult to imagine that they were constructed only by client farmers as part of their obligations. Whilst they may have collected the materials, brought them to the site and helped manoeuvre them into position, only skilled masons could have ensured the smooth facing and the tight and solid fit of the blocks on a consistent and stable batter. Various gangs may have worked each under a separate foreman, as the straight joints at some sites such as Cahercommaun suggest (Hencken 1938). Many of the stone gateways with their symmetrically battered jambs and large slab lintels are also indicative of specialist planning, but as with so much other fine stonework are late in date when any chronological precision can be inferred (Manning 1988).

Ecclesiastical sites provide the best evidence for the presence of specialist builders. Not only were some of the boundary walls well constructed, as were the domestic cells, but the finest skills are reserved for the oratories. The constructional techniques are those of the secular buildings except that oratories are rectangular when most if not all secular ones were, at least to start with, round. Rectangular buildings, because of the presence of potentially weak corners, presented different challenges for the builders, and the stone corbelling of a roof to a rectangular plan needed some adaptation of technique. It is likely that expert advice was obtained from abroad, probably from Britain where under Roman influence rectangular buildings in both timber and stone had long been part of the architecture even along the Irish Sea littoral. The proportions of the oratories were significant and standard, and followed on from those built in wood.

Most architectural stonework survives in the west of Ireland. This is partly because in this rocky region stone would have been an obvious material for building, but also survival there has been much more frequent because there has been less robbing of abandoned structures. Those buildings and enclosures using stone in the east have more frequently been robbed and only isolated sites such as Glendalough have survived in a reasonable state. Regional styles are therefore difficult to recognise because of differential survival, but even in the west local traditions cannot be recognised with any certainty. One problem is the dependence of technique on the form of the local stone. Even within limestone areas, for example, some cashel walls were beautifully formed whilst others were quite rough. Yet this was often due to the different ways in which the rock breaks into more or less regular blocks.

The other architectural form in stone which is suggestive of specialists is that of the souterrain, known also in wood. Whilst some are simple single chambers, others involve considerable design skills to incorporate numerous chambers and connecting tunnels, together with creeps and recesses. Moreover, construction of souterrains involved complex excavation and spoil removal, followed by careful building and infilling. Whilst some of these underground structures may be within the period of discussion here the vast majority are ninth century or later in date on the basis of archaeological evidence and documentary references to their use (Warner 1979b, 1980).

Other crafts

Boneworking (Figure 6:13)

Although late evidence from the High Street excavations in Dublin indicates specialist comb makers, boneworking does not previously seem to have been a distinct craft. No early site has produced sufficient quantities of boneworking debris to suggest specialisation, and even allowing for post-depositional destruction of bone in some areas because of acid soils, the presence of small amounts of waste on a range of sites does suggest large-scale activity. The only possible exception to this is at the unpublished site of Dooey where, along with much metalworking debris, there was apparently evidence for manufacture of combs, knife handles and pins. Even here, however, it would seem that the working of bone was carried out by those engaged in the other activities, and was not a distinct speciality.

It is likely that some of the bone artefacts were made, as with some in stone and wood, by non-specialists. One of the most common but simplest bone artefacts is the pin made from a pig's fibula. This needs very slight modification (MacGregor 1985, 120), and was extremely common; 82 were found at Cahercommaun and 131 at Lagore, but most of these belonged to deposits of the ninth century and later. Another very simple artefact is the spindle whorl made from the articular condyle of a cattle femur. This hemispherical head of the long bone is ideally shaped, and merely needs perforating. Bone and antler were also used for disc-shaped spindle whorls, and incompletely perforated examples were found at Cahercommaun.

A relatively easily produced item is the scoop or gouge, made from sheep tibiae or metacarpals and, more rarely, pig femurs. The purpose of this implement is uncertain, but the long bone cut was at an angle to produce a scoop or gouge; the remaining end was usually perforated. Such implements also occur in Iron Age contexts in Britain, and whilst rare in the lowland province continued in the north and west during the Roman period. Various interpretations have been put forward for their use, including beaters used in weaving (Crowfoot 1945). They have also been identified as apple scoops, and similar eighteenth century bone scoops were also used to remove samples of cheese for tasting (MacGregor 1985, 180). Despite a substantial number of bone finds, not one scoop was found at Ballinderry 2, and only 10 came from Lagore; examples came from all parts of the Carraig Aille sites. Once the real function of these enigmatic artefacts is determined, they should provide a diagnostic indicator on settlements. Whilst unfinished examples are not rare, it is interesting to note that several were found at Raheen-amadra, Co. Limerick (Stenberger 1966).

Red deer antler was used as well as bone, the tines being chopped with an axe, cut with a knife or sawn. It was used for a wide range of artefacts including handles, points and rings.

It is likely that handles of iron objects were made by blacksmiths and fitted to the requisite tools, particularly knives. As the number of bone handles on any site is always low compared

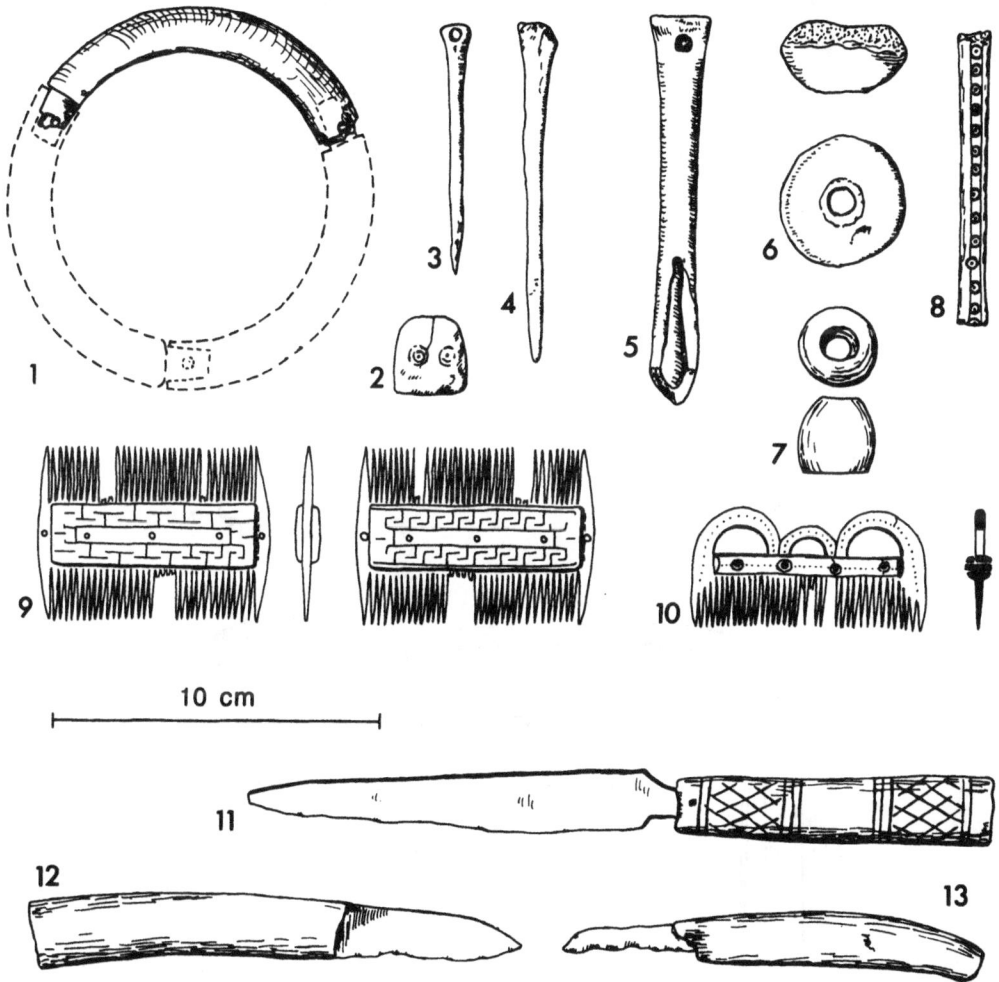

Figure 6:13 Bone and antler artefacts. Ballinderry 2, Co. Offaly: **1** segment of armlet; **2** gaming piece; **3** needle; **4** pig scapula pin. Lagore, Co. Meath: **5** bone gouge; **6** bead; **7** spindle whorl; **8** decorated handle; **9, 10** combs; **11–13** iron knives with bone or antler handles (**1–4** Hencken 1942, **5–13** Hencken 1950).

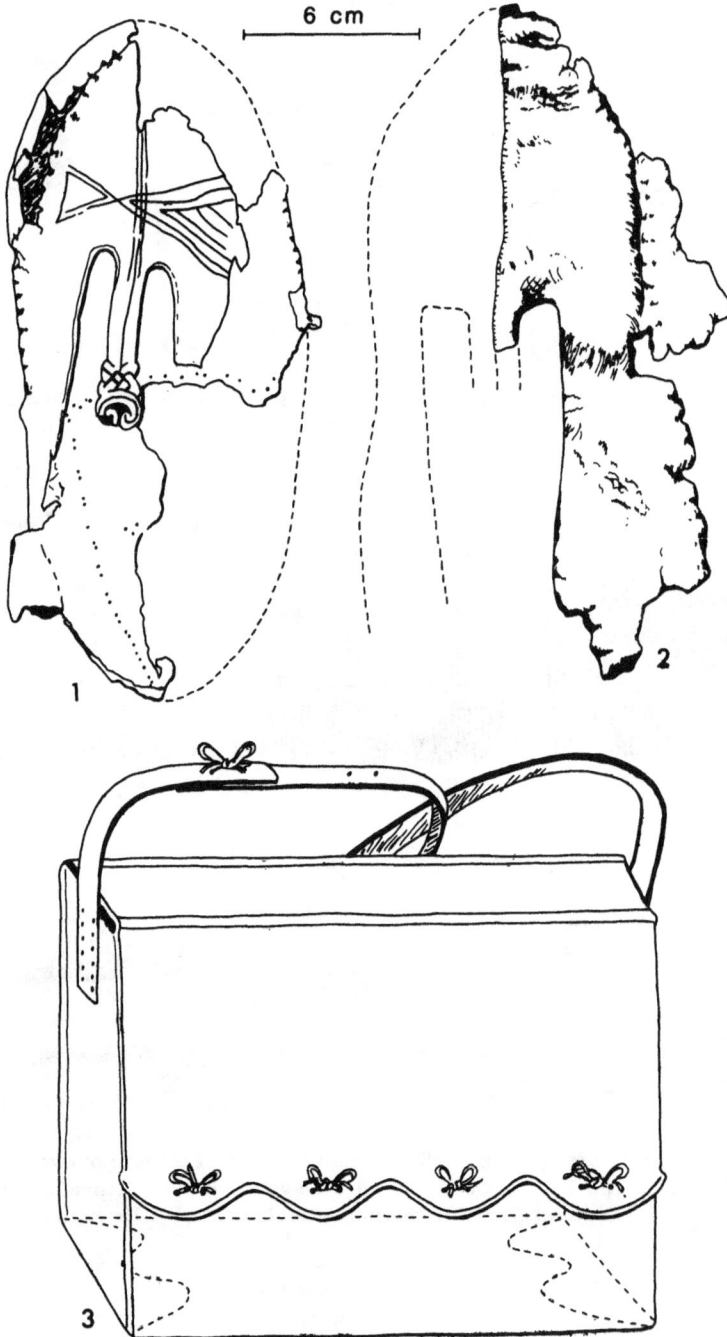

Figure 6:14 1, 2 Leather shoes from Ballinderry 2, Co. Offaly; **3** the Corpus Christi book satchel (**1, 2** Hencken 1942, **3** Waterer 1968).

with the number of knives this would suggest that few handles were of bone, unless they were re-used as the blades wore out and were discarded. The most common bones used for handles were ox or sheep metacarpals, but ox radius and antler were also used.

Combs occur at a range of Early Christian sites, but evidence of manufacture is limited. A probable side-plate for a double-sided comb was found at Clea Lakes crannog, Co. Down but there was no other bone waste (Collins and Proudfoot 1959, 96). Composite combs were held together by bronze or iron rivets, and so may have been made by metalworkers. However, the range of designs on combs does not equate with those on metalwork, being limited in general to ring and dot and simple knife-cut patterns. Whilst this may reflect more the different cultural role of combs compared to metalwork than their different makers, the general range of boneworking activities may be compared more with woodworking than any other craft.

Leatherworking (Figure 6:14)

A great deal of information about leatherworking can be gained from extant ecclesiastical artefacts such as manuscripts and book satchels. These products of highly specialised craftsmen indicate the skill in the medium that could be reached at this time, and being relatively well preserved, place the stained and fragmentary excavated fragments in a wider context.

Manuscript production consumed large numbers of sheep or calf skins to make the vellum, and this must have had an impact on husbandry management on ecclesiastical estates or those of secular suppliers. The skins had to be cleaned and cured, cut to the appropriate size and shape, and then stitched together into book form. Normally each calf could produce two pages, with the line of the spine of the animal running down the spine of the book. A more extravagant method of orienting the skins with the backbone across the page was used on the Book of Kells, involving the consumption of 150 animals (Meehan 1983, 48).

Much of the skill in the scriptoria, however, was associated with the transcribing and illustrating of the manuscripts, activities which involved many processes not associated with leatherworking, though it is appropriate to briefly mention them here. The preparation of inks and paints took place using some local products but mainly imported ones. On the Book of Kells, two types of ink were used, one made from soot and the iron-gall ink involving the combination of sulphate of iron, oak apples and gum. The colours were derived from a wide range of sources and could be made into various shades (Meehan 1983, 50). Minerals used included yellow arsenic trisulphide or yellow ochre (yellow), white lead (white), red lead (red), verdigris (bright green) and lapis lazuli (blue). Organic components were ox gall (yellow), indigo or woad (blue) and from the Mediterranean the plant *Crozophora tinctoria* (maroon or mauve) and insect *Kermococcus vermilio* (red). The elaborate designs of the later manuscripts within this period involved motifs derived from a wide range of media, and the adept translation of these onto the manuscript page. Once completed the manuscripts were placed between leather covers, often sumptuously decorated with metal fittings of which some have survived.

Book satchels or budgets rarely survive from this period, but two examples provide important information on the high level of sophistication that could be reached in leatherworking during the Early Christian period (Waterer 1968, O'Meadhra 1987). Most notable is the *Breac Moedóic* budget, adapted to act as a reliquary case, but originally for a manuscript. It was basically made from a single piece of leather, and stitched together in an extremely intricate manner. The leather was cattle hide, tanned in oak. It had been shaved down to make it thinner, and then had been stained. The tooled decoration, presumably carried out with the leather dampened, was done freehand with a bone or wooden scriber before it was assembled. The other surviving budget of this period, that at Corpus Christi, Oxford, was made in a very similar way to the *Breac Moedóic* example, including fine stitching which did not come through onto the exterior surface of the artefact. It would be reasonable to assume that book satchels, being required only by the ecclesiastical community, were made by them.

The *Hisperica Famina* gives an account of the manufacture of budgets (Herren 1974, 105–7). Here, sheepskin was used, flayed by a butcher and then stretched on a wall and smoked. Once prepared, the hide was subsequently used by the satchel maker. Here it is clear that the flesh of the sheep was available for human consumption, and that preliminary processing was carried out not by the skilled leatherworker but by others, presumably of lower status. Both the archaeological and documentary evidence point to highly skilled craftworkers in leather.

The nearest parallels for fine secular craftsmanship in leather come from some of the shoes excavated at crannog sites (Lucas 1954). The one-piece shoe was made from a complicated pattern, and some were subsequently decorated with tooled or occasionally incised designs. At Lagore, not only was a selection of shoes recovered, but a wooden shoe last was also found, indicating that manufacture must have taken place at the site. Numerous leather off-cuts are merely noted in the report, and so it is uncertain how wide a range of products were made at the site. Off-cuts were also recovered in quantity at Ballinderry 2 and here patches with their edges stitched and pieces stitched together were also found.

Woodworking

A large number of wooden artefacts found on waterlogged sites were relatively crude and may have been made by non-specialists. There is evidence, however, that some individuals must have been highly skilled in woodworking during this period. There are also clear indications from documentary sources of the value and purposes appropriate to different woods (see Chapter 5), and this is supported by archaeological finds.

Most wooden artefacts were probably relatively large and included furniture, carts and tools. Few survive, usually in a fragmentary state so that the original design cannot be appreciated. Exceptions are parts of containers. Stave-built vessels from Lagore and Ballinderry 2 indicate considerable skill; both yew and oak were used. Lathe-turned objects, particularly vessels, also must have been produced by craftsmen; two complete and several other reconstructable profiles were found at Lagore (Figure 6:15).

Woodworking tools have been found at a range of sites, but do not necessarily indicate the presence of specialist craftsmen (Figure 6:16). A wide range of tools are known, similar in form to modern types. These include a socketed gouge with bone handle from Clea Lakes crannog, and axes, an adze, saw knives, a draw knife, wedges, socketed chisel and gouges from Lagore, but all unstratified. A gouge was found at Cahercommaun. An axe and saw came from Carraig Aille 1, and the latter also appeared at Carraig Aille 2, and at Garryduff 1 with chisels. Awls have come from many sites, but could be used in a range of crafts.

Presumably ship-building must have been a skilled craft practised in Ireland during this period. Documentary sources indicate that vessels of leather and larger ones of wood were in use. However, no wrecks of this date have yet been found in coastal or inland waters. The only vessels yet located for the period are simple dug-out canoes. Large numbers have been found in drainage operations but most are undated. A few, however, have been found during site excavations and those at Ballinderry 2 and Lagore support the general finds in that oak was

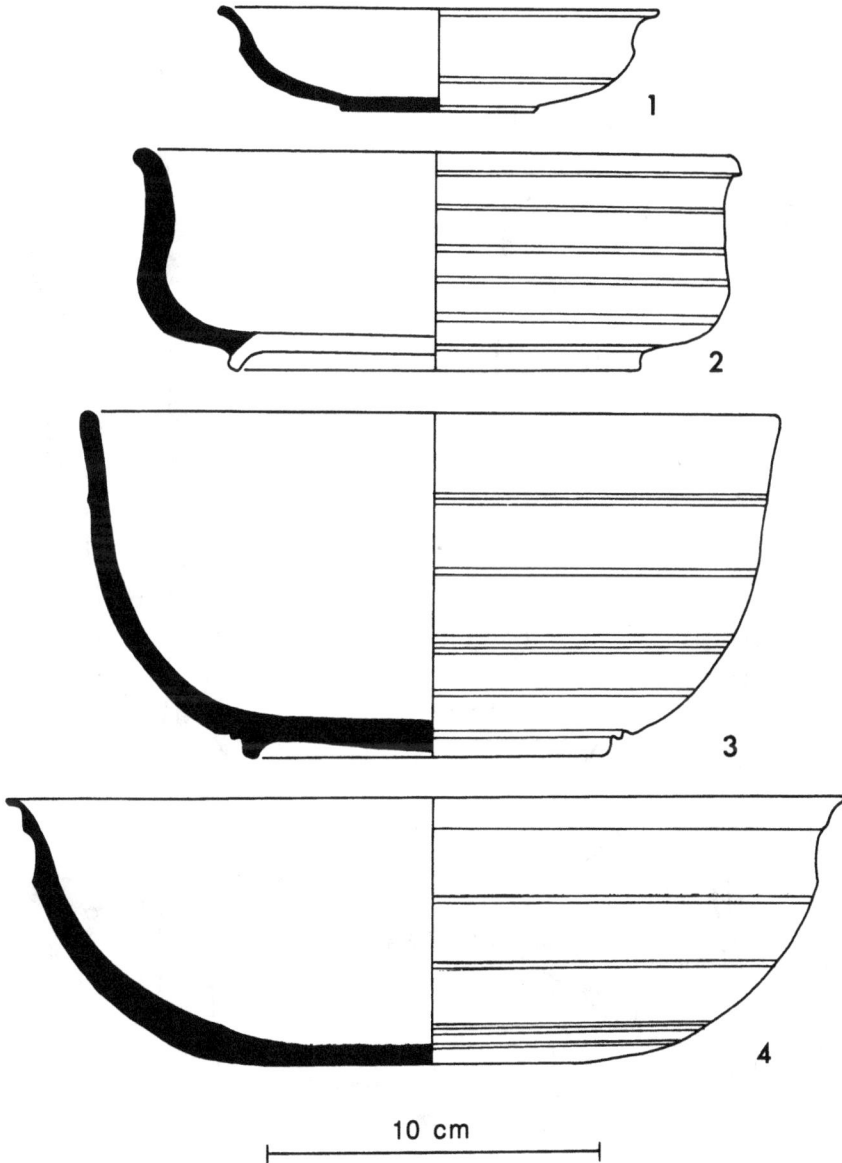

Figure 6:15   Wooden lathe-turned bowls from Lagore, Co. Meath (Hencken 1950).

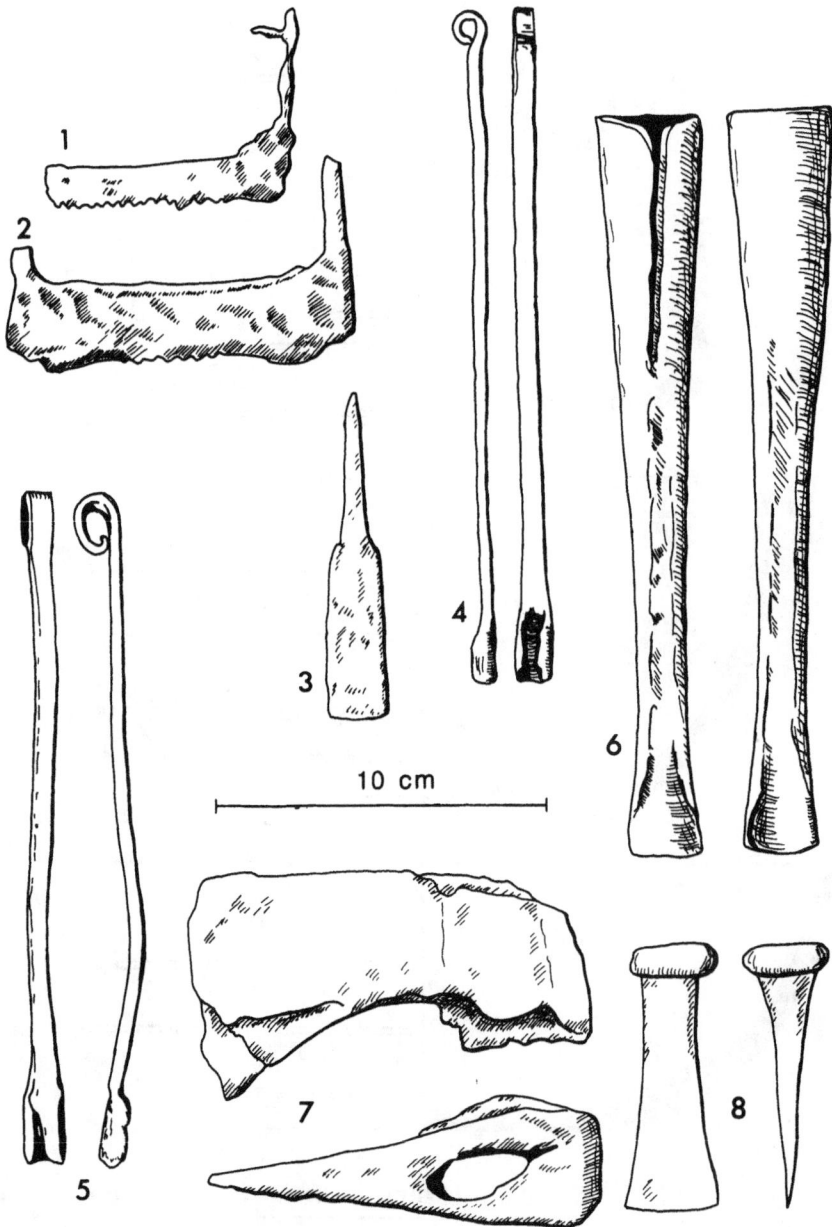

Figure 6:16   Woodworking tools. Garryduff 2, Co. Cork: **1, 2** saws; **3** punch. Lagore, Co. Meath: **4, 5** hand-gouges; **6** socketed gouge; **8** wedge. Killederdadrum, Co. Tipperary: **7** axe (**1–3** O'Kelly 1962, **4–6, 8** Hencken 1950, **7** Manning 1986).

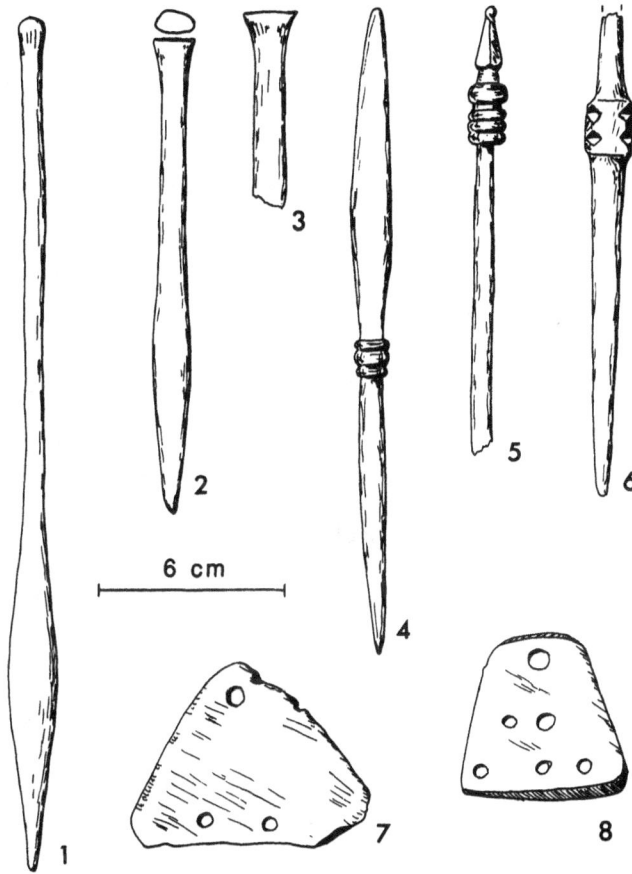

Figure 6:17 Spindles: **1, 6** Ballinderry 2, Co. Offaly; **2–5** Lagore, Co. Meath. Weaving tablets: **7** Lagore, Co. Meath; **8** Killederdadrum, Co. Tipperary (**1, 6** Hencken 1942, **2–5, 7** Hencken 1950; **8** Manning 1986).

the raw material. Evidence was found for the use of four pairs of oars at Lagore, and three at Ballinderry 2. Such boats require some skill of manufacture, but need not have been made by specialists; experiments conducted by W. A. Seaby (pers. comm.) have shown how such boats could be made.

Textiles

There is archaeological evidence of widespread interest in textile manufacture, particularly through the presence of spindle whorls. There are, however, a few but significant cases of other equipment and finished products being found, and these can be usefully set beside the considerable documentary evidence (Figure 6:17). The law tracts clearly indicate that both wool and flax processing were important female activities.

At Lagore, material was excavated which indicated that many of the stages of textile manufacture took place on the crannog (Start 1950). Samples of sheep's wool were recovered.

From the appearance of the yarn in the cloth fragments it would seem that some but not all wool was carded before being spun. Hair, probably from goat, was also examined and two cases were partly spun into threads. Examples of spindles in a range of woods were recovered, and 25 spindle whorls in wood, shale and bone were found. This number of whorls was, however, a very small proportion of the total finds and perhaps indicates that other sites where whorls are relatively common such as Carraig Aille 1 were more important for textile production. Spindles were usually of wood, and have been found not only at Lagore but also at Ballinderry 2 and Lough Faughan. Most thread was spun as two-ply. Twisted cords of two and six strands have been found, as was a three-stranded plaited cord.

The surviving textiles at Lagore indicate that most of the cloth was a simple tabby weave. These were made on a narrow horizontal loom which may or may not have had warp and cloth beams at the ends. There was also one sample, however, of a more elaborate twill or diagonal weave manufactured to a very high standard on a complex loom with four heddles; this must have been created by a weaver with considerable expertise (Start 1950, 212). All extant textiles are of sheep's wool, except for a few examples in goat hair; as yet no linen has been recovered, though a few sites have produced flax seeds (Monk 1986).

The only possible fragment of a loom that has been recovered from excavation is from Lough Faughan crannog. It could have easily been assembled and dismantled, and would presumably have been from a beam loom. Many looms would have been very small and easily portable whole; they produced narrow lengths of cloth between 25 cm and 35 cm wide. Although a few large perforated stones have been claimed as loom weights these have never been found in sufficient numbers, or intimately associated with other artefacts of textile manufacture at any site, to make this interpretation very likely. The extant fabrics suggest that beam looms were the norm.

There is also evidence of tablet weaving of braids. Whilst actual examples were excavated at Lagore (Start 1950, 214), the small, perforated tablets necessary for the production of these items are rare. They may be related to high status women or to particular craft centres; both interpretations would apply to Lagore.

Dyeing, from the surviving examples, took place after weaving rather than at the yarn stage. However, documentary references to multicoloured fabrics and embroidery would suggest that the latter practice was also known. Bleaching could take place prior to dyeing (Plummer 1968, 120) so that the colour could be even and bright. Fabric preserved in waterlogged conditions usually becomes too stained to allow identification of the original colour, though red was recognised at Lagore; this may have been made from the madder plant. The law tracts mention the intensive though small scale cultivation of *glaisin*, woad, which would have produced a blue dye. The dog whelk produces a purple dye, and large numbers of shells with their ends broken off in the process of extraction were found in middens at Inishkea North. Unfortunately it is not possible to determine whether dye was merely made at this site or whether cloth was actually processed there. Most other dyes are vegetable and mineral based, and would leave little or no trace in the archaeological record.

Textile manufacture was widespread, and according to documentary sources heavily associated with women. Certain stages, such as dyeing, even appear to have had taboos concerning the presence of men whilst they were carried out (Plummer 1968, 120). What is less clear, however, is whether textile production was purely at a household level or whether there were specialist producers, whether men or women. There is a greater spread of spindle whorls than pin beaters (if that be the function of bone scoops) even when only those sites with good bone preservation are considered, though this may only be due to depositional or even recovery factors. It is possible, however, that whilst spinning was widespread, the thread was then sold or exchanged to more specialised centres of weaving with the capital invested in looms and skilled operators. The fact that spindles of wool could be used for the payment of certain fines in the law tracts may suggest that they were made up to amounts of set value.

The manufacture of garments is an unknown stage in the textile craft. Although the daughters of the *aire désso* were taught sewing, cutting out and embroidery they were presumably only being trained to make clothes for themselves and their immediate family.

7
Long distance trade
and exchange

Whilst most economic activity took place within a local system there was the need to acquire both certain raw materials which were not widely found and finished goods which because of lack of either skills or resources were not manufactured locally. The organisation and control of long distance trade activity has been suggested as a major force in the development of states in many parts of the world (Brumfiel and Earle 1987), including early medieval Europe (Hodges 1982). Although the degree of concentration of power in the Early Christian period to AD 800 was limited, it is possible to consider how far such external contacts served both as a stimulus for change and as a response to internally generated change.

It is worthwhile first, however, to summarise the archaeological and historical evidence for long distance trade and exchange from Ireland. The subject has long been of interest and has attracted many specific and generalising interpretations, but the database is in fact quite small. It is worthwhile considering its limitations first, so that no great explanatory edifice is constructed on insufficient data. However, it will be possible to offer some tentative interpretations which relate Ireland to other developments elsewhere in western Europe at the time.

Imported pottery

The most carefully studied category of material relating to long distance trade is that of pottery, particularly that which derives from the Mediterranean and, probably, western Gaul. This has been largely due to the work of Thomas (1959, 1976, 1981b, 1990). The ceramics were almost certainly not the main import but are by-products; nevertheless they can be of significance because they can be provenanced, their distributions plotted and the mechanics of trade and distribution suggested (Figure 7:1).

Red Slip Wares

A fine tableware of bowls and dishes, some with stamped decoration, has been found mainly in south-west England and south Wales (Figure 7:2). This used to be called A ware (Radford 1956), subsequently subdivided into Ai (also called Late Roman C) and Aii (North African Red Slip) (Thomas 1976). These have now been further re-named Phocaean Red Slip Ware and African Red Slip Ware respectively now that provenances can be discerned for some at least of the products. A single Phocaean Red Slip Ware vessel was recovered from Garranes and a possible one from Garryduff, both in Co. Cork. The Garranes form of dish was current just after 500 and 23 examples came from Tintagel with single or small numbers of vessels from the other sites. No African Red Slip Wares have been found in Ireland although a single vessel has been noted from Iona. The table wares were almost certainly only space-fillers in more substantial cargoes, represented ceramically by the more numerous B ware amphorae.

Amphorae

The Bi ware amphorae seem to be contemporary with the Phocaean Red Slip Wares, and are all of the 'Agora' form which belonged to the first third of the sixth century (Figure 7:3). The globular vessels have a short neck and are decorated with deep lines of grooving in a band on the upper part of the amphorae. They came from the Aegean, probably the Peloponnese (Fulford 1989). The Bi amphorae are rare in Ireland, occurring as single examples at Garranes and also at the royal site of Clogher, Co. Tyrone. In Scotland only Dumbarton Rock and Whithorn have yielded this form. In contrast, Tintagel yielded at least 14 examples, and Cadcong and Glastonbury Tor each produced at least 3.

The few Biv amphorae, possibly from Asia Minor, have a long neck, shallow ribbing over most of the container and two handles. Thomas (1981b, 27) suggests that these British finds are perhaps water jars that may have been discarded on arrival after the long journey and had little direct significance in the trade. However, the fact that at least one such vessel reached Dinas Emrys in north Wales, a site which otherwise has none of the ceramics associated with the initial phase, suggests that the vessels were used in subsequent exchange, though none have yet been recorded in Ireland.

The Phocaean Red Slip Ware and the Bi 'Agora' amphorae both suggest an early long distance contact early in the sixth century, probably only with south-west England. From thence material (of which only the pottery survives) emanated in small quantities as far as Ireland and western Scotland, but there is nothing to suggest that, in this phase of contact, there was any direct link between Ireland and the Mediterranean. The evidence can, instead, be used to suggest secondary contact across the Irish Sea to the power centres which were, themselves, involved in exchange. The whole cargo may have come from the eastern Mediterranean; the forces behind such trade, and the mechanisms by which it operated, can best be discussed later.

The Bii amphorae form has diagnostic ribbing which is wider in the centre of the vessel than elsewhere; the handles are thick but the walls are thin (Figure 7:3). Within the region of the eastern Mediterranean there is considerable dispute concerning the centre of production, and the date range is broad, from the early fifth to the mid-seventh century (Peacock and Williams 1986, 187). The B misc category contains a range of forms and fabrics which may also cover a wide date range. Whilst all might have been derived from the same phase of activity as the early Red Slip Wares and the Bi and Biv amphorae, they may belong to a later contact. In this context the three Form 10 Phocaean Red Slip Ware dishes dated to perhaps around 580 from Tintagel may suggest a more precise temporal horizon for a voyage which, from the distribution of Bii assemblages, included a visit to Ireland. The Bii amphorae are found both on the east coast at Dalkey Island, and in the west at Reask and Inishcaltra, as well as at the sites of Garranes and Clogher already represented through earlier wares. In Scotland, however, Dumbarton Rock is the sole representative at present.

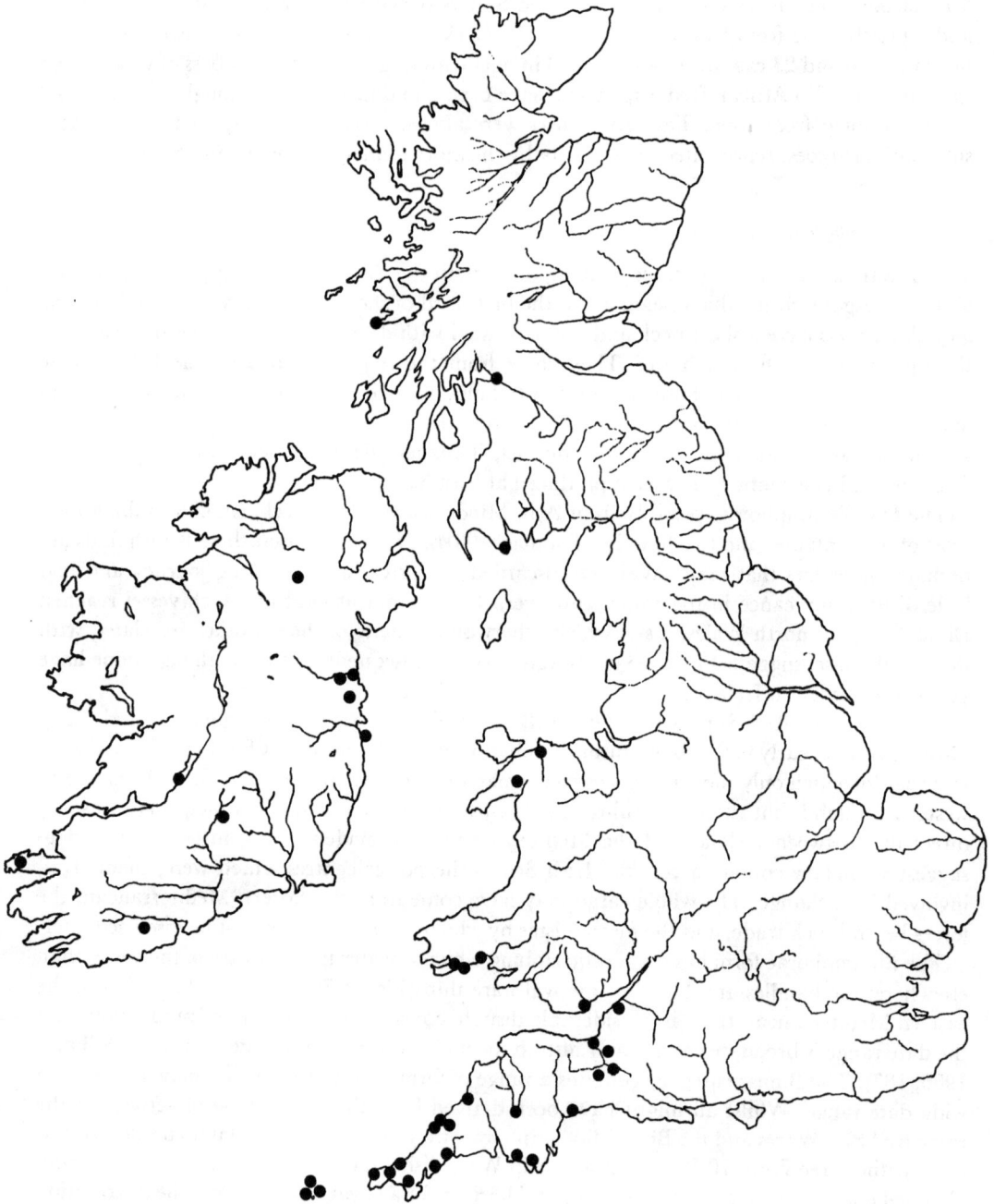

Figure 7:1 Distribution of Red Slip Wares and B ware amphorae in western Britain and Ireland (Thomas 1990).

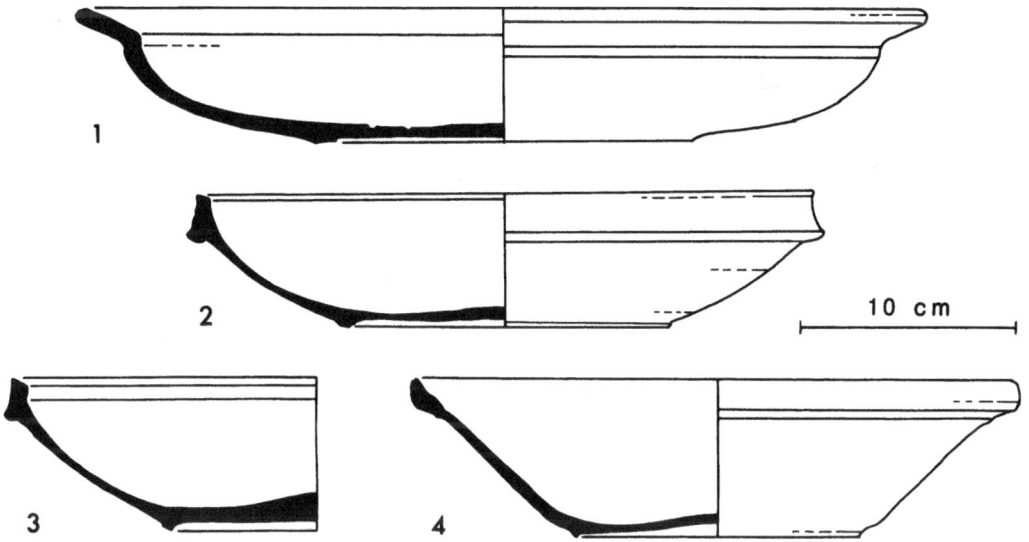

Figure 7:2 Common Red Slip Ware forms in western Britain and Ireland (Hayes 1972).

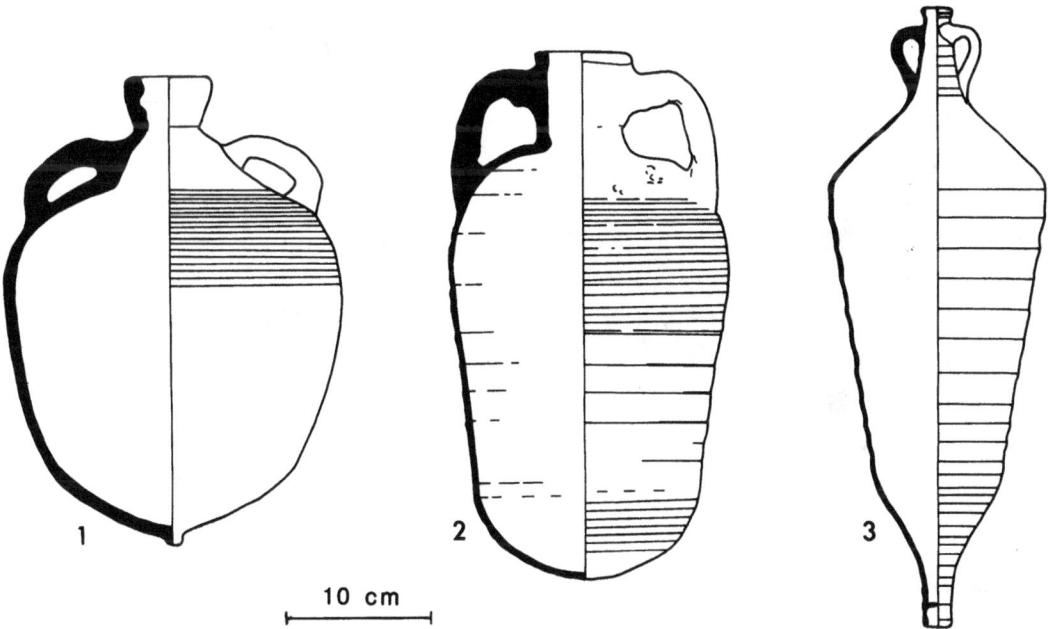

Figure 7:3 Amphora forms found in western Britain and Ireland. **1** Bi 'Agora'; **2** Biv; **3** Bii (Peacock and Williams 1986).

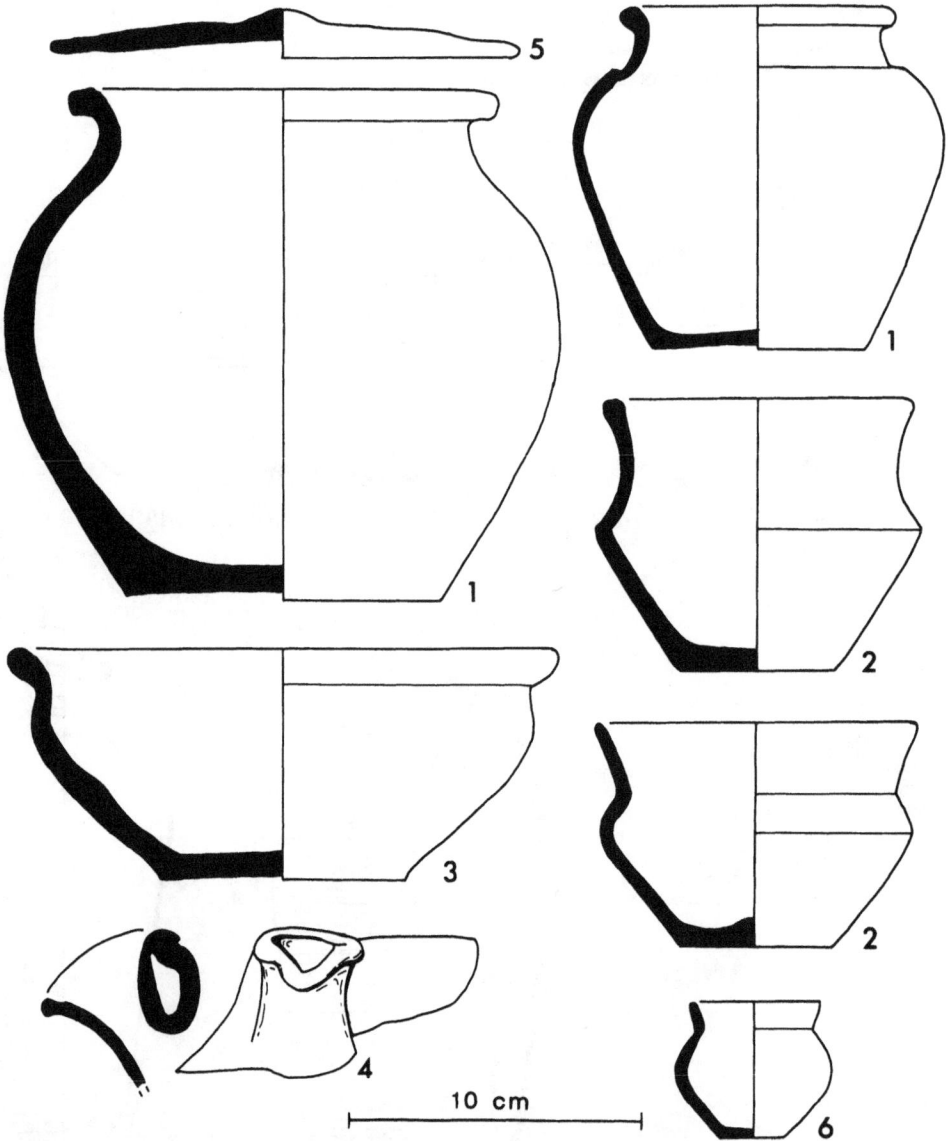

Figure 7:4   E ware forms found in Ireland. Numbers refer to forms: **1** everted rim jar; **2** carinated beaker; **3** flared carinated bowl; **4** jug; **5** lid for jar form **1**; **6** unguent jar (Thomas 1990).

Kitchen vessels

Not all ceramic evidence relates to sources of material as distant as the Mediterranean. A fine, grey kitchenware in a range of standard forms has been found in small quantities at many sites in western Britain and Ireland. This pottery has been labelled E ware, and consists of everted rim jars which could have lids, small beakers and flared bowls, and strap-handled jugs with trefoil-mouthed or tubular spouts (Figure 7:4). By far the most common forms, both in Ireland and elsewhere, were the jar and, much rarer, the beaker; all other forms were most unusual. The origin of E ware has still to be resolved. The most likely source is in the west of France on the basis of petrological evidence (Peacock and Thomas 1967, Peacock 1984) though this has been challenged (Campbell 1984). By a process of eliminating other potential areas, Hodges (1984) favours Aquitaine although he admits that Iberia may be a possible alternative.

The dating evidence for E ware is accumulating and suggests that it has a long period of production. Repeated associations with Bii amphorae suggest that some of the ware belongs to the later sixth century phase of importation. However, the stratigraphy at sites such as Clogher suggests that it lasts longer than this and continues into the seventh century. Campbell (1988) has, through study of the Welsh material, suggested only a few batches of imports. The extent of primary importation to Britain and Ireland may, therefore, have been once again restricted.

Unlike the earlier distributions of exotic pottery, Ireland and to a lesser extent Scotland were clearly very actively involved in importation (Figure 7:5). The widespread distribution of E ware within the Irish Sea zone may, however, have more to do with secondary redistributive processes than primary long distance contacts. The amount of material does allow some consideration of likely centres of importation, and the mechanisms of distribution. These may also be relevant in some respects to the earlier Red Slip Wares and B ware amphorae, but the focus of attention seems to have shifted westwards between the early sixth and seventh centuries, reflecting the growing international importance of Ireland by this date.

Another category of imported pottery, designated D ware, occurs at a few sites in Britain and Ireland. Probably originating in the Bordeaux area, it is largely restricted to south-west Britain with just one vessel known from Clogher and a presence noted at Dunadd and the Mote of Mark in Scotland. It may, in chronological terms, overlap with the B and E wares. It occurs at Tintagel, Cadcong and South Cadbury, from none of which has there been a single sherd of E ware in contrast to the quantities present of all other fabrics. But it also occurs at the Scottish sites mentioned above which have only E ware and nothing earlier.

Glass

The glass from Ireland and western Britain was studied by Harden but there has been little subsequent work. Major assemblages have come from the Mote of Mark (Harden 1956), Dinas Powys (Harden 1963) and Dalkey Island. He concludes that all these items come from the same north France/Rhineland area, are fifth to sixth century in date and come in the form of bowls and cone beakers. Such vessels occur in Anglo-Saxon graves and it is possible that the material reached Ireland via England and south Wales rather than directly from the production centre. Whether it came as complete vessels or scrap is also difficult to ascertain.

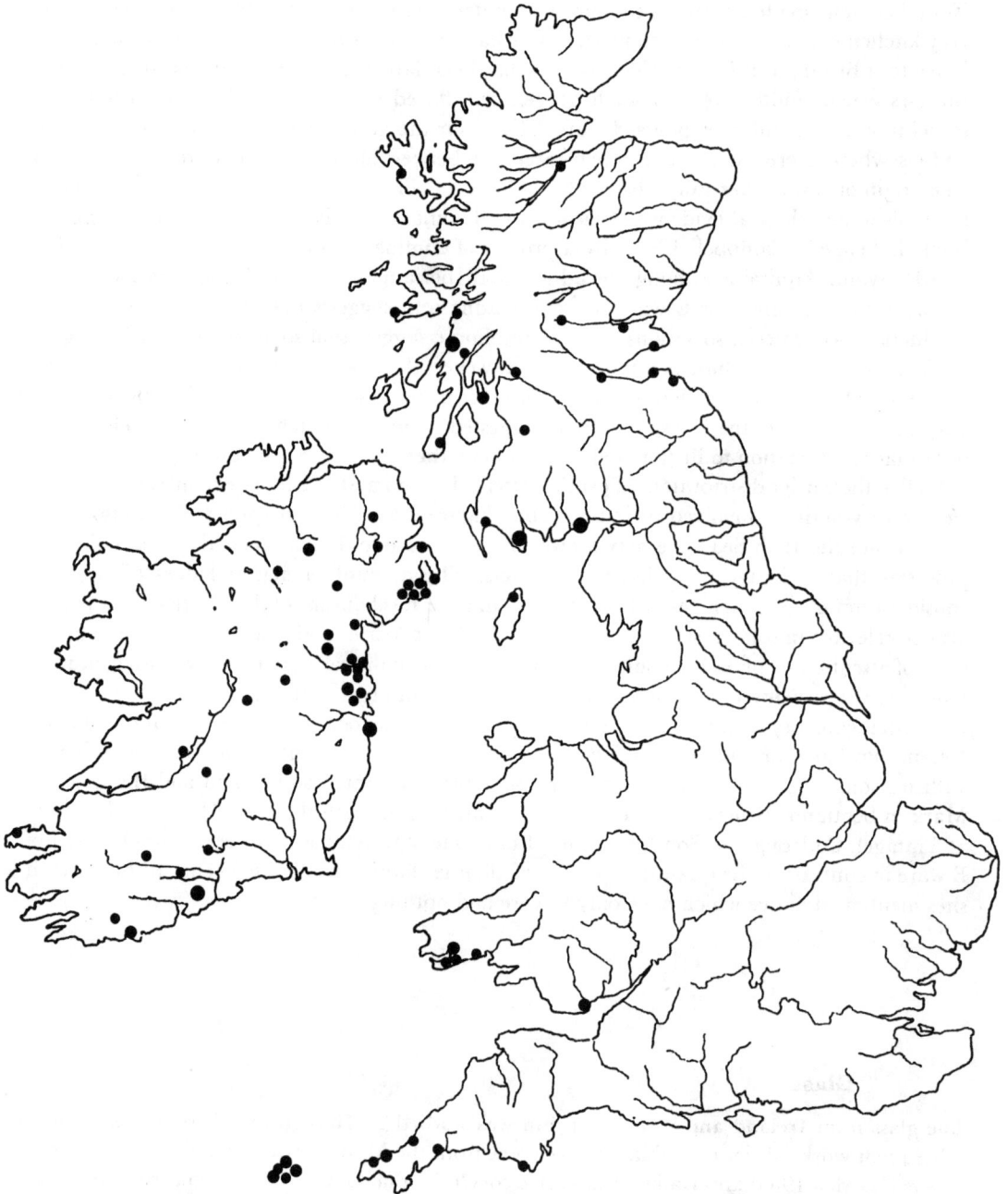

Figure 7:5   Distribution of E ware in western Britain and Ireland (Thomas 1990).

Metalwork

There is only a very limited amount of metalwork that may have been manufactured abroad. Many more items show foreign influences, including much of the ecclesiastical material discussed in Chapter 3, and this might imply actual imports. However, designs and ideas may have spread without large quantities of imports.

The Franks were noted for their production of high quality metalwork, particularly swords, and some of the exotic military equipment from Ireland can be identified with such a source. By far the largest assemblage of such material is from the royal crannog of Lagore where high status and suitable contexts for deposition and survival have fortuitously and fortunately combined. Most notable is the Frankish sword, but there are also several single-edged scramasaxes among the old finds from the site (Figure 7:6).

Lagore also produced a Continental style shield boss, though Hencken (1950, 99) comments that these are smaller than normal, as most Irish weapons seem to be (Figure 7:7); another example came from Lough Faughan crannog. The shield illustrated in the Book of Kells is of this small type. An iron horse bit from the earliest period of the crannog (Figure 7:8) is best paralleled by an example from a late seventh-century German grave (Hencken 1950, 101), and a fragment of another has been found at Gwithian (Thomas 1990).

Documentary evidence

One of the important lines of historical enquiry which is relevent in the examination of the imported pottery is that concerning the links between Iberia and Ireland over this period. Hillgarth (1962, 1984) has argued forcefully that these links were of some significance, and this

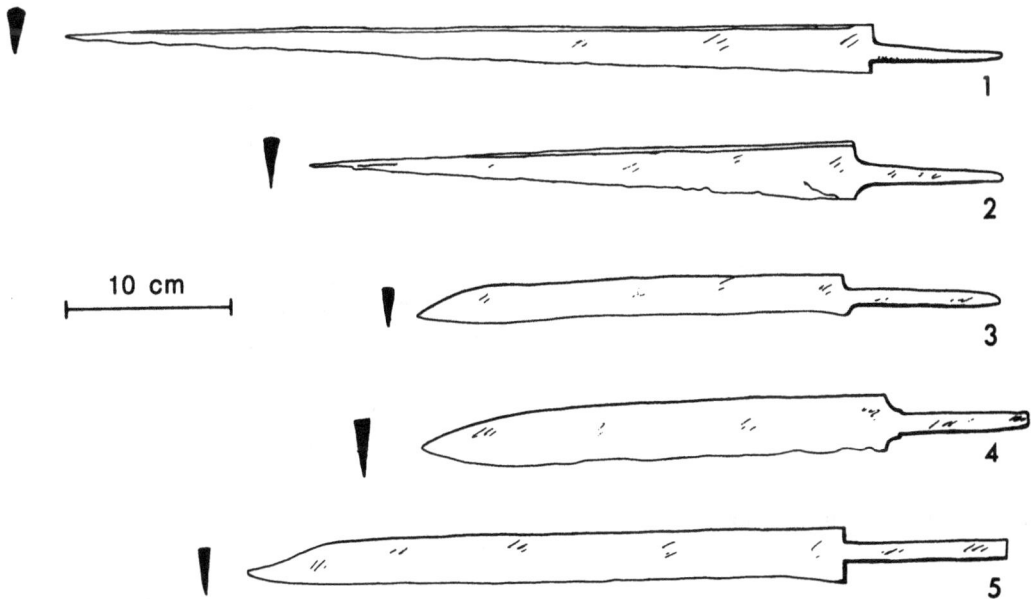

Figure 7:6 Swords and scramasaxes with Frankish influence or origin from Lagore (Hencken 1950).

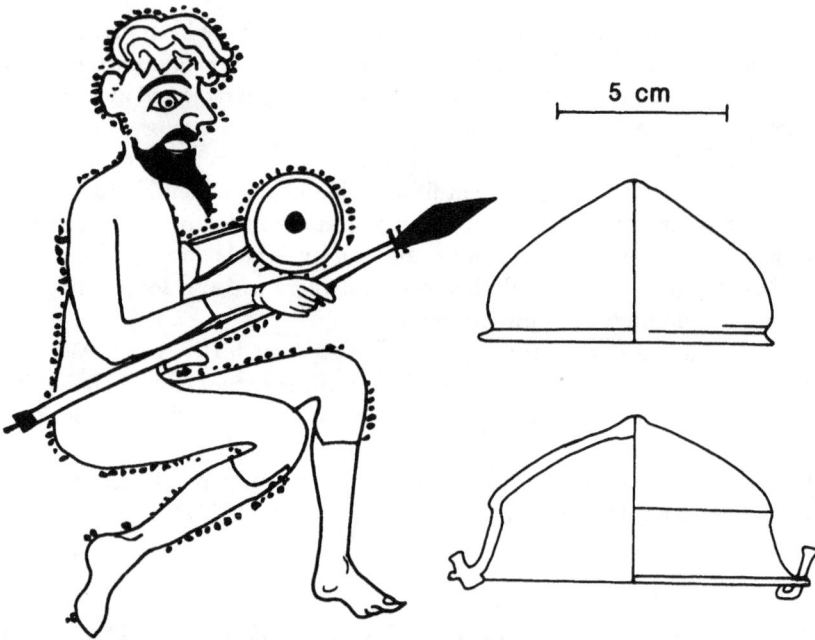

Figure 7:7   Shield bosses from Lagore and illustration of a warrior in the Book of Kells (Lagore, Hencken 1950; Book of Kells, Henry 1974).

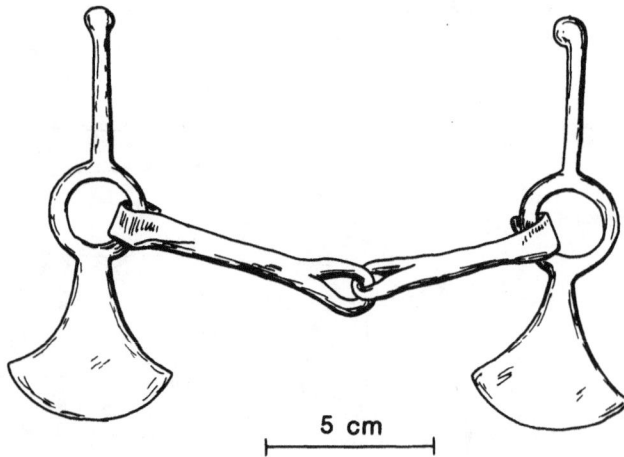

Figure 7:8   Horse bit from Lagore (Hencken 1950).

is supported by Herren (1980). He considers that Vergil – Vergilius Maro Grammaticus – was a seventh century Irishman, probably with some Continental experience, who used Isidore of Seville (Herren 1980). However, Vergil misunderstood the background of Isidore, seeing him as a convert, and thus emphasising the indirect link between Ireland and Spain. This may be a timely reminder with regard to the pottery that the amount of Mediterranean or Continental information that was transferred along with the cargoes – of pottery, wine or erudite texts – may have been extremely limited. This might explain in part how, despite such contacts, developments in Ireland over this period can be seen as largely internally generated.

The law tracts give some indications of trade and exchange, although these are not easy to interpret. The *Corus Bescna* lists foreigners or exiles amongst those with whom contracts should not be made. These may have included merchants and so suggested a limitation on those who could deal with traders, but more likely it was a protection against those from whom retribution for any wrongs would be impossible.

The silence of law tracts in dealing with any royal control and taxation of trading activity may be taken to suggest that such promotion did not take place, but Gerriets (1987, 68) points out that there are few references to household taxation compared with those payments through systems of clientship, yet this may be due to the survival of certain categories of sources. The same lack of survival could apply to commercial controls, but archaeological evidence should be expected to demonstrate major trading activity; at present it does not.

Interpretations

Whilst simple assertions of the movement of traders, whether from the Mediterranean or western France, may at one level provide an explanation of the material found in western Britain and Ireland, it is not a very satisfactory one. Indeed, such a statement might be inferred as a simplistic imposition of modern capitalist values onto a past culture. The form of trade, if that it be, may have been complex and more related to social, political or ideological factors than simple profit-led motives. This may, indeed, have been the case with regard to some of the activity for the exporters as well as the importers of goods. The use of models and terminology from economic anthropology can be usefully employed at this juncture to allow various threads of economic and other forces to be woven into the interpretation.

There are only a limited number of ways in which exotic materials can enter a country: distribution can be limited to personal contacts between individuals such as kings; it can be restricted to particular points of entry controlled by the elite; or there can be relatively uncontrolled access. Each of these three categories leads to an increase in the amount of goods that can be mobilised, but also decreases the amount of control exercised by an elite. All have been claimed for the material described above, in varying degrees of detail, and each will be examined in turn working from the least to the most controlled.

Uncontrolled access: the trading entrepreneur

Though not clearly expressed, there are implicit assumptions within the writings of Thomas and Alcock that the main impetus for some of the long distance trade came from the merchants who brought goods from the Mediterranean. The western British and Irish then responded to this trade, which was organised through high status individuals and places. It would be in this context that Tintagel, Cadcong and Dinas Powys would have acquired the large quantities of such artefacts, other processes (described below) leading to the presence of material at other sites. This idea has been briefly outlined by Thomas (1990). Whilst the Mediterranean traders can be considered as independent and entrepreneurial, and part of a wide-ranging market economy, this may not be a worthwhile framework within which to interpret the trade and exchange systems *within* Ireland and western Britain.

Fulford (1989) has recently suggested that the trade which brought the Red Slip Wares and B ware amphorae came directly from the eastern Mediterranean, possibly from Byzantium itself. The period of intense contact was approximately from 475 to 550, though there may have been some trading both before and after this. Fulford suggests that the impetus was the search for tin and if this was the case, Cornwall would have been the main target for merchants. The dominance of Tintagel in the artefact counts could be taken as support for this, but the far from insignificant quantities of imports at Cadcong and Dinas Powys then need explanation. Alternative products or complex and large scale redistribution of imports from Cornwall are both possible.

Restricted entry: gateway communities

Gateway communities are located at entry points to regions defined either politically or physically. They may be urban, but in less complex economies such as Ireland during this period, they are periodic and not necessarily even very large. Hodges (1982) has defined Type A gateway communities as ones where unloading and distribution are features. They are dependent on personal relationships inland for the dispersal of goods (Figure 7:9). The boundary location allows control over access to the imported goods so that the elite can then use such materials within the pattern of internal distributions associated with the socially horizontal movements through gift giving and the vertical ones through clientage.

There is one Irish site which suggests itself as a gateway community. Dalkey Island lies just south of Dublin Bay off the eastern coast of Ireland, the side of the island least favoured with

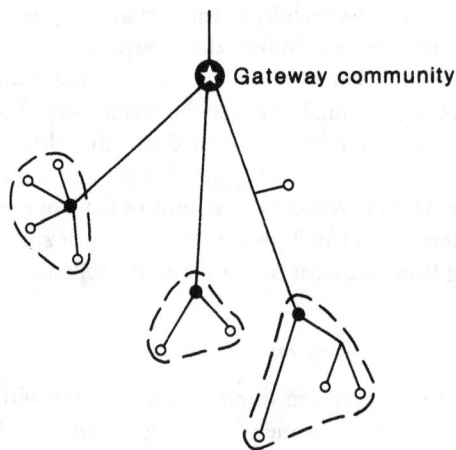

Figure 7:9 The relationships between a gateway community and its hinterland (Hodges 1982).

natural harbours on the mainland. The island also had certain advantages as a base for trading relations. Hodges (1982) has suggested the site would be a good site for a simple gateway community because its separation from the mainland provides it with a vital characteristic of such early trading centres; it is in a neutral, frontier position. This allows the traders certain protection and also gives the elite control over access to the trading location from within their territory. Thus, lines of exchange could be controlled, and the prestige goods so acquired by the elite could then be manipulated through internal exchange systems to help to preserve their position. Hodges (1978) emphasises that personal relationships underpinned such trading centres, and that they were probably not permanent.

The archaeological evidence at Dalkey Island suggests that the trading community was small, being restricted to a small promontory on the north-west end of the island. It is at this end of the island that the present harbour is situated, although the ships of the early traders probably pulled up their vessels on the adjacent shingle beach (Figure 7:10). Occupation was first unenclosed, but during the Early Christian period whilst E ware was in use the promontory was demarcated by a ditch and bank and habitation continued. Three pins from the lowest levels may be from Britain rather than Ireland, but the other metalwork is probably native in origin. The imported goods are limited to ceramics and glass. The range of imported pottery is interesting at Dalkey Island. Not only are Bii, B misc and E ware represented, but also a deliberately shaped sherd of Samian which can be compared with others from Lagore, Dundrum and Lough Faughan. Considerable debate has been generated by these Roman sherds, their functions being claimed as decorative inlays (Radford in Collins 1955), as relics or souvenirs of Rome (Warner 1976). The rarity of Roman material in Ireland suggests that such finds in Early Christian contexts are late imports and may have a symbolic significance; Liversage (1968) considered that they were charms. Such material could have come from Britain or the Continent. The glass includes several possible Roman pieces, but most is post-Roman in date and sixth century. It is yellow or yellow-green, from four bowls and three cone beakers. Only small parts of each vessel were recovered.

Whether other sites acted as gateway communities is difficult to say. It has been suggested (Hodges 1982) that Nendrum in Strangford Lough may have functioned as such in the north-east, but the absence of Red Slip Ware and amphorae indicates no part in the early trade and a single E ware vessel hardly hints at such a significant role in the slightly later importation. As parallels for Dalkey Island, one might expect a similar focal point in or near Cork Harbour, and one or more sites along the Shannon could have served the midlands. There are several possibilities in the north of Ireland. Thomas (1976, 254) has suggested that the *Bordgal* place-names in Ireland may relate to Gaulish traders and so to centres of such exchange activity. However, James (1982, 383) is doubtful on the basis of the dating and alternative meanings of the name; moreover the locations indicated by the placenames are not those most obviously suited to a long distance trading function.

Restricted entry: the church

Thomas (1959) suggested that the main impetus for the long distance trade reflected in the imported pottery was that of wine needed for the Eucharist. The B ware amphorae can be seen as the direct by-product of the imported wine, with the Red Slip Wares being space-fillers perhaps on occasion used as communion vessels. The presence of stamped crosses on some has been suggested as support for some religious function, although it was normal for such vessels

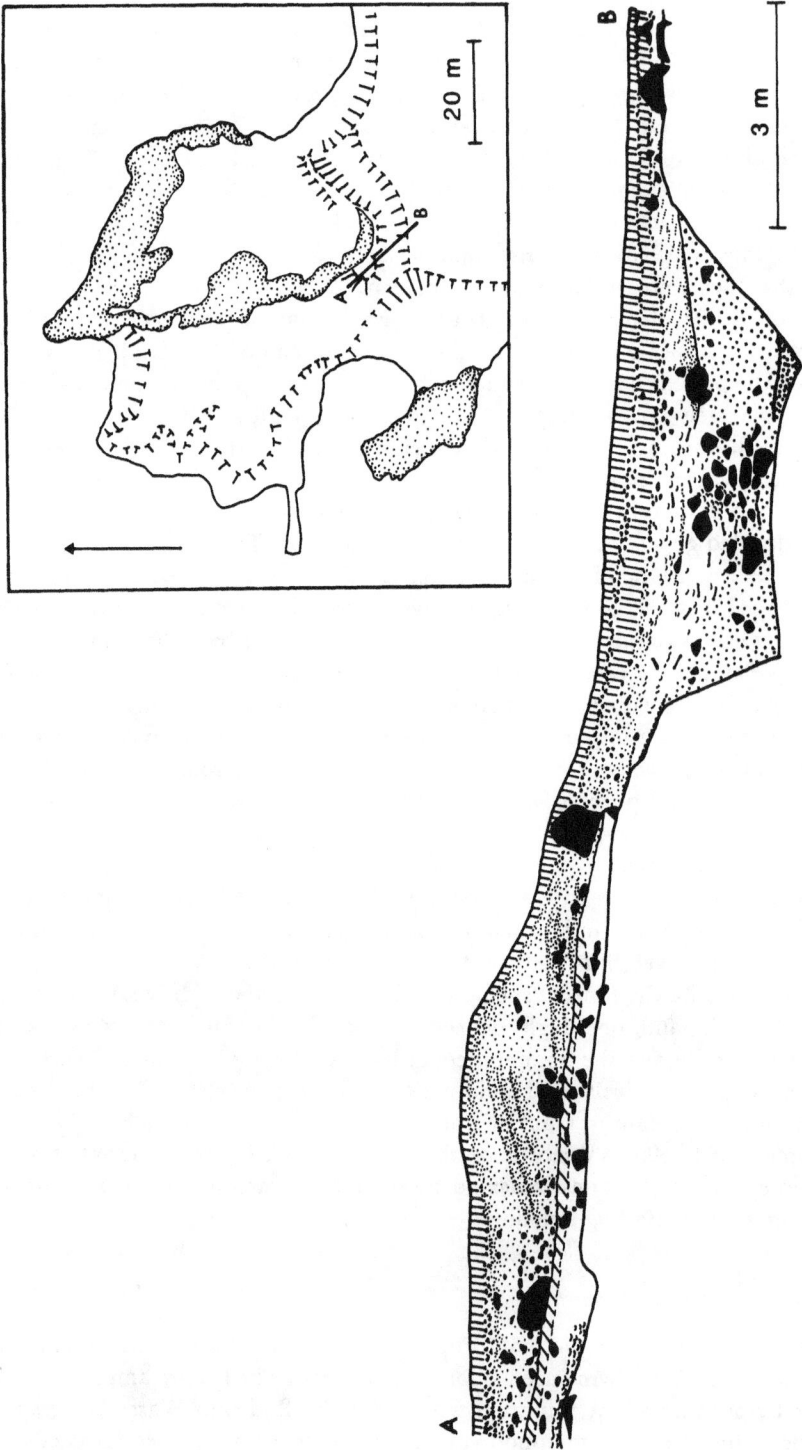

Figure 7:10 Dalkey Island promontory fort plan and section across bank and ditch (Liversage 1968).

to be stamped with a design and the cross was very common on the vessel forms found in western Britain (Hayes 1972, 348–9). With regard to the kitchenwares it is less certain that they were to be linked directly with wine, but here the presence of barrel staves and hoops on the waterlogged E ware sites of Lough Faughan and Lagore may indicate the containers for the liquid (Figure 7:11). However, both of these sites are secular, indicating that even if the church was the initial importer it was not the sole user of the products. Indeed, the importance of secular sites not only in Ireland but also in western Britain required Thomas (1981b, 4) to reduce the significance of the church as an impetus for importation.

All the sites with major assemblages of imported pottery, whether of the early material (Tintagel, Cadcong, Dinas Powys, Gwithian, South Cadbury, Glastonbury Tor, Clogher, Garranes) or the later D and E wares (Dinas Powys, Garryduff, Dunadd, Clogher, Tean, Dalkey Island), are secular. It was originally thought that Tintagel was monastic, although this has now been disproved and it is now considered a royal site (Padel 1981, Dark 1985). Therefore,

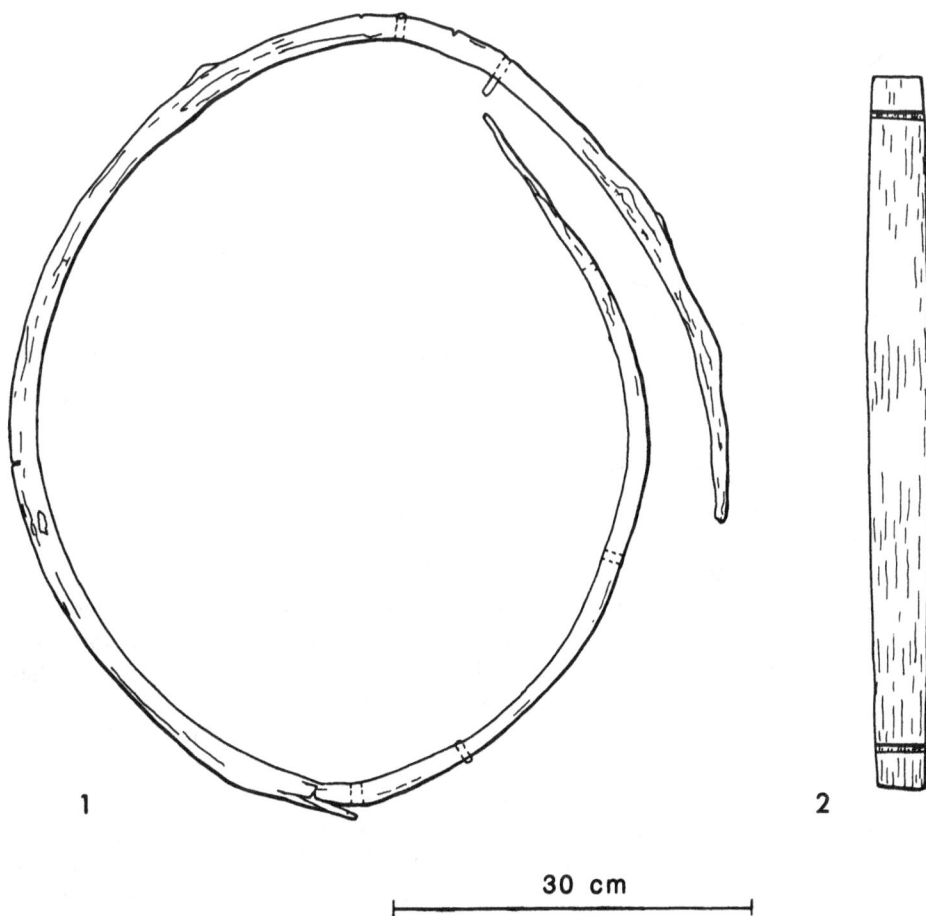

30 cm

Figure 7:11 Fragments of wooden barrels from waterlogged sites. **1** Barrel hoop, Lough Faughan, Co. Down; **2** stave, Lagore, Co. Meath (**1** Collins 1955, **2** Hencken 1950).

it can be seen that amphorae, and presumably wine, did reach religious sites such as Reask and Inishcaltra, but only in small quantities. Whether there were any religious import centres is still uncertain as the most likely religious houses have not been subjected to modern excavation, but the extensive clearances at Nendrum produced only one E ware vessel. Moreover, the documentary references to the travels of saints suggest that the traders who carried them were operating independently of religious centres. Unfortunately the texts do not give any indication, even as incidental information, of the mechanics and contexts of the mariners' activities.

At present it is possible only to recognise that the church would have desired wine for sacramental purposes but that it may have not instigated the trade visible archaeologically. That wine could come to north-west Europe from the eastern Mediterranean can be demonstrated in documentary sources. Peacock and Williams (1986, 59) emphasise the role of the church in redistribution during this period, and note that the virtues of Palestinian Gaza wine were recognised by Gregory of Tours, and that it was used for the Eucharist.

Restricted access: controlled markets

There is no evidence in the period up to 800 of the secular elite promoting internal market centres, although it is possible that towards the very end of the period some religious institutions were beginning to take on this role. Churches and monasteries may have been located near to existing small scale local marketing centres which, as successful religious houses extended their contacts, became regional, national and even international. How active the church was in expanding this form of marketing at this early date is unclear. The earliest reference to a monastic fair, óenach, noted by Doherty (1980, 81) was in 799 at Lusk, Co. Dublin. In the eighth century some may well have deliberately expanded their undoubted local exchange and secure storage roles to a wider circle as monasteries became involved in political manoeuvring and were associated with the aggrandising tendencies of major dynastic groups. It is to a later period, however, that this trend is more apposite.

Personal contacts: gift exchange

Doherty (1980) has indicated the widespread use of gift exchange in Ireland from documentary sources, and has emphasised the need to place this activity within a wider historical and anthropological perspective.

Gift exchange is used to cement new and reinforce old social and political relationships. These may be between equals, to bind them together, or may be between unequals, to confirm the asymmetrical relationship. Within the internal social and economic clientage system it has been demonstrated conclusively that the law tracts describe mutual obligations involving exchange of materials. This was also undertaken at a higher level between political groups through tribute payments and provision of services. Within such a context, the giving of gifts could allow permeation of high status items to a lower level of the hierarchy.

The separation of gift-giving between equals and distribution down through the system is important. It may well be that certain categories of artefact, such as imported pottery, had two separate values. The first was related to the initial importation and the contents (certainly in the case of the B ware amphorae but perhaps with other vessels such as E ware jars with lids). Here, wine, oils, perfumes or spices could have been the most important active elements in consumption. At a secondary level, however, the ceramic containers still remained after the fillings had been consumed. Though now empty of contents they were not necessarily empty of meaning, since they still indicated to a largely aceramic audience long distance contacts and, indirectly, the original contents. It may be that in this secondary use the objects could be distributed downwards, no longer able to function within a mode of conspicuous consumption (there was nothing left to consume) but as a display item which would still reflect back to the original giver and consumer. Such vessels could even have been given as souvenirs of feasts given by the king to his entourage, a sign of association with the highest in the social system which could be displayed thereafter. The *Bethu Brigte* indicates that breakable vessels could have value in their own right at this time, and such a context would explain this (Mytum 1986b).

Thomas (1990) has recently suggested that the significance of metalwork finds may be rather different to that of ceramics and even glass. Weapons and horse harness could have come with independent mercenaries who served under Irish kings. He considers that the expertise and renown of Frankish mercenaries could have been appreciated by Irish kings who happily accepted them into their retinues. The result is that items of equipment which had been brought with these foreigners were on occasion lost. However, the few items of Continental metalwork could have come within normal trading activity or as part of long distance gift exchange by the elite. The latter process may even seem more likely considering the characteristics of the items; it is worth noting that the late seventh-century Life of Columba mentions the saint giving a decorated sword to Libran (Anderson and Anderson 1961, 424–5). The sword was an artefact rich in symbolism aptly associated with power; this artefact had little functional value to churchmen but could be used as an element in the complex, intermittent matrix of gift-giving with all that it entailed. Therefore, the presence of foreign military hardware does not necessarily indicate the presence of Franks but could indicate the cementing of elite alliances and agreements with the exchange of high quality, ostentatious and powerful gifts (both symbolically and in practice). We know about the movement of secular aristocracy to and from Ireland through the few documented examples such as Dagobert II who was dispatched to Ireland by Grimoald (James 1982, 379), and the presence of Anglo-Saxons benefiting from monastic education. The adoption of Continental and Anglo-Saxon metalworking techniques, motifs and styles also indicates a range of contacts, perhaps to be associated with retinues travelling with these elite visitors.

The distribution of E ware may indicate the process of a widespread network of social relations, though restricted in quantity, as evidenced by this one archaeologically visible commodity. There presumably were centres of importation, but the material may then have been almost completely dissipated in the process of social relations (Figure 7:5). It may be that many of the E ware vessels themselves were only of great significance once dispersed to lesser kings and aristocracy who then retained them until breakage and deposition. Other imported goods which had accompanied the ceramics may have been consumed at the archaeologically less visible major centres.

Long distance trade was utilised within the power politics of Early Christian Ireland, but in the period up to 800 cannot be seen as a major stimulus to cultural change. In subsequent centuries, however, regional, national and wider ranging trade can be seen to play a powerful part in the development of larger political confederations and entities, and in the continued transformation of Early Christian Ireland towards greater levels of complexity.

8
Conclusion

This book has attempted to map the changes which led to the emergence of Early Christian culture in Ireland, and its subsequent development up to around AD 800. To this end, primarily archaeological but also historical material has been used. Material culture can be interrogated, as can historical documents, to answer questions about the past. The difficult task is making the mute artefacts speak, a skill only now being developed within archaeology.

We are fortunate that the period under study has a rich supply of both documents and archaeological remains which, moreover, are undergoing a renewed period of intense and critical study. Whilst historical syntheses have been attempted on a number of occasions, those heavily relying on archaeological data have been rare, relatively brief and largely descriptive. In using a processualist model involving the definition and analysis of a series of systems – beliefs, society, subsistence economy, craft, exchange – it has been possible to assess the internal dynamics of each and the interrelations of one with another. It has also been possible to consider the external forces which affected particular systems, sometimes with unforeseen consequences caused by 'knock-on' effects.

The origins for change are seen to lie outside Ireland, which was during the preceding Iron Age relatively isolated and moribund. Contacts, particularly with Britain, though also at times with the Continent, engendered changes which began in the fourth century when we know that there were Christians in Ireland and Irish migrations to parts of western Britain. The many ways in which contact between members of the different cultures could have taken place, and their relative efficacy in stimulating cultural change, have been outlined. Undoubtedly the kinship ties across the Irish Sea, and the spread to Ireland of the new belief system of Christianity along with Roman views of land ownership, agriculture and manufacture, were highly significant. These initial external triggers led to the subsequent internal generation of change.

With the gradual but steady demise of pagan beliefs and practices, a new world view came to dominate Ireland. Two major factors can be discerned that had implications in other systems, namely the increased definition of the individual and the creation of an institution, namely the church. Individual responsibility, decision-making and choice were supported by the Christian belief in individual salvation. During the period up to 800, one major change was largely completed which was caused by the increasing perception of the individual over the wider kin.

Early in the period, obligations of kinship were held by those within the *derbfine*, united by descent from a common great-grandfather. This was changed to the *gelfine*, descendants of a common grandfather. The individual's perception of socially significant kinship proximity was drastically reduced by this. Obligations were thereby reduced but so were the stabilising forces of mutual support. This allowed for the development of a more fluid system of relationships in the social sphere, with the growth of clientship. Here, relationships were chosen by those involved, although many of the disadvantaged may have in reality had little room for manoeuvre. Kinship was restrictive in the development of social strategies since it was largely inherited, but with clientship the politically active were able to manipulate their support. This adaptability increased instability and thereby allowed for the initiation of change that would, in the period after AD 800, lead to the emergence of political structures approaching that of states.

The institution of the church also introduced a new element in the social structure. At one level law codes had to be adapted to include this new hierarchy; at another, the initial separation of the church from the pagan secular elite gave way to intimate co-operation as Christian conversion spread. The presence of an institution that began to be given resources, but which never died and released these resources back into the system for redistribution, emphasised the ideas of ownership, including private ownership, particularly of land. This was to have a significant impact on the subsistence economy. Social relations between the sacred and profane sectors of society became the norm. By the end of the period the church, or more specifically, blocks of churches aligned with particular tribal political groups, acted fully within the political arena. This was a feature which was to continue and intensify in the period after 800.

In the economic sphere, the rise of the individual led to the initiation of colonising and agricultural intensification that had not been possible under a kin-based communal land ownership system. Whilst kin land remained, its relative importance, particularly for the powerful with large estates, dwindled. In its place the clientship system allowed capital to be lent by the elite, in return for economic payment as well as social use. The capital, in the form of animals, land or tools, was lent at a rate that allowed the fortunate and able to increase their own economic base, and the social system was, with some checks, fluid. It was possible to be upwardly mobile although, as power became more concentrated and as population rose, more people slid down the social scale than climbed it. The lower levels of workers tied to the land or working as slaves have left relatively little in the archaeological and historical record, but must have been numerically the largest sector of the population, an expendable resource. The increased economic activity was still conducted through a relatively rigid system of barter and payments in kind, with cows being the basic unit of wealth. Silver was beginning to play a role, but still only a marginal one. Therefore the subsistence economy was literally wealth-generating in that it created the goods directly utilised in economic and social activity.

The landscape of Ireland filled up during the period to 800, with the social and economic pressures to have children combining to create a population increase which could be supported by colonisation and intensification. However, as land became scarce, the social system came under pressure and the criteria required to define a freeman were relaxed, with the creation of the *ócaire* grade. There may also have been an increase in violence, something that was to become manifest in later centuries.

Churches and monasteries developed their own social and thereby economic hierarchies, with the flows of obligations and payments leading towards gradual domination by a few of the most successful monastic centres, a process which continued after 800. They acquired resources through gifts, or used their political power to obtain crucial estates. The larger monasteries could operate on a scale that may have allowed agricultural specialisation which was an option open to few if any secular landholders.

In craft production, the organisation certainly changed as large scale production of a wide range of goods became common. For example, the number of iron objects can be explained by the widespread exploitation of local sources of ore, particularly from bogs. This might be seen as part of the freedom offered to individuals, and as a response to the increased subsistence base and consequent demand. Moreover, the demand for more elaborate artefacts increased rapidly also. With a more dynamic social system, and the emphasis on the individual, personal display became more important. The nature of artefacts emphasised the control of patronage, such as in the use of a wide range of materials such as millefiori, gilding, and enamels on jewellery. Precious metals, notably silver, played a part but it was through the display of commissioned skills that power was manifested. In the period after 800, it is possible to see a gradual change to the use of silver as the dominant feature in adornment, as a bullion economy took over from one where the control of less mobile wealth in the form of land, cattle and manpower was central.

The church was an extremely important factor in the development of high quality craft products, since it created a demand for communion vessels, reliquaries and furniture within churches, the largest of which were probably built on a scale greater than any secular structure. The context of manufacture for ecclesiastical products is still unclear, but there were probably specialist workshops within major houses. Certainly, manuscript production was dominated by the church and was initiated by it, and the same may be the case for almost all stone sculpture. After 800, this last craft area became a particularly important focus for investment, with the use of the standing stone cross for display. The process had begun slightly earlier, but cannot be understood without looking at later developments. Architecture in stone within the Early Christian period tends to be later rather than earlier even though dating is still notoriously difficult. Again, it would seem that the church played a significant role in such developments, mainly after 800.

Trade and exchange were on an increasing scale throughout the Early Christian period up to AD 800, but most of this was at a local or at best regional level. This was in part caused by the cumbersome barter arrangements, and by the dominance of clientship payments when such relationships were themselves local or regional. Long distance trade undoubtedly was used by both the secular and religious elite to bolster their position, but it was in no way fundamental to their survival. As Ireland entered more fully into the European world, through both secular political contacts and religious exchanges, and subsequently after 800 by the intervention of the Vikings, the situation changed. Again, these are developments beyond consideration here, but their origins can in a limited way be already perceived.

In conclusion, the change from the Iron Age to the Early Christian period can be seen as of momentous importance in the cultural development of Ireland. The changes wrought by a new religion, and attendant Roman-influenced beliefs and techniques, had effects which continued to promote changes within Ireland for centuries to come. By 800, a new state of equilibrium and stability had not been reached, but certain factors were beginning to limit the development of further complexity. Most notable of these were the constraints of an economy based on cattle. Economic activity in terms of long distance trade and further intensification of local production and consumption was being stifled, as was social and political manipulation beyond a region. It may be that a new level of stability in the various systems would have emerged in the ninth century, had it not been for the further external trigger of the Viking arrival. This, again, set off in manifold and complex ways a new chain of reactions within and between the systems that led to yet further changes. These belong to another story, but one closely related to the one outlined in this book. In one sense 800 is an arbitrary date; in another, it can be taken to represent a watershed after which the trajectory of change along which Early Christian Ireland had been travelling was altered.

The origins of Early Christian Ireland were long gone by 800; the culture had a maturity and strength which in many aspects would last to the fifteenth century and beyond. The fifth to eighth centuries represent perhaps the most significant period in Ireland's history; this book has sought to describe how and explain why it happened the way it did.

Bibliography

Abbreviations used:

BAR British Archaeological Reports
CBA Council for British Archaeology
CMCS *Cambridge Medieval Celtic Studies*
JCHAS *Journal of the Cork Historical and Archaeological Society*
JIA *Journal of Irish Archaeology*
JRSAI *Journal of the Royal Society of Antiquaries of Ireland*
NMAJ *North Munster Archaeological Journal*
PRIA *Proceedings of the Royal Irish Academy*
UJA *Ulster Journal of Archaeology*

Aalen, F. H. A. (1978) *Man and the Landscape in Ireland*, London: Academic Press.
Adams, R. M. (1966) *The Evolution of Urban Society*, Chicago: Aldine.
Alcock, L. (1971) *Arthur's Britain*, Harmondsworth: Penguin.
——(1981) 'Early historic fortifications in Scotland', in G. Guilbert (ed.) *Hillfort Studies*, pp. 150–81, Leicester: Leicester University Press.
Alcock, L., Alcock, A. A. and Foster, S. M. (1986) 'Reconnaissance excavations on early historic for- tifications and other royal sites in Scotland, 1974–84: I', *Proceedings of the Society of Antiquaries of Scotland* 116: 255–79.
Alexander, J. J. G. (1978) *A Survey of Manuscripts Illuminated in the British Isles*, Vol. 6: *Insular Manuscripts Sixth to Ninth Century*, London: Miller.
Anderson, A. O. and Anderson, M. O. (1961) *Adomnan's Life of Columba*, London: Nelson.
Armstrong, E. C. R. and Macalister, R. A. S. (1920) 'Wooden book with leaves indented and waxed found near Springmount Bog, Co. Antrim', *JRSAI* 50, 160–6.
Arnold, C. J. (1988) *An Archaeology of the Early Anglo-Saxon Kingdoms*, London: Routledge.
Ashby, W. R. (1965) *An Introduction to Cybernetics*, New York: Wiley.

Bachmann, H. G. (1976) 'Crucibles from a Roman settlement in Germany', *Journal of the Historical Metallurgy Society* 10, 34–5.
Bailey, R. N. (1980) *Viking Age Sculpture in Northern England*, London: Collins.

Baillie, M. G. C. (1975) 'A horizontal mill of the eighth century AD at Drumard, Co. Derry', *UJA* 38, 25–32.

——(1979) 'An interim statement on dendrochronology at Belfast', *UJA* 42, 72–84.

——(1985) 'Irish dendrochronology and radiocarbon calibration', *UJA* 48, 11–23.

——(1986) 'A sherd of souterrain ware from a dated context', *UJA* 49, 106.

Bannerman, J. (1974) *Studies in the History of Dalriada*, Edinburgh: Scottish Academic Press.

Barker, P. W. (1979) 'The latest occupation of the site of the Baths Basilica at Wroxeter', in P. J. Casey (ed.) *The End of Roman Britain*, pp. 175–81, Oxford: BAR British Series 71.

Barrett, G. F. (1972) 'The ringfort: a study in settlement geography with special reference to southern Co. Donegal and the Dingle area, Co. Kerry', unpublished Ph.D. thesis, Queen's University, Belfast.

——(1980) 'A field survey and morphological study of ring-forts in southern County Donegal', *UJA* 43, 39–51.

——(1982) 'Aerial photography and the study of early settlement structures in Ireland', *Aerial Archaeology* 6, 27–37.

——(1983) 'The reconstruction of proto-historic landscapes using aerial photographs: case studies in County Louth', *County Louth Archaeological Journal* 20, 215–36.

Barrett, G. F. and Graham, B. J. (1975) 'Some considerations concerning the dating and distribution of ring-forts in Ireland', *UJA* 38, 33–47.

Barry, T. B. (1981) 'Archaeological excavations at Dunbeg promontory fort, County Kerry, 1977', *PRIA* 81C, 295–329.

Barth, F. (1966) *Models of Social Organization*, RAI Occasional Paper 23, London: Royal Anthropological Institute.

Bateson, J. D. (1973) 'Roman material from Ireland: a re-consideration', *PRIA* 73C, 21–98.

Bee, R. L. (1974) *Patterns and Processes*, New York: Free Press.

Bertalanffy, L. von (1962) 'General systems theory – a critical review', *General Systems* 7, 1–20.

Bethel, D. L. T. (1981) 'The originality of the early Irish church', *JRSAI* 111, 36–49.

Bieler, L. (1953) *The Works of St Patrick*, London: Longmans, Green & Co.

——(1963) *The Irish Penitentials*, Scriptores Latini Hiberniae V, Dublin: Institute for Advanced Studies.

Binchy, D. A. (ed.) (1941) *Críth Gablach*, Medieval and Modern Irish series, II, Dublin: Institute for Advanced Studies.

——(1943) 'The linguistic and historic value of the Irish law tracts', *Proceedings of the British Academy* 29, 195–228.

——(1956) 'Some Celtic legal terms', *Celtica* 3, 221–8.

——(1958) 'The fair of Tailtiu and the feast of Tara', *Ériu* 18, 113–38.

——(1961) 'The background of early Irish literature', *Studia Hibernica* 1, 7–18.

——(1962) 'Patrick and his biographers', *Studia Hibernica* 2, 7–173.

——(1966a) 'Ancient Irish law', *Irish Jurist* 1, 84–92.

——(1966b) '*Bretha Déin Chécht*', *Ériu* 20, 1–66.

——(1968) 'St Patrick's "First Synod"', *Studia Hibernica* 8, 49–59.

——(1971) 'An archaic legal poem', *Celtica* 9, 152–68.

——(1973a) 'Distraint in Irish law', *Celtica* 10, 22–71.

——(1973b) 'A text on the forms of distraint', *Celtica* 10, 72–86.

——(1981) 'Brewing in eighth-century Ireland', in B. G. Scott (ed.) *Studies on Early Ireland: Essays in Honour of M. V. Duignan*, pp. 3–6, Belfast: Association of Young Irish Archaeologists.

Binford, L. R. (1962) 'Archaeology as anthropology', *American Antiquity* 28, 217–25.

——(1972) *An Archaeological Perspective*, London: Academic Press.

——(1978) *Nunamiut Ethnoarchaeology*, London: Academic Press.

——(1982) 'Meaning, inference and the material record', in A. C. Renfrew and S. Shennan (eds) *Ranking Resource and Exchange*, pp. 160–3, Cambridge: Cambridge University Press.

Bitel, L. (1984) 'Women's donations to the churches in early Ireland', *JRSAI* 114, 5–23.

Boddington, A. (1987) 'From bones to population: the problems of numbers', in A. Boddington, A. N. Garland and R. C. Janaway (eds) *Death, Decay and Reconstruction. Approaches to Archaeology and Forensic Science*, pp. 180–97, Manchester: Manchester University Press.

Boon, G. C. (1960) 'A temple of Mithras at Caernarvon-Segontium', *Archaeologia Cambrensis* 109, 136–72.

——(1976) 'The shrine of the head, Caerwent', in G. C. Boon and J. M. Lewis (eds) *Welsh Antiquity: Essays. Presented to H. N. Savory*, pp. 163–75, Cardiff: National Museum of Wales.

Boserup, E. (1965) *The Conditions of Agricultural Growth*, London: Allen & Unwin.

Bourke, C. (1985) 'An enamelled object from Rathmullan, County Down', *UJA* 48, 134–7.

Bowen, E. G. (1954) *Settlements of the Celtic Saints in Wales*, Cardiff: University of Wales Press.

——(1969) *Saints, Seaways and Settlements in the Celtic Lands*, Cardiff: University of Wales Press.

——(1972) *Britain and the Western Seaways*, London: Thames & Hudson.

Bradley, J. (1982) 'A separate-bladed shovel from Moynagh Lough, County Meath', *JRSAI* 112, 117–22.

Bradley, R. J. (1984) *The Social Foundations of Prehistoric Britain*, London: Longman.

——(1987) 'Time regained: the creation of continuity', *Journal of the British Archaeological Association* 140, 1–17.

Brady, N. D. K. (1988) 'A late ploughshare type from Ireland', *Tools and Tillage* 5.4, 228–42.

Brandt, R. and Slofstra, J. (eds) (1983) *Roman and Native in the Low Countries*, Oxford: BAR International Series S184.

Branigan, K. (1977) *The Roman Villa in South-West England*, Bradford on Avon: Moonraker Press.

Brannon, N. F. (1980) 'Excavation of a tree-ring at Gallanagh, County Tyrone, and some observations on tree-rings', *UJA* 43, 97–101.

Bray, D. A. (1987) 'The image of St Brigit in the early Irish church', *Études Celtiques* 24, 209–15.

de Brisay, K. W. and Evans, K. A. (eds) (1975) *Salt: The Study of an Ancient Industry*, Colchester: Colchester Archaeological Group.

Brumfiel, E. M. and Earle, T. K. (1987) 'Specialization, exchange and complex societies: an introduction', in E. M. Brumfiel and T. K. Earle (eds) *Specialization, Exchange and Complex Societies*, pp. 1–9, Cambridge: Cambridge University Press.

Buchanan, R. H. (1973) 'Field systems of Ireland', in A. R. H. Baker and R. A. Butlin (eds) *Studies of the Field Systems of the British Isles*, pp. 580–618, Cambridge: Cambridge University Press.

Buckley, V. M. (1986) 'Ulster and Oriel souterrains – an indication of tribal areas?', *UJA* 49, 108–10.

Buckley, W. (1967) *Sociology and Modern Systems Theory*, Englewood Cliffs, NJ: Prentice-Hall.

Bury, J. B. (1905) *The Life of St Patrick, and His Place in History*, London: Macmillan.

Byrne, F. J. (1971) 'Tribes and tribalism in Early Ireland', *Eriu* 22, 128–66.

——(1973) *Irish Kings and High-Kings*, London: Batsford.

——(1980) 'Derrynavlan: the historical context', *JRSAI* 110, 116–26.

Campbell, E. (1984) 'E ware and Aquitaine – a reconsideration of the petrological evidence', *Scottish Archaeological Review* 3.1, 35–8.

——(1988) 'The post-Roman pottery', in N. Edwards and A. Lane (eds) *Early Medieval Settlements in Wales AD 400–1100*, pp. 124–37, Bangor/Cardiff: Research Centre Wales/Department of Archaeology, University College.

Carney, J. (1955) *Studies in Irish Literature and History*, Dublin: Institute for Advanced Studies.

——(1975) 'The invention of the Ogam cipher', *Eriu* 26, 53–65.

Caulfield, S. (1977) 'The beehive quern in Ireland', *JRSAI* 107, 104–38.

——(1981) 'Some Celtic problems in the Irish Iron Age', in D. Ó Corráin (ed.) *Irish Antiquity*, pp. 205–15, Cork: Tower Books.

Chadwick, H. (1967) *The Early Church*, Harmondsworth: Penguin.

——(1985) 'Augustine on pagans and Christians: reflections on religious and social change', in D. Beales and G. Best (eds) *History, Society and the Church: Essays in Honour of Owen Chadwick*, pp. 9–27, Cambridge: Cambridge University Press.

Charles-Edwards, T. M. (1972a) 'Notes on common farming', in K. Hughes *Early Christian Ireland: Introduction to the Sources*, pp. 61–4, London: Hodder & Stoughton.

——(1972b) 'Kinship, status and the origins of the hide', *Past and Present* 56, 3–33.

——(1984) 'The church and settlement', in P. Ní Chatháin and M. Richter (eds) *Ireland and Europe*, pp. 167–75, Stuttgart: Klett-Cotta.

Charles-Edwards, T. M. and Kelly, F. (1983) *Bechbretha*, Dublin: Institute for Advanced Studies.

Clark, G. (1966) 'The invasion hypothesis in British archaeology', *Antiquity* 40, 172–89.

Clarke, D. L. (1968) *Analytical Archaeology*, London: Methuen.

——(1972) 'A provisional model of an Iron Age society and its settlement system', in D. L. Clarke (ed.) *Models in Archaeology*, pp. 801–69, London: Methuen.

——(1973) 'Archaeology: the loss of innocence', *Antiquity* 47, 6–18.

Cole, J. R. (1980) 'Cult archaeology and unscientific method and theory', in M. Schiffer (ed.) *Advances in Archaeological Method and Theory* 3, 1–33.

Collins, A. E. P. (1955) 'Excavations at Lough Faughan crannog, Co. Down, 1951–2', *UJA* 18, 45–81.

——(1959) 'A rath group at Craigaphuile, Co. Down', *UJA* 22, 88–92.

——(1966) 'Excavations at Dressogagh Rath, Co. Armagh', *UJA* 29, 117–29.

——(1968) 'Excavations at Dromore ring-work, Co. Antrim', *UJA* 31, 59–66.

Collins, A. E. P. and Proudfoot, B. (1959) 'A trial excavation in Clea Lakes crannog, Co. Down', *UJA* 22, 92–101.

Collins, C. (1982) 'Appendix 1: report on the osteological material from excavations at Rathmullen, County Down', *UJA* 45, 156–62.

Connolly, S. and Picard, J.-M. (1987) 'Cogitosus: *Life of St Brigit*', *JRSAI* 117, 11–27.

Cooter, W. S. (1984) 'Environmental, ecological and agricultural systems: approaches to simulation modelling applications for medieval temperate Europe', in K. Biddick (ed.) *Archaeological Approaches to Medieval Europe*, pp. 159–70, Kalamazoo, Mich.: Western Michigan University, Studies in Medieval Culture 18.

Coplestone-Crow, B. (1982) 'The dual nature of the Irish colonization of Dyfed in the Dark Ages', *Studia Celtica* 16–17, 1–24.

Corish, P. J. (1971) 'Pastoral mission in the early Irish church', *Léachtaí Cholm Cille* 2, 15.

Craddock, P. T. (1989) 'Metalworking techniques', in S. Youngs (ed.) *The Work of Angels: Masterpieces of Celtic Metalwork, Sixth to Ninth Centuries AD*, pp. 170–4, London: British Museum Publications.

Cramp, R. (1967) *The Monastic Arts of Northumbria*, London: Arts Council of Great Britain.

Crawford, H. S. (1912) 'A descriptive list of early cross-slabs and pillars', *JRSAI* 42, 217–44.

——(1913) 'Descriptive list of early cross-slabs and pillars', *JRSAI* 43, 151–69, 261–5, 326–34.

——(1916) 'Supplementary list of early cross-slabs and pillars', *JRSAI* 46, 163–7.

——(1923) 'A descriptive list of Irish shrines and reliquaries', *JRSAI* 53, 74–93, 151–76.

Crehan, J. H. (1976) 'The liturgical trade route: east to west', *Studies* 65, 87–99.

Crowfoot, G. M. (1945) 'The bone "gouges" of Maiden Castle and other sites', *Antiquity* 19, 157–8.

Culleton, E. B. and Mitchell, G. F. (1976) 'Soil erosion following deforestation in the Early Christian period in south Wexford', *JRSAI* 106, 120–3.

Cunliffe, B. W. (1978a) *Iron Age Communities in Britain*, 2nd edition, London: Routledge & Kegan Paul.

——(1978b) 'Settlement and population in the British Iron Age: some facts, figures and fantasies', in B. W. Cunliffe and R. T. Rowley (eds) *Lowland Iron Age Communities in Europe*, pp. 3–24, Oxford: BAR International Series S48.

Cuppage, J. (1986) *Archaeological Survey of the Dingle Peninsula*, Ballyferriter: Oidhreacht Chorca Dhuibne.

Curwen, E. C. (1938) 'Early agriculture in Denmark', *Antiquity* 12, 135–53.

——(1944) 'The problems of early water mills', *Antiquity* 18, 130–46.

Dalton, G. (1961) 'Economic theory and primitive society', *American Anthropologist* 63, 1–25.

Dalton, G. (1971) (ed.) *Studies in Economic Anthropology*, Washington, DC: American Anthropological Association.

Daniel, G. E. (1962) *The Idea of History*, Harmondsworth: Penguin.

Dark, K. R. (1985) 'The plan and interpretation of Tintagel', *CMCS* 9, 1–17.

Davies, J. G. (1962) *The Architectural Setting of Baptism*, London: Barrie & Rockliffe.

Davies, J. L. (1984) 'Soldiers, peasants and markets in Wales and the Marches', in T. F. C. Blagg and A. C. King (eds) *Military and Civilian in Roman Britain*, pp. 93–127, Oxford: BAR British Series 136.

Davies, O. (1939) 'Excavations at Lissachiggel', *County Louth Archaeological Journal* 9, 209–43.

——(1942) 'The Twomile Stone, a prehistoric community in Co. Donegal', *JRSAI* 72, 98–105.

Davison, B. K. (1962) 'Excavations at Ballynarry Rath, Co Down', *UJA* 24–5, 39–87.

Deetz, J. (1977) *In Small Things Forgotten*, New York: Anchor.

Dickinson, C. W. and Waterman, D. M. (1960) 'Excavations at Castle Skreen, Co. Down', *UJA* 23, 63–77.

Dillon, E. P. (1983) 'Karren analysis as an archaeological technique', in T. Reeves-Smyth and F. Hamond (eds) *Landscape Archaeology in Ireland*, pp. 81–94, Oxford: BAR British Series 116.

Dillon, M. (1951) 'The taboos of the kings of Ireland', *PRIA* 54C, 1–36.

——(1977) 'The Irish settlements in Wales', *Celtica* 12, 1–11.

Doherty, C. (1980) 'Exchange and trade in early medieval Ireland', *JRSAI* 110, 67–89.

——(1984a) 'The basilica in early Ireland', *Peritia* 3, 303–15.

——(1984b) 'The use of relics in early Ireland', in P. Ní Chatháin and M. Richter (eds) *Ireland and Europe*, pp. 89–101, Stuttgart: Klett-Cotta.

Duignan, M. (1944) 'Irish agriculture in early historic times', *JRSAI* 74, 124–45.

Dumezil, G. (1968) *L'Ideologie des trois fonctions dans les épopées des peuples indo-européens*, Paris: Gallimard.

Dumville, D. (1984) 'Some British aspects of the earliest Irish Christianity', in Ní Chatháin and M. Richter (eds) *Ireland and Europe*, pp. 16–24, Stuttgart: Klett-Cotta.

——(1985a) 'Late-seventh- or eighth-century evidence for the British transmission of Pelagius', *CMCS* 10, 39–52.

——(1985b) 'On editing and translating medieval Irish chronicles: the Annals of Ulster', *CMCS* 10, 67–86.

Edwards, N. (1986) 'The south cross, Clonmacnois (with an appendix on the incidence of vine-scroll on Irish sculpture)', in J. Higgitt (ed.) *Early Medieval Sculpture in Britain and Ireland*, pp. 23–48, Oxford: BAR British Series 152.

Ervin, A. M. (1980) 'A review of the acculturation approach in anthropology with special reference to recent change in native Alaska', *Journal of Anthropological Research* 36, 49–70.

Esposito, M. (1912) 'On the earliest Latin life of St Brigid of Kildare', *PRIA* 30C, 307–16.

Evans, E. E. (1954) 'Dairying in Ireland through the ages', *Journal of the Society of Dairy Technology* 7, 179–87.

——(1966) *Prehistoric and Early Christian Ireland*, London: Batsford.

Fahy, E. M. (1969) 'Early settlement in the Skibbereen area', *JCHAS* 74, 147–56.

Fanning, T. (1981) 'Excavation of an Early Christian cemetery and settlement at Reask, Co. Kerry', *PRIA* 81C, 3–172.

Fenton, A. (1969) 'Draught oxen in Britain', *Národopisny vestník ceskoslovensky* 3–4: 17–59; reprinted in A. Fenton (1986) *The Shape of the Past 2*, pp. 2–33, Edinburgh: John Donald.

Finch, T. F. (1971) *Soils of Co. Clare*, Soil Survey Bulletin 23, Dublin: An Foras Talúntais.

Finch, T. F. and Ryan, P. (1966) *Soils of Co. Limerick*, Soil Survey Bulletin 16, Dublin: An Foras Talúntais.

Flanagan, D. (1984) 'The Christian impact on early Ireland: place-names evidence', in P. Ní Chatháin and M. Richter (eds) *Ireland and Europe*, pp. 25–51, Stuttgart: Klett-Cotta.

Flannery, K. V. (1967) 'Culture history v. culture process: a debate in American archaeology', *Scientific American* 217, 119–22.

——(1973) 'Archaeology with a capital S', in C. Redman (ed.) *Research and Theory in Current Archaeology*, pp. 47–58, New York: Wiley.

Fletcher, R. (1977) 'Settlement studies (micro and semi-micro)', in D. L. Clark (ed.) *Spatial Archaeology*, pp. 47–162, London: Academic Press.

Ford, R. I. (1977) 'Evolutionary ecology and the evolution of human ecosystems: a case study from the midwestern USA', in J. N. Hill (ed.) *Explanation of Prehistoric Change*, pp. 153–84, Albuquerque, N. Mex.: University of New Mexico Press.

Fowler, P. J. (1966) 'Ridge-and-furrow cultivation at Cush, Co. Limerick', *NMAJ* 10, 69–71.

Fulford, M. G. (1989) 'Byzantium and Britain: a Mediterranean perspective on post-Roman Mediterranean imports in western Britain and Ireland', *Medieval Archaeology* 33, 1–6.

Gerriets, M. (1983) 'Economy and society: clientship according to the Irish Laws', *CMCS* 6, 43–61.

——(1987) 'Kingship and exchange in pre-Viking Ireland', *CMCS* 13, 39–72.

——(1988) 'The king as judge in early Ireland', *Celtica* 20, 29–52.

Glassie, H. (1975) *Folk Housing of Middle Virginia*, Knoxville, Tenn.: University of Tennessee Press.

Godel, W. (1979) 'Irish prayer in the Middle Ages, I', *Milltown Studies* 4, 60–83.

Gould, R. A. (1980) *Living Archaeology*, Cambridge: Cambridge University Press.

Greene, D. (1968) 'Some linguistic evidence relating to the British church', in M. W. Barley and R. P. C. Hanson (eds) *Christianity in Britain, 300–700*, pp. 75–86, Leicester: Leicester University Press.

Grosjean, P. (1957) 'Notes d'hagiographie celtique', *Analecta Bollandia* 75, 158–226.

Guido, M. (1978) *The Glass Beads of the Prehistoric and Roman Periods in Britain and Ireland*, London: Thames & Hudson for the Society of Antiquaries of London.

Hamlin, A. (1972) 'A chi-rho carved stone at Drumaqueran, Co. Antrim', *UJA* 35, 22–8.

——(1977) 'A recently discovered enclosure at Inch Abbey, County Down', *UJA* 40, 85–8.

——(1981) 'Using mills on a Sunday', in B. G. Scott (ed.) *Studies on Early Ireland: Essays in Honour of M. V. Duignan*, p. 11, Belfast: Association of Young Irish Archaeologists.

——(1982) 'Early Irish stone carving: content and context', in S. Pearce (ed.) *The Early Church in Western Britain and Ireland*, pp. 287–96, Oxford: BAR British Series 102.

——(1984) 'The study of early Irish churches', in P. Ní Chatháin and M. Richter (eds) *Ireland and Europe*, pp. 117–26, Stuttgart: Klett-Cotta.

——(1985) 'The archaeology of the early Irish churches in the eighth century', *Peritia* 4, 279–99.

Hamlin, A. and Foley, C. (1983) 'A women's graveyard at Carrickmore, County Tyrone, and the separate burial of women', *UJA* 46, 41–6.

Hanson, R. P. C. (1968) *Saint Patrick: His Origins and Career*, Oxford: Clarendon Press.

——(1983) *The Life and Writings of the Historical St Patrick*, New York: Seabury Press.

Harbison, P. (1970) 'How old is Gallarus oratory?', *Medieval Archaeology* 14, 34–59.

——(1979) 'The inscriptions on the Cross of the Scriptures at Clonmacnois, Co. Offaly', *PRIA* 79C, 177–88.

——(1982) 'Early Irish churches', in H. Löwe (ed.) *Die Ireland und Europa im früheren mittelalter*, Vol. 2, pp. 618–29, Stuttgart: Klett-Cotta.

Harden, D. B. (ed.) (1956) *Dark Age Britain: Studies Presented to E. T. Leeds*, London: Methuen.

——(1963) 'Glass', in L. Alcock (ed.) *Dinas Powys: An Iron Age, Dark Age and Early Medieval Settlement in Glamorgan*, pp. 178–88, Cardiff: University of Wales Press.

——(1968) 'Appendix 10: note on glass fragments from Dalkey Island', *PRIA* 66C, 193–5.

Harper, A. E. T. (1972) 'The excavation of a rath in Mullaghbane Townland, Co. Tyrone', *UJA* 35, 37–44.

——(1974) 'The excavation of a rath in Crossnacreevy Townland, Co. Down', *UJA* 36–7, 32–41.

Harrison, P. (1986) 'A group of Early Christian carved stone monuments in County Donegal', in J. Higgitt (ed.) *Early Medieval Sculpture in Britain and Ireland*, pp. 49–85, Oxford: BAR British Series 152.

Hartnett, P.J. and Eogan, G. (1964) 'Feltrim Hill, Co. Dublin: a neolithic and Early Christian site', *JRSAI* 94, 1–37.

Harvey, A. (1987) 'Early literacy in Ireland: the evidence from ogam', *CMCS* 14, 1–15.

Hassan, F. A. (1978) 'Demographic archaeology', in M. B. Schiffer (ed.) *Advances in Archaeological Method and Theory*, Vol. 1, pp. 49–103, London: Academic Press.

——(1981) *Demographic Archaeology*, London: Academic Press.

Haverfield, F. (1923) *The Romanization of Roman Britain*, Oxford: Clarendon Press.

Hawkes, C. F. C. (1954) 'Archaeological theory and method: some suggestions from the Old World', *American Anthropologist* 56, 155–68.

Haworth, R. G. (1975) 'Archaeological field survey in Ireland – past, present and future', *Irish Archaeological Research Forum* 2.1, 7–19.

Hayes, J. W. (1972) *Late Roman Pottery*, London: British School at Rome.

Hencken, H. O'N. (1938) *Cahercommaun*, Dublin: Royal Society of Antiquaries of Ireland extra volume.

——(1942) 'Ballinderry crannog no. 2', *PRIA* 47C, 1–76.

——(1950) 'Lagore crannog: an Irish royal residence of the seventh to tenth centuries AD', *PRIA* 53C, 1–247.

Henderson, G. (1899) *Fled Brickrend: The Feast of Bricriu*, London: Irish Texts Society.

Henry, F. (1947) 'The antiquities of Caher Island, Co. Mayo', *JRSAI* 77, 23–38.

——(1952) 'A wooden hut on Inishkea North, Co. Mayo', *JRSAI* 82, 163–78.

——(1957) 'Early monasteries, beehive huts, and dry-stone houses in the neighbourhood of Caherciveen and Waterville (Co. Kerry)', *PRIA* 58C, 45–166.

——(1965) *Irish Art in the Early Christian Period (to 800 AD)*, London: Methuen.

——(1967) *Irish Art during the Viking Invasions 800–1020 AD*, London: Methuen.

——(1974) *The Book of Kells*, London: Thames & Hudson.

——(1980) 'Around an inscription: the Cross of the Scriptures at Clonmacnois', *JRSAI* 110, 36–46.

Herbert, M. (1988) *Iona, Kells, and Derry: The History and Hagiography of the Monastic Familia of Columba*, Oxford: Clarendon Press.

Herity, M. (1974) *Irish Passage Graves*, Dublin: Irish University Press.

——(1983) 'A survey of the royal site of Cruachain in Connacht, I: introduction, the monuments and topography', *JRSAI* 113, 121–42.

——(1984) 'The layout of Irish Early Christian monasteries', in P. Ní Chatháin and M. Richter (eds) *Ireland and Europe*, pp. 105–16. Stuttgart: Klett-Cotta.

——(1987) 'A survey of the royal site of Cruachain in Connacht, III: ringforts and ecclesiastical sites', *JRSAI* 117, 125–41.

Herren, M. W. (1974) *The Hisperica Famina: I, the A-Text*, Toronto: Pontifical Institute of Medieval Studies.

——(1980) 'On the earliest acquaintance with Isidore of Seville', in E. James (ed.) *Visigothic Spain: New Approaches*, pp. 243–50, Oxford: Clarendon Press.

Higgins, J. G. (1987) *The Early Christian Cross Slabs, Pillar Stones and Related Monuments of County Galway*, 2 volumes, Oxford: BAR International Series S375.

Higgins, V. (1984) 'The animal remains', in C. G. Brown and A. E. T. Harper 'Excavations on Cathedral Hill, Armagh, 1968', *UJA* 47, 109–61.

Higgitt, J. (1986) 'Words and crosses: the inscribed stone cross in early medieval Britain and Ireland', in J. Higgitt (ed.) *Early Medieval Sculpture in Britain and Ireland*, pp. 125–52. Oxford: BAR British Series 152.

Higham, N. and Jones, B. (1985) *The Carvettii*, Gloucester: Alan Sutton.

Hill, J. N. (1977) 'Systems theory and the explanation of change', in J. N. Hill (ed.) *Explanation of Prehistoric Change*, pp. 59–103, Albuquerque, N. Mex.: University of New Mexico Press.

Hillgarth, J. (1961) 'The east, Visigothic Spain and the Irish', *Studia Patristica* 4, 442–56.

——(1962) 'Visigothic Spain and Early Christian Ireland', *PRIA* 62C, 167–94.

——(1984) 'Ireland and Spain in the seventh century', *Peritia* 3, 1–16.

Hingley, R. (1989) *Rural Settlement in Roman Britain*, London: Seaby.

HMSO (1952) *Climatological Atlas of the British Isles*, London: HMSO.

Hodder, I. (1982) *Symbols in Action*, Cambridge: Cambridge University Press.

——(1986) *Reading the Past*, Cambridge: Cambridge University Press.

Hodges, R. (1977) 'Some early medieval French wares in the British Isles: an archaeological assessment of the early French wine trade with Britain', in D. Peacock (ed.) *Pottery and Early Commerce*, pp. 239–56, London: Academic Press.

——(1978) 'Ports of trade in early medieval Europe', *Norwegian Archaeological Review* 11, 97–101.

——(1982) *Dark Age Economics*, London: Duckworth.

——(1984) 'The date and source of E ware', *Scottish Archaeological Review* 3.1, 39–41.

Hogan, J. (1932) 'The Irish law of kingship with special reference to Ailech and Cenél Eoghain', *PRIA* 40C, 186–254.

Hollingsworth, T. H. (1969) *Historical Demography*, London: Hodder & Stoughton.

Hughes, K. (1962) 'The church and the world in Early Christian Ireland', *Irish Historical Studies* 13, 99–116.

——(1963) 'Irish monks and learning', in *Los Monjes y los estudios, IV: Semana de estudios monasticos Poblet 1961*. Poblet: Abadia de Poblet.

——(1966) *The Church in Early Irish Society*, London: Methuen.

——(1972) *Early Christian Ireland: Introduction to the Sources*, London: Hodder & Stoughton.

Hurley, V. (1982) 'The early church in the south-west of Ireland: settlement and organisation', in S. Pearce (ed.) *The Early Church in Western Britain and Ireland*, pp. 297–332, Oxford: BAR British Series 102.

Ivens, R. J. (1985) 'Dunmisk', in S. M. Youngs, J. Clark and T. Barry, 'Medieval Britain and Ireland in 1984', *Medieval Archaeology* 29, 212–13.

——(1986) 'Dunmisk', in S. M. Youngs, J. Clark and T. Barry, 'Medieval Britain and Ireland in 1985', *Medieval Archaeology* 30, 182–3.

——(1987) 'The Early Christian monastic enclosure at Tullylish, Co. Down', *UJA* 50, 55–121.

Ivens, R. J., Simpson, D. D. A. and Brown, D. (1986) 'Excavations at Island MacHugh 1985 – interim report', *UJA* 49, 99–103.

Jackson, J. S. (1978) 'Metallic ores in Irish prehistory: copper and tin', in M. Ryan (ed.) *The Origins of Metallurgy in Europe: Proceedings of the Fifth Atlantic Colloquium, Dublin*, pp. 107–25, Dublin: National Museum of Ireland.

Jackson, K. H. (1951) *A Celtic Miscellany*, London: Routledge & Paul.

——(1953) *Language and History in Early Britain*, Edinburgh: Edinburgh University Press.

——(1964) *The Oldest Irish Tradition: A Window on the Iron Age*. Cambridge: Cambridge University Press.

——(1965) 'The ogham inscription at Dunadd', *Antiquity* 39, 300–2.

James, E. (1982) 'Ireland and western Gaul in the Merovingian period', in D. Whitehead, R. McKitterick and D. Dumville (eds) *Ireland and Medieval Europe*, pp. 362–85, Cambridge: Cambridge University Press.

James, T. (forthcoming) 'Recent results from aerial photography', in N. Edwards and A. Lane (eds) *The Early Church in Wales and the West*.

Jobey, G. (1962) 'An Iron Age homestead at West Brandon, Durham', *Archaeologia Aeliana* 60, 1–34.

Jochim, M. (1983) 'Optimization in context', in J. A. Moore and A. S. Keene (eds) *Archaeological Hammers and Theories*, pp. 157–72, London: Academic Press.

Johnson, G. A. (1978) 'Information sources and the development of decision-making organizations', in C. L. Redman, M. J. Berman, E. V. Curtin, W. T. Langhorne Jr, N. M. Versaggi and J. C. Warner (eds) *Social Archaeology: Beyond Subsistence and Dating*, pp. 87–112, New York: Academic Press.

——(1982) 'Organisational structure and scalar stress', in C. Renfrew, M. J. Rowlands and B. A. Segraves (eds) *Theory and Explanation in Archaeology: The Southampton Conference*, pp. 389–421, New York: Academic Press.

Johnson, N. and Rose, P. (1982) 'Defended settlement in Cornwall – an illustrated discussion', in D. Miles (ed.) *The Romano–British Countryside*, pp. 151–207, Oxford: BAR British Series 103.

Jones, M. (1981) 'The development of crop husbandry', in M. Jones and G. Dimbleby (eds) *The Environment of Man: The Iron Age to the Anglo-Saxon Period*, pp. 95–127, Oxford: BAR British Series 87.

Jope, E. M. (1955) 'Chariotry and paired draught in Ireland during the early Iron Age: the evidence of some horse-bridle-bits', *UJA* 18, 37–44.

——(ed.) (1966) *An Archaeological Survey of Co. Down*, Belfast: HMSO.

——(1981) 'Michael Duignan and the study of Irish archaeology and history', in B. G. Scott (ed.) *Studies on Early Ireland: Essays in Honour of M. V. Duignan*, pp. 1–2, Belfast: Association of Young Irish Archaeologists.

Jope, M. (1953) 'Report on animal remains', in V. B. Proudfoot 'Excavation of a rath at Boho, Co. Fermanagh', *UJA* 16, 51–3.

Keene, A. S. (1979) 'Economic optimization models and the study of hunter-gatherer subsistence settlement systems', in C. Renfrew and K. Cooke (eds) *Transformations: Mathematical Approaches to Culture Change*, pp. 369–404, London: Academic Press.

Kelly, D. (1985) 'The capstones at Kilkieran, County Kilkenny', *JRSAI* 115, 160–2.

Kelly, F. (1976) 'The Old Irish tree-list', *Celtica* 11, 107–24.

Kelly, R. S. (1980) 'Metalworking in north Wales during the Roman period', *Bulletin of the Board Celtic Studies* 27, 127–47.

Kenney, J. F. (1929) *Sources for the Early History of Ireland*, Vol. I: *Ecclesiastical*, New York: Columbia University Press.

Kilbride-Jones, H. E. (1938) 'Glass armlets in Britain', *Proceedings of the Society of Antiquaries of Scotland* 72, 366–95.

——(1980) *Zoomorphic Penannular Brooches*, London: Society of Antiquaries, Research Report 39.

Kristiansen, K. (1981) 'A social history of Danish archaeology (1805–1975)', in G. Daniel (ed.) *Towards a History of Archaeology*, pp. 20–38, London: Thames & Hudson.

Kunkel, J. H. (1970) *Society and Economic Growth*, New York: Oxford University Press.

Lacy, B. (1983) *The Archaeological Survey of County Donegal*, Lifford: Donegal County Council.

de Laet, S. J. (ed.) (1976) *Acculturation and Continuity in Atlantic Europe, mainly during the Neolithic Period and the Bronze Age*, Brugge: De Tempel.

Laing, L. (1975) *Late Celtic Britain and Ireland c. 400–1200 AD*, London: Methuen.

——(1985) 'The Romanisation of Ireland in the fifth century', *Peritia* 4, 261–78.

Lawlor, H. J. (1916) 'The *Cathach* of St Columba', *PRIA* 16C, 241–443.

Leask, H. G. (1955) *Irish Churches and Monastic Buildings*, Vol. 1: *The First Phases and the Romanesque*, Dundalk: Dundalgan Press.

——(n.d.) *St Patrick's Rock, Cashel, Tipperary*, Dublin: Stationery Office.

Leeuw, S. E. van der (1983) 'Acculturation as information processing', in R. Brandt and J. Slofstra (eds) *Roman and Native in the Low Countries*, pp. 11–41, Oxford: BAR International Series S184.

Leone, M. (1978) 'Time in archaeology', in C. L. Redman, M. J. Berman, E. V. Curtin, W. T. Langhorne Jr, N. M. Versaggi and J. C. Warner (eds) *Social Archaeology: Beyond Subsistence and Dating*, pp. 25–36, New York: Academic Press.

Lins, P. A. and Oddy, W. A. (1975) 'The origins of mercury gilding', *Journal of Archaeological Science* 2.4, 365–73.

Lionard, P. (1961) 'Early Irish grave-slabs', *PRIA* 61C, 95–169.

Liversage, G. D. (1968) 'Excavations at Dalkey Island, Co. Dublin', *PRIA* 66C, 53–233.

Lowe, E. A. (1935) *Codices Latini Antiquiores II, Great Britain and Ireland*, Oxford: Clarendon Press.

Lowe, J. W. G. and Barth, R. J. (1980) 'Systems in archaeology: a comment on Salmon', *American Antiquity* 45, 568–75.

Lowry-Corry, D., Wilson, B. C. S. and Waterman, D. M. (1959) 'A newly discovered statue at the church on White Island', *UJA* 22, 59–66.

Lucas, A. T. (1953) 'The horizontal mill in Ireland', *JRSAI* 83, 1–36.

——(1954) 'Footwear in Ireland', *County Louth Archaeological Journal* 13, 309–94.

——(1955) 'A horizontal mill at Ballykilleen, Co. Offaly', *JRSAI* 85, 100–13.

——(1958a) 'Cattle in ancient and medieval Irish society', *O'Connell School Union Record* (1937–58), Dublin.

——(1958b) '*An fhóir*: a straw rope granary', *Gwerin* 1.1, 2–20.

——(1959) '*An fhóir*, a straw rope granary: further notes', *Gwerin* 2.2, 1–10.

——(1960) 'Irish food before the famine', *Gwerin* 3, 1–36.

——(1967) 'The plundering and burning of churches in Ireland, seventh to sixteenth centuries', in E. Rynne (ed.) *North Munster Studies*, pp. 172–229. Limerick: Thomond Archaeological Society.

——(1968) 'Irish ploughing practices', *Tools and Tillage* 2, 52–83.

——(1986) 'The social role of relics and reliquaries in ancient Ireland', *JRSAI* 116, 5–37.

Lynch, A. (1981) *Man and Environment in SW Ireland*, Oxford: BAR British Series 85.

Lynn, C. J. (1975) 'The medieval ringfort – an archaeological chimera?', *Irish Archaeological Research Forum* 2.1, 29–36.

——(1978) 'Early Christian period structures: a change from round to rectangular plans?', *Irish Archaeological Research Forum* 5, 29–46.

——(1982) 'The excavation of Rathmullan, a raised rath and motte in County Down', *UJA* 44–5, 65–171.

——(1983a) 'Some "early" ring-forts and crannogs', *JIA* 1, 47–58.

——(1983b) 'Two raths at Ballyhenry, Co. Antrim', *UJA* 46, 67–91.

——(1985) 'Excavations on a mound at Gransha, County Down, 1972 and 1982: an interim report', *UJA* 48, 81–90.

——(1986) 'Lagore, County Meath, and Ballinderry No. 1, County Westmeath, crannogs: some possible structural reinterpretations', *JIA* 3, 69–73.

——(1989) 'Deer Park Farms', *Current Archaeology* 113, 193–8.

McAdam, R. (1856) 'Ancient water-mills', *UJA* 4, 6–15.

Mac Airt, S. (1958) '*Filidecht* and *Coimgne*', *Ériu* 18, 139–52.

Macalister, R. A. S. (1909) *The Memorial Slabs of Clonmacnois, King's County*, Dublin: Royal Society of the Antiquaries of Ireland, extra volume.

——(1931) *Tara: A Pagan Sanctuary of Ancient Ireland*, London: Charles Scribner.

——(1948) *Corpus Inscriptionum Insularum Celticarum*, Vol. 2. Dublin: Stationery Office.

Mac Cana, P. (1970) *Celtic Mythology*, Feltham: Hamlyn.

——(1973) 'Conservation and innovation in early Celtic literature', *Études Celtiques* 13, 61–119.

McCone, K. R. (1986) 'Werewolves, cyclopes, *díberga* and *fíanna*: juvenile delinquency in early Ireland', *CMCS* 12, 1–22.

McCormick, F. (1983) 'Dairying and beef production in Early Christian Ireland: the faunal evidence', in T. Reeves-Smyth and F. Hamond (eds) *Landscape Archaeology in Ireland*, pp. 253–67, Oxford: BAR British Series 116.

McCracken, E. (1971) *Irish Woods since Tudor Times: Distribution and Exploitation*, Newton Abbot: David & Charles.

Mac Eoin, G. (1981) 'The early Irish vocabulary of mills and milling', in B. G. Scott (ed.) *Studies on Early Ireland: Essays in Honour of M. V. Duignan*, pp. 13–19, Belfast: Association of Young Irish Archaeologists.

MacFarlane, A., Harrison, S. and Jardine, C. (1977) *Reconstructing Historical Communities*, Cambridge: Cambridge University Press.

MacGregor, A. (1985) *Bone Antler Ivory and Horn*, London: Croom Helm.

McManus, D. (1983) 'A chronology of the Latin loan-words in early Irish', *Ériu* 34, 21–72.

Mac Neill, E. (1911) 'Early Irish population groups: their nomenclature, classification and chronology', *PRIA* 29C, 59–114.

——(1921) *Celtic Ireland*, Dublin: L. Parsons.

——(1923) 'Ancient Irish law: law of status or franchise', *PRIA* 26C, 265–316.

——(1931) 'Archaisms in the ogham inscriptions', *PRIA* 29C, 59–114.

Mac Niocaill, G. (1968) 'The "heir-designate" in early medieval Ireland', *The Irish Jurist* 3, 326–9.

——(1971) '*Tír cumaile*', *Ériu* 22, 81–6.

——(1972) *Ireland before the Vikings*, Dublin: Gill & Macmillan.

——(1981) 'Investment in early Irish agriculture', in B. G. Scott (ed.) *Studies on Early Ireland: Essays in Honour of M. V. Duignan*, pp. 7–9, Belfast: Association of Young Irish Archaeologists.

McRoberts, D. (1965) 'The ecclesiastical character of the St Ninian's Isle treasure', in A. Small (ed.) *Fourth Viking Congress*, pp. 224–46, Edinburgh: University of Aberdeen/Oliver & Boyd.

Mac White, E. (1961) 'Contributions to a study of ogam memorial stones', *Zeitshrift für Celtische Philologie* 28, 294–308.

Mallory, J. P. and Woodman, P. C. (1984) 'Oughtymore: an Early Christian shell midden', *UJA* 47, 51–62.

Manning, C. (1984) 'The excavation of the Early Christian enclosure of Killederdadrum in Lackenavenora, Co. Tipperary', *PRIA* 84C, 237–68.

——(1986) 'Archaeological excavation at a succession of enclosures at Millockstown, Co. Meath', *PRIA* 86C, 135–81.

——(1987) 'Excavation at Moyne graveyard, Shrule, Co. Mayo', *PRIA* 87C, 37–70.

——(1988) 'The stone-built ring-fort entrance at Cahirvagliair, Cappeen, Co. Cork', *JIA* 4, 37–54.

Manning, W. H. (1976) 'Blacksmithing', in D. Brown and D. Strong (eds) *Roman Crafts*, pp. 143–53, London: Duckworth.

Meehan, D. (1958) *Adamnan's de Locis Sanctis*, Scriptores Latini Hiberniae III, Dublin: Institute for Advanced Studies.

——(1983) 'Irish manuscripts in the early Middle Ages', in M. Ryan (ed.) *Treasures of Ireland: Irish Art 3000 BC–1500 AD*, pp. 48–55, Dublin: Royal Irish Academy.

Melia, D. F. (1982) 'The Irish church in the Irish laws', in S. Pearce (ed.) *The Early Church in Western Britain and Ireland*, pp. 363–78, Oxford: BAR British Series 102.

Merdrignac, B. (1987) 'Folklore and hagiography: a semiotic approach to the legend of the immortals of Landevennec', *CMCS* 13, 73–86.

Messenger, J. C. Jr (1959) 'Religious acculturation among the Anang Ibibio', in W. R. Bascom and M. J. Herskovits (eds) *Continuity and Change in African Culture*, pp. 279–99, Chicago: University of Chicago Press.

Michelli, P. E. (1986) 'Four Scottish croziers and their relation to the Irish tradition', *Proceedings of the Society of Antiquaries of Scotland* 116, 375–92.

Miller, D. (1982) 'Artefacts as products of human categorisation processes', in I. Hodder (ed.) *Symbolic and Structural Archaeology*, pp. 17–25, Cambridge: Cambridge University Press.

Miller, D. and Tilley, C. (eds) (1984) *Ideology, Power and Prehistory*, Cambridge: Cambridge University Press.

Miller, M. (1978) 'Date-guessing and Dyfed', *Studia Celtica* 12–13, 33–61.

Mitchell, G. F. (1965) 'Littleton Bog, Tipperary: an Irish agricultural record', *JRSAI* 95, 121–32.

——(1976) *The Irish Landscape*, London: Collins.

——(ed.) (1977) *Treasures of Early Irish Art 1500 BC to 1500 AD*, New York: Metropolitan Museum of Art.

Moloney, M. (1964) 'Beccan's hermitage in Aherlow: the riddle of the slabs', *NMAJ* 9, 99–107.

Monk, M. A. (1981) 'Post-Roman drying kilns and the problem of function: a preliminary statement', in D. Ó Corráin (ed.) *Irish Antiquity*, pp. 216–30, Cork: Tower Books.

——(1986) 'The evidence of macroscopic plant remains for crop husbandry in prehistoric and early historic Ireland: a review', *JIA* 3, 31–6.

Moore, J. A. (1983) 'The trouble with know-it-alls: information as a social and ecological resource', in J. A. Moore and A. S. Keene (eds) *Archaeological Hammers and Theories*, pp. 173–91, London: Academic Press.

Morris, J. (1973) *The Age of Arthur*, London: Weidenfeld & Nicolson.

Morris, R. K. (1989) *Churches in the Landscape*, London: Dent.

Moss, R. J. (1927) 'A chemical examination of the crucibles in the collection of Irish antiquities of the Royal Irish Academy', *PRIA* 37C, 175–93.

Munton, R. J. C. (1973) 'Systems analysis: a comment', in C. Renfrew (ed.) *The Explanation of Culture Change*, pp. 685–90, London: Duckworth.

Mytum, H. C. (1981) 'Ireland and Rome: the maritime frontier', in A. King and M. Henig (eds) *The Roman West in the Third Century*, pp. 445–9, Oxford: BAR International Series S109.

——(1982) 'The location of early churches in northern County Clare', in S. M. Pearce (ed.) *The Early Church in Western Britain and Ireland*, pp. 351–61, Oxford: BAR British Series 102.

——(1986a) 'Dark Age', in T. Darvill *The Archaeology of the Uplands: A Rapid Assessment of Archaeological Knowledge and Practice*, pp. 35–7, London: RCHME and Council for British Archaeology.

——(1986b) 'High status vessels in early historic Ireland: a reference in the *Bethu Brigte*', *Oxford Journal of Archaeology* 5, 375–8.

——(1988) 'On-site and off-site evidence for changes in subsistence economy: Iron Age and Romano-British West Wales', in J. L. Bintliff, D. A. Davidson and E. G. Grant (eds) *Conceptual Issues in Environmental Archaeology*, pp. 72–81, Edinburgh: Edinburgh University Press.

——(forthcoming) *The Vikings and Early Christian Ireland AD 800–1100*, London: Routledge.

Nagy, J. F. (1982) 'Liminality and knowledge in Irish tradition', *Studia Celtica* 16–17, 135–43.

Nash-Williams, V. E. (1950) *The Early Christian Monuments of Wales*, Cardiff: University of Wales Press.

Ní Chatháin, P. (1980) 'The liturgical background of the Derrynavlan altar service', *JRSAI* 110, 127–48.

Nicholaisen, W. F. (1965) 'Scottish placenames: 24, *slew* and *sliabh*', *Scottish Studies* 9, 91–106.

Nisbet, R. A. (1967) *The Sociological Tradition*, London: Heinemann.

Norman, E. R. and St Joseph, J. K. S. (1969) *The Early Development of Irish Society*, Cambridge: Cambridge University Press.

O'Briain, F. (1940) 'The hagiography of Leinster', in J. Ryan (ed.) *Féil-sgríbhinn Eoín Mhic Néill: Essays and Studies Presented to Professor Eoin MacNeill*, pp. 454–64. Dublin: The Sign of the Three Candles.

Ó Corráin, D. (1971) 'Irish regnal succession: a reappraisal', *Studia Hibernica* 11, 7–39.

——(1972) *Ireland before the Normans*, Dublin: Gill & Macmillan.

——(1981) 'The early Irish churches: some aspects of organisation', in D. Ó Corráin (ed.) *Irish Antiquity: Essays and Studies Presented to Professor M. J. O'Kelly*, pp. 327–41. Cork: Tower Books.

——(1983) 'Some legal references to fences and fencing in early historic Ireland', in T. Reeves-Smyth and F. Hamond (eds) *Landscape Archaeology in Ireland*, pp. 247–51. Oxford: BAR British Series 116.

Oddy, W. A. (1983) 'Bronze alloys in Dark Age Europe', in R. L. S. Bruce-Mitford *The Sutton Hoo Ship-Burial*, Vol. III, pp. 945–62, London: British Museum Publications.

Oddy, W. A. and Tite, M. S. (1983) 'Appendix: report on the analysis of metal samples from a recently found early Irish chalice, paten and ladle', in M. Ryan (ed.) *The Derrynavlan Hoard, I: A Preliminary Account*, Dublin: National Museum of Ireland.

Odner, K. (1972) 'Ethno-historic and ecological settings for economic and social models of an Iron Age society: Valldalen, Norway', in D. L. Clarke (ed.) *Models in Archaeology*, pp. 623–51. London: Methuen.

O'Donnabháin, B. (1986) 'The human remains', in C. Manning 'Archaeological excavation at a succession of enclosures at Millockstown, Co. Meath', *PRIA* 86C, 171–9.

O'Dwyer, M. (1964) 'A survey of the earthworks in the district of Old Pallasgrean, III', *NMAJ* 9, 94–8.

O'Dwyer, P. (1981) *Célí Dé Spiritual Reform in Ireland 750–900*, Dublin: Editions Tailliura.

O'Kelly, M. J. (1951) 'An early Bronze Age ring-fort at Carrigillihy, Co. Cork', *JCHAS* 56, 69–86.

——(1952) 'St Gobnet's house, Ballyvourney, Co. Cork', *JCHAS* 57, 18–40.

——(1956) 'An island settlement at Beginish, Co. Kerry', *PRIA* 57C, 159–94.

——(1958) 'Church Island near Valencia, Co. Kerry', *PRIA* 59C, 57–136.

——(1961) 'The ancient method of smelting iron', in *V. Internationalen Kongress Fur Von-Und Fruhgeschichte, Hamburg 1958*, pp. 459–91, Hamburg: Congress for Pre- and Protohistory.

——(1962) 'Two ring-forts at Garryduff, Co. Cork', *PRIA* 63C, 17–125.

——(1965) 'The belt-shrine from Moylough, Co. Sligo', *JRSAI* 95, 149–88.

——(1967) 'Knockea, Co. Limerick', in E. Rynne (ed.) *North Munster Studies*, pp. 72–101, Limerick: Thomond Archaeological Society.

——(1975) *Archaeological Survey and Excavation of St Vogue's Church Enclosure and Other Monuments at Carnsore, Co. Wexford*, Dublin: Electricity Supply Board.

O'Leary, P. (1988) 'Honour-bound: the social context of early Irish historic Geis', *Celtica* 20, 85–107.

Ó Laoghaire, D. (1984) 'Irish spirituality', in P. Ní Chatháin and M. Richter (eds) *Ireland and Europe*, pp. 73–82, Stuttgart: Klett-Cotta.

Ó Loan, J. (1965) 'A history of Irish farming', *Department of Agriculture Journal* 62, 131–98.

O'Meadhra, U. (1979) *Early Christian, Viking and Romanesque Art: Motif Pieces from Ireland, an Illustrated Catalogue*, Theses and Papers in North European Archaeology 7, Stockholm: Almqvist & Wiksell.

——(1987) *Early Christian, Viking and Romanesque Art: Motif Pieces from Ireland, 2: A Discussion*, Theses and Papers in North European Archaeology 17, Stockholm: Almqvist & Wiksell.

Ó'Rahilly, T. F. (1946) *Early Irish History and Mythology*, Dublin: Institute for Advanced Studies.

——(1952) 'Buchet the herdsman', *Ériu* 16, 7–20.

——(1967) *Tain Bo Culange from the Book of Leinster*, Dublin: Institute for Advanced Studies.

Ó Riain, P. (1972) 'Boundary association in early Irish society', *Studia Celtica* 7, 12–29.

——(1974) 'Battle-site and territorial extent in early Ireland', *Zeitschrift für Celtische Philologie* 33, 67–80.

Ó Ríordáin, S. P. (1940) 'Excavations at Cush, Co. Limerick', *PRIA* 45C, 83–181.

——(1942) 'The excavation of a large earthern ring-fort at Garranes, Co. Cork', *PRIA* 47C, 77–150.

——(1949) 'Lough Gur excavations: Carraig Aille and the "Spectacles"', *PRIA* 52C (1948–50), 39–111.

——(1951) 'Lough Gur excavations: the great stone circle (B) in Grange Townland', *PRIA* 54C, 37–74.

——(1954a) 'Lough Gur excavations: neolithic and Bronze Age houses on Knockadoon', *PRIA* 56C, 297–459.

——(1954b) *Tara: The Monuments on the Hill*, Dundalk: Dundalgan Press.

Ó Ríordáin, S. P. and Foy, J. B. (1941) 'The excavation of Leacanbuaile stone fort, near Caherciveen, Co. Kerry', *JCHAS* 46, 85–91.

Ó Ríordáin, S. P. and Hartnett, P. J. (1943) 'The excavation of Ballycatteen Fort, Co. Cork', *PRIA* 49C, 1–43.

Ó Ríordáin, S. P. and Mac Dermott, M. (1952) 'The excavation of a ring-fort at Letterkeen, Co. Mayo', *PRIA* 54C, 89–119.

Orme, A. R. (1970) *Ireland*, The World's Landscapes 4, London: Longman.

O Sé, M. (1948) 'Old Irish cheeses and other milk products', *JCHAS* 53, 82–7.

——(1949) 'Old Irish butter making', *JCHAS* 54, 61–7.

Padel, O. J. (1981) 'Appendix III. Tintagel: an alternative view', in C. Thomas *A Provisional List of Imported Pottery in Post-Roman Britain and Ireland*, pp. 28–9, Redruth: Institute of Cornish Studies Special Report 7.

Paine, R. (1974) *Second Thoughts about Barth's Models*, RAI Occasional Paper 32, London: Royal Anthropological Institute.

Painter, K. S. (1965) 'A Roman silver treasure from Canterbury', *Journal of the British Archaeological Association* 28, 1–15.

de Paor, L. (1955) 'A survey of Sceilg Mhichíl', *JRSAI* 85, 174–87.

de Paor, M. and de Paor, L. (1958) *Early Christian Ireland*, London: Thames & Hudson.

Pauw, B. A. (1965) 'Patterns of Christianization among the Tswana and the Xhosa-speaking peoples', in M. Fortes and G. Dieterlen (eds) *African Systems of Thought*, pp. 240–57, London: International African Institute/Oxford University Press.

Payer, P. J. (1984) *Sex and the Penitentials: The Development of the Sexual Code, 550–1150*, Toronto: University of Toronto Press.

Peacock, D. P. S. (1984) 'E ware and Aquitaine', *Scottish Archaeological Review* 3.1, 38–9.

Peacock, D. and Thomas, C. (1967) 'Class E imported post-Roman pottery: a suggested origin', *Cornish Archaeology* 6, 35–46.

Peacock, D. P. S. and Williams, D. F. (1986) *Amphorae and the Roman Economy: An Introductory Guide*, London: Longman.

Perlman, M. L. (1977) 'Comments on explanation and on stability and change', in J. N. Hill (ed.) *Explanation of Prehistoric Change*, pp. 319–33, Albuquerque, N. Mex.: University of New Mexico Press.

Petrie, G. (1839) 'On the history and antiquities of Tara Hill', *Transactions of the Royal Irish Academy* 18, 25–232.

Piggott, S. (1940) 'Timber circles: a re-examination', *Archaeological Journal* 96, 193–222.

Plog, F. (1977) 'Explaining change', in J. N. Hill (ed.) *Explanation of Prehistoric Change*, pp. 17–57, Albuquerque, N. Mex.: University of New Mexico Press.

Plummer, C. (1910) *Vitae Sanctorum Hiberniae*, Oxford: Oxford University Press.

——(1923a) 'Notes on some passages in the Brehon laws: II', *Ériu* 9, 31–42.

——(1923b) 'Notes on some passages in the Brehon laws: III', *Ériu* 9, 109–17.

——(1928) 'Notes on some passages in the Brehon laws: IV', *Ériu* 10, 113–29.

——(1968) *Lives of Irish Saints*, 2 volumes, Oxford: Oxford University Press.

Power, P. (1939) 'A decorated quern-stone, and its symbolism', *PRIA* 45C, 25–30.

Price, L. (1950) 'The history of Lagore, from the Annals and other sources', in H. Hencken 'Lagore crannog: an Irish royal residence of the seventh to tenth centuries AD', *PRIA* 53C, 18–34.

Proudfoot, V. B. (1951) 'Settlement and economy in County Down from the late Bronze Age to the Anglo-Norman invasion', unpublished Ph.D. thesis, Queen's University, Belfast.

——(1953) 'Excavation of a rath at Boho, Co. Fermanagh', *UJA* 16, 41–57.

——(1959) 'Note on a rath at Croft Road, Holywood, Co. Down', *UJA* 22, 102–6.

——(1961) 'The economy of the Irish rath', *Medieval Archaeology* 5, 94–121.

Proudfoot, V. B. and Wilson, B. C. S. (1962) 'Further excavations at Larrybane promontory fort, Co. Antrim', *UJA* 24–5, 91–115.

Rackham, O. (1980) *Ancient Woodland: Its History, Vegetation and Uses in England*, London: Edward Arnold.

Radford, C. A. R. (1956) 'Imported pottery found at Tintagel, Cornwall', in D. B. Harden (ed.) *Dark-Age Britain*, pp. 59–70, London: Methuen.

——(1977) 'The earliest Irish churches', *UJA* 40, 1–11.

Raftery, B. (1976) 'Rathgall and Irish hillfort problems', in D. W. Harding (ed.) *Hillforts: Later Prehistoric Earthworks in Britain and Ireland*, pp. 339–57, London: Academic Press.

——(1981) 'Iron Age burials in Ireland', in D. Ó Corráin (ed.) *Irish Antiquity: Essays and Studies Presented to Professor M. J. O'Kelly*, pp. 173–204, Cork: Tower Books.

——(1984) *La Tène in Ireland*, Marburg: Sonderband.

——(1987) 'Ancient trackways in Corlea Bog, Co. Longford', *Archaeology Ireland* 1.2, 60–4.

Raftery, J. (1941) 'Long stone cists of the early Iron Age', *PRIA* 46C, 299–315.

——(1951) *Prehistoric Ireland*, London: Batsford.

——(1972) 'Iron Age and Irish Sea: problems for research', in C. Thomas (ed.) *The Iron Age in the Irish Sea Province*, pp. 1–10, London: CBA Research Report 9.

——(1981) 'Concerning chronology', in D. Ó Corráin (ed.) *Irish Antiquity: Essays and Studies Presented to Professor M. J. O'Kelly*, pp. 82–92, Cork: Tower Books.

Randsborg, K. (1980) *The Viking Age in Denmark*, London: Duckworth.

——(1982) 'Rank, rights and resources: an archaeological perspective from Denmark' in C. Renfrew and S. Shennan (eds) *Ranking, Resource and Exchange*, pp. 132–9, Cambridge: Cambridge University Press.

RCAHMS (Royal Commission on the Ancient and Historical Monuments for Scotland) (1982) *Argyll: An Inventory of the Monuments*, Vol 4: *Iona*. Edinburgh: HMSO.

Reece, R. (1984a) 'Sequence is all: archaeology in an historical period', *Scottish Archaeological Review* 3.2, 113–15.

——(1984b) 'Mints, markets and the military', in T. F. C. Blagg and A. C. King (eds) *Military and Civilian in Roman Britain: Cultural Relations in a Frontier Province*, pp. 143–60, Oxford: BAR British Series 136.

Rees, A. and Rees, B. (1961) *Celtic Heritage*, London: Thames & Hudson.

Renfrew, C. (1972) *The Emergence of Civilisation*, London: Methuen.

——(1982) *Towards an Archaeology of Mind*, Cambridge: Cambridge University Press.

——(1984) *Approaches to Social Archaeology*, Edinburgh: Edinburgh University Press.

——(1986) 'Introduction: peer polity interaction and socio-political change', in C. Renfrew and J. Cherry (eds) *Peer Polity Interaction and Socio-Political Change*, pp. 1–18, Cambridge: Cambridge University Press.

Renfrew, C. and Cherry, J. (1986) *Peer Polity Interaction and Socio-Political Change*, Cambridge: Cambridge University Press.

Renfrew, C. and Shennan, S. (1982) *Ranking, Resource and Exchange*, Cambridge: Cambridge University Press.

Reynolds, P. J. (1979) *Iron Age Farm: The Butser Experiment*, London: British Museum Publications.

Reynolds, P. J. and Langley, J. K. (1980) 'Romano–British corn drying oven: an experiment', *Archaeological Journal* 136, 27–42.

Richards, M. (1960) 'The Irish settlements in south-west Wales', *JRSAI* 90, 133–62.

Richardson, H. (1980) 'Derrynavlan and other Early Christian treasures', *JRSAI* 110, 92–115.

——(1984) 'Number and symbol in Early Christian Irish art', *JRSAI* 114, 28–47.

Riley, D. N. (1980) *Early Landscape from the Air*, Sheffield: Department of Archaeology, University of Sheffield.

Roe, H. (1960) 'A stone cross at Clogher, Co. Tyrone', *JRSAI* 90, 191–206.

Ross, A. (1967) *Pagan Celtic Britain*, London: Routledge & Kegan Paul.

Ryan, J. (1962) 'The sacrament in the early Irish church', *Studies* 51, 508–20.

Ryan, M. (1973) 'Native pottery in early historic Ireland', *PRIA* 73C, 619–45.

——(1981) 'Some archaeological comments on the occurrence and use of silver in pre-Viking Ireland', in B. G. Scott (ed.) *Studies on Early Ireland: Essays in Honour of M. V. Duignan*, pp. 45–50, Belfast: Association of Young Irish Archaeologists.

——(1983) *Treasures of Ireland: Irish Art 3000 BC–1500 AD*, Dublin: Royal Irish Academy.

——(1985) *Early Irish Communion Vessels*, Dublin: National Museum of Ireland.

——(1987) 'Some aspects of sequence and style in the metalwork of eighth and ninth century Ireland', in M. Ryan (ed.) *Ireland and Insular Art AD 500–1200*, pp. 66–74, Dublin: Royal Irish Academy.

Rynne, C. (1989a) 'Early Irish watermills', *British Archaeology* 14, 13–15.

——(1989b) 'The introduction of the vertical watermill into Ireland: some recent archaeological evidence', *Medieval Archaeology* 33, 21–31.

Rynne, E. (1956) 'Excavations of a ring-fort at Ardcloon, Co. Mayo', *JRSAI* 86, 203–14.

——(1972) 'Celtic stone idols in Ireland', in C. Thomas (ed.) *The Iron Age in the Irish Sea Province*, pp. 79–93, London: CBA Research Report 9.

——(1987) 'The date of the Ardagh chalice', in M. Ryan (ed.) *Ireland and Insular Art AD 500–1200*, pp. 85–9, Dublin: Royal Irish Academy.

Salmon, M. H. (1978) 'What can systems theory do for archaeology?', *American Antiquity* 43, 174–83.

Saxe, A. A. (1977) 'On the origin of evolutionary process: state of formation in the Sandwich Islands', in J. N. Hill (ed.) *Explanation of Prehistoric Change*, pp. 105–51, Albuquerque, N. Mex.: University of New Mexico Press.

Schiffer, M. B. (1976) *Behavioral Archaeology*, New York: Academic Press.

——(1987) *Formation Processes of the Archaeological Record*, Albuquerque, N. Mex.: University of New Mexico Press.

Schrire, C. (1972) 'Ethno-archaeological models and subsistence behaviour in Arnhem Land', in D. L. Clarke (ed.) *Models in Archaeology*, pp. 653–70, London: Methuen.

Scott, B. G. (1978) 'Iron "slave-collars" from Lagore crannog, Co. Meath', *PRIA* 78C, 213–30.

——(1981) 'Some conflicts and correspondences of evidence in the study of Irish archaeology and language', in B. G. Scott (ed.) *Studies on Early Ireland: Essays in Honour of M. V. Duignan*, pp. 115–19, Belfast: Association of Young Irish Archaeologists.

——(1983) 'An early Irish law tract on the blacksmith's forge', *JIA* 1, 59–62.

Scott, E. M., Baxter, M. S. and Aitchison, T. C. (1983) 'A comparative view of calibration', in B. Ottoway (ed.) *Archaeology, Dendrochronology and the Radiocarbon Calibration Curve*, pp. 37–41, Edinburgh: Department of Archaeology, University of Edinburgh Occasional Paper 9.

Sharpe, R. (1984) 'Some problems concerning the organisation of the church in early medieval Ireland', *Peritia* 3, 230–70.

Sheehy, M. P. (1961) 'The relics of the Apostles and early martyrs in the mission of St Patrick', *Irish Ecclesiastical Review* 95, 372–6.

Sleen, W. G. N. Van der (1967) *A Handbook on Beads*, Liège: Musée de Verre.

Smith, M. A. (1955) 'The limitations of inference', *Archaeological Newsletter* 6.1, 3–7.

Spicer, E. H. (ed.) (1961) *Perspectives in American Indian Culture Change*, Chicago: University of Chicago Press.

SSRC (Social Science Research Council Seminar) (1954) 'Acculturation: an exploratory formulation', *American Anthropologist* 56, 973–1002.

Start, L. E. (1950) 'Textiles', in H. O'N. Hencken 'Lagore crannog: an Irish royal residence of the seventh to tenth centuries AD', *PRIA* 53C, 203–24.

de Ste Croix, G. E. M. (1975) 'Early Christian attitudes to property and slavery', in D. Baker (ed.) *Church, Society and Politics: Studies in Church History* 12, 1–38, Oxford: Blackwell.

Stelfox, A. W. (1942) 'Report on the animal remains from Ballinderry 2 crannog', in H. O'N. Hencken 'Ballinderry crannog no. 2', *PRIA* 47C, 67–74.

Stenberger, M. (1966) 'A ring-fort at Raheenamadra, Co. Limerick', *PRIA* 65C, 37–54.

Stephens, G. R. (1985) 'Caerleon and the martyrdom of SS. Aaron and Julius', *Bulletin of the Board of Celtic Studies* 32, 326–35.

Stevenson, J. (1989) 'The beginnings of literacy in Ireland', *PRIA* 89C, 127–65.

Stevenson, R. B. K. (1974) 'The Hunterston brooch and its significance', *Medieval Archaeology* 18, 16–42.

——(1985) 'Notes on the sculptures at Fahan Mura and Carndonagh, County Donegal', *JRSAI* 115, 92–5.

Stout, G. T. (1984) *Archaeological Survey of the Barony of Ikerrin*, Roscrea: Roscrea Heritage Society.

Swan, D. L. (1978) 'The Hill of Tara, County Meath: the evidence of aerial photography', *JRSAI* 108, 51–66.

Swan, L. (1983) 'Enclosed ecclesiastical sites and their relevance to settlement patterns of the first millennium AD', in T. Reeves-Smyth and F. Hamond (eds) *Landscape Archaeology in Ireland*, pp. 269–94, Oxford: BAR British Series 116.

Swarzenski, G. (1954) 'An early Anglo-Irish portable shrine', *Bulletin of the Museum of Fine Arts, Boston* 52 (October), 50–62.

Sweetman, D. (1983) 'Souterrain and burials at Boolies Little, Co. Meath', *Riocht Na Midhe* 7, 42–57.

Thomas, C. (1959) 'Imported pottery in Dark-Age western Britain', *Medieval Archaeology* 3, 89–111.

——(1966) 'Ardwall Isle: the excavation of an Early Christian site of Irish type', *Transactions of the Dumfriesshire and Galloway Natural History and Antiquarian Society* 43, 84–116.

——(1968) 'Grass-marked pottery in Cornwall', in J. M. Coles and D. D. A. Simpson (eds) *Studies in Ancient Europe: Essays Presented to Stuart Piggott*, pp. 311–31, Leicester: Leicester University Press.

——(1971a) *The Early Christian Archaeology of North Britain*, Oxford: Oxford University Press.

——(1971b) *Britain and Ireland in Early Christian Times AD 400–800*, London: Thames & Hudson.

——(1972) 'Irish colonies in post-Roman western Britain: a survey of the evidence', *Journal of the Royal Institution of Cornwall* n.s. 6, 251–74.

——(1973) 'Irish colonists in south-west Britain', *World Archaeology* 5, 5–12.

——(1976) 'Imported late Roman Mediterranean pottery in Ireland and western Britain', *PRIA* 76C, 245–55.

——(1979) 'Saint Patrick and fifth century Britain: an historical model explored', in P.J. Casey (ed.) *The End of Roman Britain*, pp. 81–101, Oxford: BAR British Series 71.

——(1981a) *Christianity in Roman Britain*, London: Batsford.

——(1981b) *A Provisional List of Imported Pottery in Post-Roman Western Britain and Ireland*, Redruth: Institute of Cornish Studies, Special Report 7.

——(1986) *Celtic Britain*, London: Thames & Hudson.

——(1987) 'The earliest Christian art in Ireland and Britain', in M. Ryan (ed.) *Ireland and Insular Art AD 500–1200*, pp. 7–11, Dublin: Royal Irish Academy.

——(1990) '"Gallici nautae de Galliarum provinciis" – a sixth/seventh century trade with Gaul, reconsidered', *Medieval Archaeology* 34, 1–26.

Thomas, D. H. (1972) 'A computer simulation model of Great Basin Shoshonean subsistence and settlement patterns', in D. L. Clarke (ed.) *Models in Archaeology*, pp. 671–704, London: Methuen.

Thompson, E. A. (1985) *Who Was St Patrick?*, Woodbridge: Boydell Press.

Trigger, B. G. (1980) *Gordon Childe: Revolutions in Archaeology*, London: Thames & Hudson.

Twohig, D. C. (1990) 'Excavation of three ring-forts at Lisduggan North, County Cork', *PRIA* 90C, 1–32.

Tylecote, R. F. (1976) *A History of Metallurgy*, London: Metals Society.

——(1986) *The Prehistory of Metallurgy in the British Isles*, London: Institute of Metals.

Waddell, J. (1978) 'The invasion hypothesis in Irish prehistory', *Antiquity* 52, 121–8.

——(1983) 'Rathcroghan – a royal site in Connacht', *JIA* 1, 21–46.

Wallace, P. F. (1982) 'Irish Early Christian "wooden" – oratories – a suggestion', *NMAJ* 24, 19–28.

Warhurst, C. (1971) 'Excavation of a rath at Shane's Castle, Co. Antrim', *UJA* 34, 58–64.

Warner, R. B. (1976) 'Some observations on the context and importation of exotic material in Ireland, from the first century BC to the second century AD', *PRIA* 76C, 267–92.

——(1979a) 'The Clogher yellow layer', *Medieval Ceramics* 3, 37–40.

——(1979b) 'The Irish souterrains and their background', in H. Crawford (ed.) *Subterranean Britain*, pp. 100–44, London: John Baker.

——(1980) 'Irish souterrains: later Iron Age refuges', *Archaeologia Atlantica* 3, 81–99.

——(1983) 'Ireland, Ulster and Scotland in the earlier Iron Age', in A. O'Connor and D. Clark (eds) *From the Stone Age to the Forty-Five*, pp. 161–87, Edinburgh: John Donald.

——(1986a) 'Comments on Ulster and Oriel souterrains', *UJA* 49, 111–12.

——(1986b) 'The date of the start of Lagore', *JIA* 3, 75–7.

——(1987) 'Ireland and the origins of escutcheon art', in M. Ryan (ed.) *Ireland and Insular Art AD 500–1200*, pp. 19–22, Dublin: Royal Irish Academy.

——(1988) 'The archaeology of early historic Irish kingship', in S. T. Driscoll and M. R. Nieke (eds) *Power and Politics in Early Medieval Britain and Ireland*, pp. 47–68, Edinburgh: Edinburgh University Press.

Washburn, D. K. (ed.) (1983) *Structure and Cognition in Art*, Cambridge: Cambridge University Press.

Waterer, J. W. (1968) 'Irish book-satchels or budgets', *Medieval Archaeology* 12, 70–82.

Waterman, D. M. (1956) 'The excavation of a house and souterrain at White Fort, Drumaroad, Co. Down', *UJA* 19, 73–86.

——(1958) 'Excavations at Ballyfounder Rath, Co. Down', *UJA* 21, 39–61.

——(1967) 'The Early Christian churches and cemetery at Derry, Co. Down', *UJA* 30, 53–75.

——(1972) 'The group of raths of Ballypalady, Co. Antrim', *UJA* 35, 29–36.

Waterman, D. M. and Collins, A. E. P. (1952) 'The excavation of two raths at Ballypalady, Co. Antrim', *UJA* 15, 71–83.

Watson, P. J., Leblanc, S. A. and Redman, C. L. (1971) *Explanation in Archaeology: An Explicitly Scientific Approach*, New York: Columbia University Press.

Westropp, T. J. (1901) '"Slane in Bregia", County Meath: its friary and heritage', *JRSAI* 31, 404–30.

——(1902) 'The ancient forts of Ireland', *Transactions of the Royal Irish Academy* 3, 579–730.

Whimster, R. (1989) *The Emerging Past: Air Photography and the Buried Landscape*, London: Royal Commission for Historic Monuments (England).

Whitfield, N. (1987) 'Motifs and techniques of Celtic filigree: are they original?', in M. Ryan (ed.) *Ireland and Insular Art AD 500–1200*, pp. 75–94, Dublin: Royal Irish Academy.

Williams, B. B. (1980) 'The excavation of a rath in Shewis Townland, near Richhill, County Armagh', *UJA* 43, 106–8.

——(1983) 'Early Christian landscapes in County Antrim', in T. Reeves-Smyth and F. Hamond (eds) *Landscape Archaeology in Ireland*, pp. 233–46, Oxford: BAR British Series 116.

——(1984) 'Excavations at Ballyutuog, County Antrim', *UJA* 47, 37–49.

Williams, G. (1985) *Fighting and Farming in Iron Age West Wales*, Carmarthen: Dyfed Archaeological Trust.

——(1988) 'Recent work on rural settlement in later prehistoric and early historic Dyfed', *Antiquaries Journal* 68, 30–54.

Wilson, P. A. (1966) 'Romano–British and Welsh Christianity: continuity or discontinuity?', *Welsh History Review* 3, 5–21, 103–20.

Wobst, M. (1977) 'Stylistic behavior and information exchange', in G. E. Cleland (ed.) *For the Director: Research Essays in Honor of James B. Griffin*, pp. 317–42, University of Michigan Museum of Anthropology, Anthropology Paper 61, Ann Arbor, Mich.: Museum of Anthropology, University of Michigan.

Wolf, E. R. (1965) 'Aspects of group relations in a complex society: Mexico', in D. B. Heath and R. N. Adams (eds) *Contemporary Cultures and Societies of Latin America*, pp. 85–101, New York: Random House.

Wood, W. R. and Johnson, D. C. (1978) 'A survey of disturbance processes in archaeological site formation', in M. B. Schiffer (ed.) *Advances in Archaeological Method and Theory*, Vol. 1, pp. 315–81, London: Academic Press.

Wright, H. T. (1977) 'Recent research on the origin of the state', *Annual Review of Anthropology* 6: 379–97.

Wylie, A. (1985) 'The reaction against analogy', in M. B. Schiffer (ed.) *Advances in Archaeological Method and Theory*, Vol. 8, pp. 63–111, London: Academic Press.

Wynne, E. J. and Tylecote, R. F. (1958) 'An experimental investigation into primitive iron smelting technique', *Journal of the Iron and Steel Institute* 190, 339–48.

Youngs, S. (ed.) (1989) *The Work of Angels: Masterpieces of Celtic Metalwork, Sixth to Ninth Centuries AD*, London: British Museum Publications.

Index

For Product Safety Concerns and Information please contact our EU
representative GPSR@taylorandfrancis.com
Taylor & Francis Verlag GmbH, Kaufingerstraße 24, 80331 München, Germany

www.ingramcontent.com/pod-product-compliance
Lightning Source LLC
Chambersburg PA
CBHW081427270326
41932CB00019B/3122

9 781032 875767